FRANK STELLA

ANDRIANNA CAMPBELL
KATE NESIN
LUCAS BLALOCK
TERRY RICHARDSON

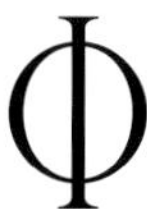

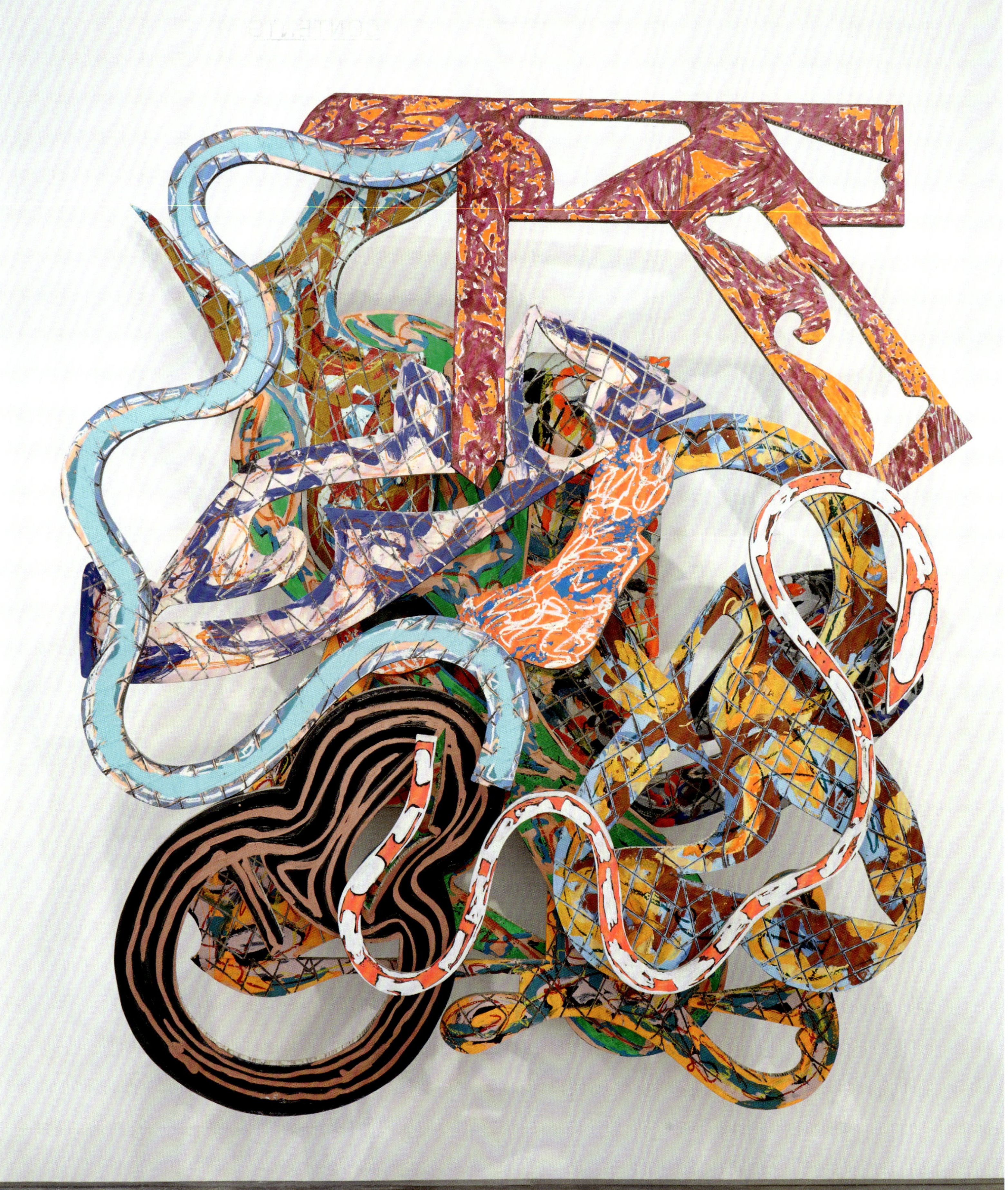

NORISRING (XVI), 4.75X, 1982
MIXED MEDIA ON ETCHED
ALUMINUM
310 X 269 X 53 CM

CONTENTS

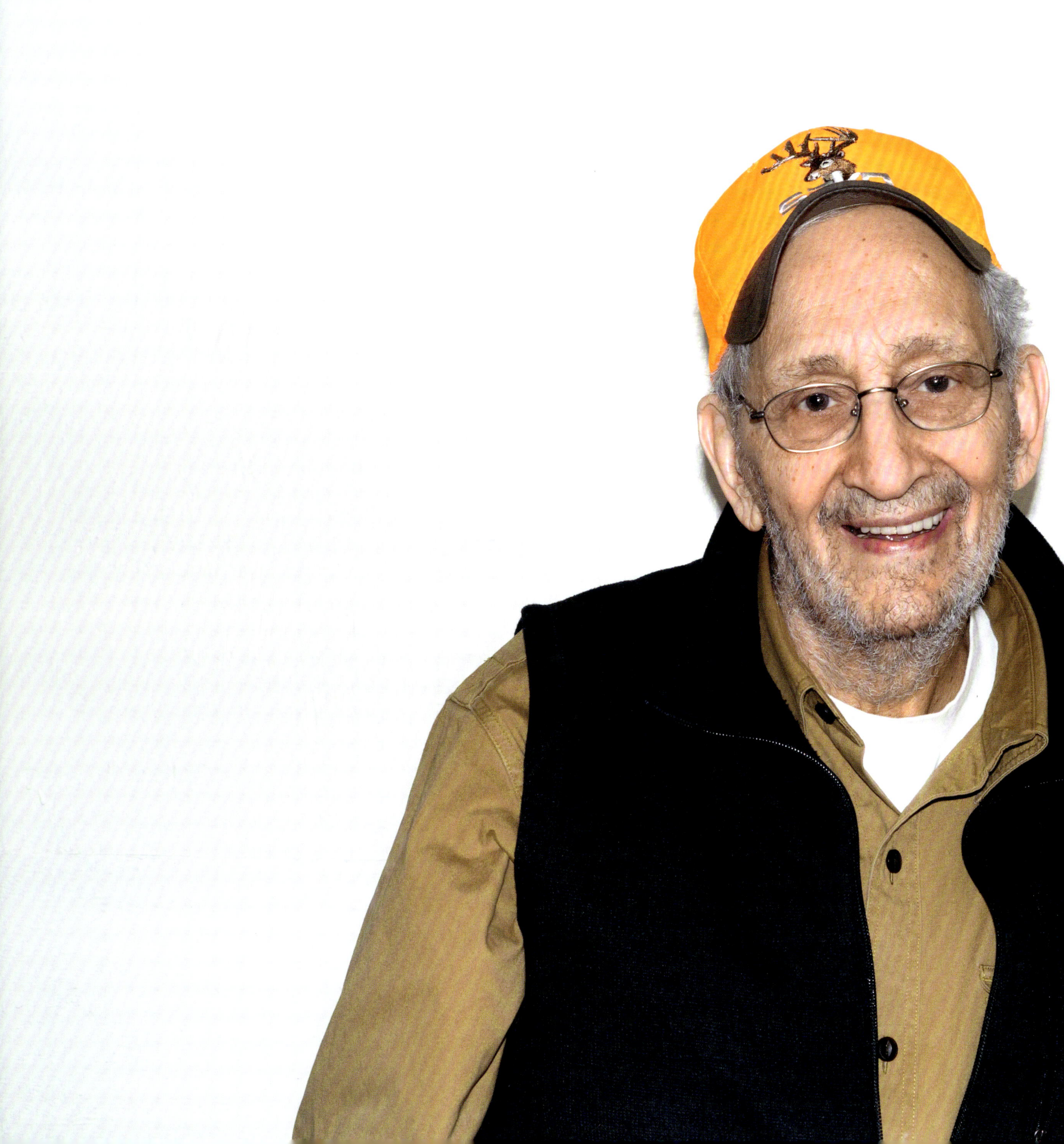

007 INTERVIEW

Andrianna Campbell in conversation with Frank Stella

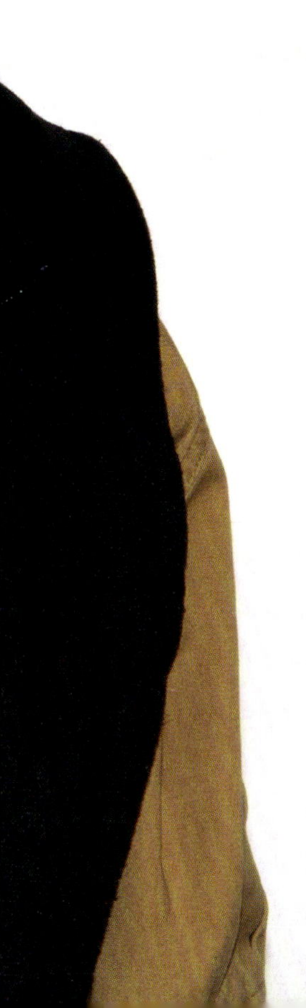

previous pages,
FRANK STELLA, NEW YORK,
2017

ANDRIANNA CAMPBELL: *While walking through your survey exhibition at the Whitney Museum in 2015, Roberta Smith asked me what work I'd choose to discuss if I were to write about the show. I said* Die Fahne hoch! *(1959). She just smiled – an uncharacteristic smirk – and said maybe I could think of something less obvious. Looking around I was struck by* Das Erdbeben in Chili [N#3] *(1999), with its irregular scale shifts, so much colour, so much gesture and a radical redefinition of space. The newer work didn't make sense to so many people for so long: what happened to the elegant striped paintings and the irregular polygons? Now, a generation of younger artists often bring up these paintings that you've been making since the early 1990s, and they tell me there's so much to mine there. What brought about this transition from the Minimalism – or reductive abstraction – in your early work and the decorative decadence of your current practice?*

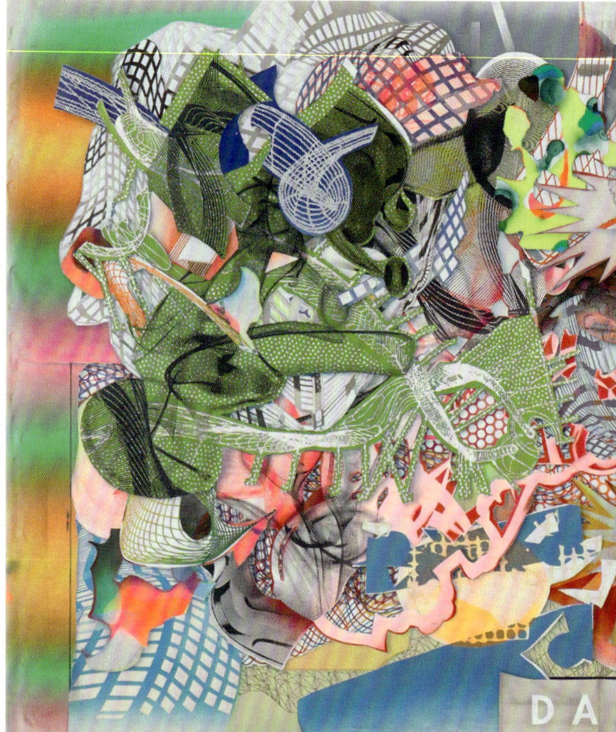

FRANK STELLA: Well with Minimalism, I was there, but I'm not there now, except in a literal way: in the paintings that are extant from then. When you see them, you can say, 'Oh, that's from the 1960s.' But the 1960s didn't live on, and so I think it doesn't have any real resonance anymore, except in the work that's made to look like art, but isn't art. I didn't want my work to live on continuously as a conversation or product of the 1960s, the product of who I was as a very young artist.

CAMPBELL: *Can you talk about the making of* Das Erdbeben in Chili [N#3]?

STELLA: We used engraving – many of those lines are engraved lines. It's a two-dimensional interpretation of smoke. We hired an engraver from Sweden, who'd worked on the country's currency. He used some kind of digital process. The smoke rings are fairly simple to render in that way.

CAMPBELL: *Smoke is so important in your later work. Your interest in smoke originated when you were smoking a cigar during the time that you gave the Charles Norton lectures series at Harvard in 1982–84. From the smoke, you began to rethink the working space of painting. Smoke is tangible, and intangible: it interfaces structure. The problem of space and painting – which in the past had been tied to perspective, illusionism, architecture, sitedness, objecthood, opticality on the surface – could now be approached in an interactive way. And the photographic capture of smoke, a gambit, which led to the eventual digital rendering of it (through AutoCad and other digital mapping programs) between 1991 and 1992, allows you to generate non-Euclidean scalar and pictorial delineations.*

STELLA: Yes, but we weren't trying to get at the digital look, because that's kind of obvious. We were trying to get at another type of space.

CAMPBELL: *Exactly. What were the first computer processes you used to reconfigure your relationship with space? I know the smoke sculptures came first, but what were the two-dimensional rather than three-dimensional formats? How do these contribute to your conception of working space in painting and the ways in which we started to interface with pictorial space around the late 1980s and early 1990s?*

STELLA: When we first started with the smoke rings, it was as if I could envision what I wanted to do before it was possible to do it, so we faked it a bit until 1991, when Michael [O'Rourke] figured out how to digitally convert the photographs of smoke and I incorporated them into the 'French Mining Town' series. It's one version or another of a 3-D prototype but it's not all rapid prototyping. For instance, in *Fishkill* (1995), there was a smoke ring and that was made from a cast, because that's the way

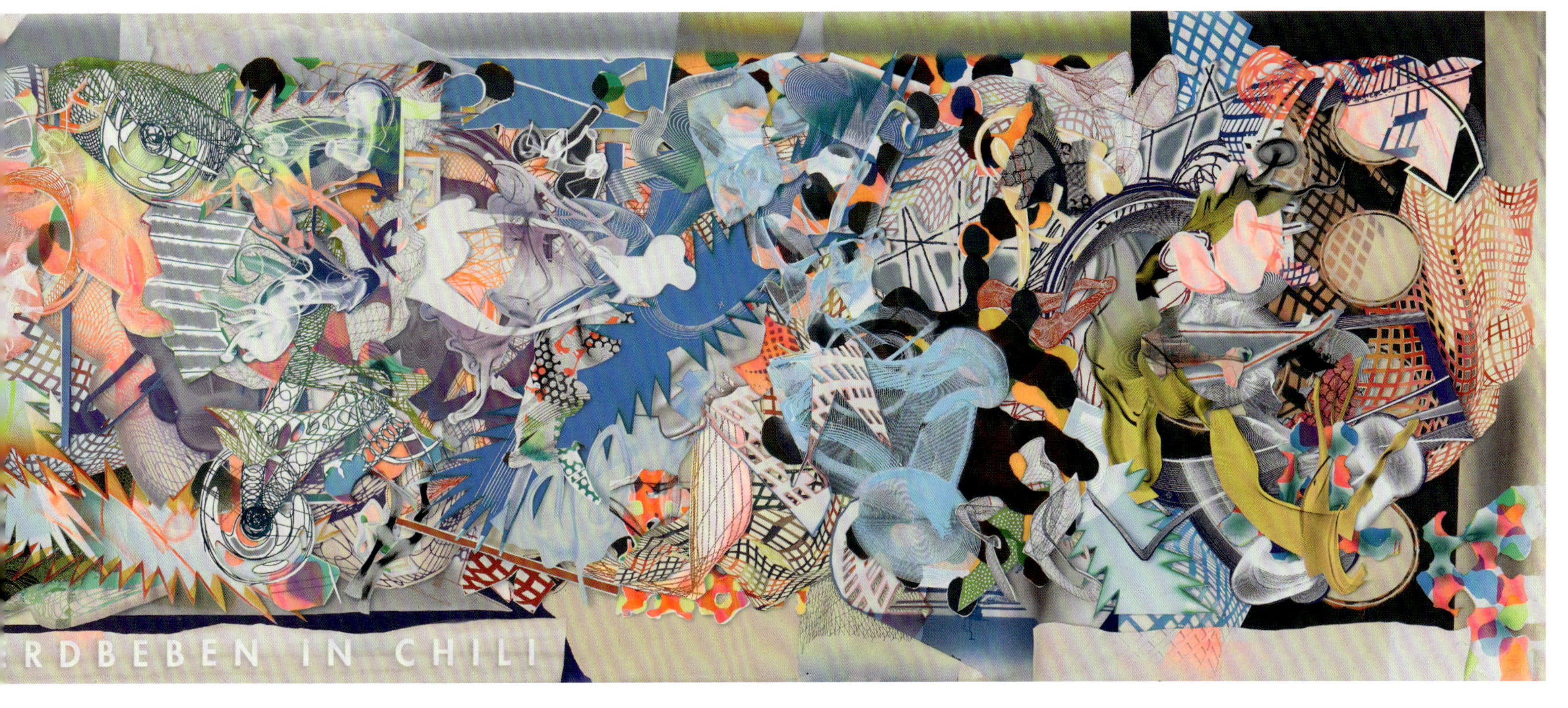

DAS ERDBEBEN IN CHILI [N#3],
1999
ACRYLIC ON CANVAS
366 X 1234 CM

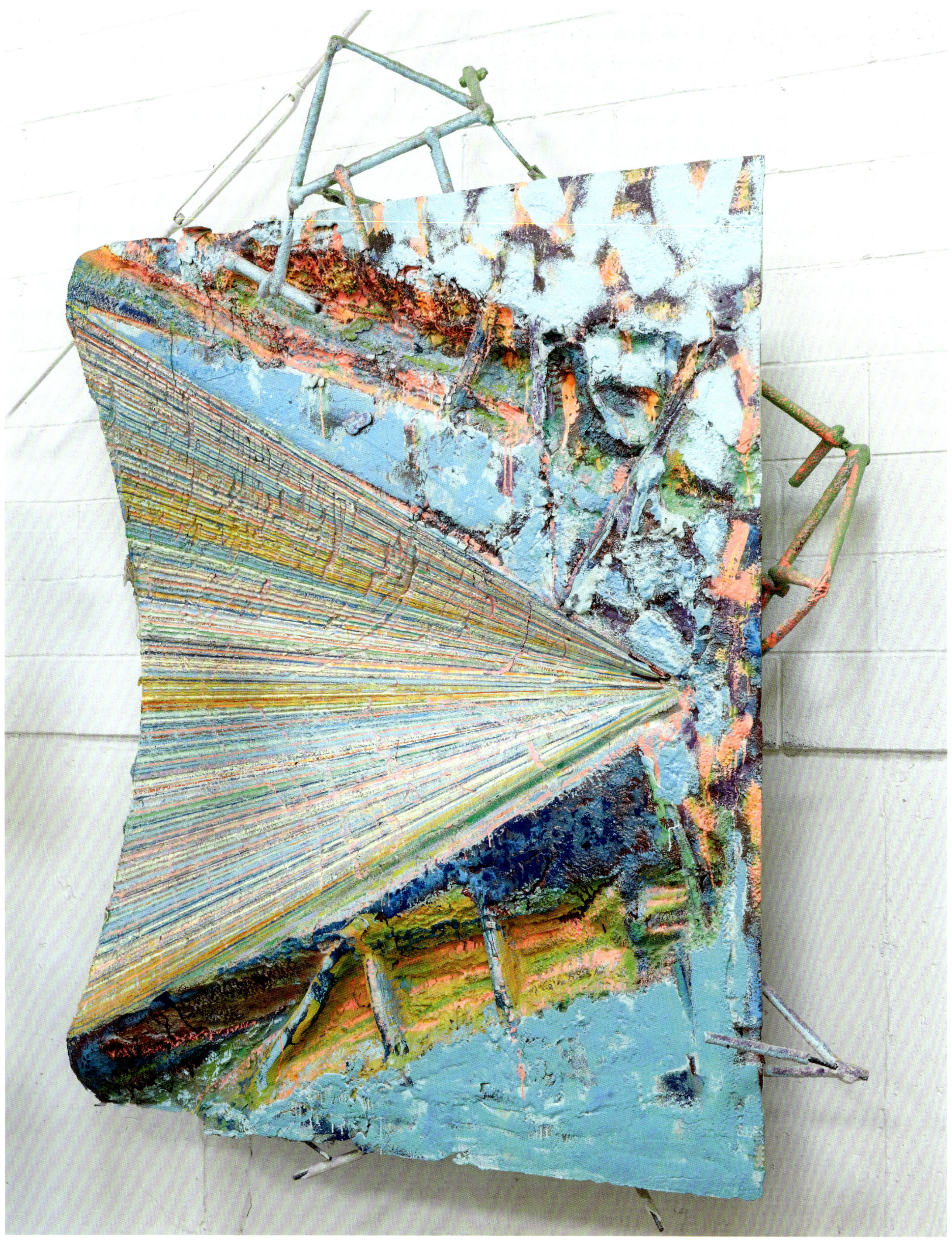

previous page,
MERSIN XX, 2001
MIXED MEDIA ON CAST ALUMINUM, CERAMIC AND CARBON STEEL
252 X 209 X 56 CM

ETANG D'AMBACH, 1992
ALUMINIUM
147 X 135 X 114 CM

next pages,
THE MICHAEL KOHLHAAS CURTAIN, 2008
MIXED MEDIA ON CANVAS
457 X 3050 CM

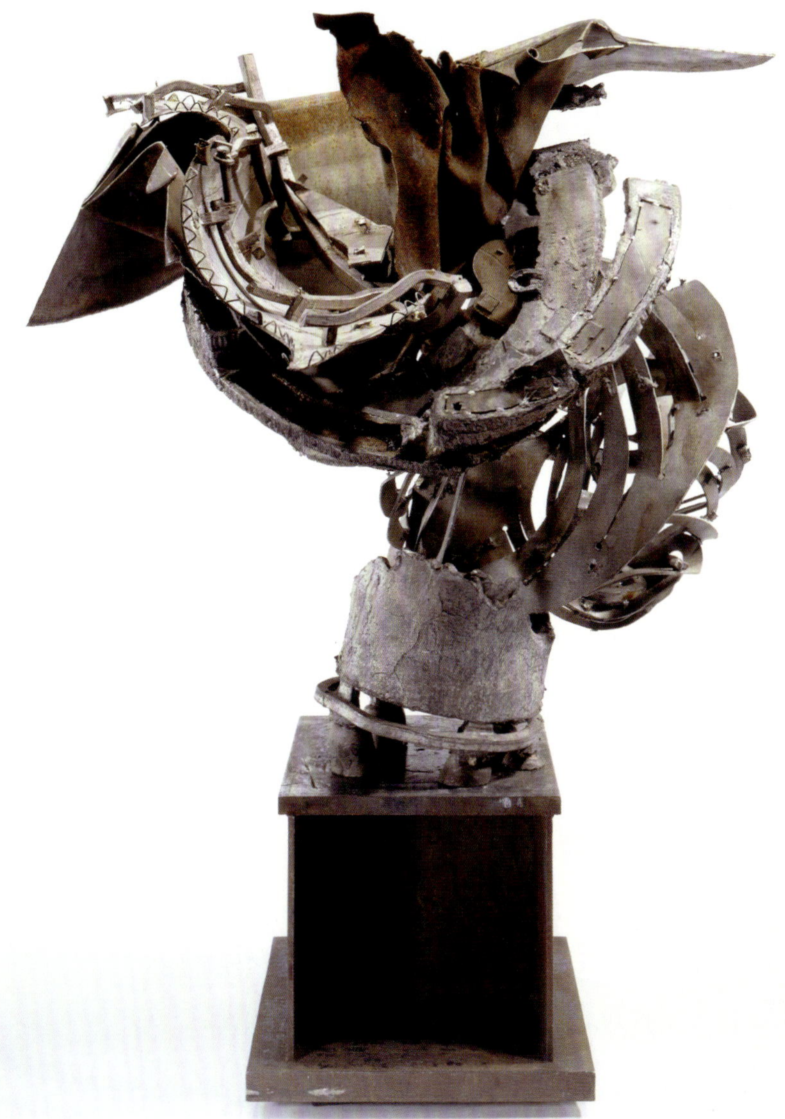

it was done in the early 1990s. By 1999 in *Das Erdbeben in Chili [N#3]*, the smoke ring is a newer, primarily digital version.

CAMPBELL: *In your work, it's often the intersection of so many different types of mark-making that's striking. For you, these works are still paintings. The illusionism of the smoke rings or even the bas-relief of striation marks in* Mersin XX *(2001) are engaged with the legacy of the drawn mark or the painted brushstroke. Layers of paint emerge flecked and variegated; this is innovative. These deep relief lines – are they a happy mistake? Could you get rid of them in the casting?*

STELLA: No, we liked them.

CAMPBELL: *You liked them and so they're deliberate.*

Stella: We could get rid of them, but that's the way I wanted it done.

CAMPBELL: *Rapid prototyping is a set sequence of processes that's used in fabrication and derived from computer data of a three-dimensional rendering. I wonder if this kind of sequence of scale modelling is integral to your work, like the found small structure making up the larger structure in your processes in the 1960s? You've been dealing with issues of space since the 1960s.*

STELLA: Well, in *The Michael Kolhaas Curtain* (2008) space is way more complicated than what you see. Even with some of these small sketches, rapid prototyping can be a way of introducing something unknown into the work of art. It is very physical. Doing it is fairly tricky compared to how it comes across. Initially, it was just a way to create some kind of inner expression from what you can do with material. We cast all kinds of things. In *Mersin XX* we used sand casting to generate the lines that emerge from the wax. Those are from extruded wax, so we use a lot of processes, but they're all fairly straightforward. You can view the processes – so-called computer processes – which are relatively primitive.

CAMPBELL: *For you, the computer is merely a tool that enables you get at this idea of floating space, interactive space, a means to control the feeling of floating unmoored in the work of art. I wonder if using the computer allows you further entry into the illusionism that we see in the two-dimensional plane?*

STELLA: I don't do the computer work. I draw and this gets translated into AutoCad or some other digital-imaging programme. It's merely a tool. So I don't think about it; I only think about the imagery. Then I have to arrange it in space, when it gets to be physical.

CAMPBELL: *But you acknowledge that the computer is the only way to get this digital effect that you're after – not the look of interfacing but the non-Euclidean feel of that space? When we look at the works that incorporate smoke rings, there's an interfolding – almost a liquidity – more so than say, some of the more geometrically rigid earlier paintings.*

STELLA: Yes, each is different.

CAMPBELL: *Would you make work for the internet?*

STELLA: No. If it's used for information, it's fine with me, but I find the aesthetic uses of it … it's going to happen, something inevitably will be good. But I don't see it and it's hard for me to see it.

CAMPBELL: *You or your assistants just use the tools to map certain geometries that you weren't able to do before computers came along.*

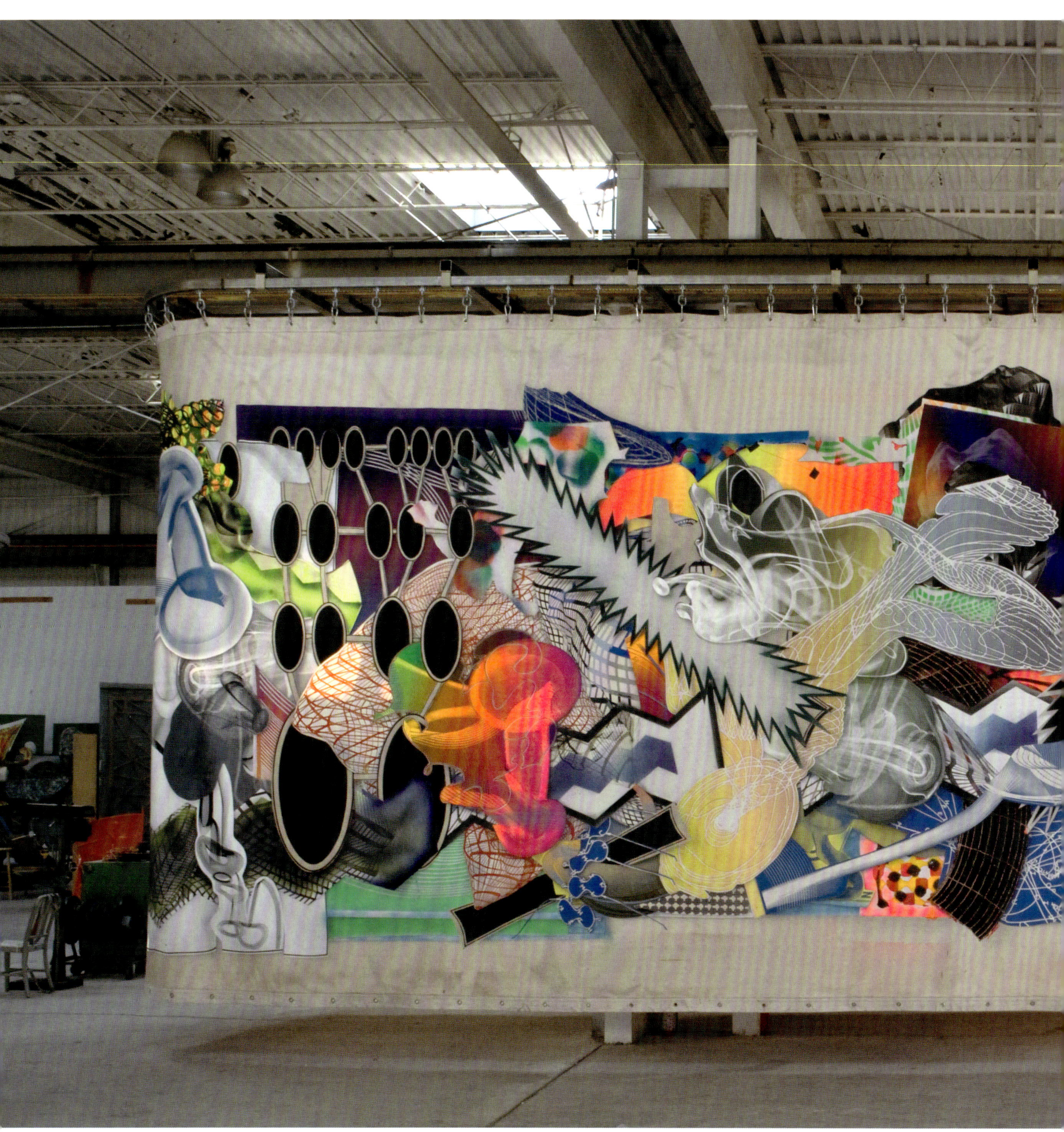

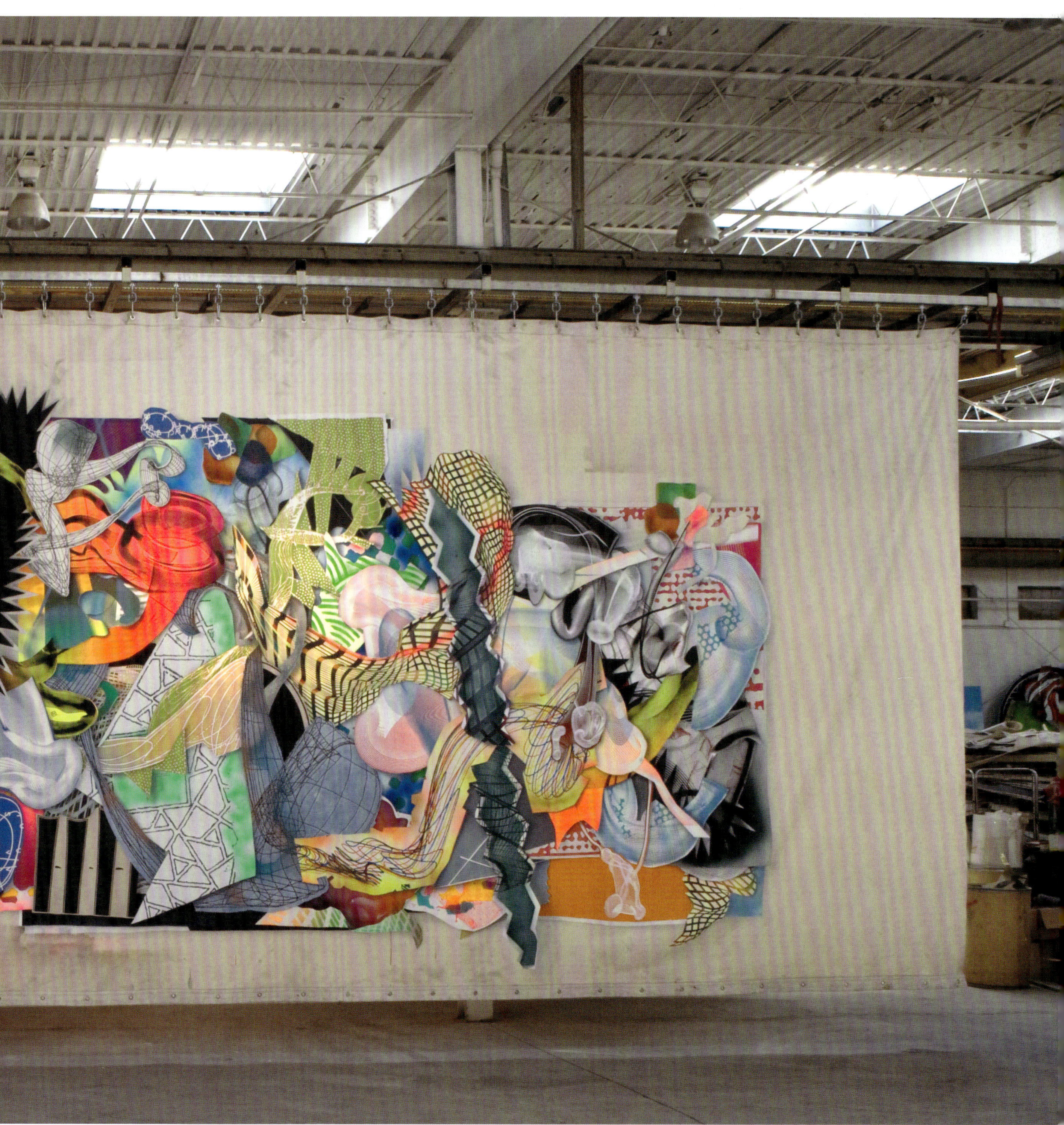

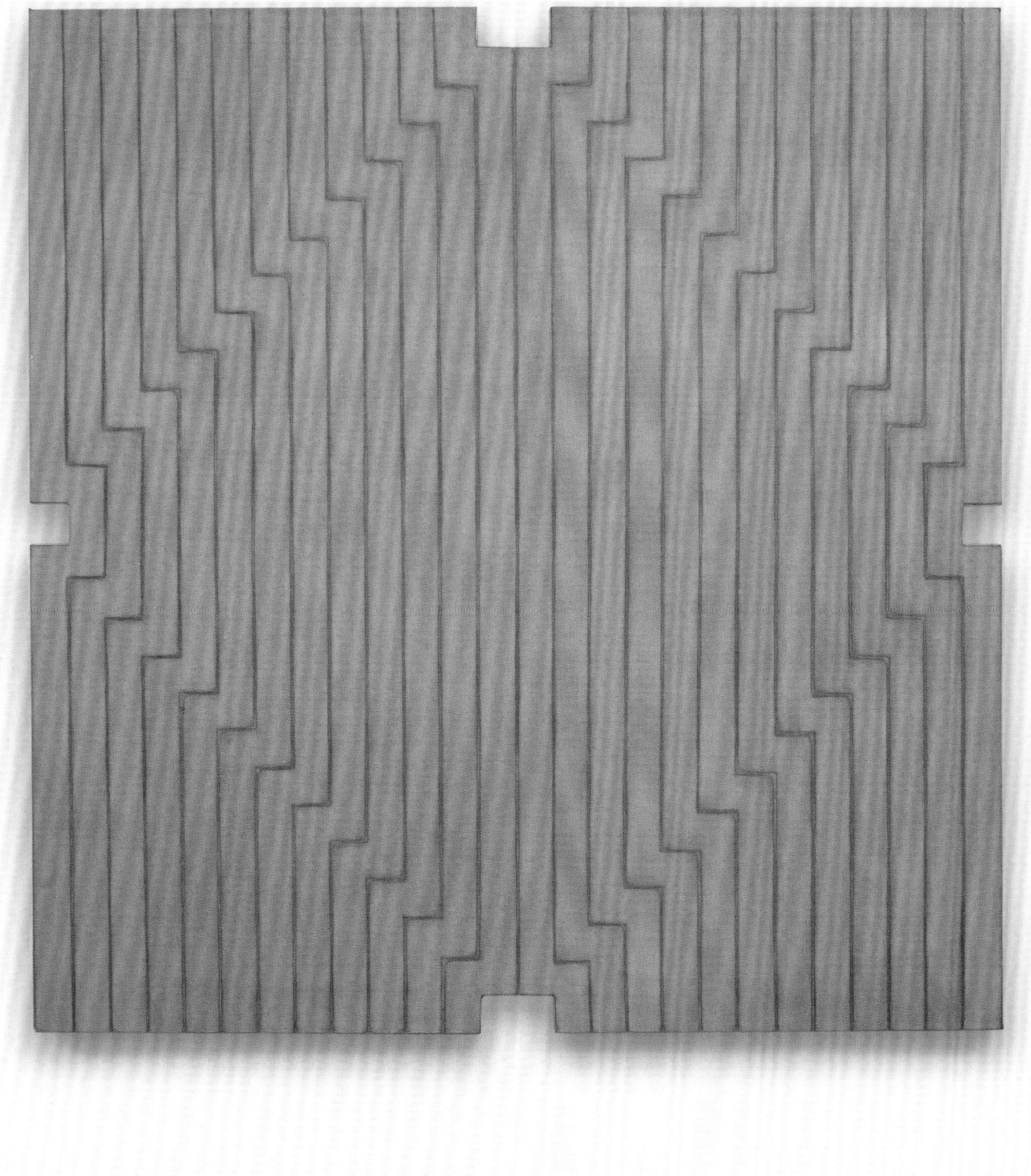

AVERROES, 1960
ALUMINIUM PAINT ON CANVAS
185 X 180 CM

next page,
VALPARAISO FLESH AND GREEN, 1963
METALLIC PAINT ON CANVAS
198 X 343 CM

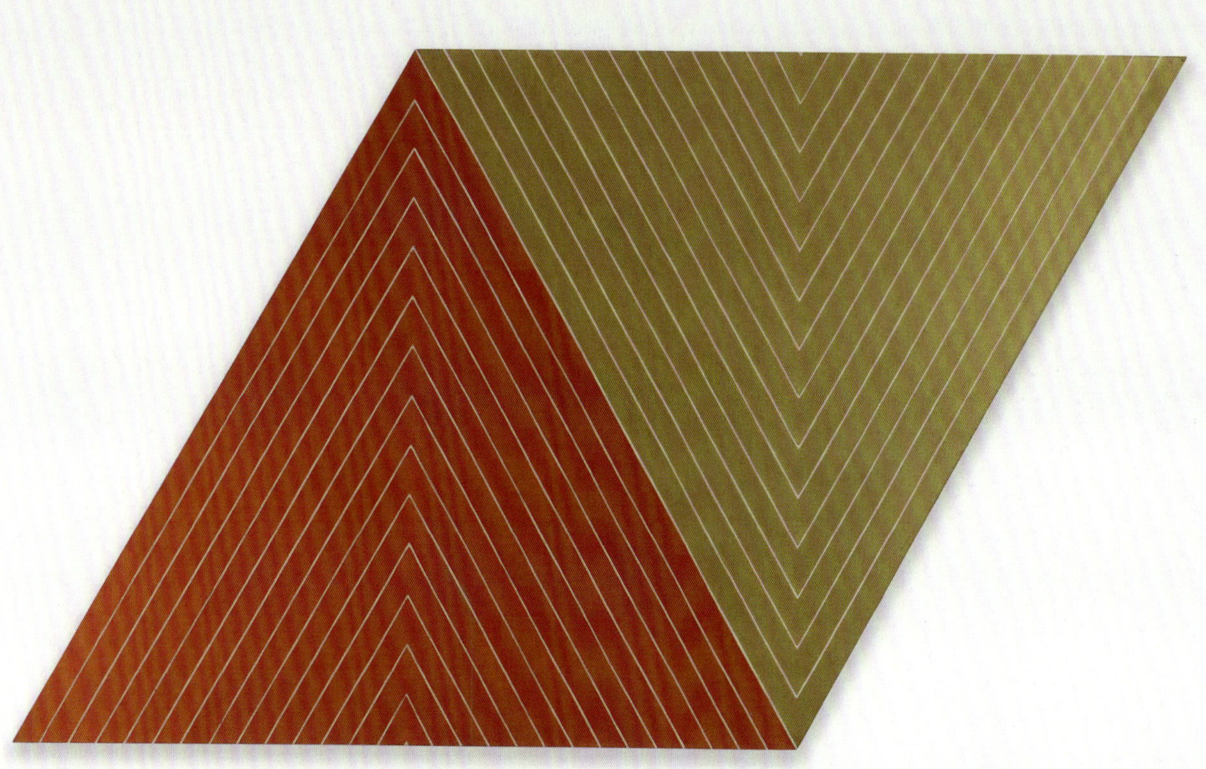

STELLA: Yes, we do very complicated things that are done with three-dimensional programming. I drew them and then we weren't able to actualize them until later. The question is, do you want to spend that much time doing it, and do you really need to have it done in elephant ivory? I don't know why they use ivory, but ivory works quite well for doing complicated things. For me, it's a geometric form that's been made organic – actually it was a shell originally and so it's gone both ways: it's gone from hard geometry to organic expression and then back to hard geometry. We wanted to digitize the smoke rings and they laughed at us when we asked them. But the point wasn't to make the images. What was interesting, but what never happened was to use the kind of modelling that they use for weather forecasts, which is to change the conditions: to see what would happen to the smoke ring if you set it on fire or watched it drip or something. I wanted to do it but it didn't happen and I couldn't find a good enough way to approach it. I'm not sure exactly why. It's to do with the limit of your experience and the way you feel things. Actually, strangely enough, on the computer, the way you put these elements together almost inevitably, for me anyway, has to do with a kind of cross between equilibrium and symmetry. Anyway, it pretty much almost always comes out how it would come out in your hands if you could put the pieces together. So you shouldn't get beyond the idea of the lump of clay in your hands. Because if the clay really could be saved and restretched, would you bend it around the back of your neck? It should stay within the limits of your hands and then the extension of your hands with your body. And if you're clever you can … you know like the guys in India, who can hold things with their feet? That would be nice. You could use all four limbs. It could get really complicated, but you don't do that very much. The tools allow you to get something different in your hands.

CAMPBELL: *Could you talk about the shift from, say, the pieces you were working on in the 1970s to what started happening in the late 1980s and early 1990s in terms of that kind of fluidity and biomorphism?*

STELLA: The earlier works are plain geometry and these later paintings are all about surface: how you work on the surface and make more complicated, freer surfaces rather than always a rigid surface. Often we talk about the difference between Euclidean geometry and the geometry of curves – rubber space, rubber surfaces – so I wanted in these later paintings surfaces that are stretchable, malleable and manipulable.

CAMPBELL: *Is this something that you're reading about?*

STELLA: Yes. It's really about computing the faces of polygons.

CAMPBELL: *What is the text you're reading?*

STELLA: It's a book on Euler's Formula. The text isn't very interesting. The idea is what counts, and it allows for a lot of different ways of doing things. So you can get some idea of what you might do with surfaces and spaces, or where the artwork might go.

CAMPBELL: *How long have you had this interest in geometry? It's an obvious touchstone in the work, but do you have any particular memories of being drawn to it when you were young?*

STELLA: No, I wasn't like others in the 1960s. It wasn't geometry that interested me; that was a means to an end. The thing about geometry is that you need it to measure and to be able to build things. Geometry is just part of measuring and building surfaces. You paint on surfaces, basically, and if you don't paint on surfaces, or if you take a surface for granted, then you're creating surfaces, or painting on top of the surfaces you create. It's the basic ingredient for making paintings or art.

CAMPBELL: *I know you don't want to talk about the stripe paintings anymore, but may I ask a direct question and you won't get upset?*

STELLA: Probably. [Laughter]

CAMPBELL: *The early paintings were about this idea of a kind of found measure, right? Do you think that in some ways you're thinking more about surface now than about measurement, if they're both related to geometry?*

STELLA: Well, in the stripe paintings, I picked a simple geometry. It's easy measurements. And then I painted on it. I made the surface, which was also relatively simple because it was repetitive. So that was trying to make it as easy for myself as I could.

CAMPBELL: *But now there's all of this complexity in terms of this kind of warped surface, so maybe your interest is ...*

STELLA: Well, in the end it's all the same. You have to make it look all right.

CAMPBELL: [Laughter] *That's true. I guess you can tell who the art historian is in this conversation! But your relationship to geometry has changed during your career. Visually it manifests in different ways.*

STELLA: No, I don't think it's changed. You can't fabricate anything anymore unless you provide the people who are going to work for you with the geometry. I just think at some point you need to know about whatever the people who are helping you are doing. That's the way life is now.

CAMPBELL: *So you have to know what's possible in terms of the machines in the studio?*

STELLA: Yes. Mutable space is what I want to happen even in the prototyping stage, but we don't ever really get there in machine fabrication, because in the end, after we do all of those things, and we cast them, they emerge rigid. You have to move things around and play with them.

LETTRE SUR LES SOURDS ET MUETS II, 1974
SYNTHETIC POLYMER PAINT ON CANVAS
358 X 358 CM

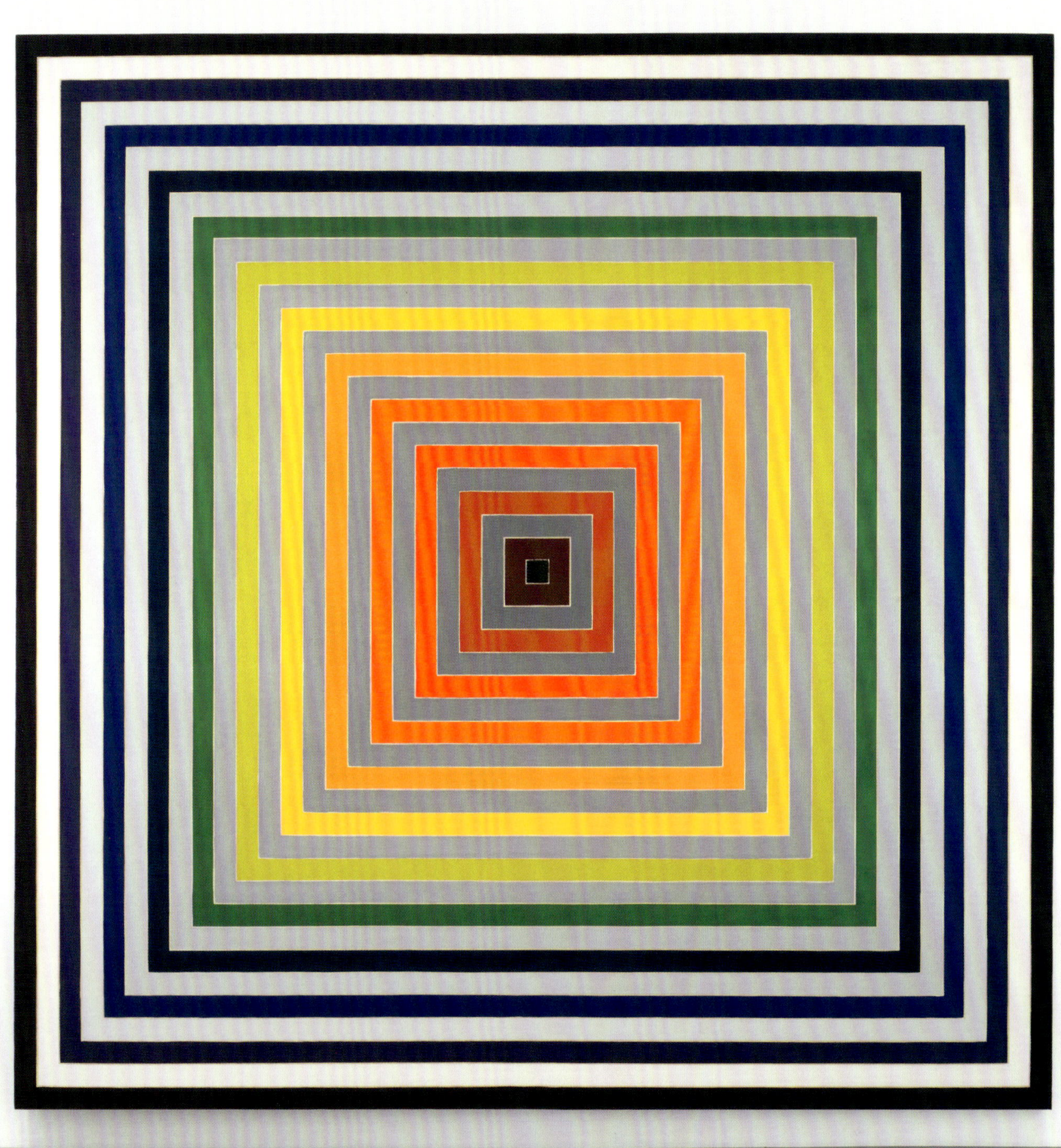

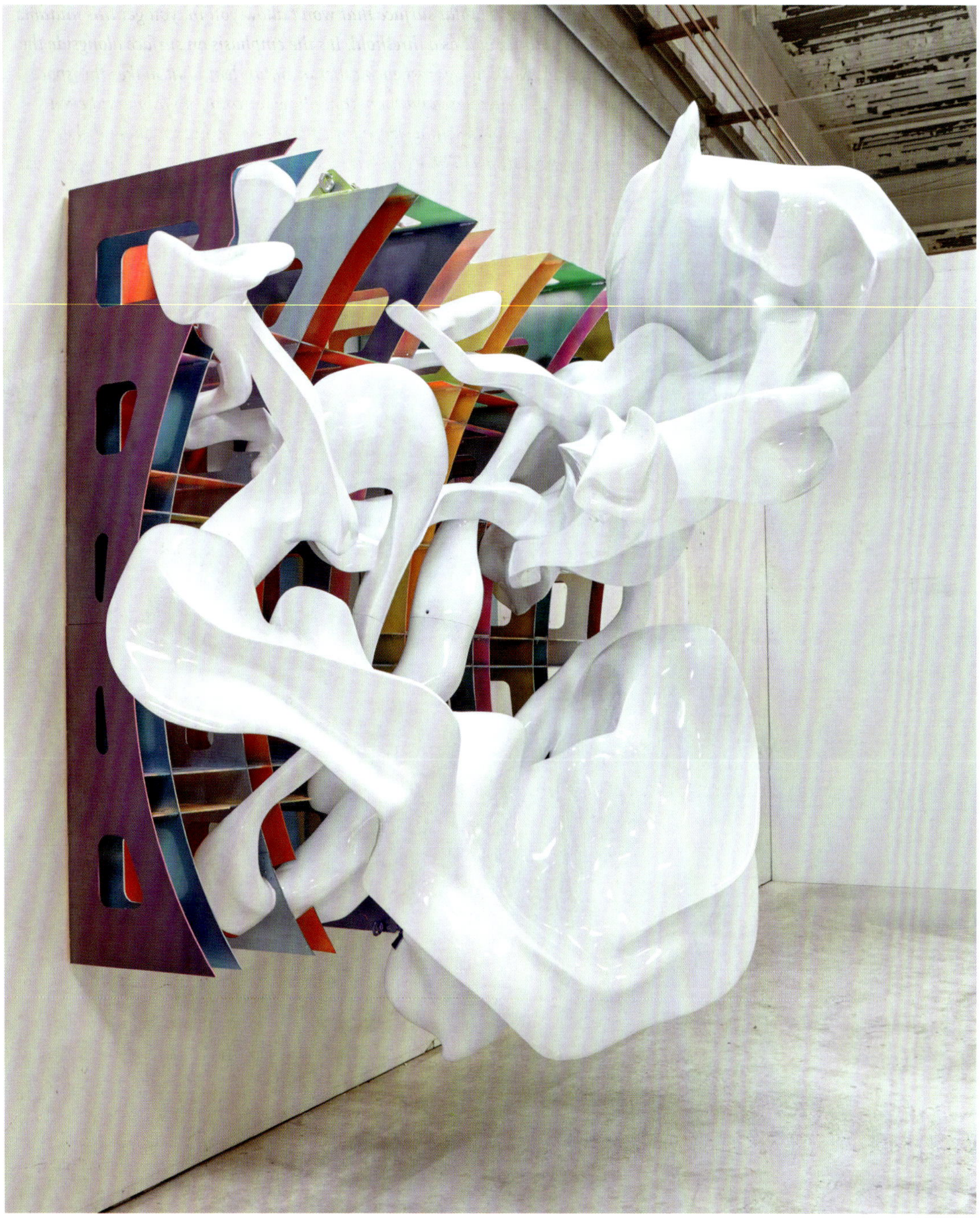

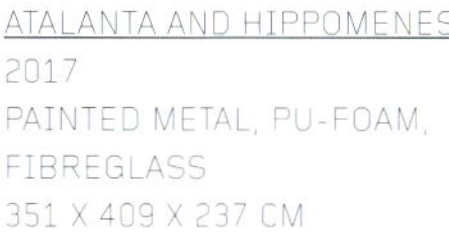

ATALANTA AND HIPPOMENES,
2017
PAINTED METAL, PU-FOAM,
FIBREGLASS
351 X 409 X 237 CM

CAMPBELL: *You've been working with a new type of plastic that's a little bit more wobbly and elastic.*

STELLA: I've always been interested in new materials. The new plastic is more flexible, but it's not working that well.

CAMPBELL: *Why?*

STELLA: It's fine in the model size, but it doesn't lend itself to scaling up. Scale changes shift everything.

CAMPBELL: *You've been writing about and exploring pictorial space for over half a century, but there is a space in the later work, as I understand it, that doesn't stem from a phenomenological interest – making the body aware of its relationship to the space in the painting – but rather where a centripetal contraction and also a centrifugal refusal happens. When you combine the almost hypnotic illusionism of the smoke rings, the*

TARGOWICA I, 1973
MIXED MEDIA COLLAGE
311 X 246 X 8 CM

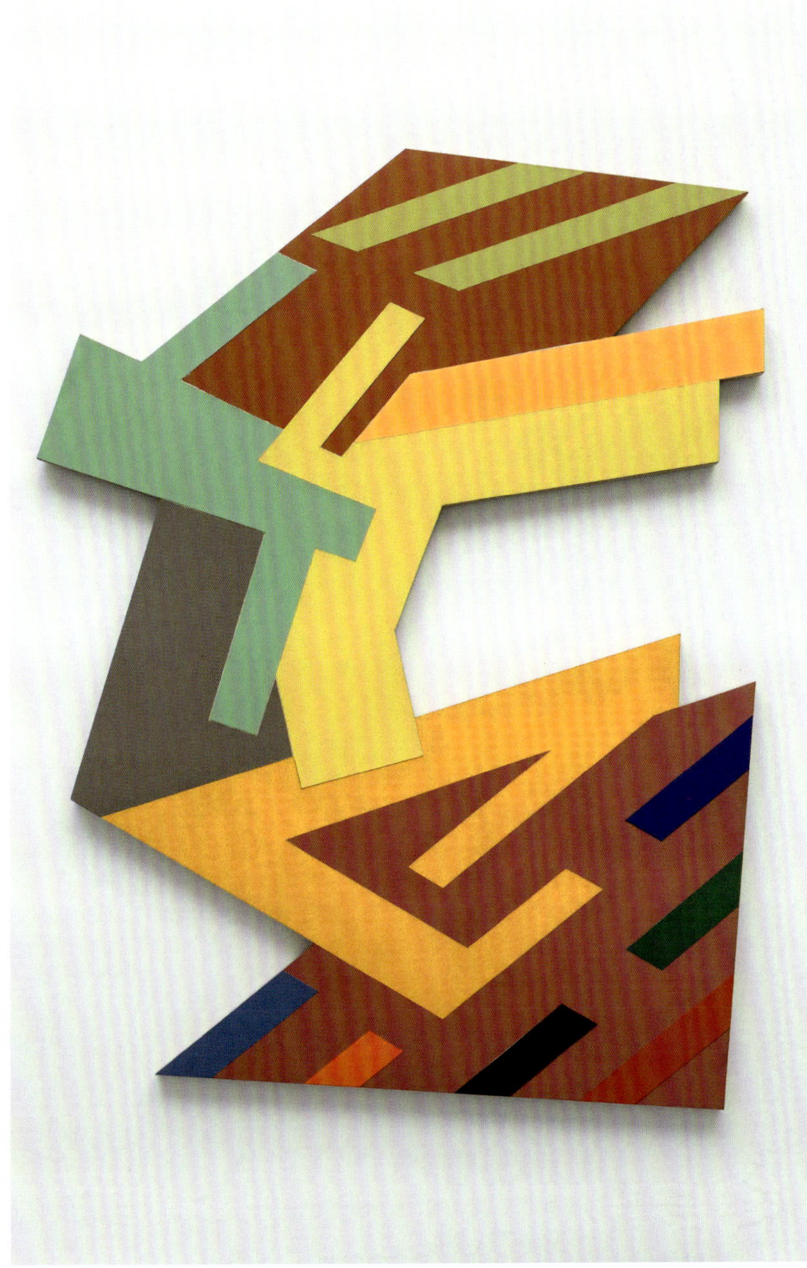

biomorphic gesture and areas of flat surface that won't allow you in, you get this mutable working space. I like to think of it as a threshold. It's the emphasis on surface alongside the imagery, as you've said, working against each other or in tandem, that makes this space disorienting and creates niches here and there that allow for contemplation and even habitation. The scale, the monumental size, allows the viewer to occupy these niches in almost an architectonic manner. There's a certain amount of generosity in that approach.

STELLA: It comes from making marks on a surface – a surface you can see so that viewers can find their way out. As long as you do research into the surface, anything that you make on the surface is generous.

CAMPBELL: *I like this idea.*

STELLA: After all, the marks that you've made get stolen from the surface, then become places of contact.

CAMPBELL: *The introduction of digital space into the work that happened around the time that you did the Norton lectures, when you started thinking about these ideas and you created a tool to make that happen through photography and smoke, for me, is an exploration of the threshold of virtual space. So I want to kind of go back and think about what you discussed in some of your writings as being the potential in painting and how you saw that potential as being very fraught in the 1990s specifically.*

STELLA: Well, I think that in the 1990s, painting was losing traction – at least in the amount of attention it was getting and the effect that it had on the art that was being made. The older painters at that time like Helen Frankenthaler, the colour-field painters, were invested in what seemed to me to be open and beautiful, but even this was disappearing. Painting was reverting to being, if it was painting at all, solely gestural: one could think here of Schnabel and Basquiat. This was timely painting and plenty interesting, but it wasn't very open; it was, again, sort of digging into the painting rather than letting the paint move. Conceptual painting. There was a loss of the dynamic that might have had potential. To me, it seemed obvious that the new emphasis in painting didn't have that much of a chance of moving forward.

CAMPBELL: *So what I call the virtual, you designate as potential. (There must be a link to Agamben there somewhere… 'a light that strives to reach us but can not.') This openness you discuss seems related to the fluidity we talked about before. In the early 1990s, the path forward that you saw was an emphasis on variegated materials but with an openness that the colour-field painters found solely using paint. Your incorporation of illusionism is a discontinuation from your early work; you started talking about illusionism a lot in the late 1980s and 1990s – how to bring that back into painting?*

STELLA: Yes, but what I talked about isn't completely relevant to what I did. Illusionism was never a reality for me, because if there's an object and that object is physical, then the illusionism is given. For example, *Targowica I* (1973): there's no need for illusionism there – the light has it's own illusionism.

CAMPBELL: *Of course, but we've spoken of the intensification of illusionism in Renaissance art, whether according to Nagel and Wood in an anachronistic juxtaposition of 'virtual life' or in terms of perspective. Your large-scale paintings, even* The Michael Kohlhaas Curtain, *integrate painted forms or sprayed forms that appear three-dimensional, or half relief, or as if they're interfacing space. Even if there is a given illusionism, those traffic in an increased illusionism that I would call the virtual space of painting – and somewhere between the virtual and physical world lies painting's potential.*

STELLA: You're right. And we tried this idea in those pieces that are central to the 'Imaginary Places' series. Think, for instance, of *Cantahar* (1998). In some of the 'Kleist Paintings', the illusionism was the illusionism of the collage. So if the collage had a depth of, say, a quarter of an inch and you blew it up four times, then you were painting a shadow representing an inch. So, there was illusionism that was a mechanical illusionism or even a digital one, depending on the tools you used to blow it up.

CAMPBELL: *In previous discussions of mechanical illusionism and its relationship to collage, you've made a connection to printmaking. Could you expand on how prints – in the way in which they repeat patterning – allowed you to play with or envision the digital illusionism that we're talking about in the 'Imaginary Places' series?*

STELLA: Patterning is basically a flat device with several different layers that, yes, generates surface illusion, but on the other hand needs a sense of tactility, which becomes a contact point for viewing. It's not about depth versus illusionism in a binary; you need to have a spherical illusionism or the kind of illusionism you would get if you're dealing with perspective or that could be warped.

CAMPBELL: *Illusionism as it relates to motion? So, maybe a kind of energy? You've written about this idea of pictorial energy versus a physical energy. Is that something you see in the 'Imaginary Places' series?*

STELLA: Well, I'd like to see it. I want to get there.

CAMPBELL: *You think the works are successful when they have that?*

STELLA: Yes. I think that's what it's all about and it doesn't matter too much how you get it. I worried when colour-field painting and the expansive gestural painting seemed to disappear in favour of a lot of heavy-handed muddiness and then a lot of conceptual painting. I wanted to find a way to achieve pictorial energy.

CAMPBELL: *Like installation art, performance, all these genres that came to the fore in this period.*

STELLA: Yes, well, they achieved primacy. But I don't know if it applies, because I'm thinking of works that are strictly speaking literal. I don't know if installation art is particularly visual. You have to look at it, but you have to do so many other things too. One of the advantages with painting, theoretically, is that you just look at it.

CAMPBELL: *Do you want to elaborate on this idea of physical energy? Is motion really important in these works? Because I always think that they're kind of torqued and you see that even in the large-scale sculpture. There seems to be movement that's happening here.*

CANTAHAR, 1998
ACRYLIC ON CANVAS
396 X 396 CM

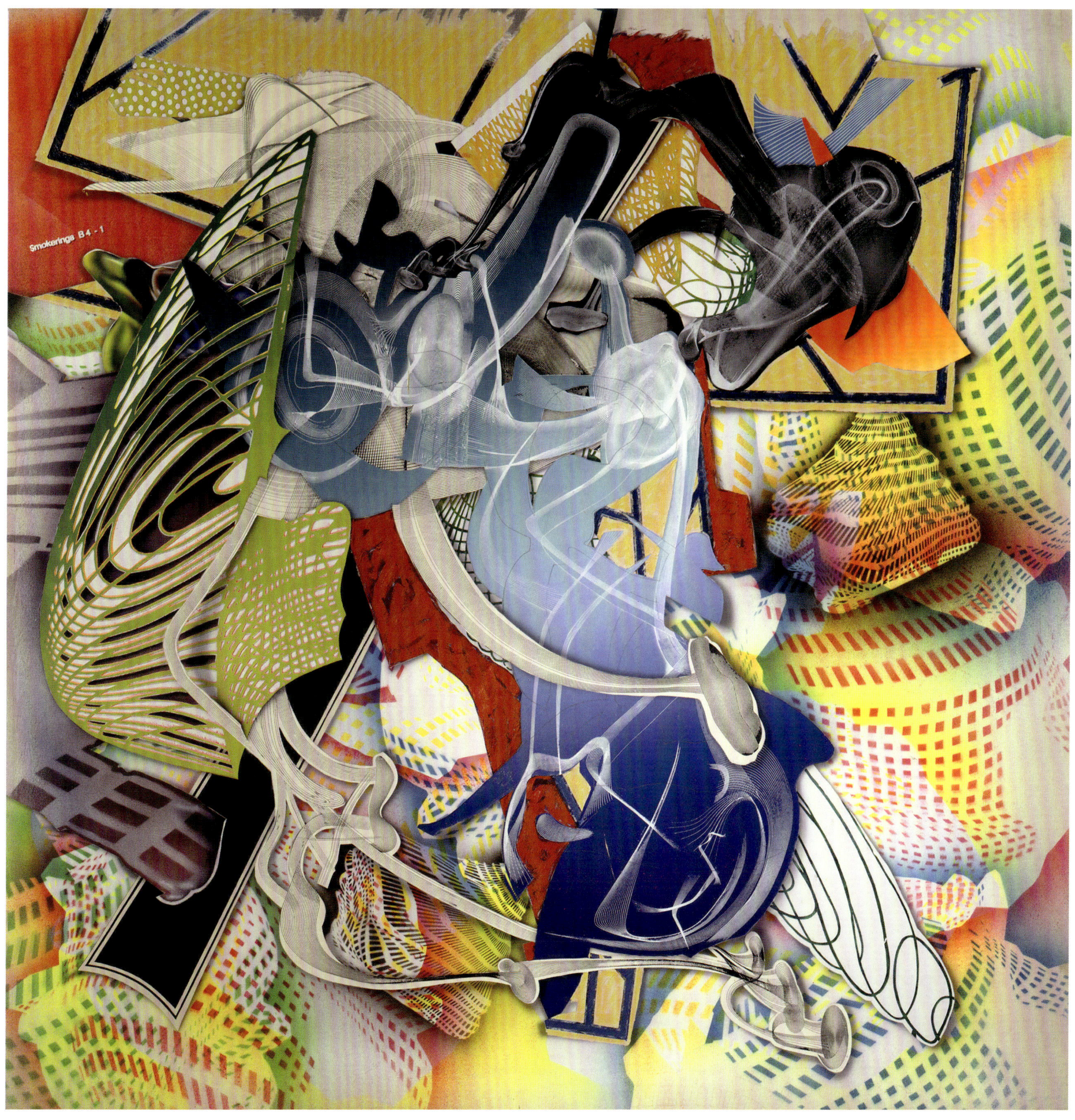

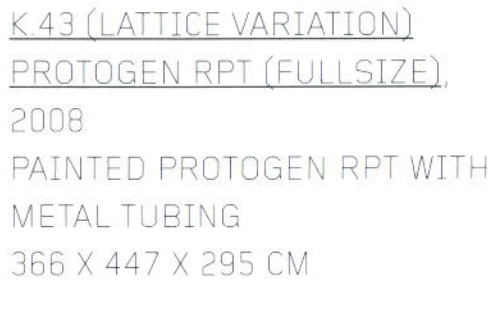

K 43 (LATTICE VARIATION) PROTOGEN RPT (FULLSIZE), 2008
PAINTED PROTOGEN RPT WITH METAL TUBING
366 X 447 X 295 CM

STELLA: Actually it's really hard to think of examples of art that are successful at portraying a static.

CAMPBELL: *In Vermeer, or even in photography, there is this emphasis on that frozen moment.*

STELLA: I don't know anything about photography, but you mean like those drops of milk? That's a frozen moment, right?

CAMPBELL: *Yes, that's the frozen moment.*

STELLA: But that's anything but a frozen moment, right? The way you experience it.

CAMPBELL: *Ha! Good one. I've been writing about Kandinsky and Klee, and their theories of motion around 1942–44 – movement that isn't line, isn't a demarcation or a boundary in space, but traverses from one part of the pictorial plane to another. I started thinking about the difference between boundaries in painting or in any controlled space, and the ways one delineates movement. So that's why I'm asking you this. Because I think there's a shift that happens in that period that's quite different from what we saw before.*

STELLA: With Kandinsky, it depends on the body of work. The ones that have the most movement are biomorphic, but no one liked his biomorphic paintings. They do depict movement. Actually, when you think of movement, there's the exterior movement – the portrayal of a person from the outside – and at the same time, biologically speaking, there's interior movement: your heart is beating, the blood is flowing. There's a lot of movement going on that's not particularly well depicted and maybe fortunately so. I wouldn't go so far … I mean I don't know how far I would go, but I don't particularly want to deny how paintings are basically static and so not moving.

CAMPBELL: *So what is a movement in a painting? Would you describe an optical sensation caused by scale shifts etc as movement?*

STELLA: Compositions are about the way forms relate to each other: they suggest movement, and if they don't, if they lack a little bit of tension, then they're boring. This is a method that implies motion.

CAMPBELL: *How does technology get you there? Caroline Jones has written about the factory in the studio, how you decided to move into this realm where you're using technology. How does technology get you to move away from something more static towards the moving surface?*

STELLA: I don't know. I actually don't know. I think the technology came to me accidentally from printmaking. When you're etching, you start with etching aluminium. And then I went wild! I etched magnesium because it took to the acid. We changed the standard etching material so when you printed from it, it was quite beautiful. Then unfortunately I had the idea to paint them, which wasn't so smart, but we won't talk about that.

CAMPBELL: *And the poured metal came out of printmaking as well, and stamping.*

STELLA: I brought that to printmaking. We were pouring metal at the foundry.

CAMPBELL: *So that idea of creating a pattern didn't come out of prints, but the other way around?*

STELLA: Yes, the other way around. When you're etching, you're working on a surface and you're digging it deeper. Then if you pour the metal over its surface, it's hard to print. But within reason you can make it work. I don't think we exploited that as much as we could have, or should have, now that I think of it.

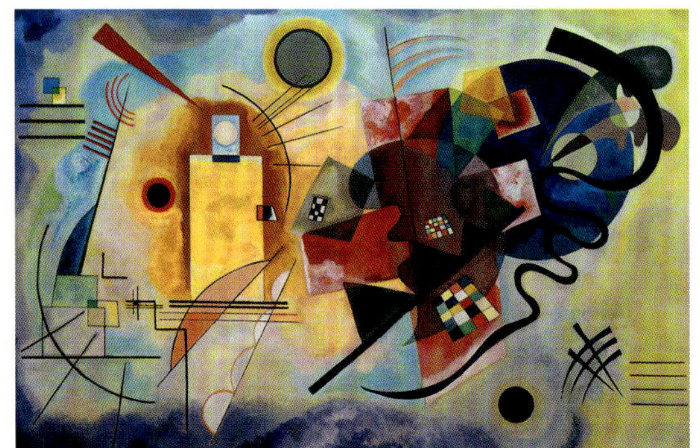

WASSILY KANDINSKY
GELB, ROT, BLAU, 1925
OIL ON CANVAS
128 X 202 CM

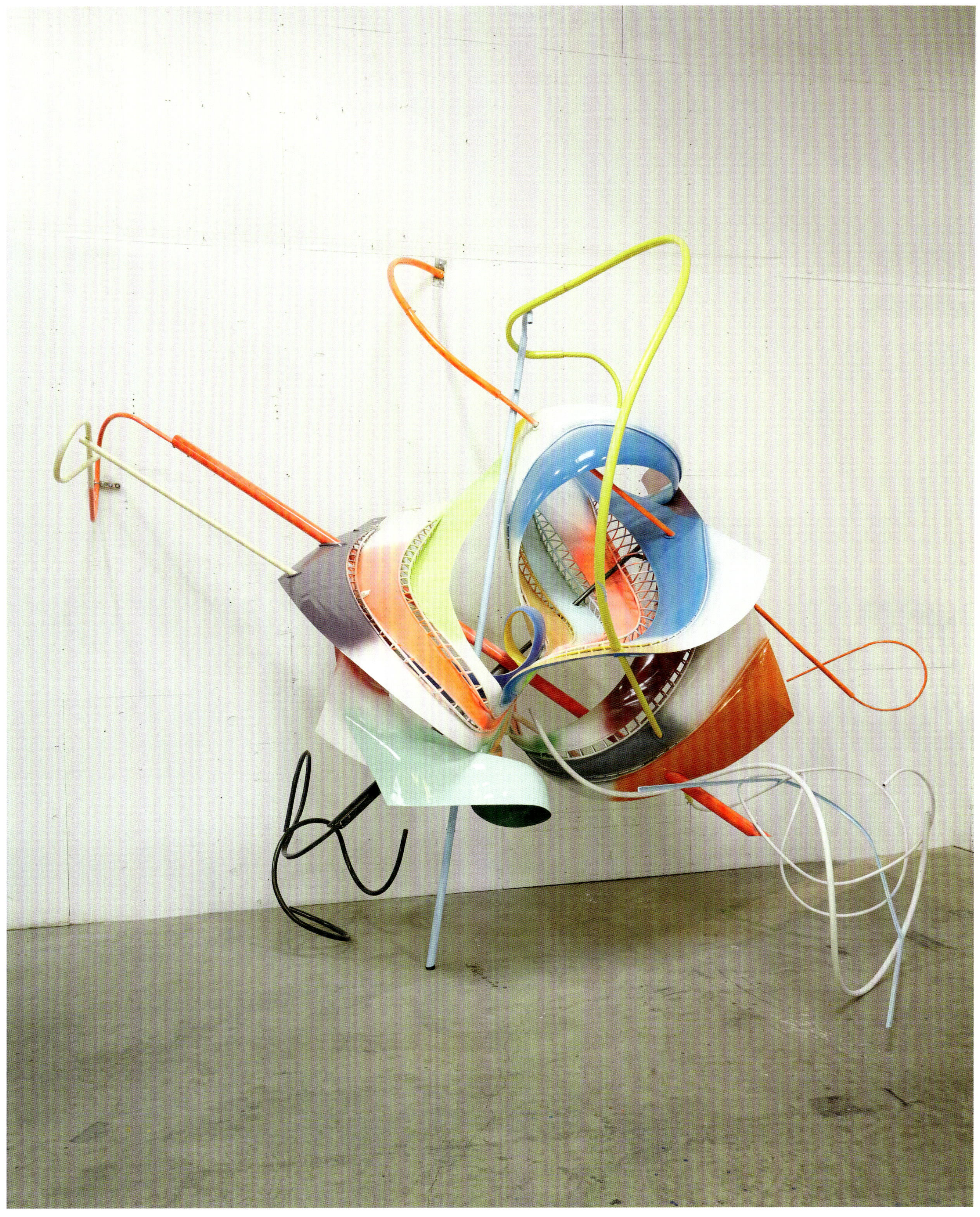

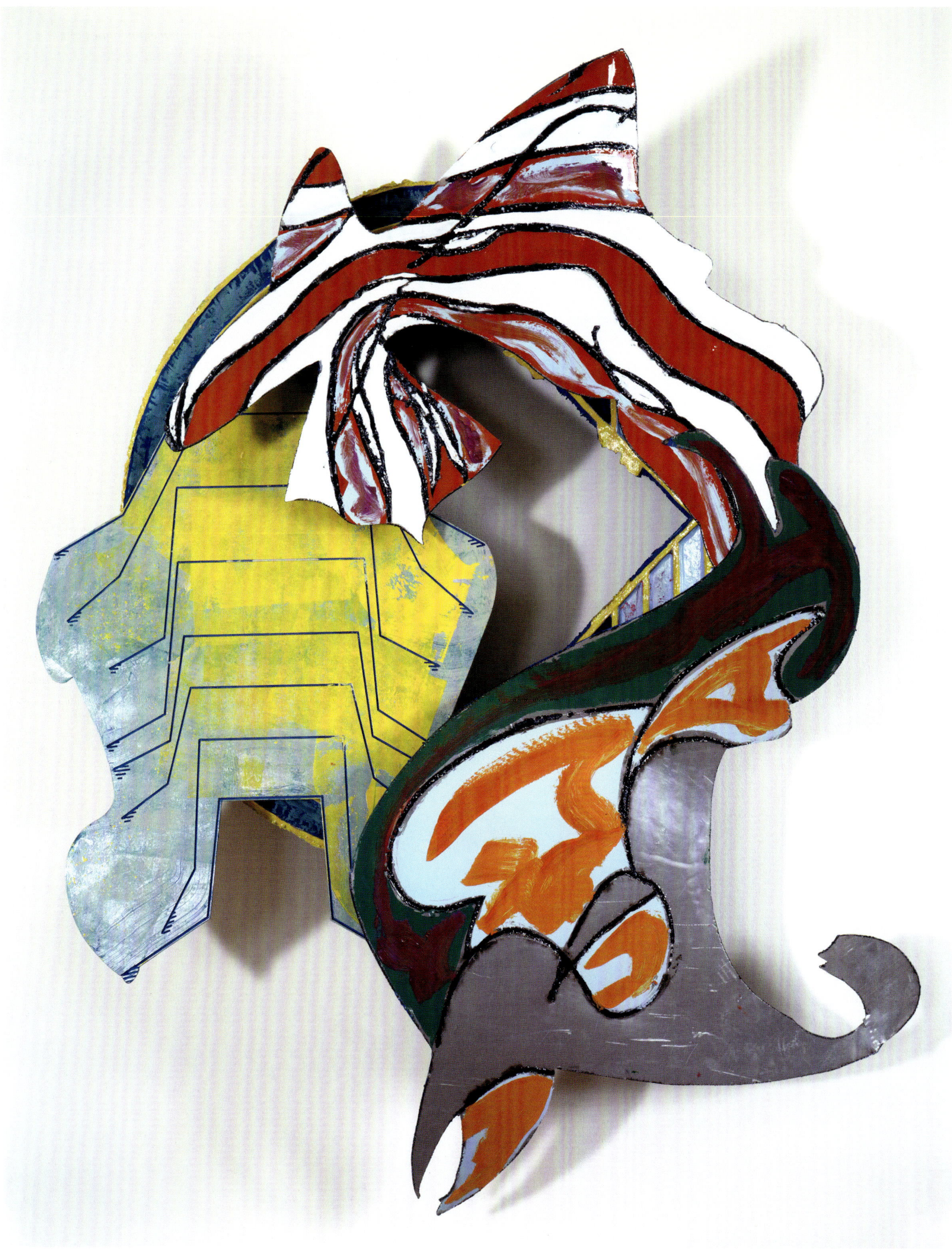

THE PEQUOD MEETS THE RACHEL, 1988
ACRYLIC AND ENAMEL ON ALUMINUM
334 X 258 X 81 CM

CAMPBELL: *You've talked about cave paintings and movement in those paintings. Where does fiction come in – the imaginary, the poetic – if at all?*

STELLA: I think the beauty of cave painting is the desperation with which they wanted to make a mystical shamanistic experience and a dream state from the observational. So it's actually the battle of reason against magic. It was about observing what was going on. And in observation we used to progress to magic, which doesn't lead anywhere except as entertainment, I guess.

CAMPBELL: *I guess so.*

STELLA: I don't think it does. You know, the titles of my works come out of what I experience and read?

CAMPBELL: *Like* Moby Dick?

STELLA: Yes, but *Moby Dick* was for me, much more. It's not fair to Melville, but it was an around-the-world adventure story about struggling with larger-than-life forces.

CAMPBELL: *I love Melville's poem on art: 'To wrestle with the angel – Art'.*

STELLA: The detail in Melville is beautiful and he tries to sustain you during the trip and to indulge you in the language. This approach gives you permission, as the author, to indulge in a fair amount of variety; it doesn't have to make sense, except at the end, when it's over. So while you're working your way through it, you do have to look back and say, 'Does it hold together, does it fit, does it work, does it make sense?' But the fact of the matter is that when you construct something like that you'll never say 'Okay, I did it; now forget about it.' It changes something. It shifts.

CAMPBELL: *I like this idea of exploration and the imaginary because I see it as being very connected virtuality or the digital. You've written about the investment in virtuality that in some ways Pollock innovated. As we know, the whole idea of the avant-garde is the consumption and digestion of what came before. You wrote about how Pollock consumed the roots of Cubism, regionalism and even Mexican muralism.*

STELLA: I didn't say that he consumed the roots of regionalism.

CAMPBELL: *You said 'destroyed the roots'.*

STELLA: Well, you could say that he did, because regionalism didn't bounce back in that era. But the roots of regionalism did in the end come back, so maybe when I said it I didn't have the insight I have now. Pollock took virtuality in painting to a level that was so abstract and yet viewers didn't want to give up on the connection to reality and felt it had to express the most literal kind of feelings. So I guess what I said was true, but only up to a point.

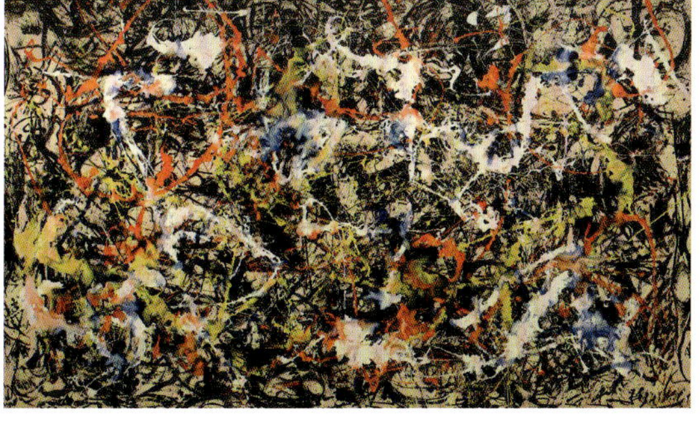

JACKSON POLLOCK
CONVERGENCE, 1952
OIL ON CANVAS
238 X 394 CM

CAMPBELL: *Your pinpointing of the return of regionalism highlights what's happening now, where there's this kind of folk-like interest in figuration. There's a rejection of process-based or 'zombie abstraction'.*

STELLA: Yes there are waves. But the disappearance of the expansive and open abstraction is too bad. I don't know why it couldn't continue. What abstraction you have now is that much more finicky and detailed; it's just not expansive. And I equate expansiveness, I suppose, with a kind of ambitiousness and a kind of generosity about what an enterprise should try to do.

CAMPBELL: *Does that relate to how you think about the relationship between art and architecture? Because you've described how in the past, for instance, architects and artists worked together and function followed form instead of the other way around. So there was a way in which that expansiveness could be about our relationship to our environment and not just the way that a painting sits on a wall. Instead, it actually is integral to the space that we're living in or residing in, or eating in, for instance.*

STELLA: Well, architecture can be big and expansive. As far as I'm concerned, architecture isn't a problem. The problem is the units – when units overwhelm the idea of building. People accept living in units when nothing else is available, but I don't know that they would necessarily choose to do that; I guess if you make the units big enough … Anyway, the repetition of units is the basic problem of architecture.

CAMPBELL: *But how do you see art relating to architecture, especially these days? Because so many of your large pieces can't sit in a home – not my house anyway – they have to be in large corporate buildings or museums.*

STELLA: Paintings don't look so great in architecture. And the other problem is, they're not so great outside in mother nature's realm either. It's a challenge to make something work in that way. And also to not get bound by rules, measurements or even phenomenology.

CAMPBELL: *Sculpture has to do with building – not necessarily architecture as a field of study, but building in general. Even autoconstruction, as Abraham Cruzvillegas calls it, has a scale and a life to it. As does a bridge or platform building, that kind of thing. I see that pretty much as sculpture.*

STELLA: Yes, the folly or the scaffolding, or the kind of confinement that's not unit-based. But isn't the folly different from the bridge? The bridge has to stand up.

CAMPBELL: *That's true.*

STELLA: The bridge has a sense of having been put together for a purpose. In some cases, it can be purposeful and in others not purposeful, but it has more purpose than the folly.

CAMPBELL: *That's interesting because in the past you've talked about the opposite. I'm interested in this newer idea of this kind of structure that's purposeful versus a structure that has formal properties that don't relate to its function.*

STELLA: Well, I mean the purposefulness is inherent in it; it doesn't really have any purpose except to be accepted as art. You might say that that quality is actually akin to what makes representationalism a meta-quality. Because representation is recognizable that is why recognizability has a purpose.

CAMPBELL: *Yes and with that recognizability, viewers feel that they can relate or maybe enter the work. You've written about how the space of abstraction in Abstract Expressionism has an even-weightedness. Greenberg writes about this as well: in Pollock, it's as if an oscillation is happening. It's on the surface and in a very shallow field, and so it's very hard to enter that space because you're feeling a kind of vibration of movement across the surface. You play with weightedness in your own work, whether it's the irregular polygons, which are differently weighted in terms of their shape, or the later works, like* Targowica I, *which is heavier on the top than on the bottom. So it's a move away from the traditional ways of weighting things in painting and even in sculptural objects.*

STELLA: This was true earlier as well. My teacher always told me to keep it heavy on the top.

CAMPBELL: *Yes? Which one?*

STELLA: William Seitz. He would say that painting should always have the weight at the top, then you work your way down.

K 236, 2016
ALUMINUM AND STAINLESS STEEL
871 X 818 X 551 CM

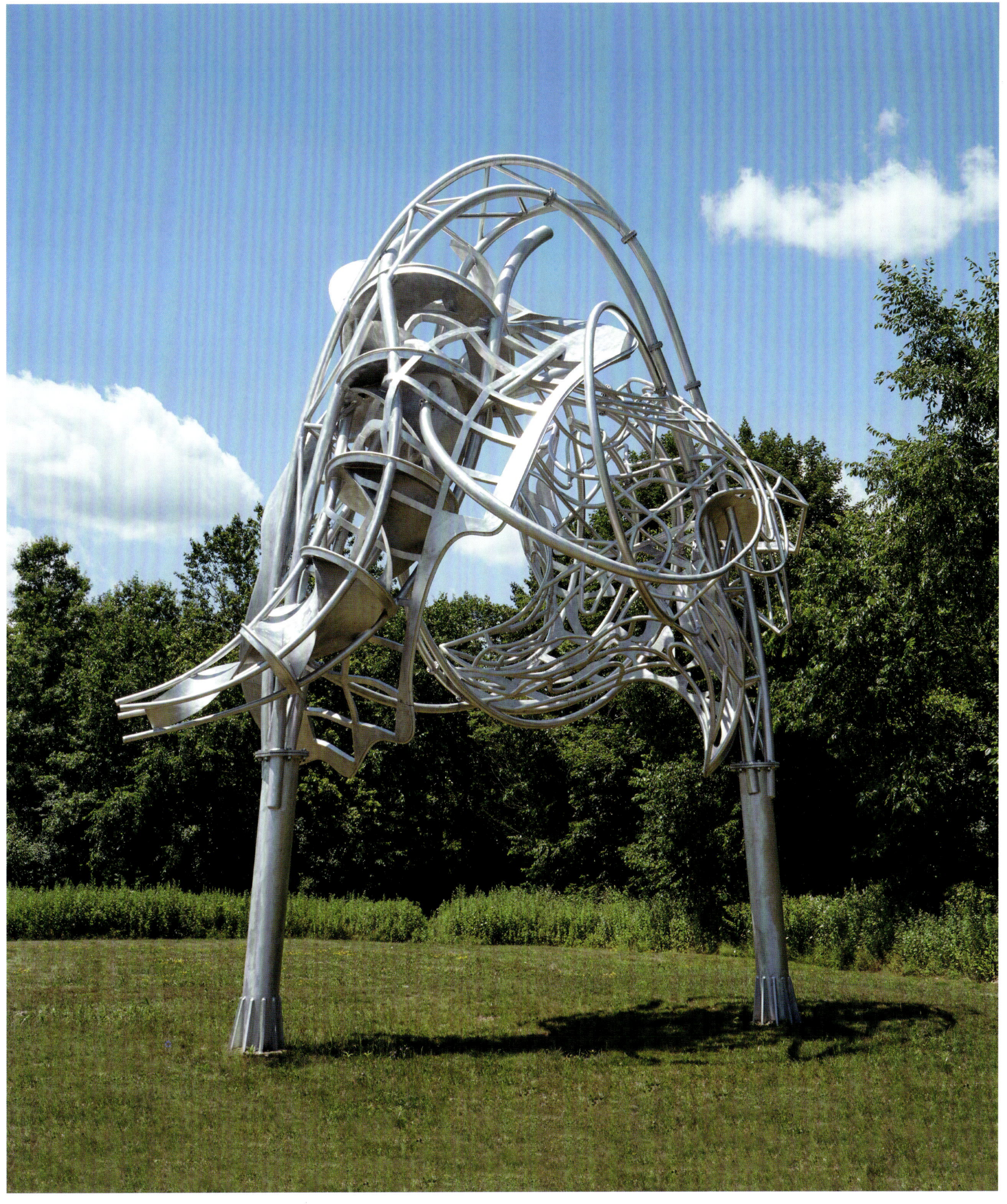

CAMPBELL: *But that's not traditional painting – Claudian or Classical – so you know what I mean.*

STELLA: I do, but I'm not sure that it's so purposeful. After a certain point, when you have a practice, you have a kind of vocabulary that you work with. And in a certain sense this dictates the way a painting will be put together, how the equilibrium is going to be expressed.

CAMPBELL: *Can you talk about some words that come to mind that constitute your own vocabulary?*

STELLA: I don't report that. I try to keep the words to a minimum and to myself.

CAMPBELL: *I know, but my job is to get these words out of you!*

STELLA: Yes and you've been good at it so far! In terms of your question, you could say 'Well, you're always talking to yourself', but you know, I'm a very poor listener so I may be talking to myself but I don't pay any attention. And so it's still the apprehension of the forms that makes the art. I'm not trying to be picky about the works: once you see what the forms are and once you know them and what you want to do with them, then they have their own sense of how they go together. There are some things they'll do and some things they won't do.

CAMPBELL: *You talk about this idea of 'spatial averaging' that happens with Abstract Expressionism, and then you come on the scene and you're making the striped paintings, and there's this feeling of averaging using the found shape of the stretcher bar. But then with the later work, we don't get averaging at all. It seems like you moved out in multiple directions – rethinking averaging and illusionism all at once. Are you in fact consuming the roots?*

STELLA: Yeah, yeah, okay. All right. So I wanted that when spatial averaging began and it was a very literal impression. Probably it's modern in the sense that it is impressionism. That's really what it is. The Impressionists were seeking to relate to what they see of the atmosphere, but what they did with that was on the surface – that was the all-over surface.

CAMPBELL: *The broken brushstroke.*

STELLA: Yes. Now, what was the point of that?

CAMPBELL: *I guess my point was that I see this trajectory that happens with the work where you shift to irregularity, to a kind of fragmentation and maybe even what one would describe as a pictorial effect of interface, which I don't see in the early work in the same way. Would you discuss this patterning, this spatial averaging in the work after the 1990s, and the shift from the protractors to the more recent work?*

STELLA: If you go from the pattern paintings or the striped paintings and then to the 'Irregular Polygons' and 'Protractor' paintings, these became in a way a kind of colour-field painting. But it turned back on itself with the 'Polish Village' series, when I had to 'construct' and build the actual painting. The physicality of the painting became more important than the painting of it.

CAMPBELL: *So you see it as a much more fluid process, rather than say a hard shift?*

STELLA: Yes, but I think it was inevitable. You know, in a funny way the surface idea or the given surface of the canvas or easel painting is abstract. It's just another square, or another little off-square. So what size are you going to make it? It's really an issue about the perimeter, defining the perimeter of what you're doing, finding the edges. And once you get into that, then you'll think of things a little bit differently.

MOULTONBORO III, 1966
ALKYD AND EPOXY ON
SHAPED CANVAS
279 X 305 CM

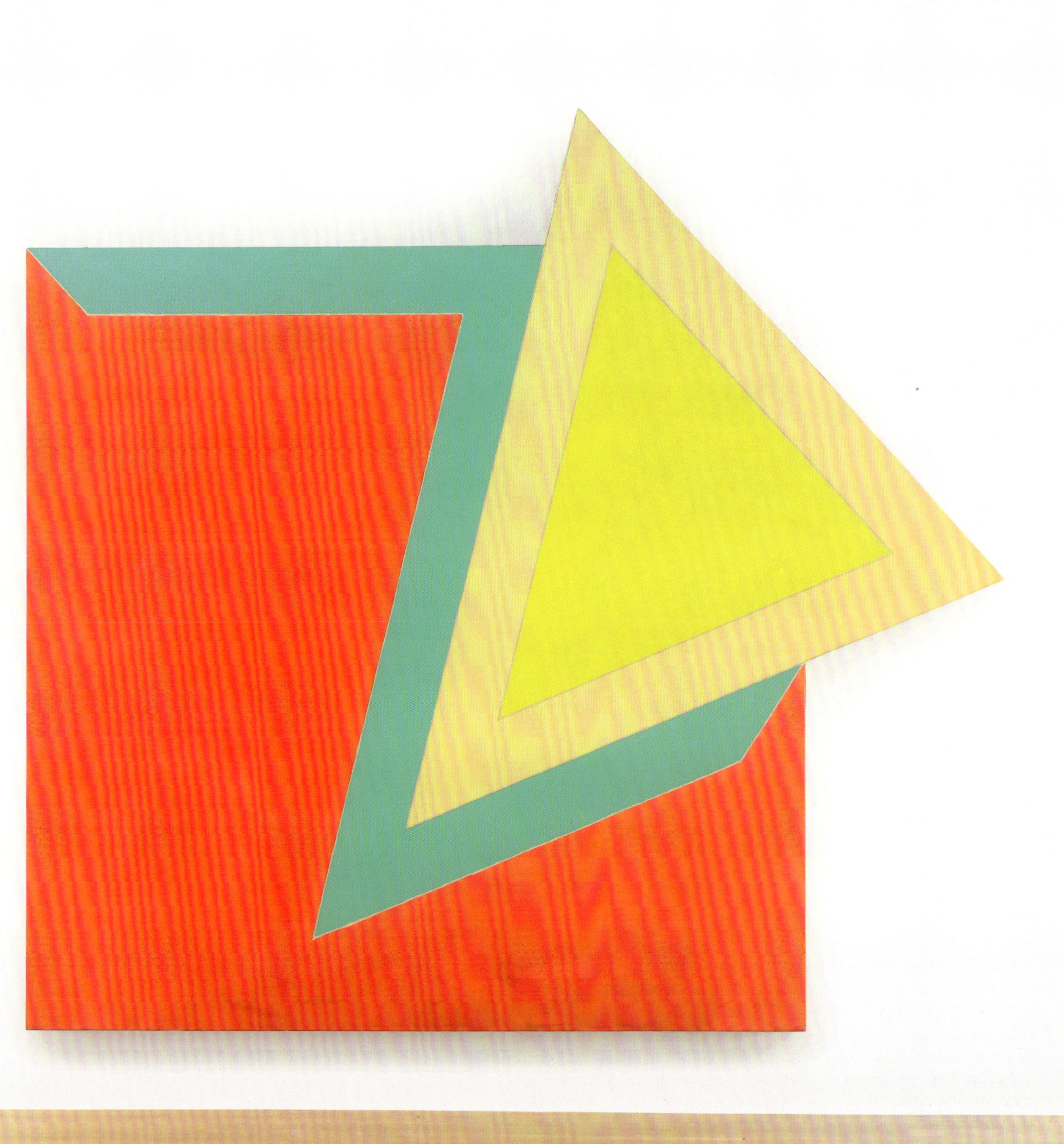

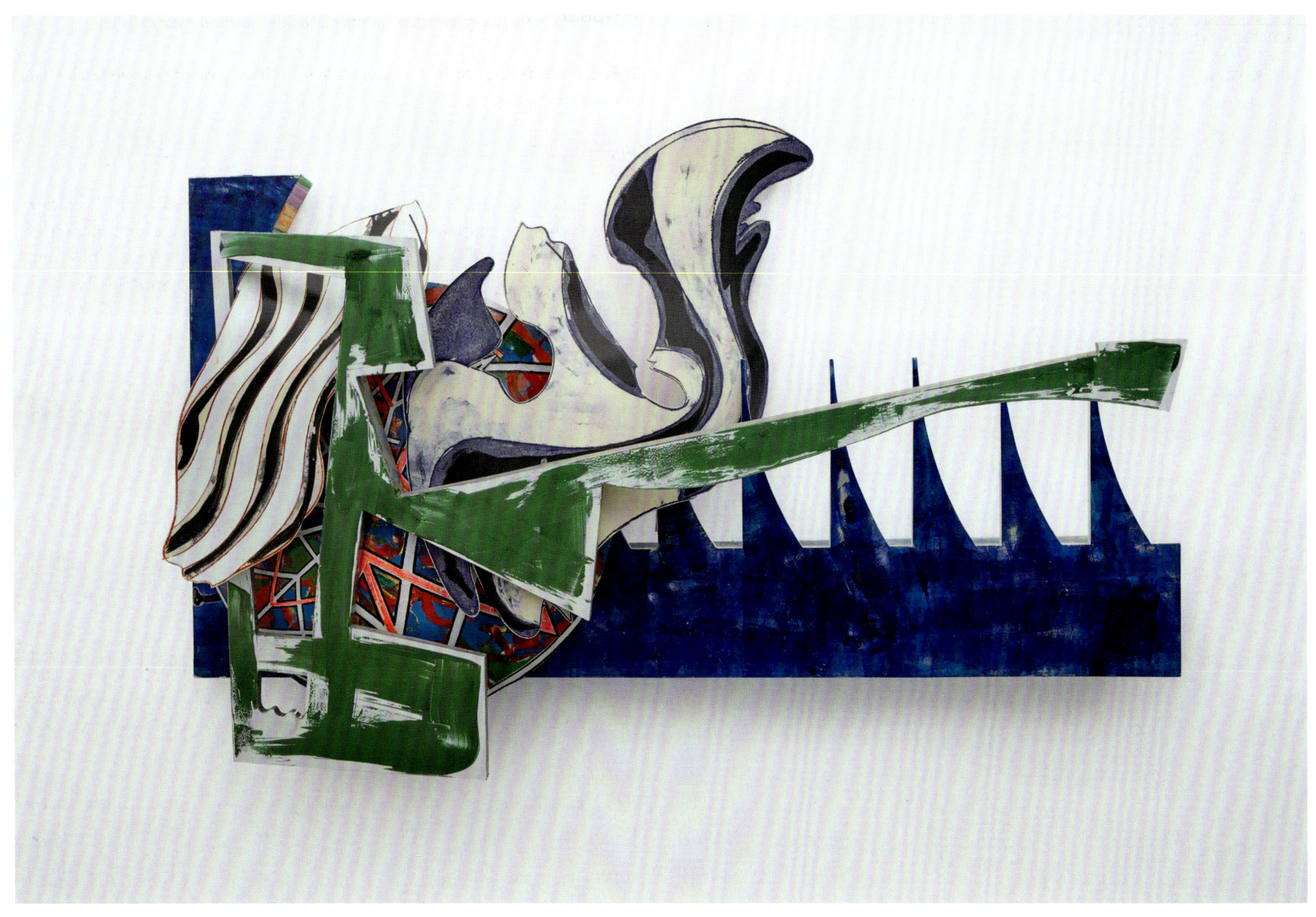

CAMPBELL: *You've spent so much time in Italy and I know your thinking about working space and the innovation of perspective comes from the Renaissance. Have you been to Italy recently?*

STELLA: Yes, I stayed in Rome. I love the museums there.

CAMPBELL: *Me too. I haven't been there for a year since the last Venice Biennale. Was Europe different because of all the security measures that are going on everywhere?*

STELLA: Yes, there's more of the same. It's very different from when I first started going. I can remember when you went to the airport and bought your ticket just before you got on the plane.

CAMPBELL: *I'm curious about that change in travel and the changes that you've seen in how your work sells. I ask because, having had a long career, you've seen many highs and some more fallow periods, but of late you've been very busy with your survey show in multiple venues and shows in Aspen, Poland and elsewhere. Was it strange to change your work so much, even though there was already a market for these earlier bodies of work?*

STELLA: The market is an illusion, a fantasy that's all about the money. It shouldn't affect you. I mean, nobody chooses to be an artist. Once you're practising, you realize that there are other jobs you could do if you want to make money.

THE SHARK MASSACRE, 1988
MIXED MEDIA ON ETCHED
MAGNESIUM AND ALUMINIUM
154 X 243 X 70 CM

CAMPBELL: *Are you speaking as someone who was successful quite early on?*

STELLA: I don't think so. When I taught, it was as if I was being asked to teach artists how to do marketing.

CAMPBELL: *That's horrible.*

STELLA: Marketing hurts students. Schools are just stealing their money. Then they repeat the saying to someone else and then you have another generation that think about marketing more than art. This is true even of some of the critics as well. When I was teaching at Cooper Union, I'd enjoy two hours in a history class, then I'd go to the MFA studios and they'd want a playbook on how to be successful. I said 'You know, you're in graduate school. This is the time for you to really focus on the work and on making the work better. Bring it to a place where you're happy.'

CAMPBELL: *You know graduate degrees are getting more expensive from year to year?*

STELLA: Yes.

CAMPBELL: *Awful.*

STELLA: Students look at you like, 'Art is not my problem'. Sometimes it's really exciting to see all their work, really inspiring. When they begin to realize that it takes time to get what you want.

CAMPBELL: *I also like the work that I see going on with many artists in the studio who are trying to figure out the in-between space between painting, sculpture and photography – a way in without completely turning over to sculpture, you know? Without moving to the floor you're standing on.*

STELLA: It's on the wall; it's hanging on the ceiling; it's smeared on the floor. A lot of details are in the hanging.

CAMPBELL: *As opposed to some kind of fresco where the paint is integral to the wall. With these in-between ways of working, you have the fluidity to be many things.*

STELLA: There are no schools anymore, no more styles, yet a whole number of people are working in this way.

CAMPBELL: *Yes, it feels like a funny time.* [She picks up a handwritten pencilled extensive list of colours for a painting in the spray booth] *This list is intimidating stuff. What's on the list?*

STELLA: The lists are of specific colours for my studio assistants. Sometimes I go in the spray booth, but less and less these days, now that I've gotten older. All my assistants are from the local community. Many have been with me for over a decade. I don't like having artists as assistants because I like to make the artistic decisions. Sometimes I see something we've been working on for months and I just start pulling it apart and we scrap it.

CAMPBELL: *Why did you begin to write and lecture? Especially since you're so jaded about teaching?*

STELLA: I think about painting a lot, so I wanted to beautify ways of thinking about painting and technology, especially in the late 1940s and 1950s. I admired so many critics who aren't around anymore. In writing, don't you think you're allowed more fluidity? These days, there's a false sense of objectivity. Nobody writes well anymore. We've lost that continuity and lost the understanding of materiality.

CAMPBELL: *Yes it's true. I share this concern.*

STELLA: There are some paintings now that are looking backwards. I mean they feel to me, not surprisingly, nostalgic.

CAMPBELL: *Now with a new wave of figuration, so much art looks like it's from the 1930s. I'm writing about the new materiality in photography. I don't know if you've been reading it or seeing this work?*

STELLA: In photography?

CAMPBELL: *Yes, artists are printing photography on different surfaces like aluminium, and other metals.*

STELLA: I appreciate it. Twenty years ago I did a prototype. I wish they'd had the technology then, because it was a direction in which I saw the work going. This happens.

CAMPBELL: *Would you ever return to experimenting with it?*

STELLA: No, at this point I just want to make physical objects.

CAMPBELL: *Yes. I understand the desire in a word of so much virtuality.*

STELLA: Imagery might be out, or abstraction, but after decades of making work, it doesn't matter to me. I'm happy to continue to make things.

DIAVOLOZOPPO (#2, 4X), 1984
MIXED MEDIA ON CANVAS,
ETCHED MAGNESIUM,
ALUMINIUM AND FIBERGLASS
353 X 432 X 41 CM

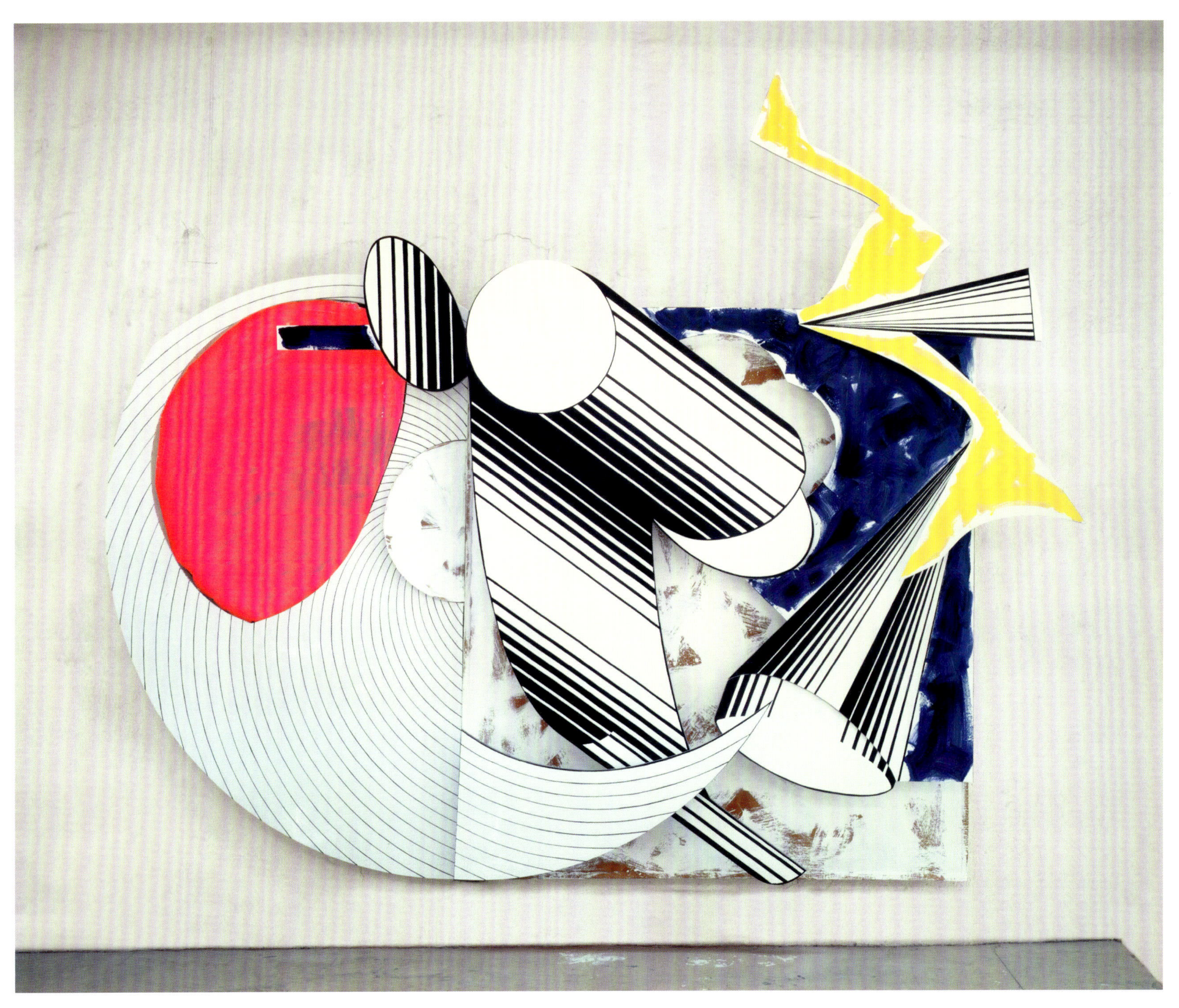

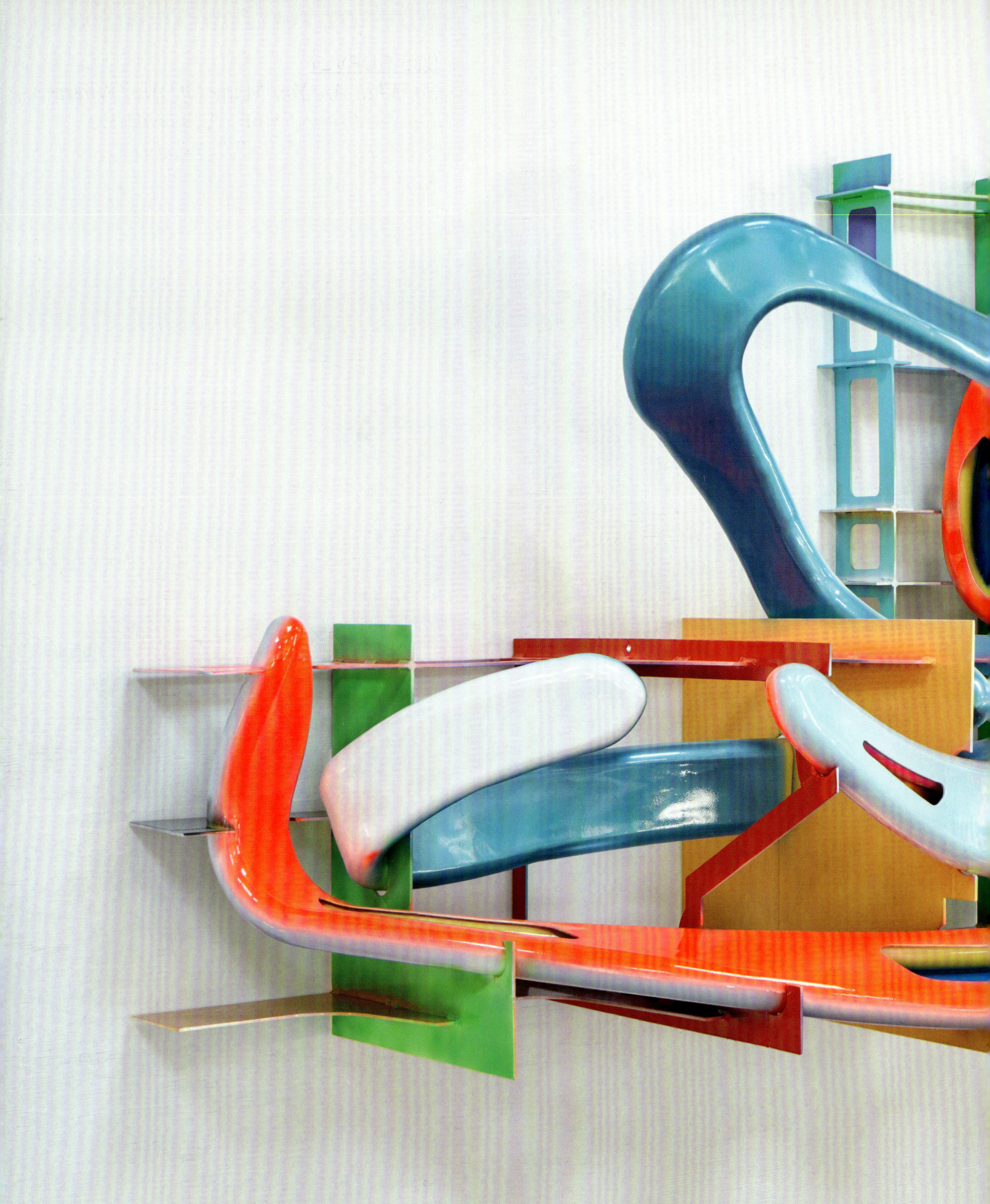

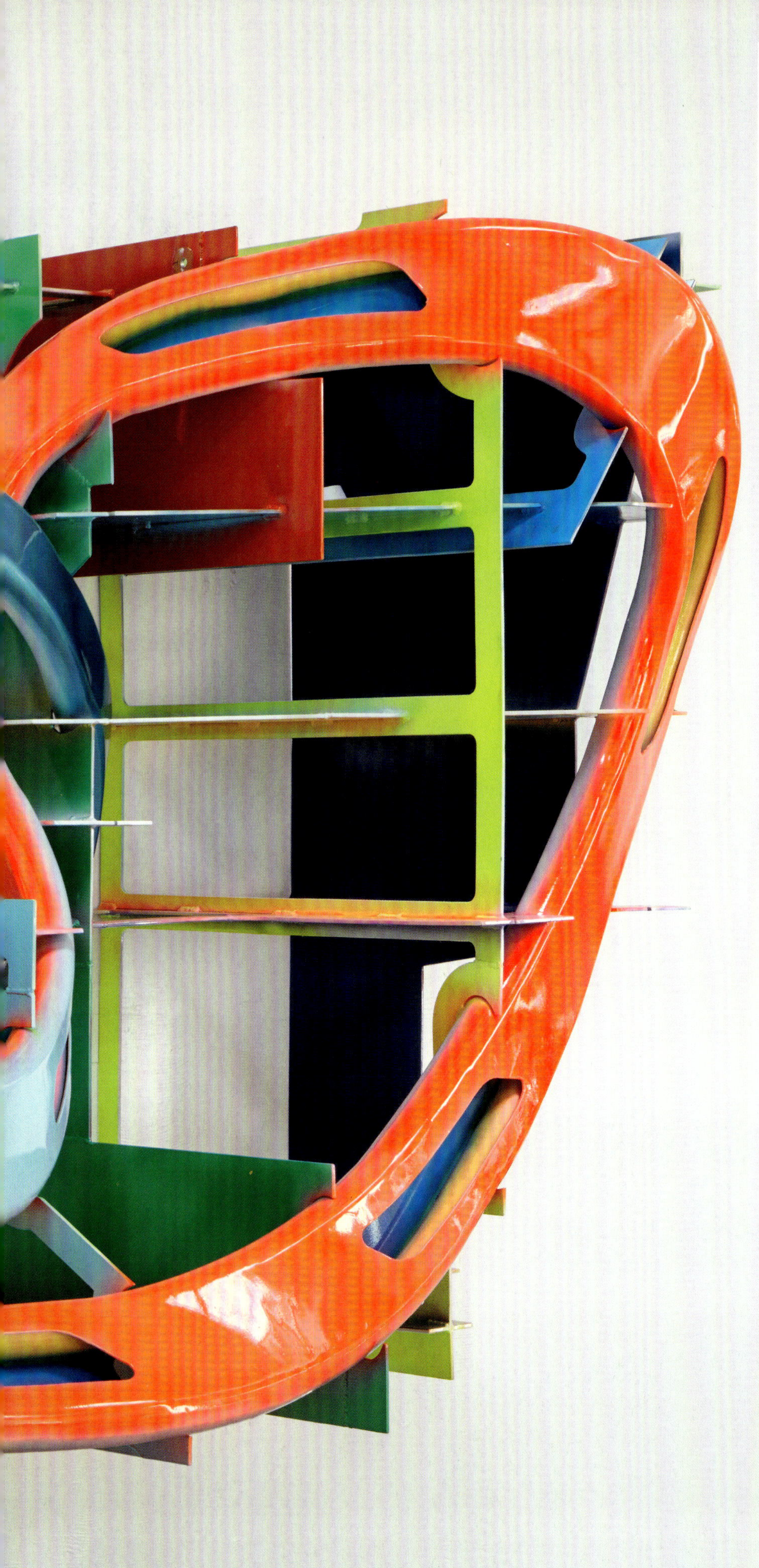

035 SURVEY

So What Are You Made Of? And Where Do You Come From? (A Speculative Survey of Frank Stella's Practice)

Kate Nesin

previous pages,
LEEUWARDEN II, 2017
PAINTED METAL
171 X 295 X 106 CM

CREUTZWALD, 1992
STEEL
166 X 150 X 119 CM

Points of Entry

Frank Stella has produced thousands of individual works across six decades, divided among more than sixty series and categorized variously (sometimes conflictingly) as paintings, prints, reliefs and sculptures; using commercial and industrial paints, canvas, paper, print media, wood, felt, cardboard, aluminium, magnesium, steel, bronze, ceramic, fibreglass, carbon fibre, foam, bamboo, numerous plastics and Corian; brushing, spraying, collaging, machine-cutting, casting, assembling, machine-carving, as well as 3-D printing and laser sintering, among other forms of rapid-prototyping. These lists are not comprehensive, nor precisely chronological, but the list format is useful insofar as it presents with concision a constitutive incommensurability.

To be sure, cogent narrative accounts of Stella's practice abound, either structured around a succession of ever more surprising breaks with convention and expectation, or around the differently surprising advance of a kind of formal logic from extreme to extreme.[1] Either way, the language of boundaries and borders pertains – a language on which my storytelling will rely as well. Indeed, this survey begins as if both in the middle and off to the side, with small sculptures made in the early 1990s, a point of possible beginning I have cultivated in part because these were the works, according to one glowing review, that show Stella the renowned and avowed painter crossing 'the sculpture threshold'.[2]

So, let's begin. In 1992 Stella displayed nearly three dozen freestanding works in steel and bronze, assembled from found as well as intentionally cast parts.[3] They were grouped as the 'Alsace-Lorraine' series, each titled after a different town in that industrial region where France borders Germany. All were sized for pedestal or table, and so, in theory, for human-scaled encounter – an invitation to bend closer, examining intricacies and irregularities as if they might be possible to parse. Theirs was an appealing intimacy, yet not one that seemed intrinsic to them. Some registered as possible models for larger works; others registered as fragments broken from a mysterious mass.

Creutzwald, for instance, appears simultaneously whole and partial. Its own parts – all steel scraps, though divergent in surface, sheen, tone and thickness – coalesce as a wing-like form, via the mottled triangular shard that angles upward from a loop of crumpled metal sheeting. The clear directionality of this 'wing', which leads the eye out from a compact material bundle into the air that circulates around it, is thus forceful in itself. At the same time, it suggests its own incompletion: a body needs two wings to fly.

More than two decades later, in 2014, Stella showed *Creutzwald* for the second time, but differently. The work sat on a squat, slatted steel platform, which underscored the pull of gravity that the 'wing', in turn, resists. Nor was it alone – there still may not be two wings, but Stella's platform did now proffer two sculptures, the works newly considered a pair. What seems from one angle like an additional, low-lying appendage to *Creutzwald* is in fact *Toul*, a nugget of similar steel components, likewise darkling, scumbled, and cut by flashes of brighter strands. The bulk of this smaller sculpture, however, is comprised of a single

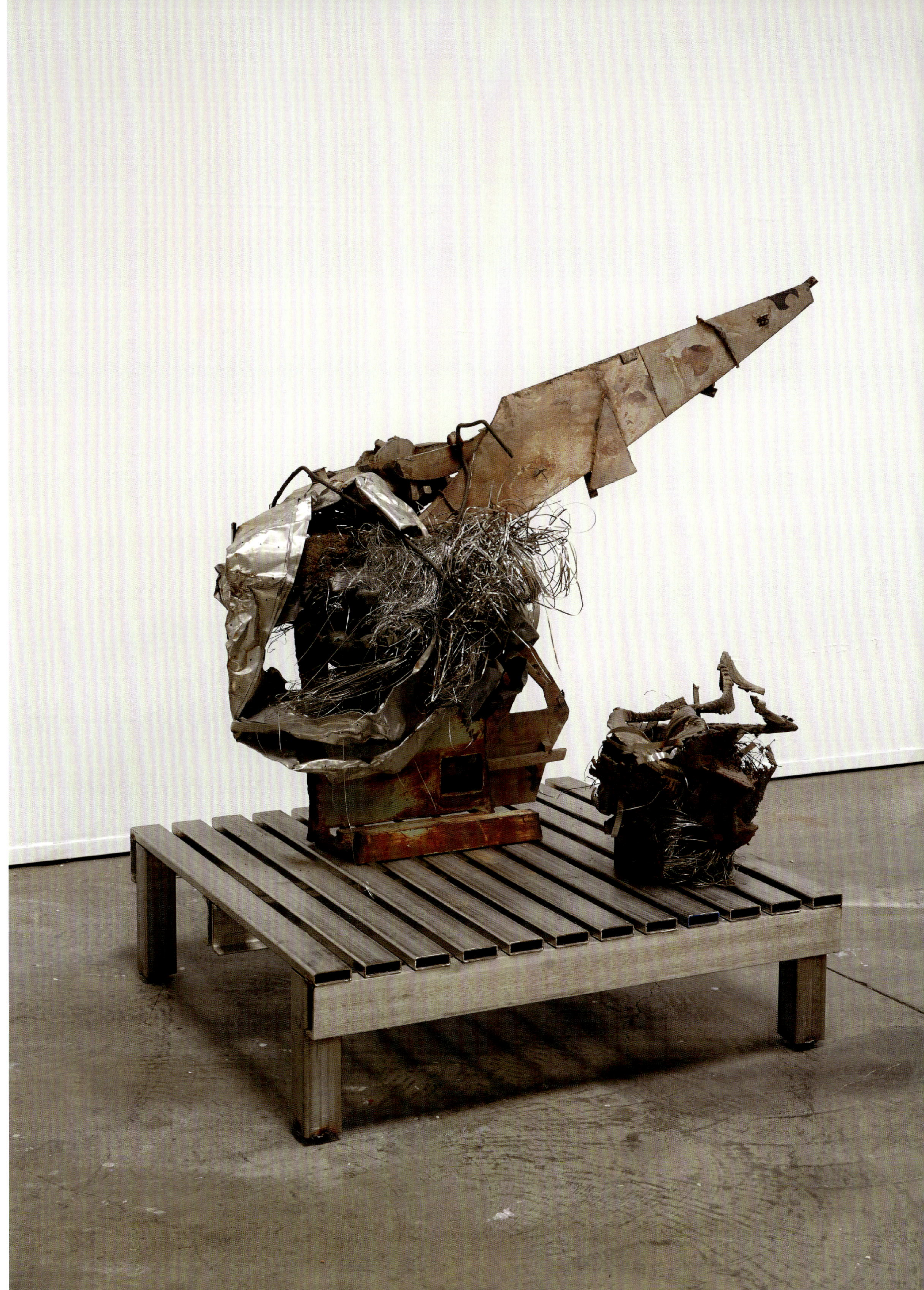

TOUL, 1992
CAST STAINLESS STEEL
46 X 51 X 46 CM

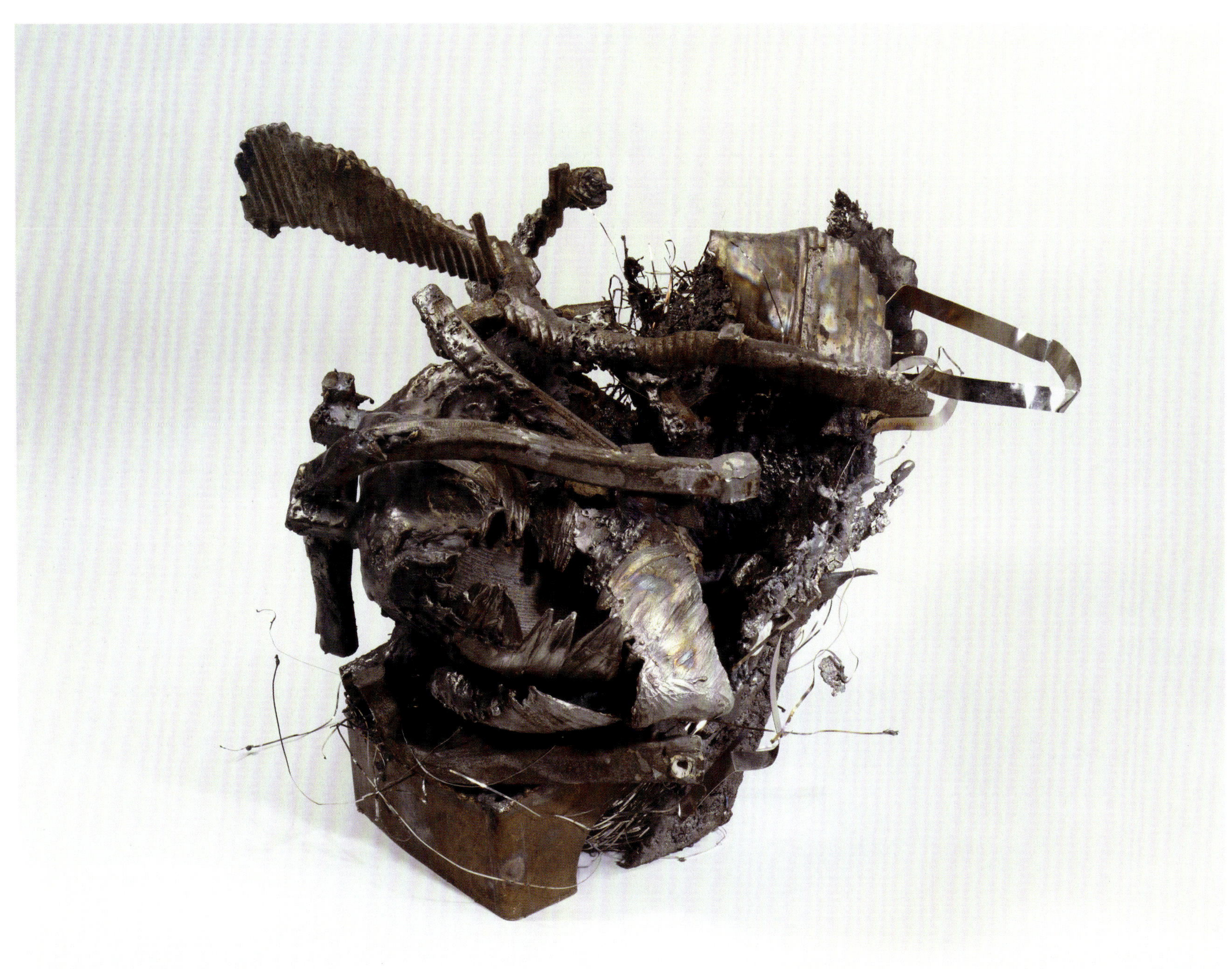

element cast from assembled parts, such that clear distinctions in texture and form nevertheless present as materially unified.

Casting is an ancient method of sculpture-making, whereby a molten material is poured into and shaped by a mould, generally solidifying into a hollow volume, a shell that is also a faithful index of the surfaces it is meant to replicate. Found-object assemblage bears a distinct historical burden – its genealogy typically traced via the critical play, the decontextualizations and juxtapositions at once aggressive, absurd and reparative, of early twentieth-century avant-gardes like Dada and Surrealism – and it was often conceived as an a-sculptural or even anti-sculptural mode.[4] The combination of casting and assemblage in a single sculpture is art-historically odd, and we find it in Stella's work on and off throughout the 1990s. Even the relatively tiny *Toul* is thus representative, for the sometimes implausible continuities of surface that casting enables, and the frequently implausible adjacencies that assemblage enables, are both central to considerations of the artist's recent practice.

Of course, Stella is best known, by far, as a painter, not a sculptor, and the terms with which he frames his own practice have long, and ardently, been those of the pictorial and the painterly. But for some time now he cannot seem to help *making* sculpturally by *thinking* (or imagining or even, these days, computer-imaging) pictorially; the vast majority of his production since the early 2000s has been more or less three-dimensional. Even so, my initial emphasis on sculpture is meant as speculative rather than corrective. What is 'the sculpture threshold', and where are we once we've crossed it? In the sculptural realm, conventionally speaking, we deal in the cast, carved, constructed or modelled; we deal in the three-dimensional or in-the-round, and so too in the time of circumnavigation, in experiential duration; we deal in weight and gravity, or their self-conscious resistance; we deal in relationships to place, either in historical terms as a kind of monument, a marker, or in modern terms as inevitably mobile, sculptures elaborating or absorbing their own bases, or to the contrary, insisting on the demonstrative responsiveness of the site-specific.[5]

The supposed capacities of painting and sculpture have for centuries seemed to distinguish them from one another as competitors, and more often than not sculpture was seen at a disadvantage, too much of and in the physical world.[6] Nor is an acknowledgement of the conventional tensions between two and three dimensions new in the Stella literature. As early as 1970 curator William Rubin wondered how much the artist could 'subsume from the neighbouring plastic arts of sculpture and architecture and still [make] paintings', articulating a tension between what is desirable and what is threatening.[7] (Where Stella himself writes in the early 1980s about 'what painting wants', it is possible to deliberately misread 'wants' as 'lacks'.)

Stella has not put brush to canvas in decades, yet he has continued to make what we might call unsanctioned paintings – paintings that do not always look like paintings precisely because they are trying to advance what painting can do. That is one way of approaching his diverse, thousands-strong body of work, and an especially persuasive one when we take his own texts about painting into account (as this essay will later do). Meanwhile I am left to reckon with the fact that I do not experience most of his works as paintings. My automatic assumption is therefore that I must experience them as sculptures. I'm not sure that's accurate, either, however; or if it is accurate, then they might be unsanctioned sculptures, so to speak.

Across the street from Stella's upstate New York studio building, on an otherwise unclaimed grassy expanse hard by the road, stand a collection of monumentally scaled three-dimensional works – as well as a large, empty pavilion designed to display a set of sculptures still underway – made across roughly twenty years, from *Fishkill* (1995) to *K.304 (Full-Size)* (2013). Even now, months after my first visit, I remember this outdoor grouping with equal parts wonderment and discomfiture. The works seemed to me as if dropped from the sky – fallen meteors, wrecked fuselage, alien ships, looming from concrete pads, all comprised of generally recognizable materials and occasionally recognizable shapes or forms but none straightforward to approach. In part this was because of their massive scale, and it is notable that most people who see them in their current location will do so from a passing car; that is, they are more often glimpsed than approached.

This essay's title is borrowed from elsewhere, but its interrogative terms have rattled around in my head in recent months as the simultaneously foundational and inane, demanding and marvelling questions I wanted to pose during my first encounter, as if to the sculptures themselves: 'So what are you made of? And where do you come from?' Precisely these questions are intoned early in the voiceover narration of Alain Resnais's 1958 short film *Le Chant du Styrène (The Song of Styrene)*. Commissioned by the French company Pechiney, the film tracks the process of fabrication in plastic, but it does so in reverse, beginning with the finished commercial product, passing backwards through plastic's variously pliable stages of formation, and ending at the ocean, in a nod towards the organic origins even of this synthetic material.[8] Perhaps, too, in a nod towards plastic's inherent liquidity.

Sculpture is called a 'plastic' art, its plasticity – its mould-ability, its model-ability – considered characteristic, if not essential. Anything cast in a mould is liquid first, and Stella had begun casting in aluminium and steel during the late 1980s in order to capitalize on a certain sense of suspended or frozen liquidity: drawing in sand and allowing molten metal to pool before hardening; or pouring molten metal over flat, undisturbed sand, which seemed to secure for the painterly gesture an ultimate autonomy from the supporting surface. These sand-cast

FISHKILL, 1995
CAST STAINLESS STEEL
WITH CARBON STEEL
343 X 434 X 330 CM

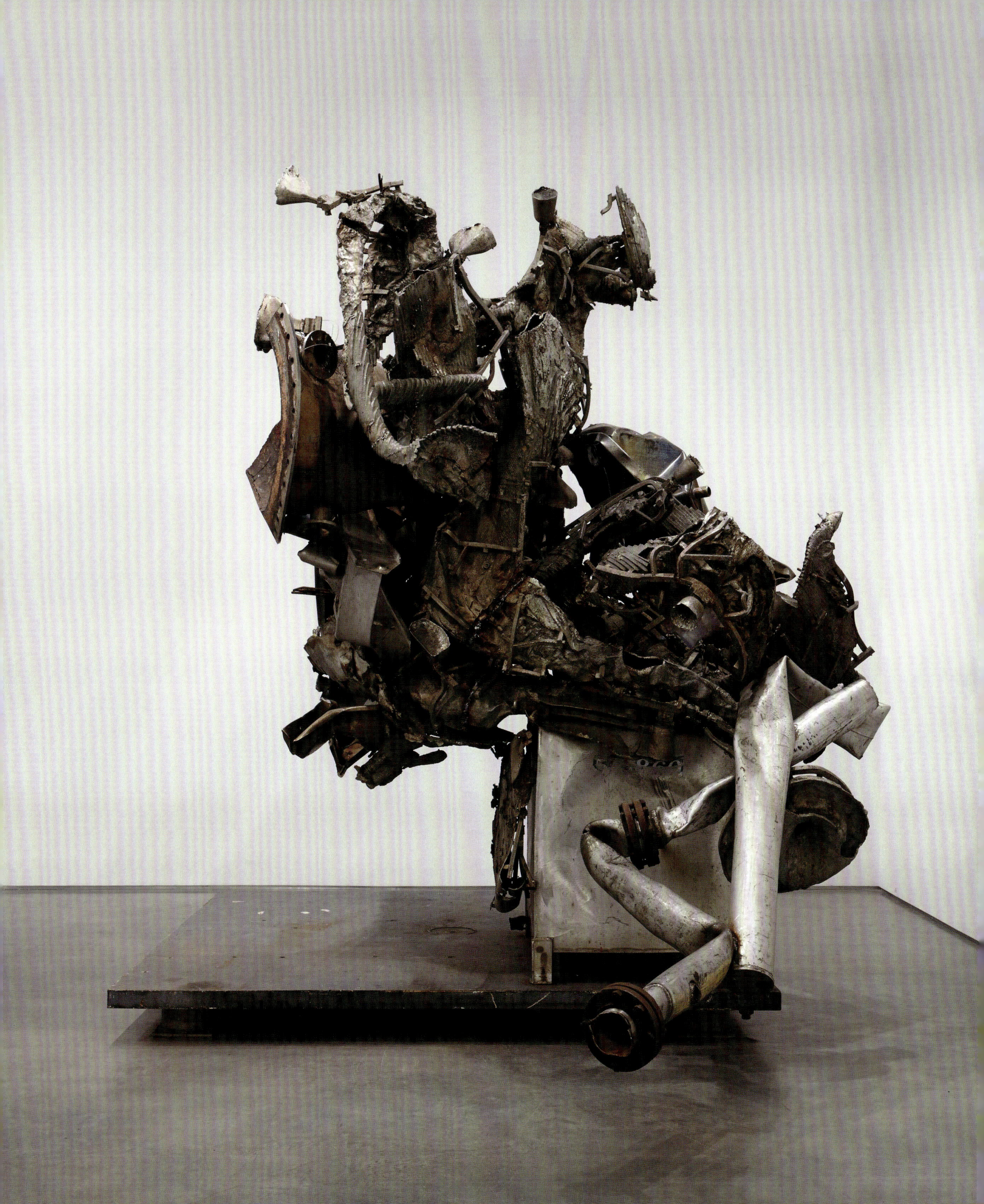

RAFT OF MEDUSA, PART I, 1990
OIL AND ENAMEL ON ETCHED HONEYCOMB ALUMINIUM WITH STEEL PIPES, BEAMS AND OTHER
METAL ELEMENTS
425 X 414 X 404 CM

and splash-cast metal forms appear, among other places, in large-scale assemblages called the 'Easel Paintings' from the early 1990s (see the shimmering friable layers, like a ghostly coral reef, in *Raft of Medusa, Part I* (1990), for instance). Stella used the solidified splashes, too, as plates or impresses in his parallel printmaking work.[9]

Thought figuratively, metal is 'plastic' – the plasticity of molten metal is what allows it to take on such a range of shapes, textures and densities. The plasticity of steel is necessarily limited by the specificity of steel; its plasticity is, in the end, different from the plasticity of aluminium, or bronze and so on. Plasticity is plastic's only quality, which means that plastic is a fundamentally abstract material.[10] It seems to me that Stella wanted plasticity before, or more than, he has ever wanted sculpture as such. In the early 1990s he progressed the plasticity of his work by turning to new computer-modelling software – software that has itself progressed in the years since, so that even an eventual two-dimensional work begins now, for Stella, as a three-dimensionally modelled and ever-mutable set of forms within the virtual space of the computer.

Since the early 2000s, most (though certainly not all) of Stella's work has been made primarily from plastic. Yet instead of the pouring and casting of liquid polymers, these works require the minute layerings of 3-D printing and the powdery coalescences of rapid-prototype laser sintering. Roland Barthes once recounted the making of plastic goods: 'At one end, raw, telluric matter, at the other, the finished, human object; and between these two extremes, nothing; nothing but a transit, hardly watched over by an attendant in a cloth cap, half-god, half robot.'[11] By comparison, Stella's recent production is almost transit-less, the materialization of something where before there was, materially speaking, nothing. Hence the yearning questions I have appropriated: 'So what are you made of? And where do you come from?' The first question can often be satisfied with enormous technical specificity. The second question may well be unanswerable.

Metaphors of transit and of threshold-crossing will prevail throughout this essay, productive most of all for the sense of motion or passage that both imply. Stella's work is so knowingly, joyfully unrestrained – stretching or transgressing boundary after boundary, between categories of media, between studio and factory, between good and bad taste. Such metaphors compel me, then, because they clarify the boundary as always already porous, a portal or passageway rather than a barrier. That said, the notion of Stella's work as potentially transit-less lingers.

So far I have skirted the fact that the Alsace-Lorraine assemblages, which do count as 'first' sculptures, represent another kind of first, too. They are the first works for which Stella attempted to produce physically, at the time by casting, three-dimensional forms modelled and manipulated virtually, by computer. They cohere as both analogue and digital, in a ratio that his newer works seem to reverse.[12] One wouldn't know it to look at them, or at least not when looking at *Creutzwald* alone. *Toul* begins to hint at its virtual derivation, with those snaking, striated protrusions along its top – about which much more later. The coincidence of these two firsts cannot but be significant. Or perhaps this simultaneity leads us to re-examine the threshold itself. If Stella crossed into sculpture's realm in 1992, one of his methods of crossing no longer required painting and sculpture to share the boundary; the threshold was instead between virtual and real space, between visualization and substantiation. Considered thus, Stella's works are physical realizations, manifestations, more than they are either paintings or sculptures.

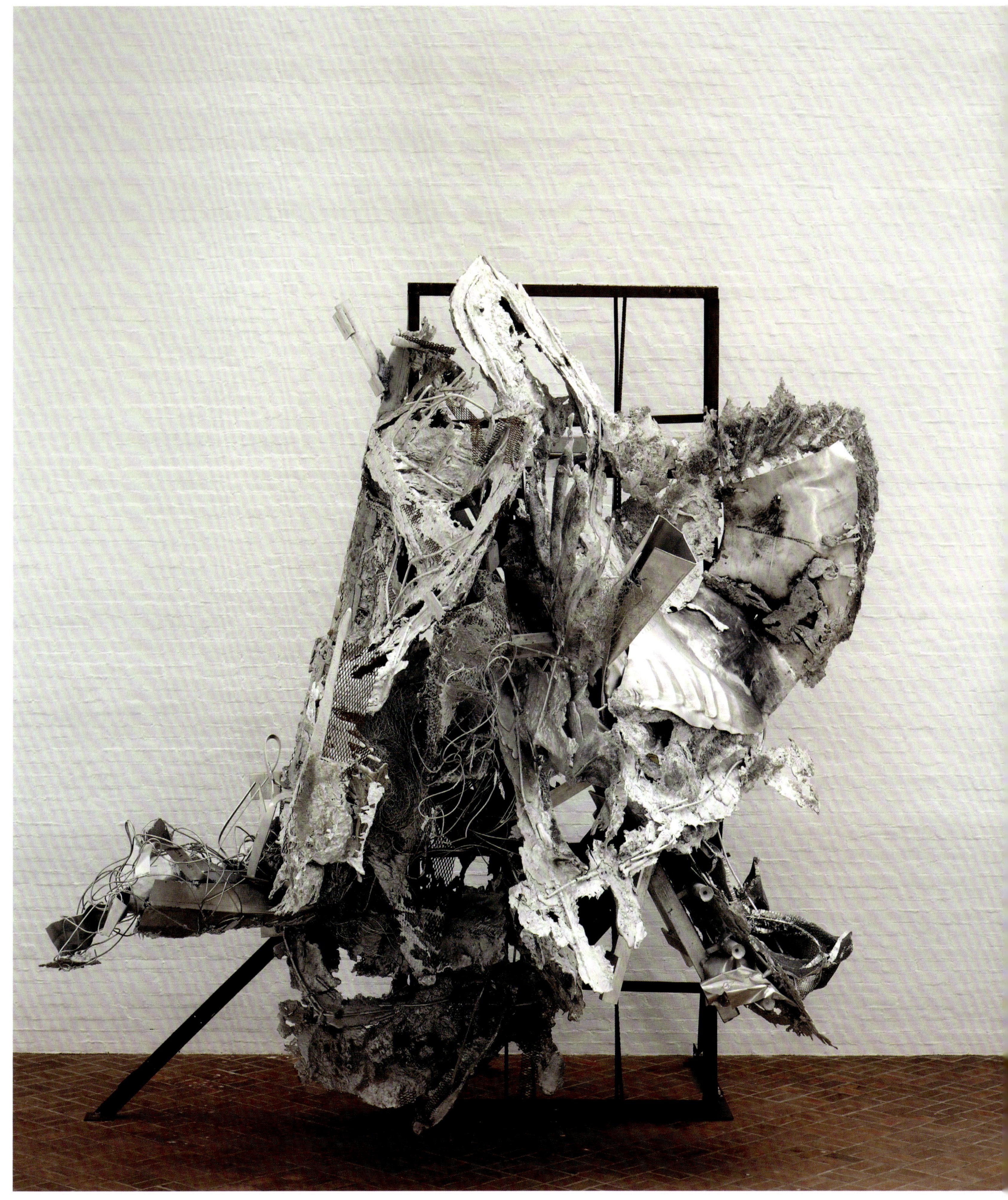

K.150, 2014
PAINTED ABS RPT WITH METAL
244 X 168 X 191 CM

next page,
PUFFED STAR II, 2014
POLISHED ALUMINIUM
570 X 570 X 570 CM

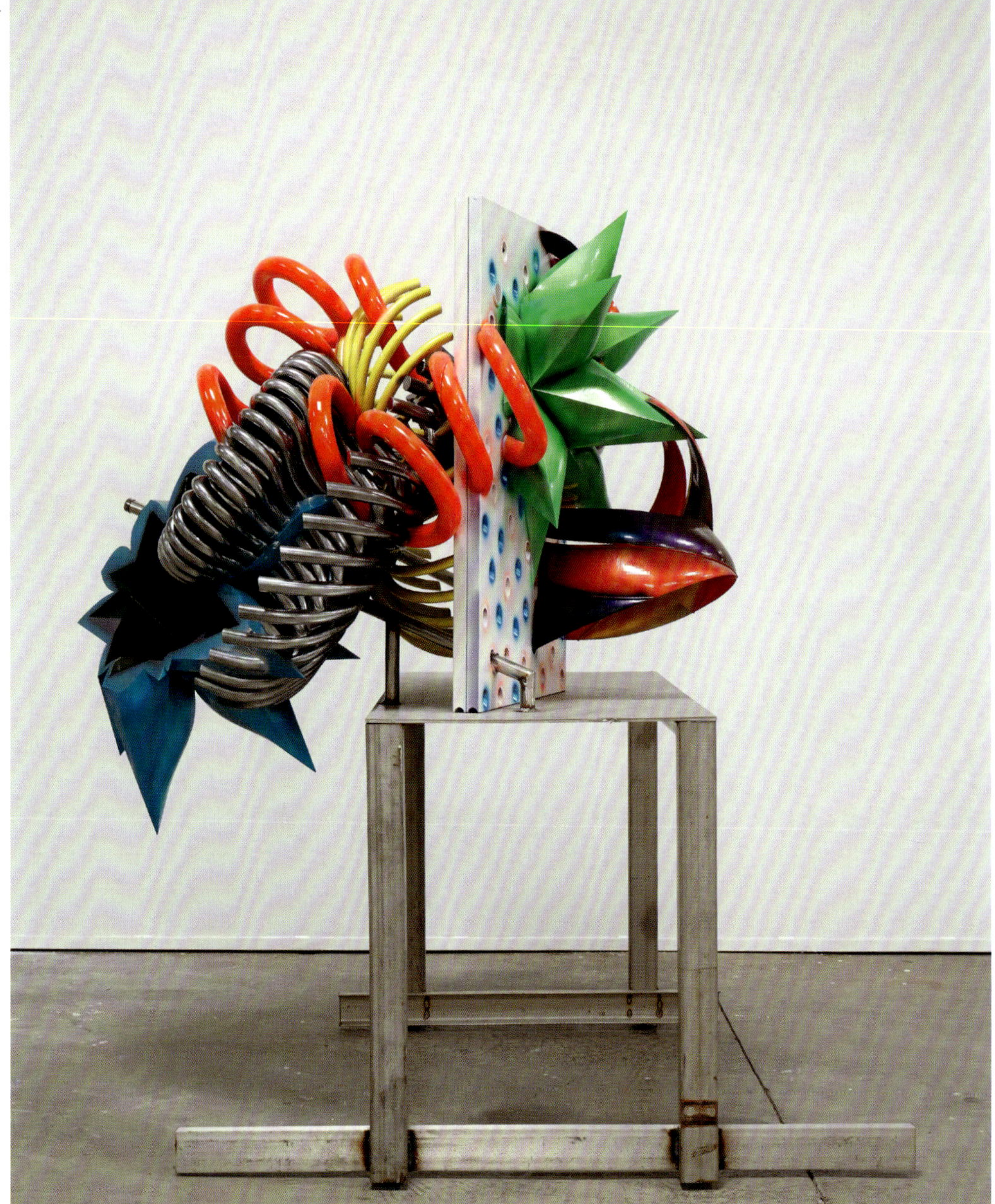

Indeed, in what follows I am guided by a language of realization, not of transformation. Where the word *realization* shades into either *recognition* or *revelation*, of course, *transformation* won't seem far off, and both de-formation and re-formation will prove meaningful throughout as well. I am also guided by the recent staging of a curious chronological collapse: in their 2014 showing, Stella brought *Creutzwald* and *Toul* together in order to share a room with the newly made *K.150*, one from a large, ongoing body of work called 'The Scarlatti K' series. Similar in size to *Creutzwald*, it is 3-D printed in the thermoplastic ABS, sprayed with a riotous combination of spectacular automotive paints, and perches on a high steel table. Where *Creutzwald* and *Toul* are compact and compressed – an impression only augmented by flares of tinsel, the wing-like shape, those snaking protrusions – the centrifugal *K.150* is downright explosive. Where *Creutzwald* and *Toul* show themselves as heavy metal, *K.150* figures as cartoon.

A similar staging occupied the large adjacent gallery. *Fishkill* from 1995 (one of the giants these days installed outside Stella's studio) shared a room with the equivalently sized *Puffed Star II* (2014), both unpainted but the latter in high-polished aluminium, dazzling beside the cast stainless and carbon steel of the former. These two pairings of 1990s works with brand new ones appear to communicate contrast rather than correlation: look how the work has changed; look how materially

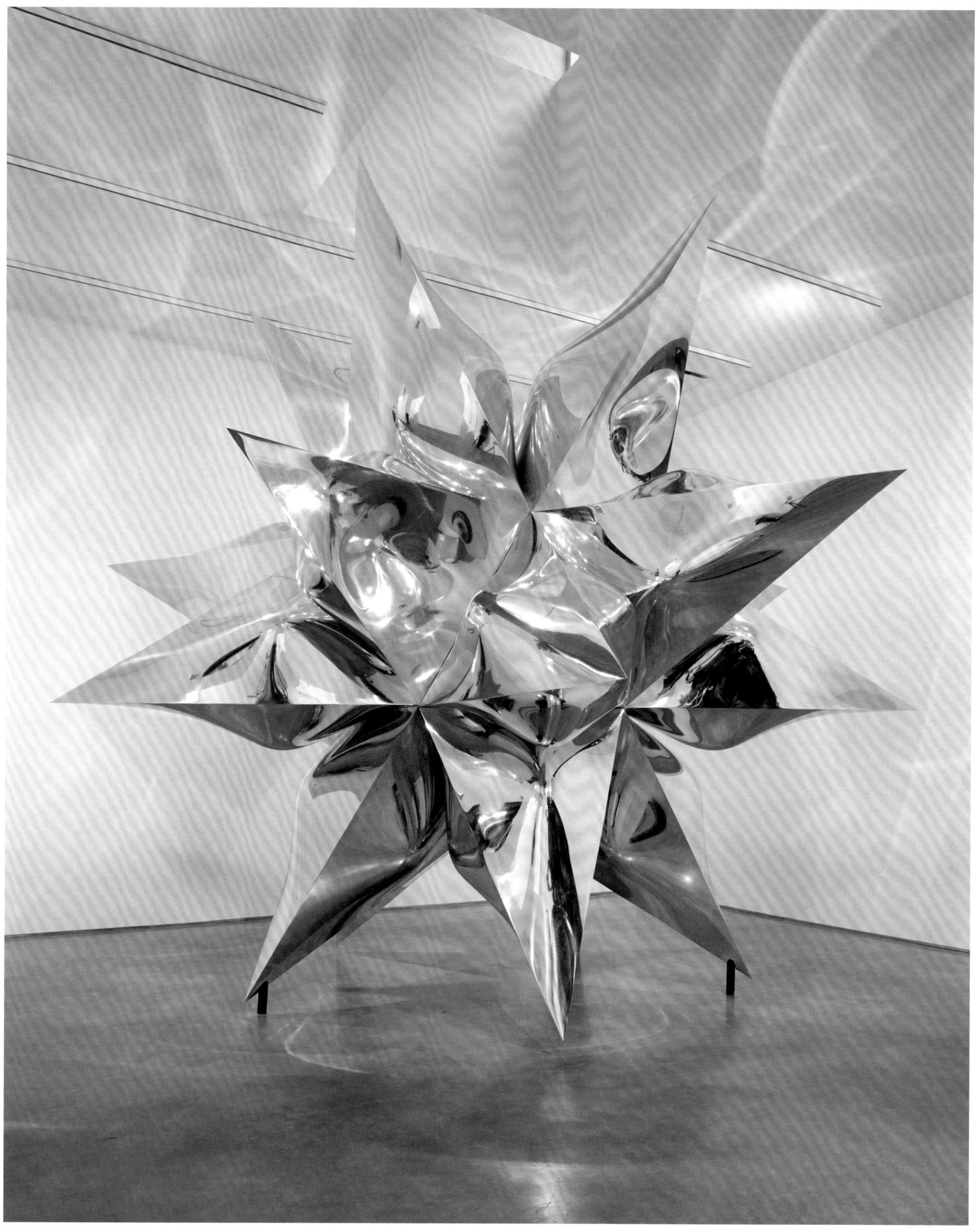

THE FOUNTAIN, 1992
WOODCUT, ETCHING, AQUATINT, RELIEF, DRYPOINT, COLLAGE AND AIRBRUSH
231 X 670 CM

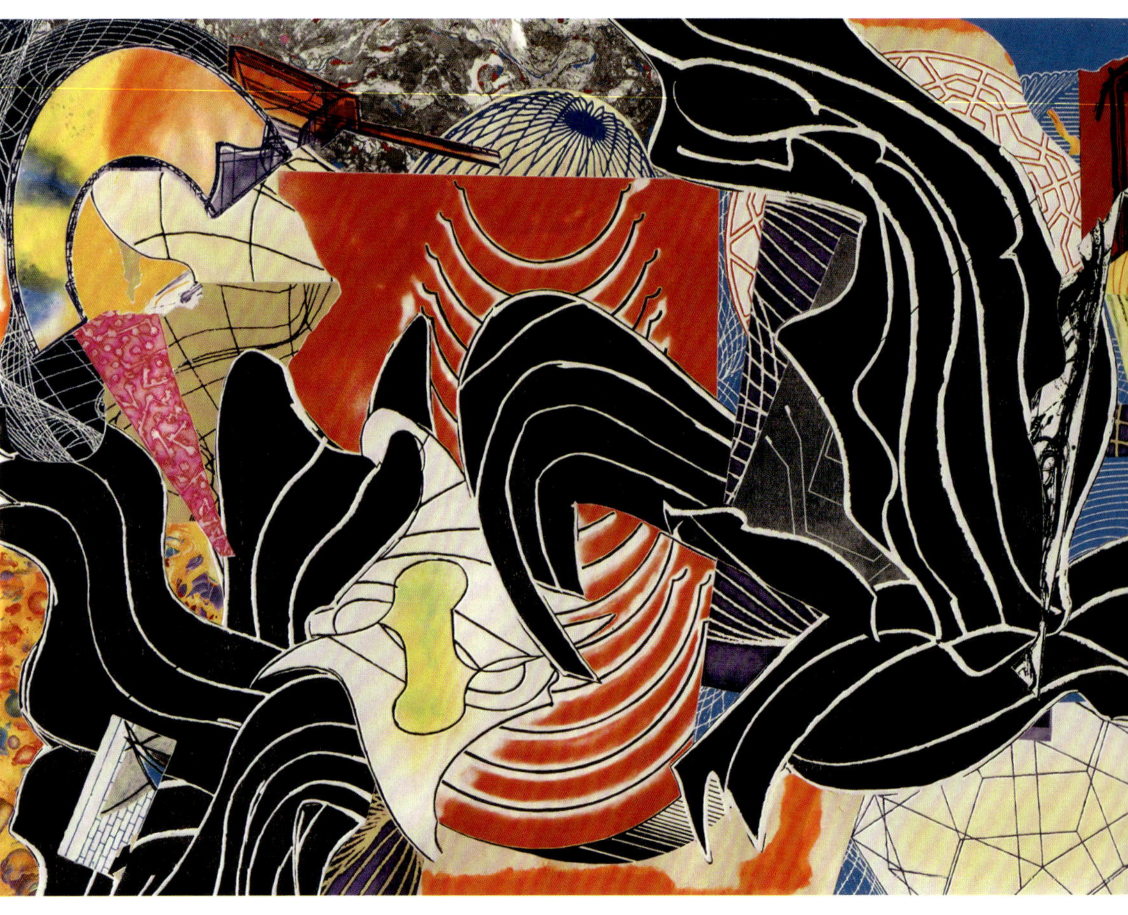

and affectively divergent they are. But we now know the earlier sculptures in both cases to contain the point of origin, or proofs of origin, for all that followed. To the extent that this overstates the case, it does so only in the interest of storytelling – and no account of Stella's work is complete without accounting, along the way, for habits of embellishment, exaggeration and excess.

Stella rarely makes one thing, or even one series, at a time. Much else was underway in 1992, when he assembled and showed the 'Alsace-Lorraine' sculptures. In that year, too, he produced his largest print to date, *The Fountain*, which extends seven feet high and 23 feet long, made via woodcut, etching, aquatint, relief, drypoint, collage and airbrush – a project that represented years of collaborative innovation, as well as accident and inspiration.[13] But so-called sculptures like *Creutzwald* and *Toul* – petite, haptic, crude – instantiate far more than one might guess. They are, indeed, nothing so much as they are points of entry.

All the Space

To many, Stella remains best known for his precocious appearance in 'Sixteen Americans' at the Museum of Modern Art, New York, in 1959. Only twenty-three years old, he was represented there by four of his 'Black Paintings', a series that eventually comprised about two dozen large-scale canvases, each composed of concentric bands or stripes in black enamel house paint on raw canvas, at once stark, deadpan, rigorous, imposing, velvety – diagrammatic but also tactile. Reproductions render the works darker and flatter than they actually are. While each black stripe derives its width from the brush Stella used, the paint itself often bled into the

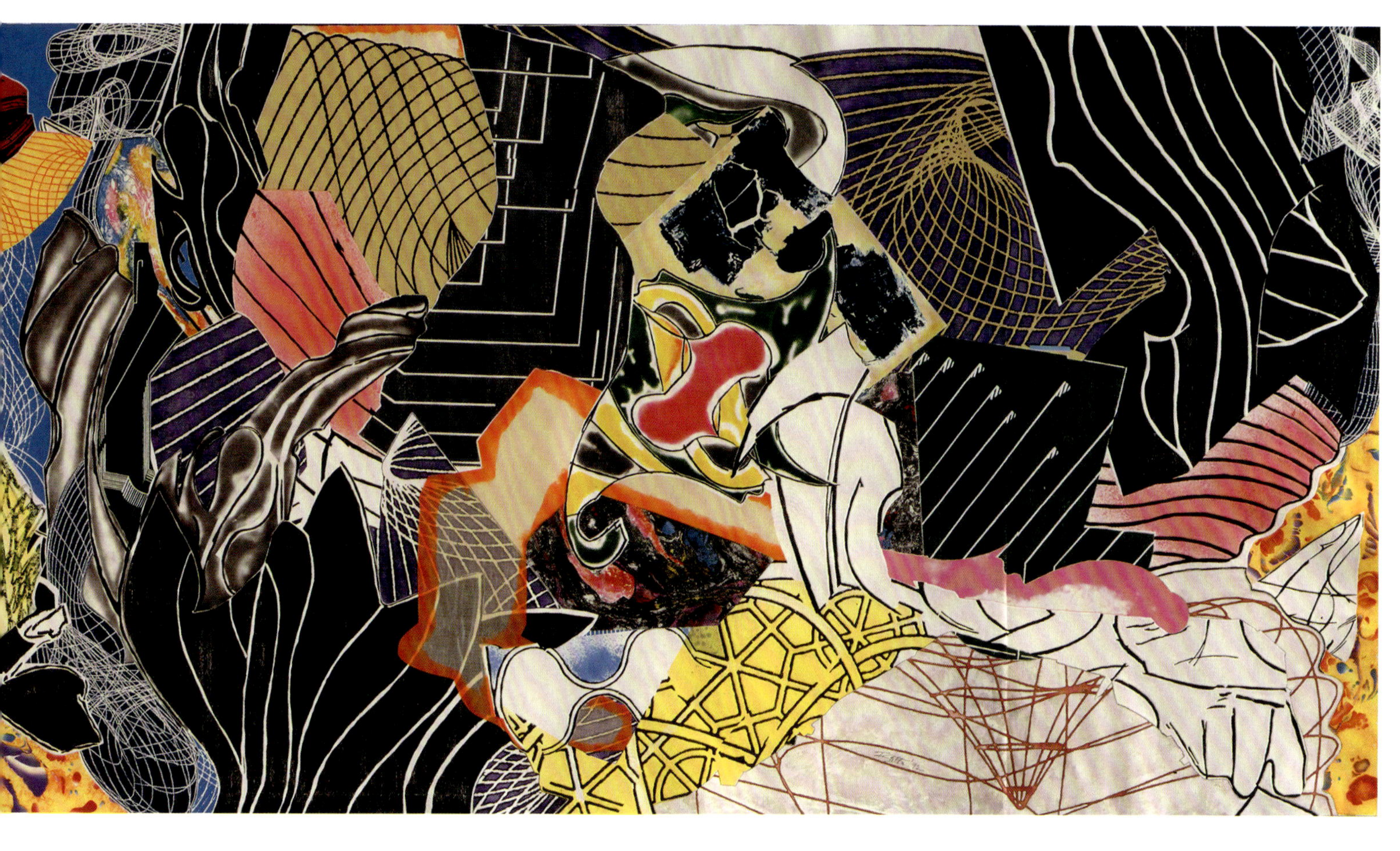

ZAMBEZI, 1959
ENAMEL PAINT ON CANVAS
231 X 200 CM

already pin-thin gaps of raw canvas between them, so that the surface can appear fuzzier, as well as more variegated, in person than one might expect. Initial responses either esteemed or censured their clarity; later responses, including most in the vast current literature, emphasize their elusiveness.

These are evidently handmade works, however purposefully flat-footed in their conception. They are at the same time crucial exponents in the history of non-compositional abstraction, by which artists have sought to produce paintings absent of subjective decision-making. Instead, emphasis is placed on the painting itself, on its materials and terms, as well as, during the 1960s in particular, on the viewer: it feels impossible to write about Stella's early paintings without citing, for the umpteenth time, his own notorious line, 'What you see is what you see' – which either sets aside the difficulty of seeing them, or simply accepts the vagaries of seeing them.[14] He offered this statement during a 1964 radio interview, and it has resounded like a Minimalist mantra ever since, treated as a kind of koan rather than as mere tautology.

Stella's first striped paintings were and often still are claimed as 'literalist', ready precursors to the Minimalist work that constituted abstraction's primary avant-garde during the early and mid-1960s: spare, geometric, serial or modular, works transparent in their fabrication and often industrial in their finish, works that blur or ignore conventional boundaries between painting and sculpture. Many then and since have acknowledged the young Stella as Minimalism's 'father'. In parallel, his striped canvases were and still are claimed as high modernist, certainly the modernism espoused primarily by mid-century critic Clement Greenberg, whom Stella had read with admiration in college. The progress of modernist abstraction, as Greenberg formulated it throughout the 1950s and into the 1960s, refined painting towards its irreducible conditions of flatness and framing edge – towards the necessities, or specificity, of the medium itself.

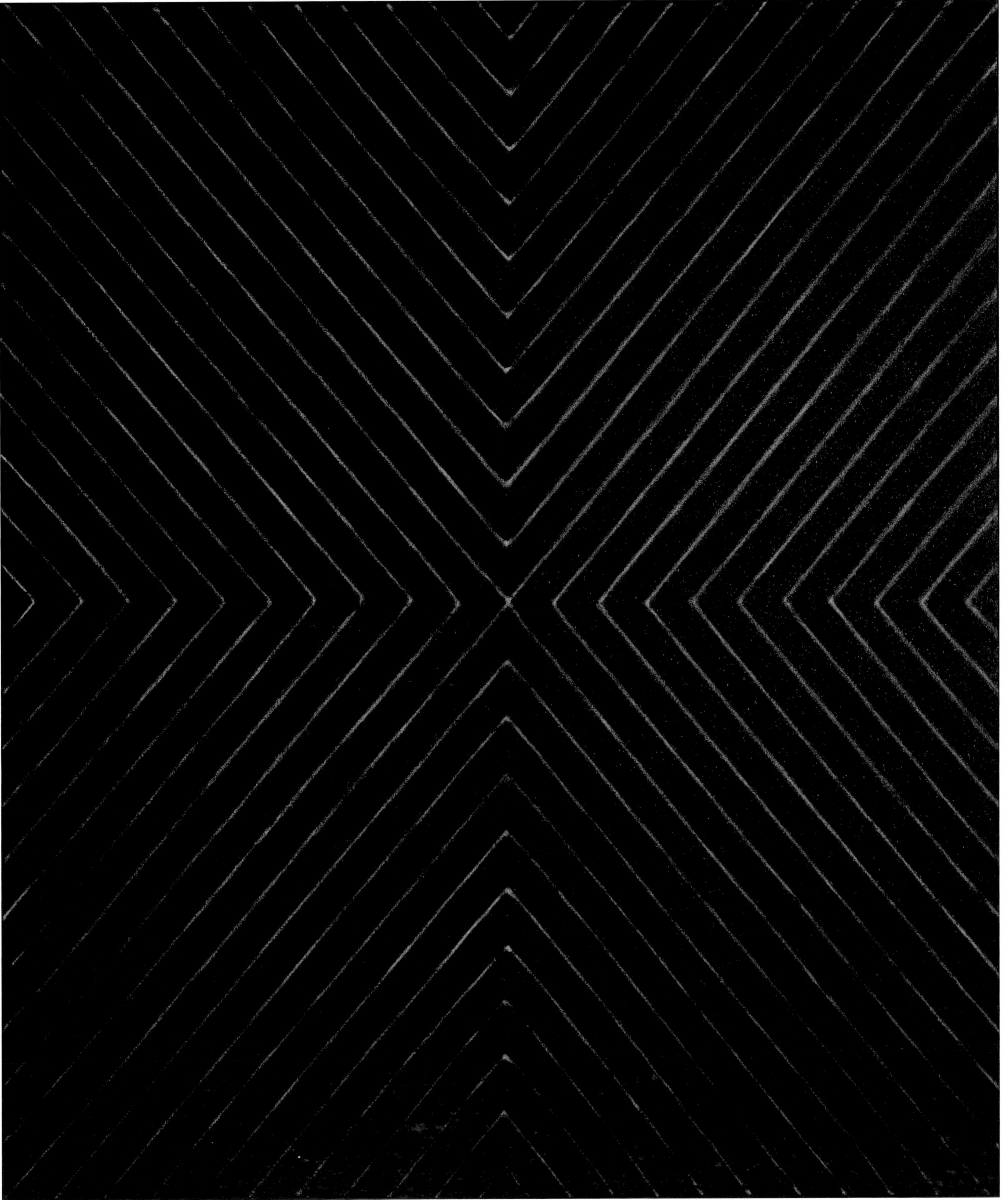

EMPRESS OF INDIA, 1965
METALLIC POWDER IN POLYMER
EMULSION PAINT ON CANVAS
200 X 570 CM

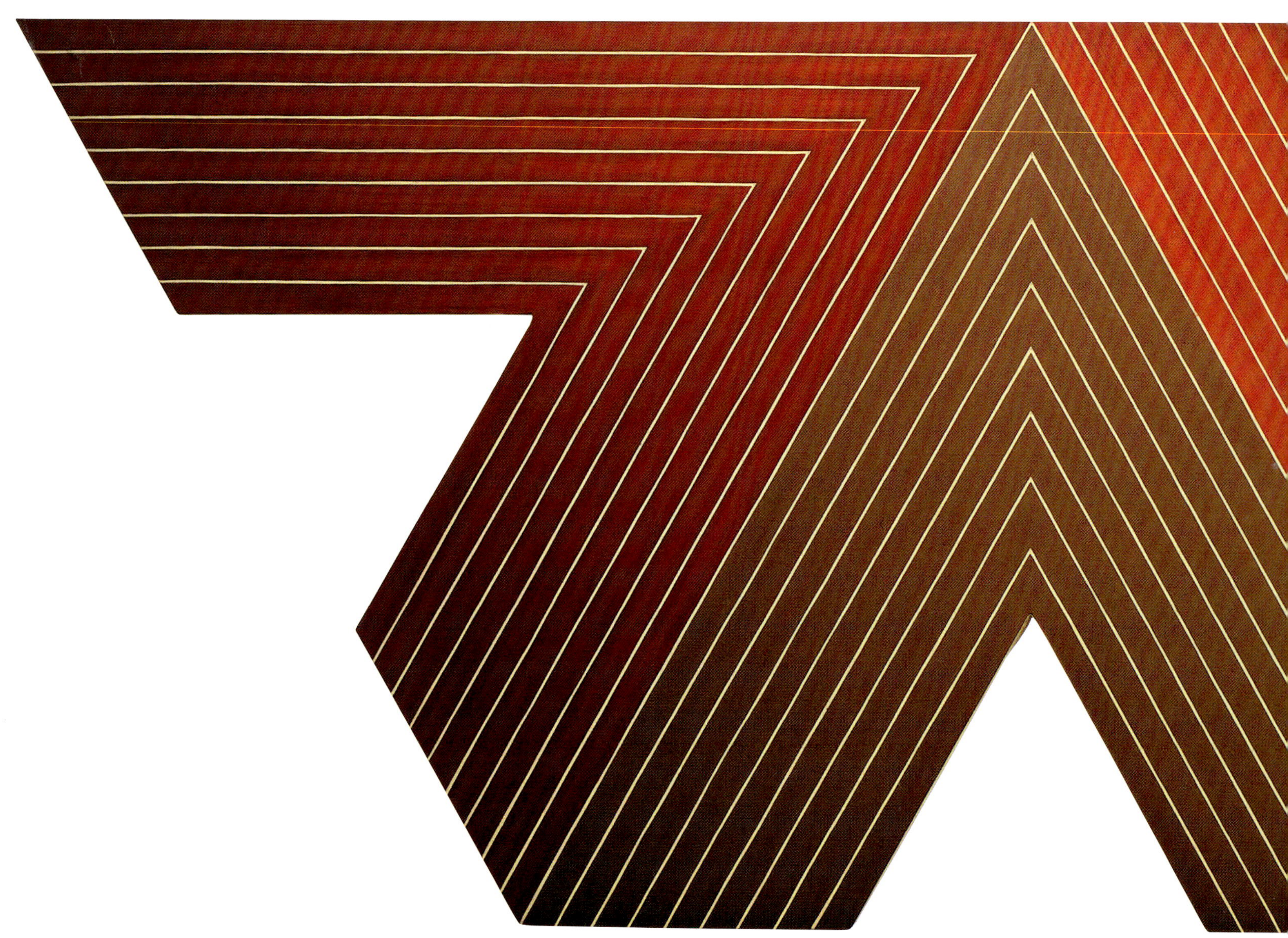

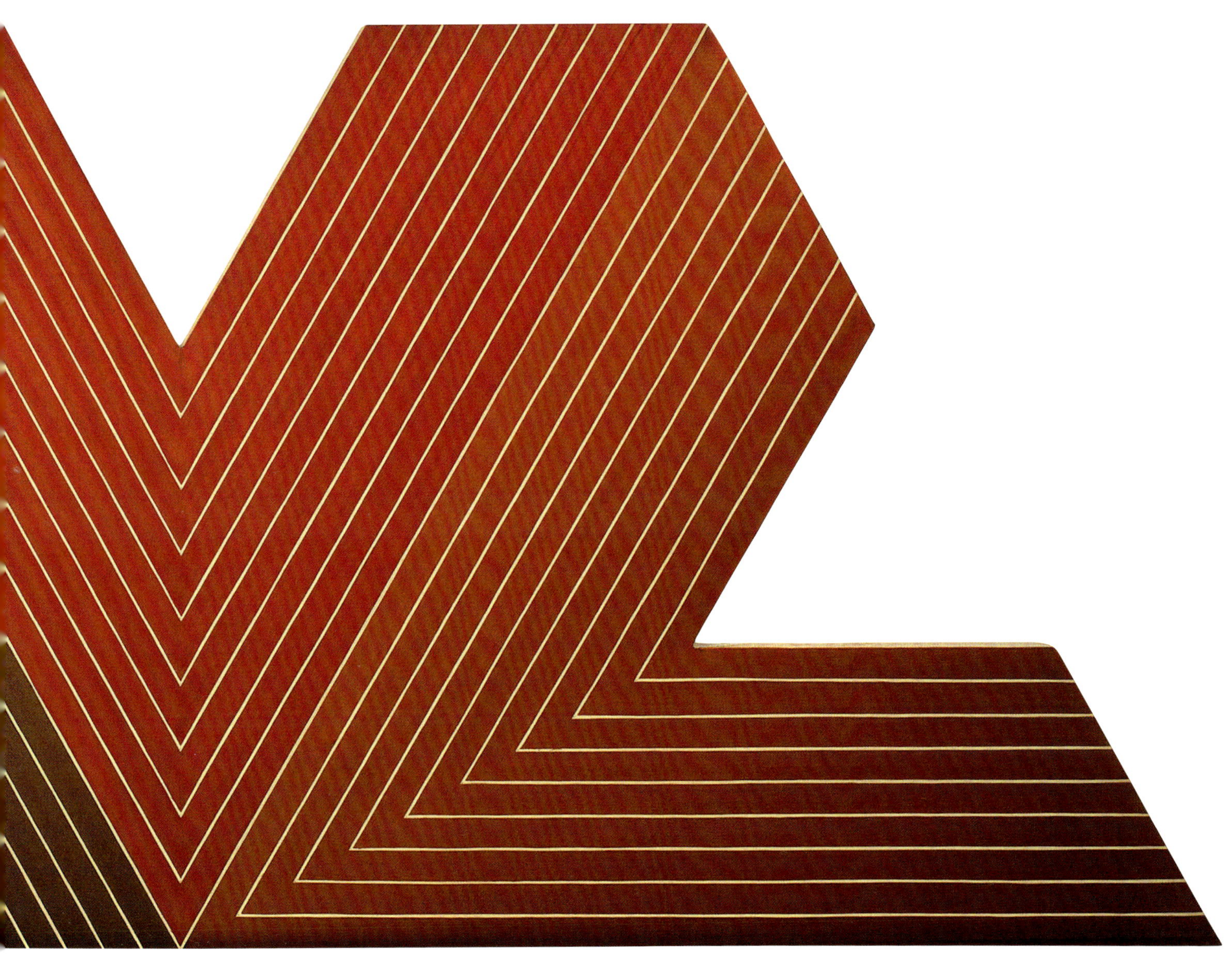

Thought one way, these two positions are entirely at odds – Minimalist physicality versus modernist opticality; spatio-temporal encounter versus 'presentness' and immediacy.[15] The art historian and critic Michael Fried, a key opponent of literalism, recounts being locked in a battle for the artist's soul during these years.[16] Thought another way, literalist art was simply the modernist ideal pushed to its logical extreme. Greenberg himself struggled to distinguish the ultimate modernist painting from a bare canvas tacked to the wall; and Fried later admitted that, 'with respect to his understanding of modernism Greenberg had no truer followers than the literalists'.[17] The circularity (and, perhaps, the shrugging frustration) of Stella's 'What you see is what you see' feels apt.

Taking a longer view, modernism is rather elided. Stella often describes the progress of his work from the late 1950s forward as one from Minimalism to 'maximalism' – as if by proclaiming his own subsequent tendencies he accepts one party's '–ism' merely in order to forsake it. Thus we arrive at what seems, in retrospect, like a concerted trajectory away from the reductiveness of the 'Black Paintings': across the 1960s alone, the striped works from the first years of that decade ceased to be rectangular – first their corners were cut away, next the canvases were more radically shaped, eventually becoming lateral and wall-spanning as well (the 'Aluminium', 'Copper', 'Purple' and 'Dartmouth Paintings', the 'Notched V' and 'Running V' Paintings); they elaborated their concentric banding

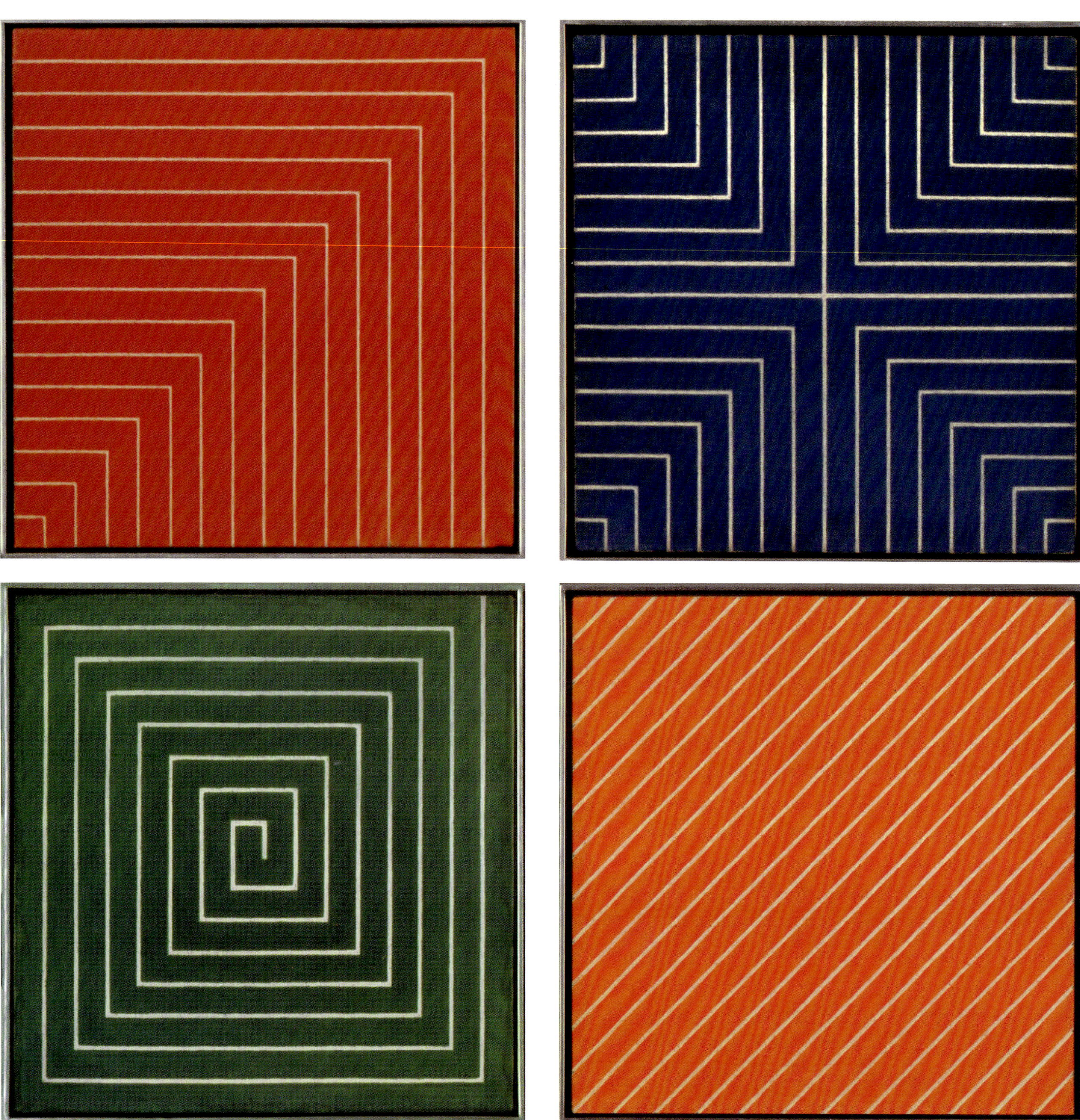

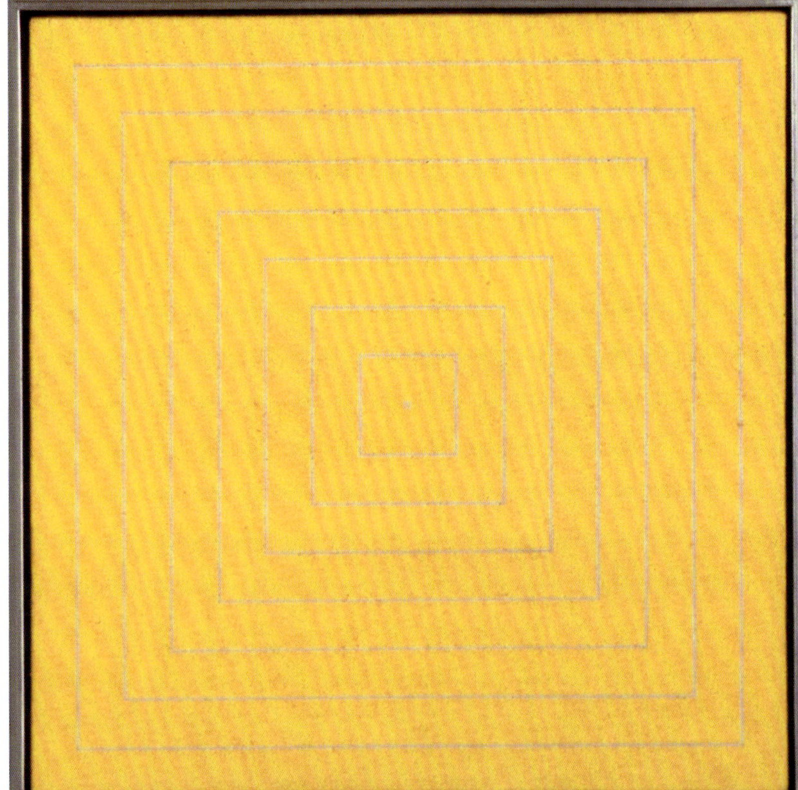

BENJAMIN MOORE PAINTINGS,
1961
ALKYD ON CANVAS
EACH 31 X 31 CM

with intentional illusionism through mitered corners or strong colour relationships (the 'Benjamin Moore Paintings', the 'Concentric Squares' and 'Mitered Mazes', the 'Moroccan' and 'Persian' Paintings); the all-over nature of the stripes gave way to intermittently woven, open, or closed bands of contouring, and the shapes of the canvases ceased to be nameable, geometrically speaking, instead circumscribing multiple, interpenetrating planes (the 'Irregular Polygons', the 'Protractor' series).[18]

Once again, the list format implies a false orderliness—the 'Notched Vs' and 'Running Vs' come after the 'Concentric Squares' and 'Mitered Mazes', and are concurrent with the 'Moroccan Paintings', for instance. But when, in 1970 at the age of thirty-three, Stella became the youngest artist to receive a survey exhibition at MoMA, viewers could track for themselves the permutations and leaps within and among twelve years' worth of striped and shaped paintings. Writing for *ARTnews* at the time, Elizabeth C. Baker delineated 'a growing ambiguity of surface-space relations' as well as a 'relative complexity of sensation', already signalled by the 'physical unevenness' of the 'Black Paintings'. Overall, she deemed Stella's output 'blunt yet illusionist, tough-hided and flat yet baroque'; seen together, these were paintings that demonstrated his 'opposing urges toward the systematic and the stunningly strange'.[19]

Few would have predicted 'opposing urges' after something like Stella's short, potent lecture delivered at Pratt in the winter of 1959, in which he explained that, through the 'regulated pattern' and symmetry of the 'Black Paintings', he had aimed to force 'illusionistic space out'.[20] In the 1964 interview already mentioned, however, Stella only allowed that the striped paintings have 'less illusionism' than others; and in 1966, he granted that there was 'an element of fantasy' to ideals of absolute flatness or evenness – that 'no matter how evenly you paint it... you're going to have an idea [perceptually, that is] of something going on anyway'.[21] Which is not to say that his growing deployment of illusionism across the 1960s was either simply circumstantial or unavoidable. Nor was Stella alone among his painter peers: James Meyer posits 1965 as 'the high season of a new illusionism'.[22] Lucy R. Lippard encompassed Stella in her 1967 essay 'Perverse Perspectives', on the emergence of 'a new incongruous illusionism' among abstract painters.[23]

Nonetheless, illusionism was anathema not only to popular Minimalist positions but also to fading high-modernist ones, and as Minimalism won out, painting in particular came under attack. In Judd's own crucial mid-1960s formulation, the 'specific objects' of Minimalist production were neither paintings nor sculptures, but they (and he) did favour three-dimensionality, for 'three dimensions are real space', which 'gets rid of the problem of illusionism' and with it 'the several limits of painting'.[24] In Judd's view, too, Stella in that moment was a maker of 'specific objects', of not-sculptures and not-paintings.[25] Such was the power of real space – of Minimalism's supposed literalism – and equally, such was the power of the art world's readiness to assimilate 'objects' as 'sculptures', that today we're accustomed to conceive of whatever breaks the two-dimensional surface or frame as actively leaving painting's realm for sculpture's.

Painting died a thousand declared deaths during this period, or was simply dismissed as irrelevant. Even the late-1960s dispersal and dematerialization of sculpture – scattered, emptied, or dissolved in Process and Earth art; rendered as intangible language or idea in Conceptual art – favoured the theorization of an 'expanded field of sculpture' rather than an expanded field of painting.[26] It is perhaps no wonder, then, that Stella doubled down on both illusionism and the pictorial, electing to identify different 'problems' for painting than those otherwise endorsed. Though that he did so not just in the face of, but somehow in concert with, the physical, literally spatial, wilder and wilder material facts of his own work is paramount.

Indeed, the professed maximalism in Stella's later work maps the eruption of illusionistic space into real space – the literalization, and then the multiplication and embellishment, of illusionistic effects. In the early 1970s, Stella fractured the surface of his works for the first time, not only imagining the interpenetration of two-dimensional planes, as in the Irregular Polygons, but also now pushing those planes physically, if at first subtly, out towards the viewer, using wood and cardboard in the 'Polish Village' series, and soon aluminium panels in the 'Brazilian' series. Across the 1970s and 1980s, when aluminium was the primary material support for increasingly exuberant wall-based reliefs, Stella introduced stencilled curves and ribbony loops, each flat or projecting surface coated with one or more different, often dissonant colours, the underlying sheen of metal countered by a variety of paint applications or, occasionally, exaggerated by passages of glitter.

Material evidence aside, Stella mostly professed ambivalence. In the striped 'Copper Paintings' of 1960–61 he had elaborated a large L-shaped unit into T, H and squared U shapes. Speaking of them several years later, he admitted that the copper works 'were a big jump, and I was aware that they raised questions about relief and sculpture'.[27] Talking in 1977 about the 'Brazilian', 'Exotic Bird' and 'Indian Bird' series made across the latter half of that decade – for each of which metal shapes were cut and then angled out from a rectangular field or mounting surface – Stella explained, 'I think of them as paintings. I know they are reliefs… I see them more as paintings because they are really meant to be seen head-on.'[28] In 1987, bracing for an unprecedented second survey exhibition at MoMA, and at the moment of his highest-relief wall works to date, he specified, 'more than two dimensions but short of three, so, for me, 2.7 is probably a very good place to be'.[29]

Significantly, while the space of relief – this incremental scale between two-dimensional painting and three-dimensional sculpture – is technically one of literal, physical rupture, it is also, historically and simultaneously, one of illusionistic suggestion. We are meant to imagine the carved figures of traditional relief, for instance, as emerging from the stone, and our corollary instinct is towards mental completion, imagining each figure's far side as available behind

CREEDE II, 1961
COPPER OIL PAINT ON CANVAS
210 X 210 CM

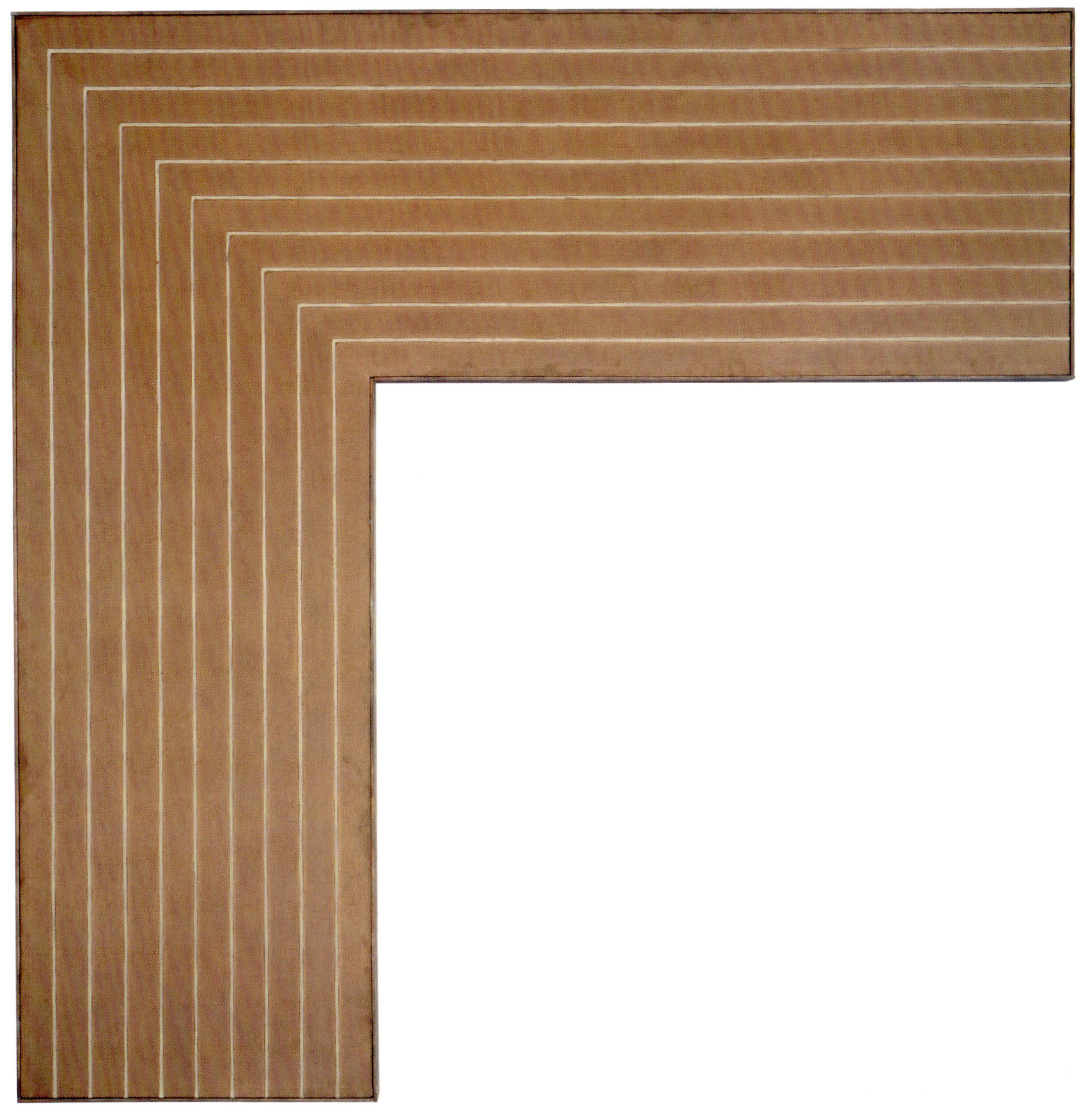

a relief's unarticulated planar support. Moreover, the relief has been called a 'diagnostic site for shifts in style.' Deemed during the Renaissance the 'dolce/amaro' (sweet/bitter) by Vincenzo Borghini, and the 'imperfetto' (imperfect) of sculpture by Giorgio Vasari, the relief form had long caused 'unease.'[30] This unease meant that relief remained essentially untheorized, until its brief summoning in the late nineteenth century as 'the foundation for all artistic forms.'[31] In 1893, at the moment of modern art history's disciplinary formation, sculptor Adolf von Hildebrand published *The Problem of Form in Painting and Sculpture*, defining sculpture via relief, and so vaunting the latter. For von Hildebrand, sculpture ('Plastik') was, ideally, the animation of the plane ('Belebung der Fläche').[32]

We would seem to have veered a long way from Stella. Yet since the early 1980s he has spoken and written at length about his own commitment to the animation of the plane, making specific recourse to the history of Baroque painting rather than to relief. In a series of lectures delivered at Harvard in 1983–84, and thereafter published as the book *Working Space*, Stella laid out a provocative, deeply felt argument about the lessons that contemporary abstract painting might learn from painterly advances of the sixteenth century: 'Can we find a mode of pictorial expression that will do for abstraction now what Caravaggio's pictorial genius did for sixteenth-century naturalism and its magnificent successors?' His impassioned analyses of Caravaggio, as well as Rubens, with forays into the early twentieth century, privilege the innovations of 'projective illusionism', a 'contained elasticity', allying the pictorial again and again with 'spatial fecundity.'[33] Caravaggio could 'explode the surface and still contain the action.'[34] 'What painting wants more than anything else', Stella proposes, 'is working space – space to grow with and expand into, pictorial space that encourages unlimited orientation and extension. Painting does not want to be confined by boundaries of edge and surface.'[35]

Duly visualized, what painting wants is to operate as a kind of relief; or at least, relief is what demonstrates – again literally, physically – Stella's vision for painting. Just after delivering the *Working Space* lectures, he began his largest series of the 1980s, known as the 'Cones and Pillars' and each titled after an Italian folktale retold by Italo Calvino.[36] The cone and pillar forms themselves were inspired by a late nineteenth-century tract by French architect Louis Monduit, *Traité théorique et pratique de la stéréotomie au point de vue de la coupe des pierres* – stereotomy being a descriptive geometry that supports the design (and the construction, through the very 'cutting of stones') of complex architectural structures. Each title in the series applies to two distinct kinds of work: one is a two-dimensional composition, in which the cone and pillar volumes are depicted through caricatures of chiaroscuro-led modelling – something like Fernand Léger meets Roy Lichtenstein – as, for example, *Giufà e la statua di gesso* (1984), with its additional, unfurling cylinder form; the other to a work in '2.7' dimensions, in which the cones and pillars exist as actual volumes, pushing out from the wall, but realized at the foreshortened angles of perspectival rendering – see, for example, *Lo sciocco senza paura* (1987). These are reliefs that revel in the funny fiction that they might remain only representations of relief (let alone of sculptural and architectural volumes).

Several years on, Stella's 1991 lecture 'Grimm's Ecstasy' rehearsed the terms of *Working Space* through an analysis of Antonio da Correggio's *Assumption of the Virgin*, painted on the ceiling of the Duomo at Parma in 1526–30.[37] Lamenting the materialist emphasis in abstract painting since the 1960s as productive of little more than 'pigmented objects', he proffers instead 'that the goal of painting is to create a *habitable illusion*' – 'pictorial space that is expansive rather than restrictive, space that is more easily understood in terms of normal vision than in terms of artistic vision'.[38] The spatiality of Stella's language grows more conspicuous as his wall-based reliefs grow more extravagant, drastic in their projection. And 'Grimm's Ecstasy' was written in the year before Stella crossed the so-called threshold into fully three-dimensional sculpture, with the Alsace-Lorraine works, as we know. Where I find this

GIUFÀ E LA STATUA DI GESSO,
1984
MIXED MEDIA ON ETCHED MAGNESIUM, ALUMINIUM AND FIBREGLASS
311 X 405 X 67 CM

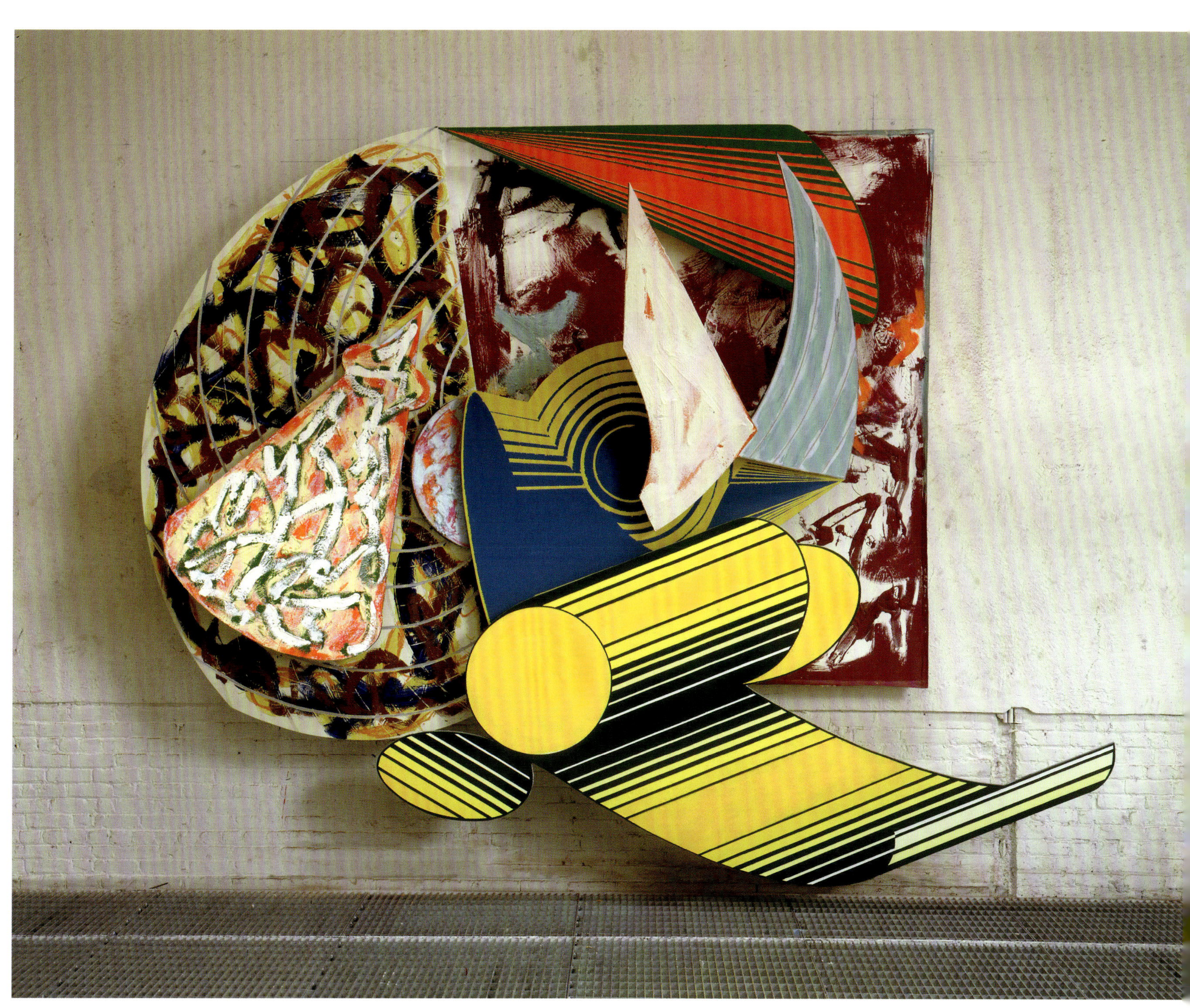

LO SCIOCCO SENZA PAURA 3D–3X, 1987
MIXED MEDIA ON ETCHED MAGNESIUM, ALUMINUM, FIBREGLASS AND CANVAS
267 X 215 X 163 CM

next page,
LO SCIOCCO SENZA PAURA 3.8X, 1984
MIXED MEDIA ON ETCHED MAGNESIUM, ALUMINUM, FIBREGLASS AND CANVAS
328 X 318 X 38 CM

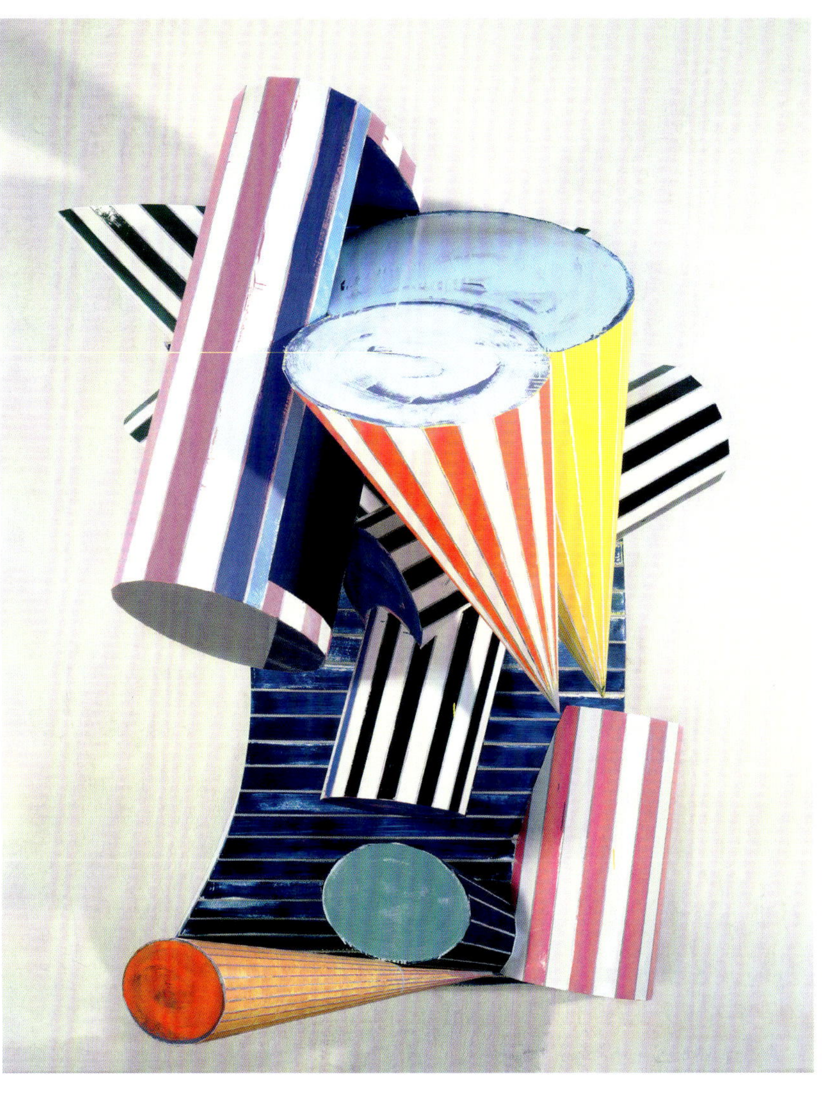

consistently eloquent text most intriguing, however, is in the moment at which the artist acknowledges a failure of language to express, or of theorization to corral, his experience. While looking at Correggio's *Assumption*, 'each time my thoughts turned to babble, circular and obvious, *That's it, that's the way painting's supposed to be, that's the way they look, and that's the way you see them*'.[39] Stella's work has shifted from Minimalism to maximalism, yet he circles back, even unwittingly, to the same fundamental, also quite personal tautology: what you see is what you see.

Stella does push himself to describe the Correggio work in question, to assess what happens within it, and his terms here are likewise telling. He speaks of its compositional awkwardness, a sense of dislocation, of 'being on edge at the edge'.[40] If this is habitable illusion, it need not also be comfortable. If Stella prizes a certain immediacy and accessibility, it need not also be easy. Nor are Old Master paintings his only explanatory devices. In a 1994 lecture called 'Broadsides', Stella asks us – ludicrously, endearingly – to imagine picking up two orange traffic cones and abutting their bases, thereby creating a 'double pylon shape' that can be read 'schematically as two cones whose bases are separated by a plane.' The plane is next to be imagined as the picture plane, and the two cones that extend on either side of it as containing 'the space of recessional illusionism… [and] the space of projective illusionism', respectively. Each cone thus 'gives us… three dimensions to work with', while the plane in between them 'represents a space of at least two dimensions. I say *at least* because it's possible to accept the notion of fractional dimensions when we consider the effects of the illusionism produced by abstract paintings in [their] exploration of flat and shallow pictorial space.'[41]

As we know, Stella does not need to be working in actual relief to achieve the illusion of an intermediate dimensionality. In this essay, it follows that,

any attempt to account for all the space, recessional, shallow/planar, and projective that pictorial thought engages is bound to exceed the three dimensions we can experience convincingly. Without much effort we have ticked off 8.5 dimensions. Seen in this context of excessive dimensionality, pictorial thought always risks being unreal and unconvincing, but this doesn't seem to hinder its usefulness.[42]

The first time Stella enumerates a dimensionality for his work beyond 2.7 – and in fact, beyond three – he

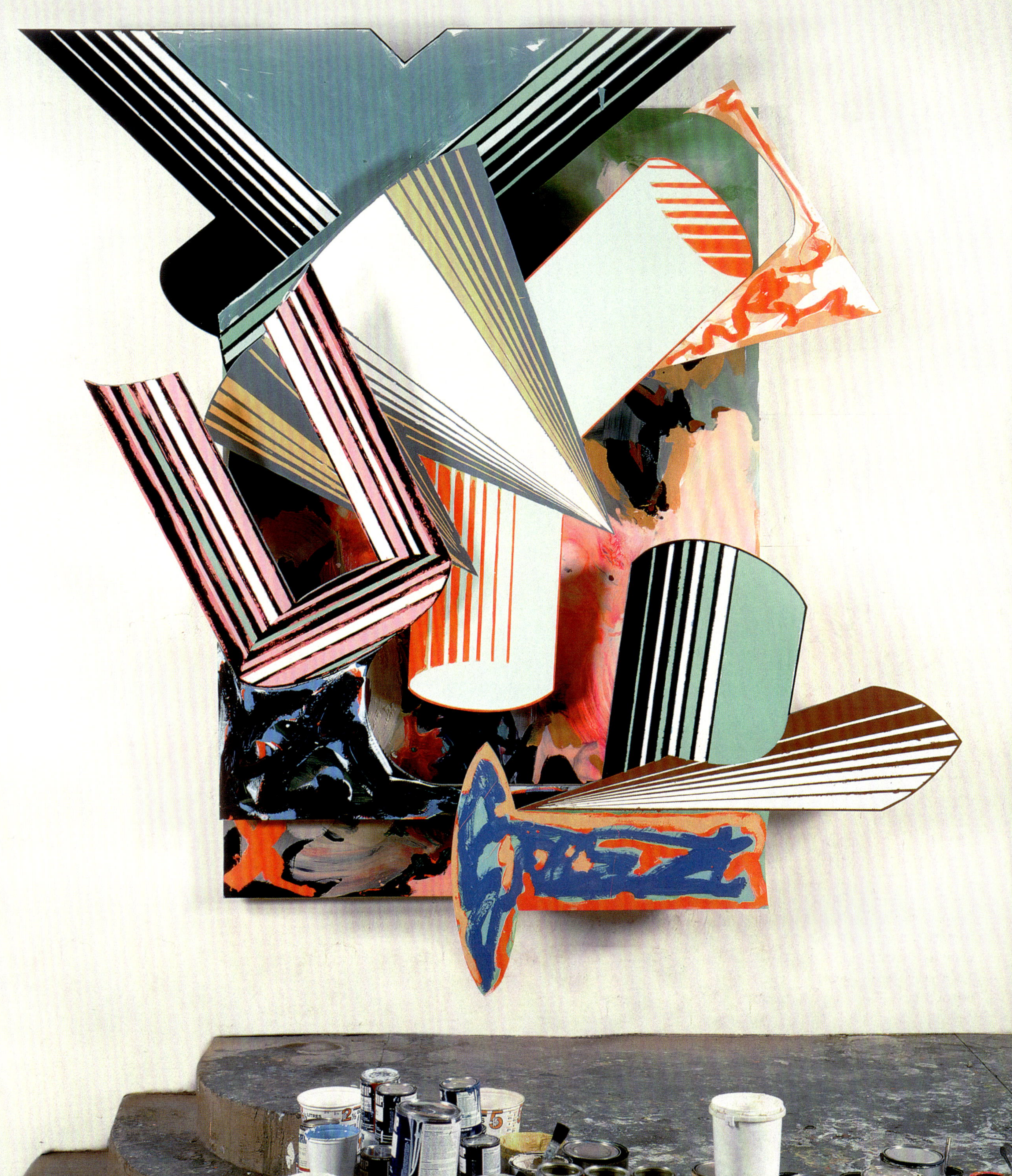

describes an excess of it, his work operational within, as well as productive of, a dimensional overdrive.

By the time of his 'Broadsides' text, Stella was relying with greater and greater frequency on computer-aided design software to model parts of, and sometimes entire, works. The 'space' that the computer opened for him in the early 1990s was, to be sure, one of 'excessive dimensionality': 'Virtual space has no ground', he has said. 'That's the beauty of it. It's about destroying the ground so you can explore all the dimensions and the viewpoints.'[43] Then again, Stella also explains that he 'need[s] the physical thing to work with or against', and what he explores in the 'excessive dimensionality' of virtual space does consistently attain some kind of physical form, realized in or somewhere between two and three dimensions.[44] It is even possible to identify points at which the artist takes the example of his own 'double pylon shape' literally – manifesting, that is, all 8.5 dimensions.

In the 'Easel Paintings' series of 1990–91 – large, unpainted and floor-bound metal assemblages – Stella seems through such a series title, and through the raw-steel framing devices that uphold the found and splash-cast elements, to indicate that he is making sculptural work by means of painting's typical support structures – easel and stretcher, however extrapolated and, crucially, pulled off the wall. In works of the last decade, he makes much of his sculptural work by pulling the relief off the wall; that is, by demonstrating the animation of the plane in its 'excessive dimensionality'. These recent works comprise one or more shapes shown as if in literal projection *and* literal recession, in the process of passing or even bursting through an independent planar form.

A work currently in the studio makes an extreme case. Its planar element is a roughly foot-thick block, formed from a delicate, crystalline grid structure – and so constituted mostly by its own negative space. Its delicacy is enhanced by how finely it is painted, in a green that fades to white wherever the wires meet in a kind of asterisk. The oxymoronic sense of thick block or slab, of an incongruous density, is itself reinforced by what this open framework contains, cradling forms that variously push into, slice through, rest within, and protrude from it – namely five fragments of painted and unpainted solid foam and two cast panels of white paper pulp, among a handful of small wire forms. This sculpture's airy matrix of green and white wire, the scattering of forms it suspends, and its disquieting clarity of scale, seem to zoom us as if close in on the very activity of intersection – on the precise points where volumetric forms cross through a plane.

We might recall, too, more representative (comparatively zoomed-out) works like *K.150* (2014), mentioned at the start of this essay, in which the 'shallow pictorial plane' is actualized as a slightly folded panel of white, punctured by an array of colourfully spraypainted holes; through this plane push fully three-dimensional spring, spiral and star shapes, differently legible on either side. Or we might look to a new group of works known as the 'Marshmallow Mold' series, where this planar form is explicitly gridded, halfway between the mostly solid panel of *K.150* and the sparse structure of the wire-matrix sculpture. The physical plane of *Little Egypt* (2016) undulates, all the more elastic in appearance. In *Midnight Blue* (2016), the plane, sprayed blue on one face and purple on its other, behaves similarly, though here we approach one of its broad, white-painted edges rather than either face. In *Corner Pocket* (2016), two gridded planes cross one another perpendicularly, while cut through by additional shapes.

Here's what I see: pictorial illusionism is not the same as virtuality, but virtual tools have clearly enabled the modelling within, and then the manifestation as if from within, the ideally elastic pictorial space Stella most values. Yet I am intrigued by a generic understanding of virtuality here as well, where the virtual means almost or nearly, but not quite. For virtual space is also not real

LITTLE EGYPT, 2016
PAINTED ELASTO PLASTIC RPT
WITH METAL
64 X 130 X 112 CM

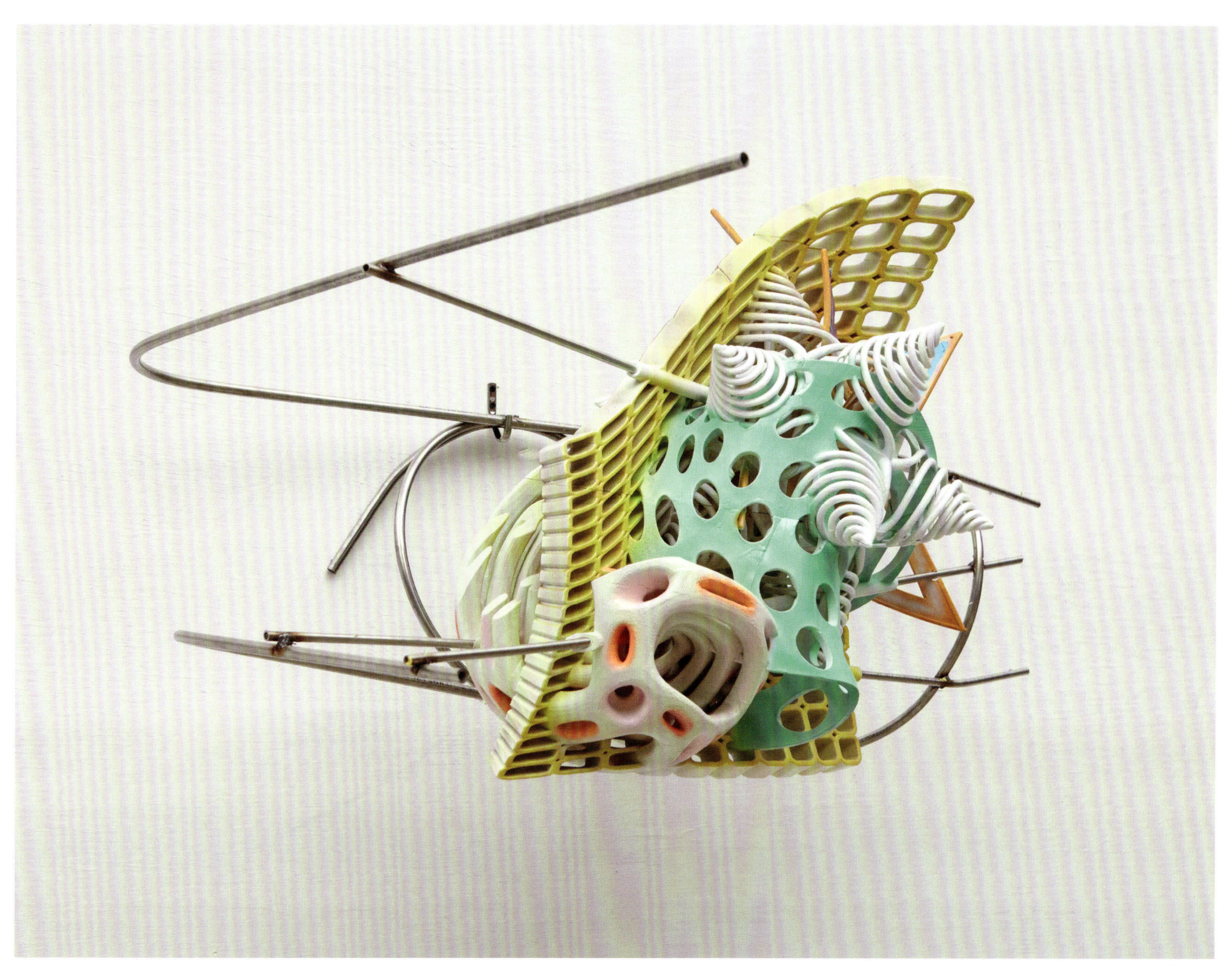

MIDNIGHT BLUE, 2016
PAINTED ELASTO PLASTIC RPT
WITH METAL
173 X 84 X 91 CM

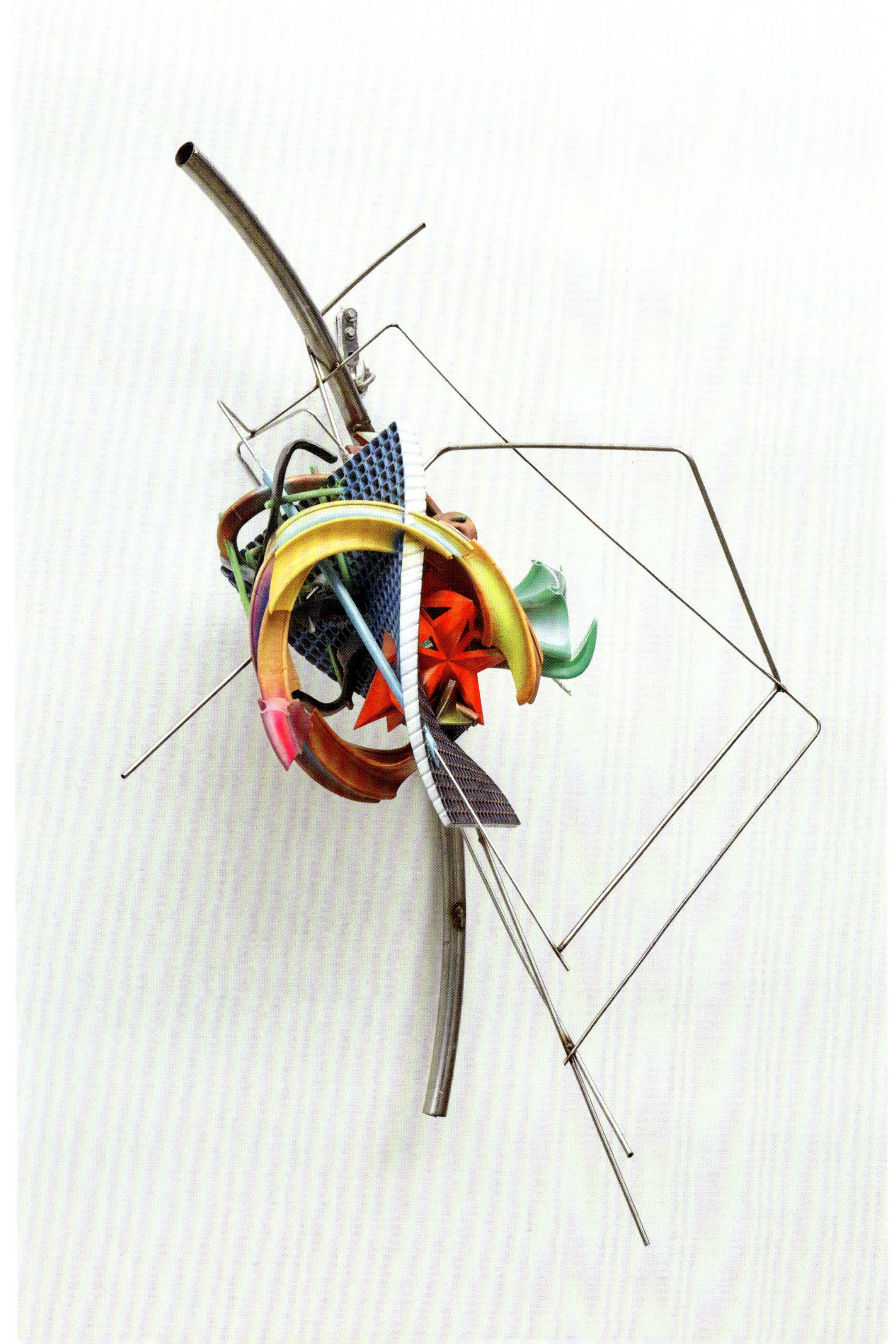

CORNER POCKET, 2016
PAINTED ELASTO PLASTIC RPT
WITH METAL
79 X 79 X 152 CM

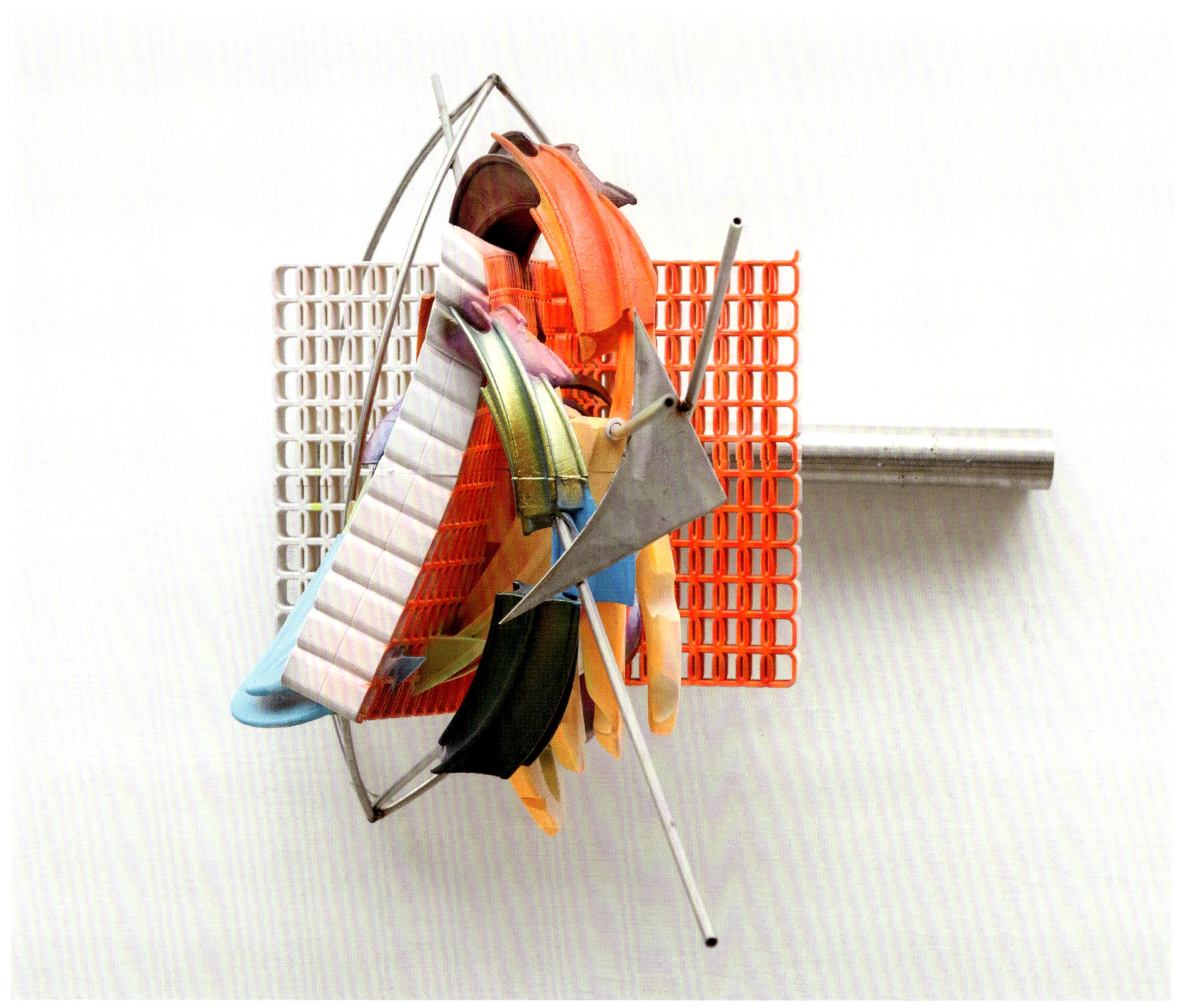

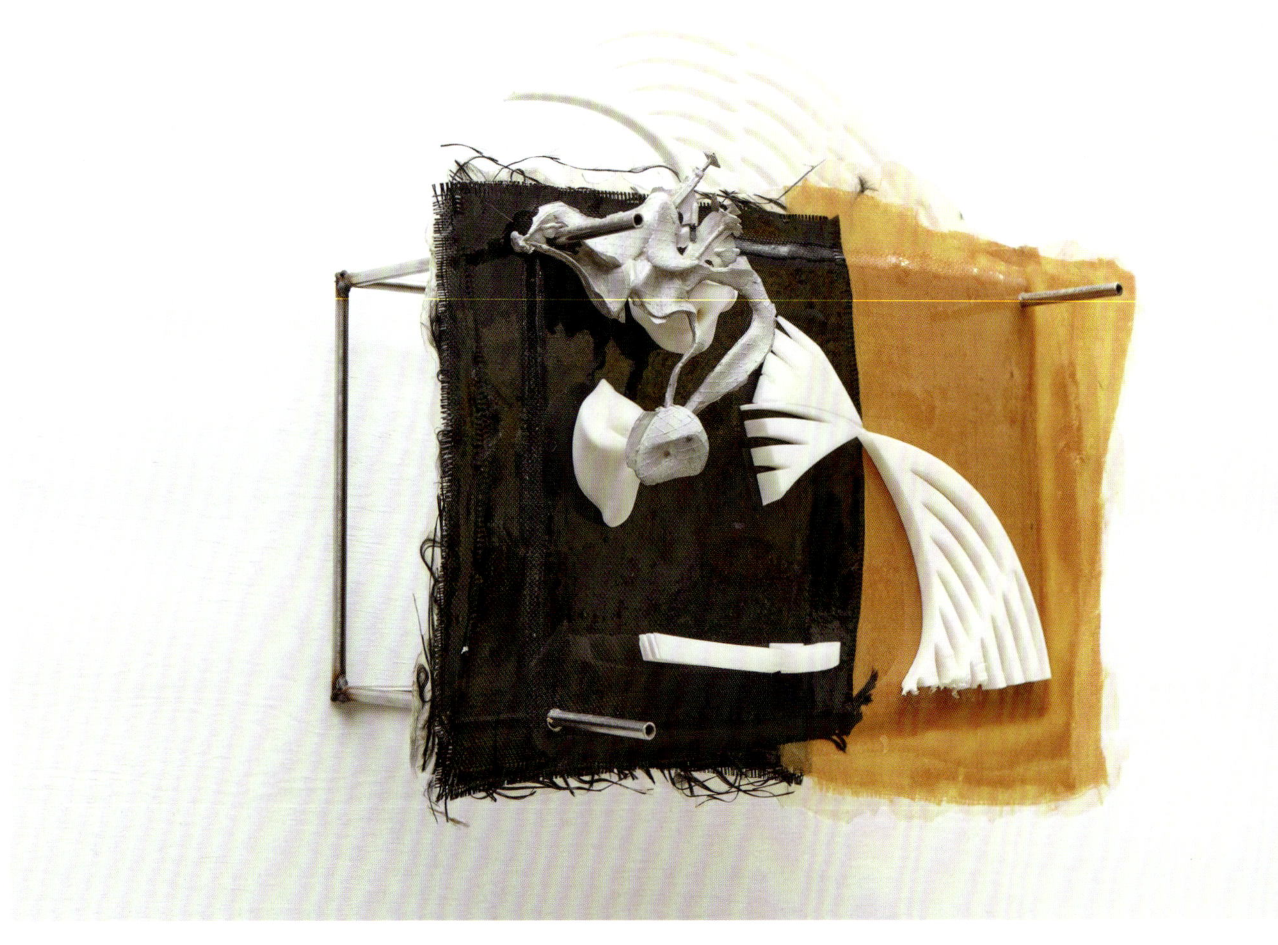

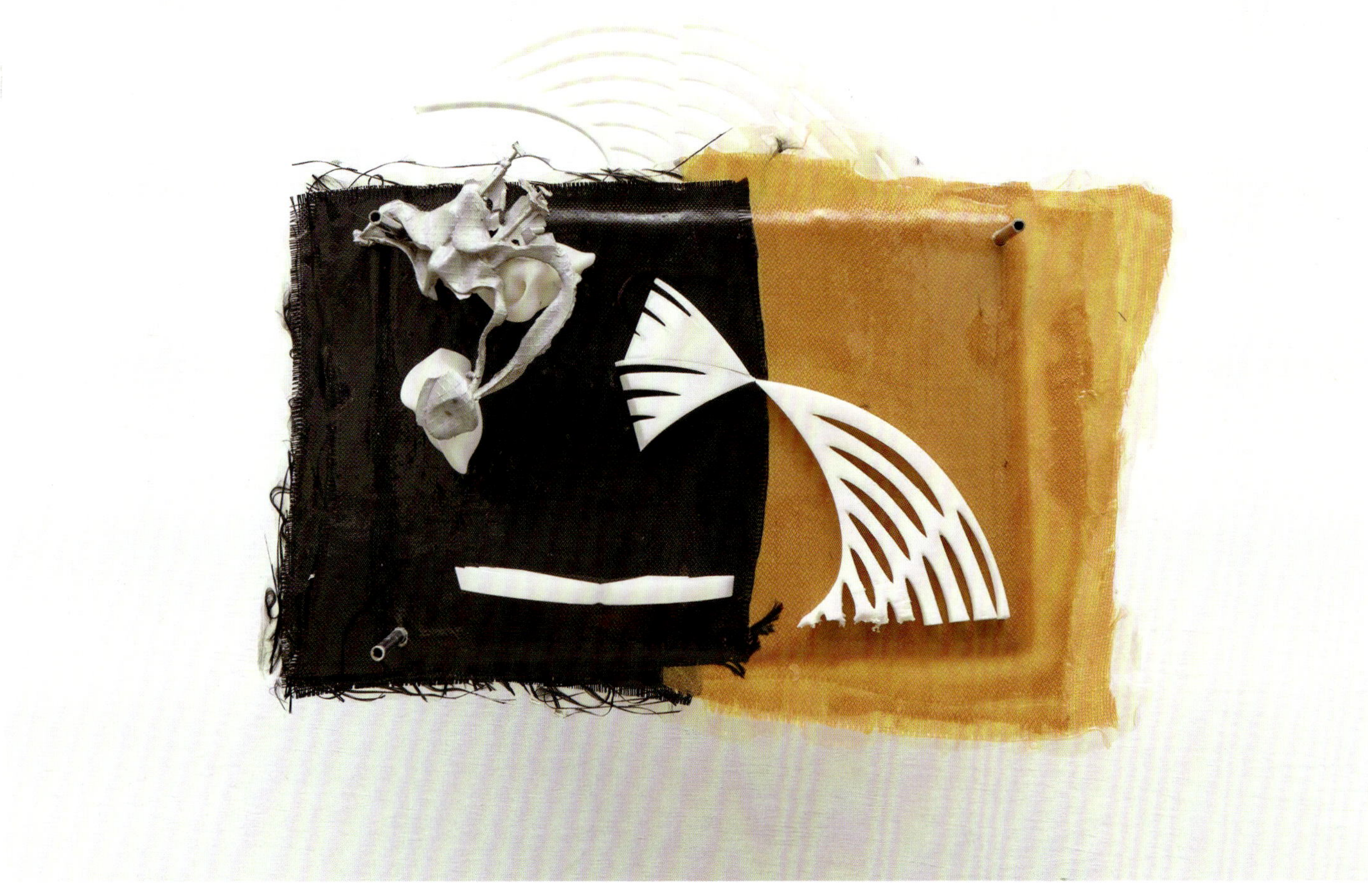

K.503 SEGMENT 1, 2015
ELASTO PLASTIC RPT WITH
METAL AND CARBON FIBRE
48 X 89 X 69 CM

space. To continue to lean on Stella's language in this regard, this lack of fundamental (or, ultimate?) equation may be why the sculptural works he has made for more than two decades now so often 'exceed the three dimensions we can experience convincingly' – why they seem to put us 'on edge at the edge'.

Here's what else I see: passing from 2.7 to 8.5 does not necessarily mean that Stella has left the relief behind. While the relief is often discerned as inter-medial, a name for a gap or interstice between two other media, the sheer time that Stella has spent working in relief encourages me to think about it as a medium in its own right. His work further encourages me to conceive of the relief as extra-medial, too – a mode not in between but somehow beyond, in excess of… what? In excess of itself? Can a relief be two-sided, or does it simply become, then, a sculpture? 'Sculpture' is the convenient term, to be sure, but 'relief' obtains for me as well because of how steadily Stella seeks to correlate spatiality with planarity. And perhaps I am persuaded by the 'excessive dimensionality' he has enumerated precisely because it 'always risks being unreal and unconvincing'.

Motifs and Motivations

Stella did, as early as 1971, rupture or fragment the pictorial plane, and then, via his later, physically multidimensional work – most literally in the new 'Marshmallow Mold' series, and in many examples from the ongoing 'Scarlatti K' series – he re-establishes it again as a thickness or density (also, a threshold?) to be crossed before our very eyes. Meanwhile some of the 'Scarlatti K' works are more formally complicated than my emphasis on either plane or threshold has seemed to allow. In *K.503 Segment 1* (2015), the central 'plane' being crossed by other forms is not only bisected by a fold but itself curled into a kind of loop, for instance – figured as a new shape in its own right. In other recent works from the series, there is no legible planar element at all, but rather two or more different shapes interleaved or interpenetrated.

Thus far I have written more about terms and trappings than about content, but many such shapes demand focused attention, the planar form being only one among them. Which is actually another way of saying that 'motif', itself, is the next term we must undertake. Motifs are key to Stella's practice both as forms that develop over time and as forms that recur over time. We might take the plumb line of the earliest striped paintings as, indeed, Stella's earliest motif, a unit that mimed, and in so doing seemed to overwrite, the bounding edge or corner of the stretched canvas. It was with a differently forceful linearity that Stella then angled out from the flat plane into his initial reliefs. Next, motifs borrowed or derived from the real world appeared in the mid-1970s, with the French, railroad and ship-builder's curves – legible stencils or templates used initially in the 'Exotic Bird' series and for several series after.[45] We know already the pillars and cones of the 1980s. The fixed curves of the stencils gave way to the increasingly melodramatic, freeform waves of the 'Moby Dick' series of the later 1980s into the late 1990s. If the planar grids of the 'Marshmallow Mold' series led me to declarations on behalf of the medium or mode of relief, they can also help us clarify aspects of Stella's material and technical means. The grid is in fact an especially mutable motif, which I first note in the openwork mounting structures of the 'Indian Bird' series of the late 1970s – likely a pragmatic solution for its comparative lightness of weight and multiplicity of points of attachment, and in this case, too, simply a support for the frenzied activity of French curve motifs atop it. Later, a grid is intentionally etched onto painted metal plates in the 'Circuits' series, and torqued, crumpled, or otherwise used as an unlikely image of pliability in paintings and prints from the early and mid-1990s onward. Beginning around 1992, one such grid stands out from the others – a fuzzy, often primary-coloured off-grid of dots as if spray-painted through a crude, jaunty stencil (see, for example, the *Moby Dick Deckle Edges* prints (1993), or prints from the 'Imaginary Places' series (1994–95), both of which demonstrate this particular motif in its transition from showing stencil-like contours to showing that which has been stencilled, or see marginal but tantalizing snippets of the motif in certain larger paintings of the later 1990s, like *Organdie* (1997); I first wondered about this grid-like dot pattern when I noticed unmoored patches of it floating high up on a couple of Stella's studio walls as well). These are computer-modelled enlargements based on the very pixels of computer-based image composition, and early on Stella hoped to manifest the resulting soft-edged grid in three dimensions as well. Preliminary efforts did not satisfy, however, and only in the last two years has he arrived at an adequate three-dimensional rendering, which he calls the 'marshmallow mould', printed in elasto plastic – the thick, undulant planar form I have interpreted at some length.

I am lingering over this marshmallow mould form once again in order, this time, to press on matters of rendering. Considered basically, the grid form tends to be a framework, a network, a matrix – for supporting, constructing, as well as for diagramming and transferring. The weave of a painter's canvas is at once echoed and amplified in certain reductive abstract painting of the twentieth century, in which a grid is given simultaneously as painting's figure and as painting's ground. But the grid is also critical for contour mapping, and so for plotting a figure within 'groundless' virtual space as well. By now, every motif that Stella uses is modelled from scratch within the computer, so that a three-dimensional form is the starting point for whatever results, whether flat or volumetric work.

This is the case even for so-called 'found' forms, such as the marshmallow mould, an ultimately three-dimensional element named after a candy-making device, though not actually modelled on one. But as a motif, the marshmallow mould is new, its exemplars

ORGANDIE, 1997
ACRYLIC ON CANVAS
396 × 396 CM

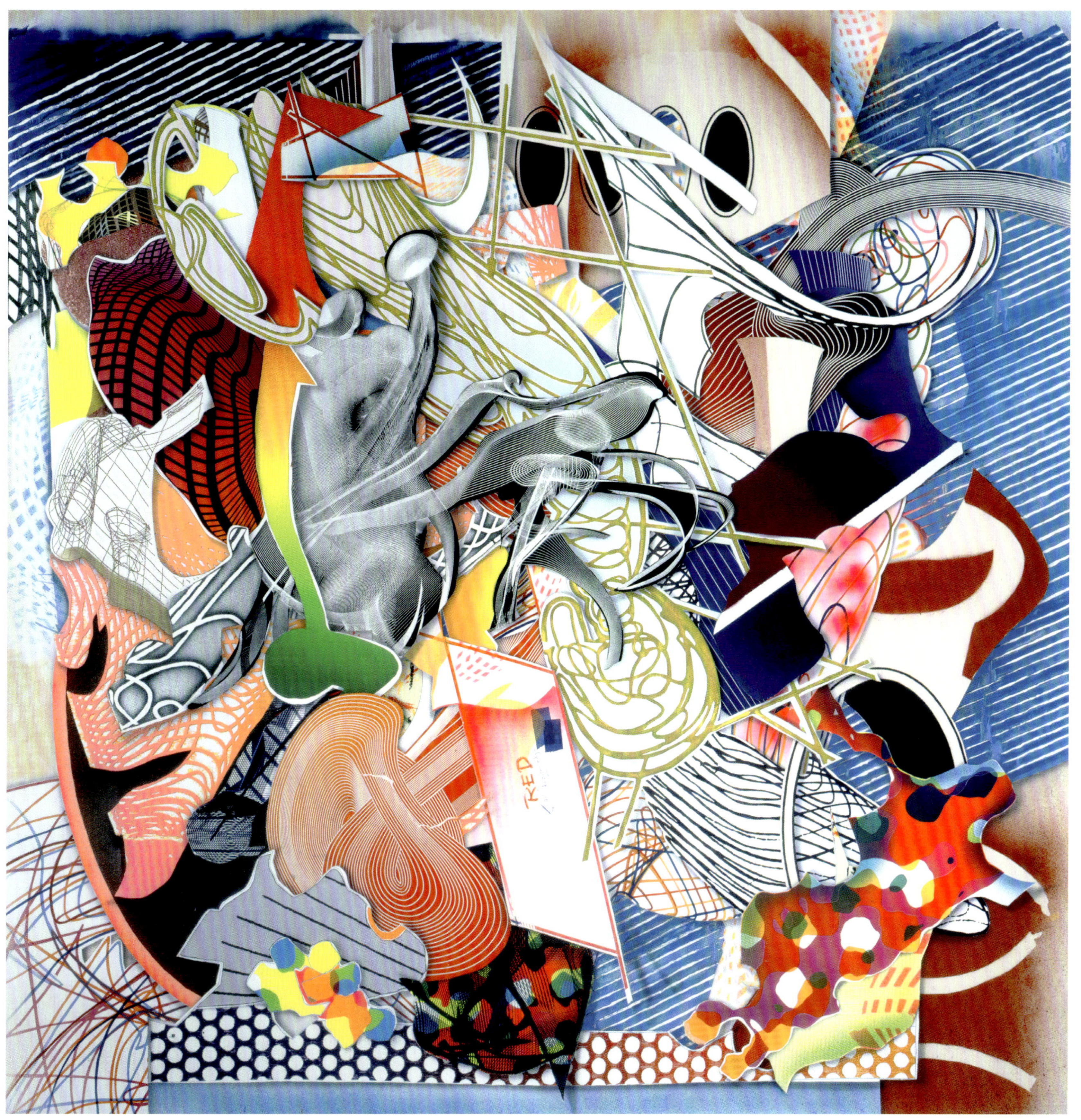

BEAR MOUNTAIN, 1995
STAINLESS STEEL, CARBON
STEEL, AND BRONZE
249 X 545 X 545 CM

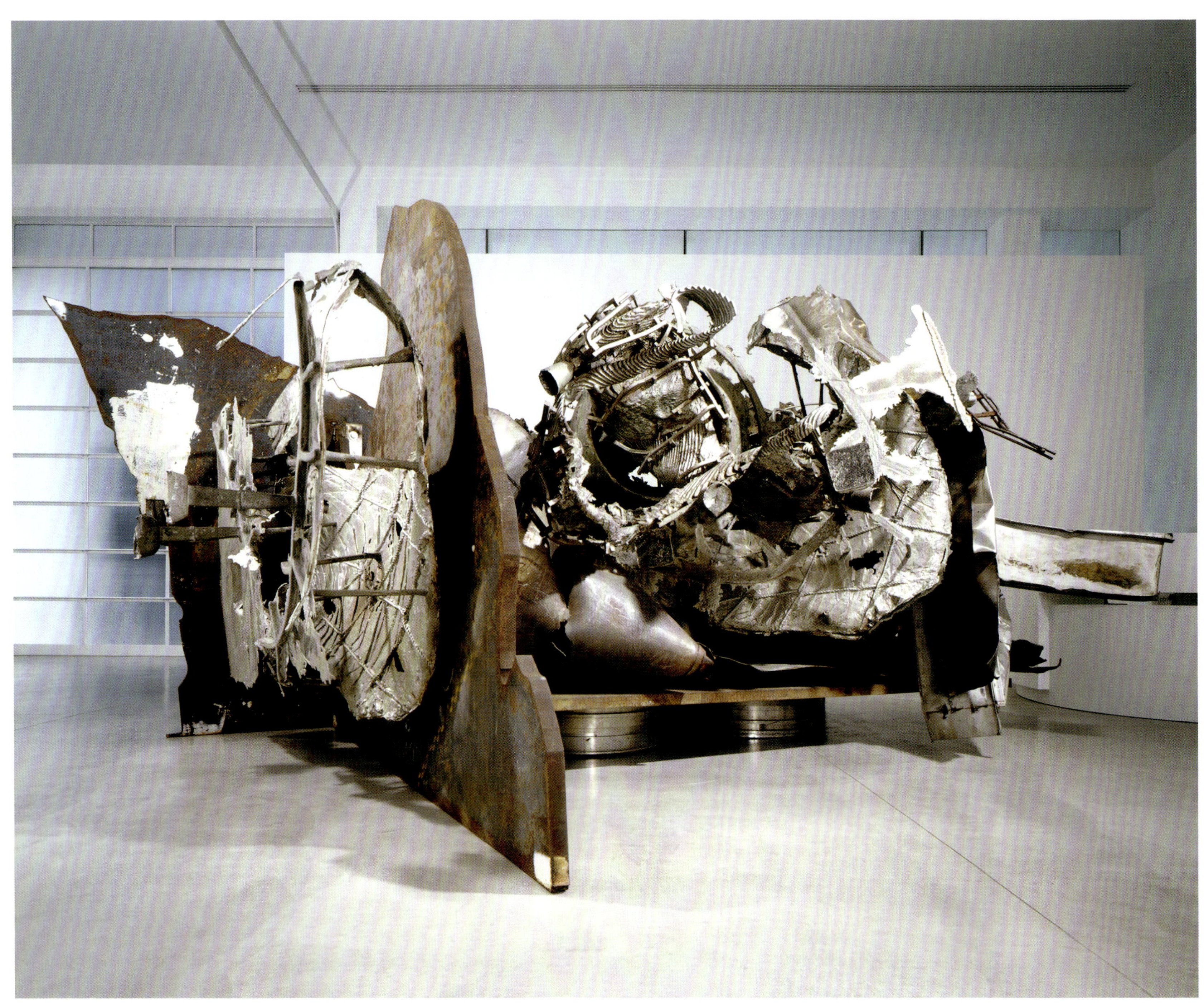

still technically few. By far the most prominent motifs in Stella's production since the early 1990s have been the smoke ring and the spiral-cut hat (along with a dog toy and a variable star form that is somehow both borrowed, because a recognizable symbol, and designed). Indeed, the smoke ring and the spiral-cut hat best elaborate the etymological relationship between motif and movement, as well as between motif and motivation, in pursuit of which this essay will conclude.

Stella had smoked cigars for years before attempting to apprehend the smoke ring as a form within his work. 'A smoke ring is a gesture that is intrinsically a part of space, integrated into it. It doesn't sit in front of space and it isn't in the background. It's like a molecular part of it. I've always wished I could do that with a painted gesture', he once explained.[46] Around 1990 he undertook rigorous efforts to isolate and capture the otherwise ephemeral: he blew smoke rings through a small hole into an eight-foot-square enclosure; cameras mounted to each of the box's interior faces indexed these rings, which were then combined within a 3-D computer imaging programme – faithfully translated by contour mapping and thereafter available for more and less radical manipulations. The smoke rings thus initiated Stella's work with computer modelling, and they have appeared in every major series since.

We see sections of smoke rings – telltale, snaking appendages that either end in or emanate from annular or lozenge-like nodes – first three-dimensionally, in the Alsace-Lorraine assemblages of 1992, or on a far grander scale in metal assemblages like *Bear Mountain* (1995) and *Çatal Hüyük (Level II) Shrine A.III.1* (1999). We

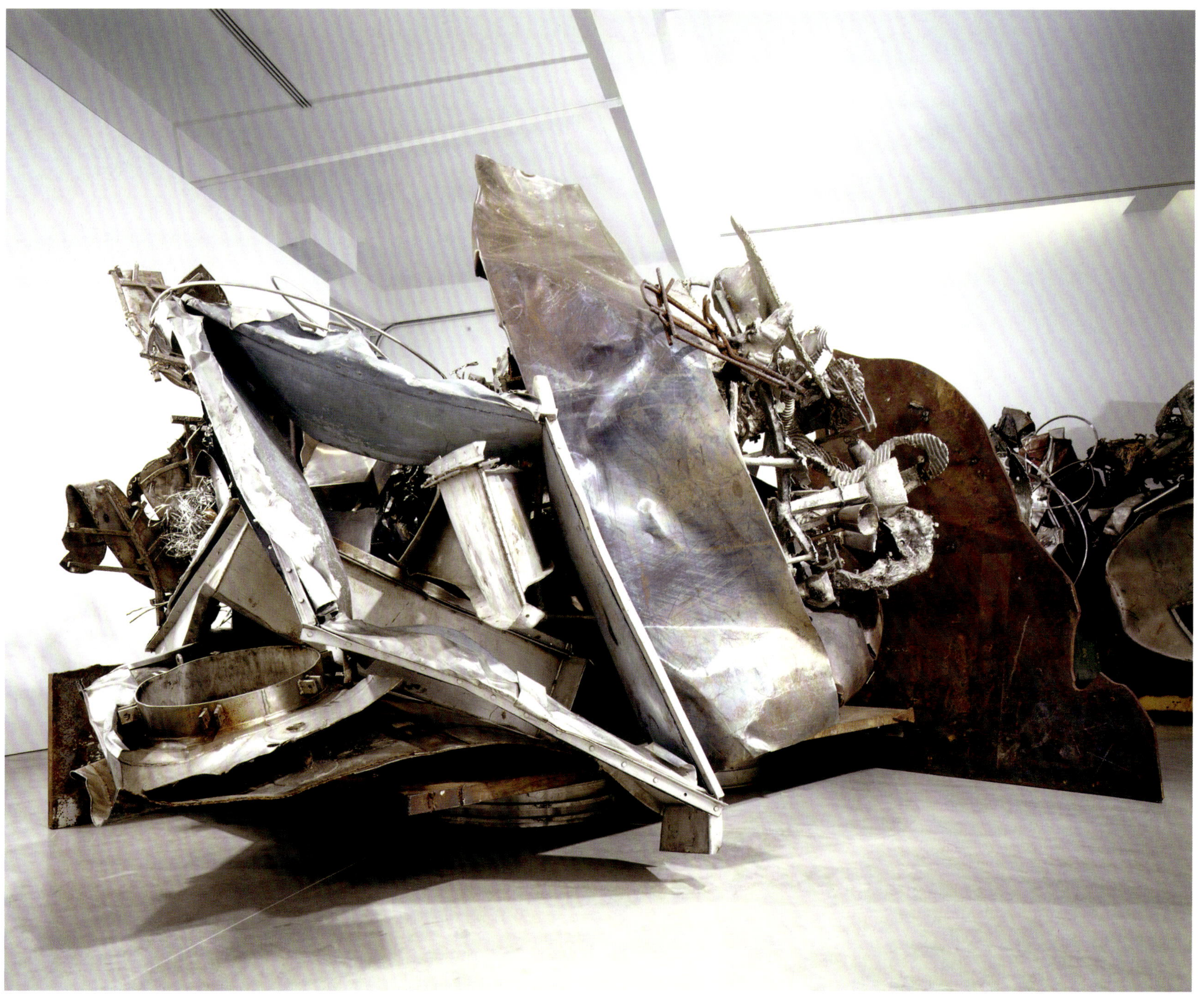

ÇATAL HÜYÜK (LEVEL II) SHRINE A III 1, 1999
CAST ALUMINUM AND STAINLESS STEEL
358 X 304 X 445 CM

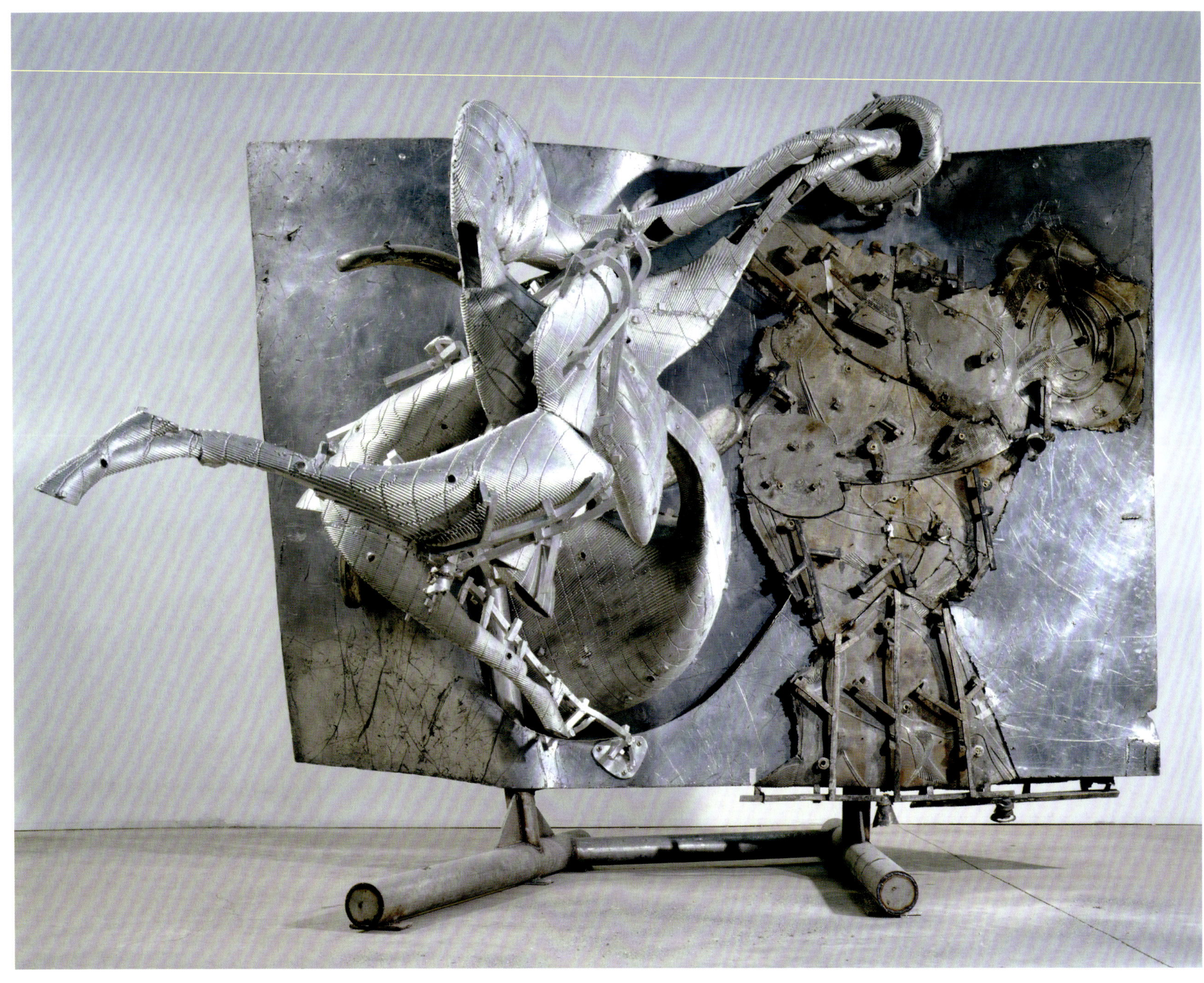

AT SAINTE LUCE! (HOANGO)
[Q#1], 1998
MIXED MEDIA ON CAST
ALUMINIUM
297 X 274 X 173 CM

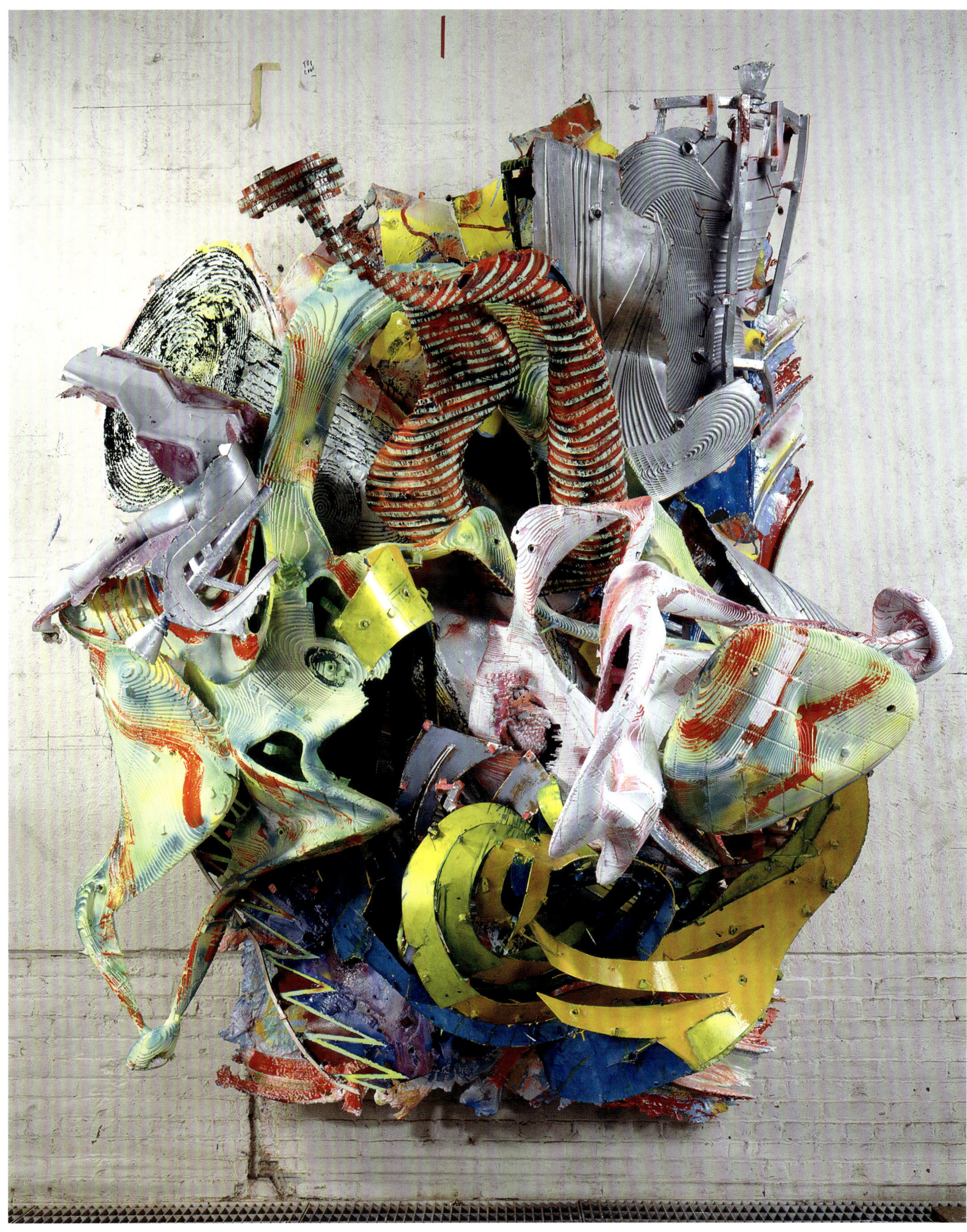

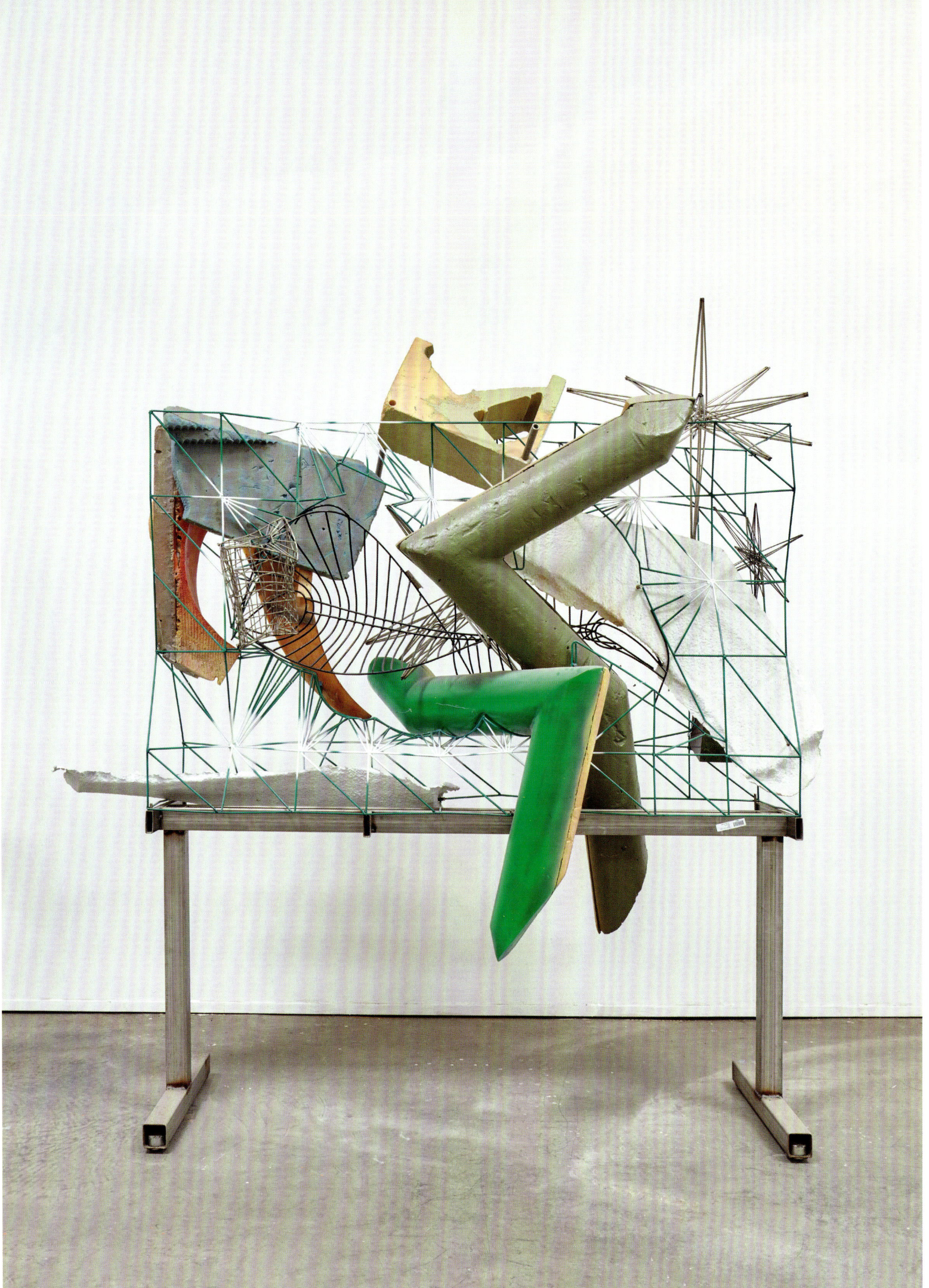

ZHORKIN CAMP, 2014
PAINTED METAL AND FOAM
178 X 236 X 86 CM

see them, or struggle to pick them out, in riotous wall reliefs of painted cast aluminium like *At Sainte Luce! [Hoango]* [Q#1] (1998), or *Calendar Thoughts [EJ#8]* (1999). We see them realized in two dimensions as well, in frenetically layered acrylic-on-canvas works like *Organdie* (1997) and the forty-foot-long *Das Erdbeben in Chili [N#3]* (The Earthquake in Chile) (1999). We see one in unpainted, 3-D-printed plastic, unusually whole, in a small recent work called *Reclining Smoke*.

In the paintings of the later 1990s, these smoke-ring forms tend to appear as they might on the computer screen, some explicitly diagrammatic, others preserving a kind of smoky translucency via the intricate surface webbing used to model them. Curiously, the cigar smoke does not read as more ephemeral, more prone to shape-shifting and ultimate dissipation, than do any of the other forms of imagery and marking against which they slide and jostle. Where the three-dimensional realizations are concerned, however, the smoke forms stand out as notably less recognizable – notably stranger – their wispiness and rippling or dimpling presented as tubular and bulbous. Stella first made the smoke rings in cast steel and aluminium, the moulds for which were achieved either by way of stereolithography, which limited their size and to some degree their contortion, or by cutting and pasting foam, which was more labour-intensive but could achieve greater scale. In the former case, a laser-based translation from computer model into polymer structure (an early process of rapid prototyping) re-formed the smoke as a physical maquette from which the foundry could make a useable mould. In the latter case, the foam was sliced and then layered back together in a hand-built analogue to the smoke form's digitally mapped cross-sections.[47]

In both cases the resulting metal casts maintain on their surfaces evidence of such complicated, experimental mould construction. Casts derived from stereolithography are surfaced by a delicately raised grid – ghostly remainders of the points of connection between the polymer, while it was still hardening in its vat, and the support structure built to steady it while it took its intricate shape.[48] (Stella could have asked that these gridded lines be polished away before each mould was made from its polymer maquette, but he preferred instead to retain them, which for me oddly foreshadows the much later marshmallow mould forms – nothing but grid, and never themselves either used as or made from a mould.) See, for instance, the bas-relief netting across the protuberant smoke forms in *Zimming*, one of the Alsace-Lorraine sculptures from 1992. Casts derived from foam-built moulds register each cross-section as a distinct ridge, as if the form has been pushed to the point of pixelation, beyond its clear or ideal resolution. These are the striations that help us identify the smoke rings in various painted aluminium reliefs from the 'Heinrich von Kleist' series of the late 1990s, as well as the smoke fragments in the earlier *Toul*, not themselves full volumes, but instead, I would wager, doubly cast – in steel from a scrapped, perhaps failed, prior cast.

To the extent that the smoke rings are recognizable as they proliferate across materials, scales and series, they are certainly never identical from one work to the next. They are a recurrent signal more than a recurrent form: a signal of that which moves constantly, of that which re-forms constantly, as if by its own agency though in fact guided by otherwise imperceptible air currents – until it has 'integrated' (to use Stella's word) so fully, so drastically, with the space around it that it seems to have disappeared. Meanwhile, around the same time as his first smoke-ring experiments, Stella had received 'a hat that my kids picked out for me in a Rio de Janeiro souvenir shop'.[49] He went on to describe its native manipulability:

It's basically a die-cut sheet of foam, circular in form, with spiral cuts radiating from its centre. If you dunk it in the surf and pull it over your head it will keep you cool on the beach. The coolest thing about it, though, is that almost any twist you give it will yield a high-class sculptural or architectonic form. The transformation accomplished by manipulating the beach hat is truly amazing. Using it without any particular effort or skill, one can create from a bland planar object complex spaces with complex surfaces. The beach hat seemed to dance off by itself, stopping every once in a while to strike a pose as a piece of architecture or as a piece of sculpture.[50]

The hat form did 'strike a pose as a piece of architecture' first. We see it in architectural maquettes like *Kunsthalle and Garden II, Dresden Project* (1992), or *Gate House (Model)* (1994). Even in 12-foot-high sculptures like the painted fibreglass *The Broken Jug [D #3] (1st version)* (1999), or the unpainted wood

KUNSTHALLE AND GARDEN II, DRESDEN PROJECT, 1992
COLORED SINTRA AND PLASTER
25 X 142 X 91 CM

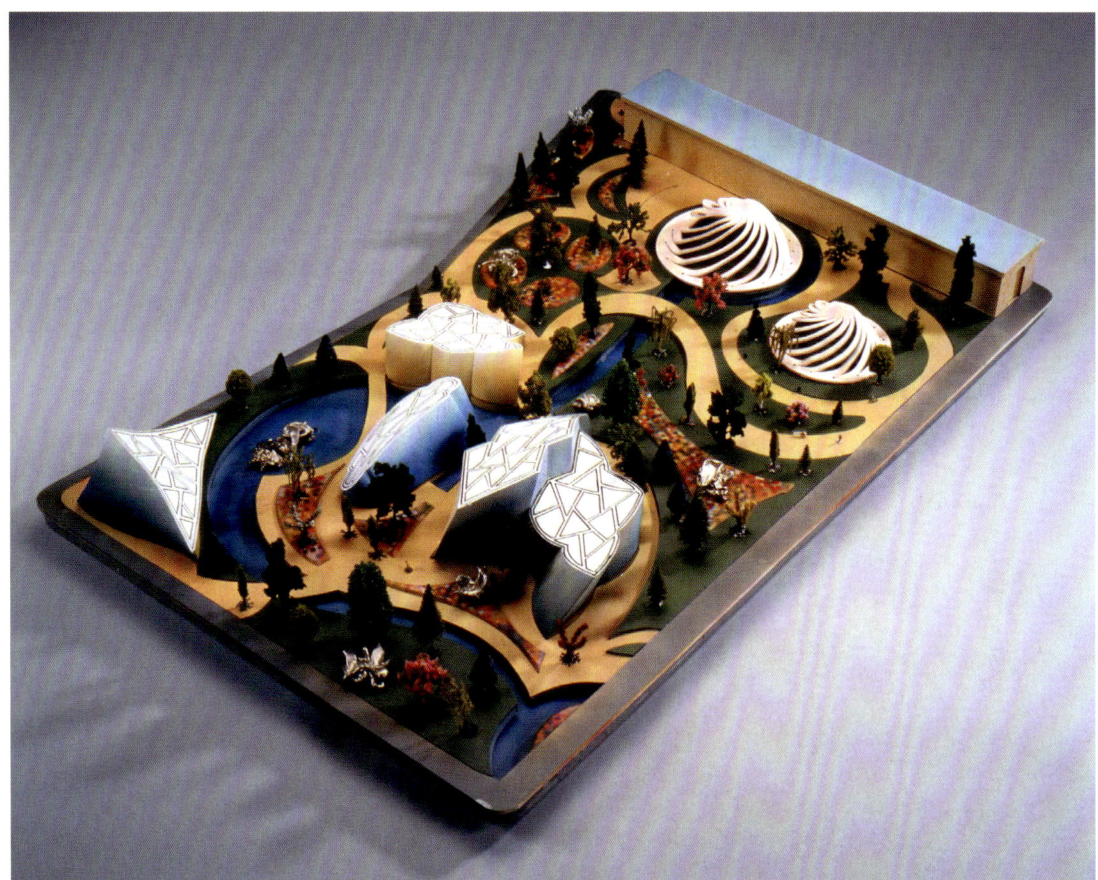

THE BROKEN JUG, A COMEDY [D#3] (LEFT HANDED VERSION), 2007
MARINE PLY AND PINE
475 X 515 X 360 CM

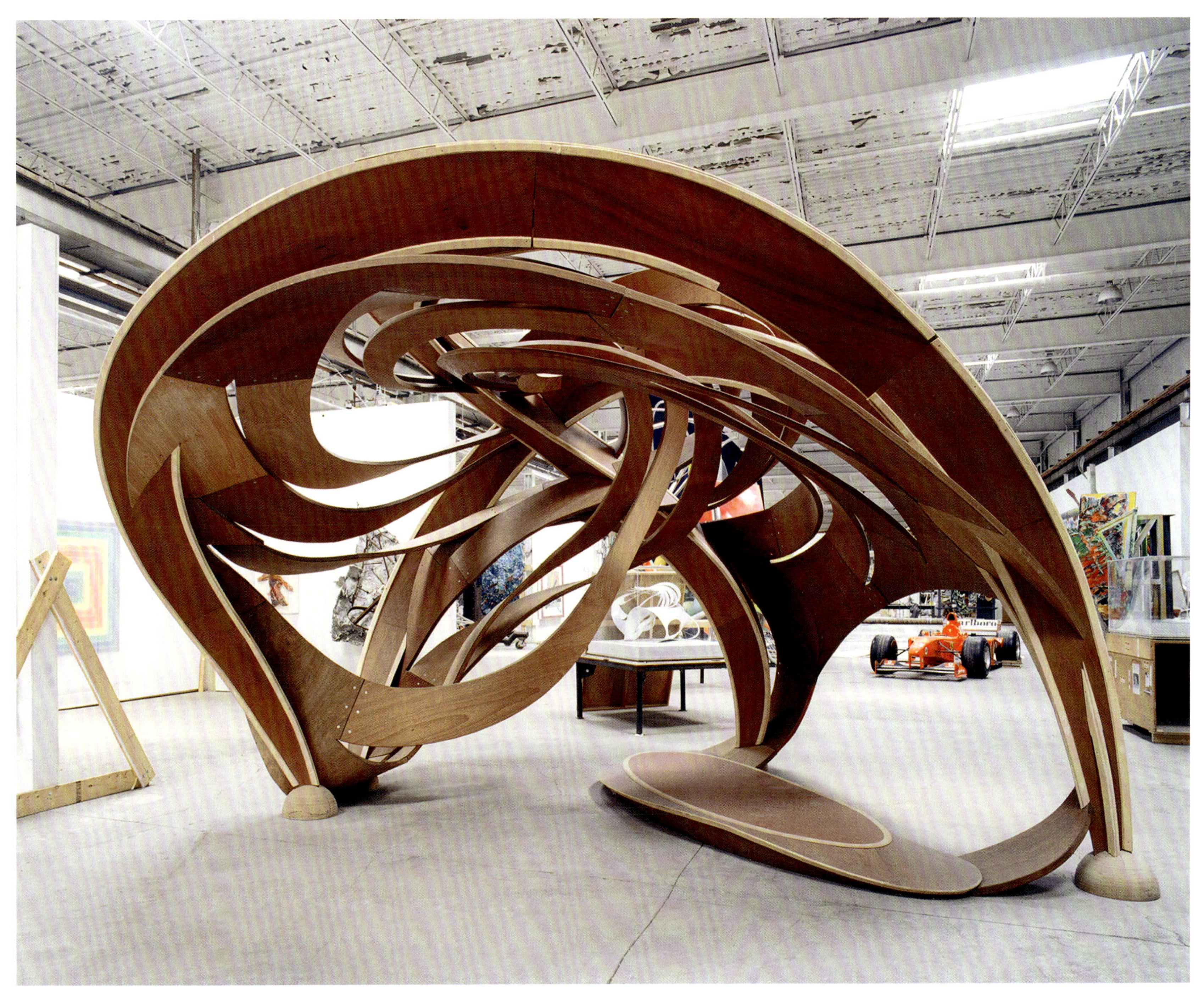

PRINZ FRIEDRICH VON HOMBURG, EIN SCHAUSPIEL, 3X, 1998–2001
STAINLESS STEEL, ALUMINIUM, PAINTED FIBREGLASS, CARBON FIBRE
945 X 1189 X 1036 CM

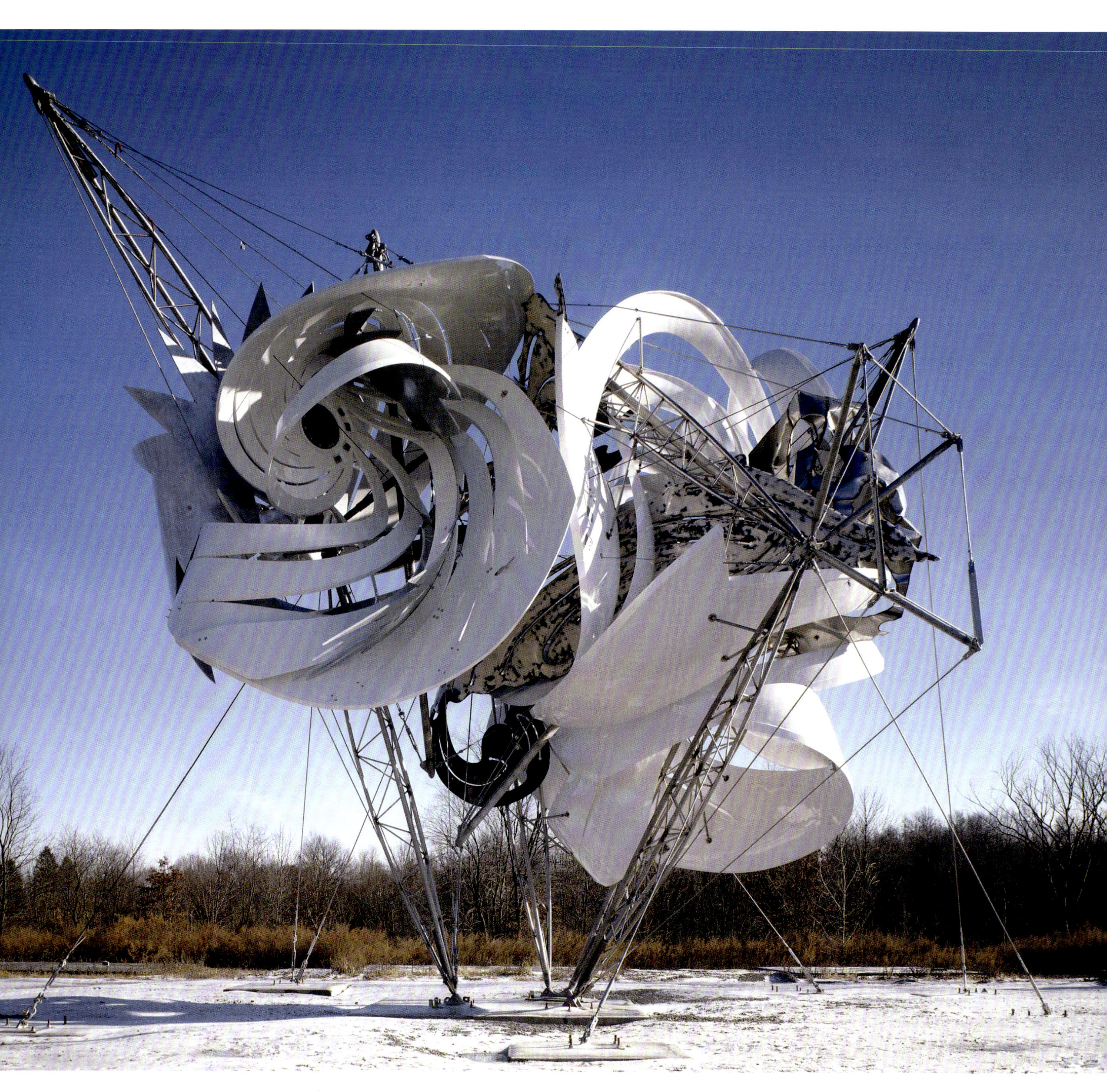

The Broken Jug. A Comedy [D#3] (Left Handed Version) (2007), we see what resembles an albeit human-scale model for a pavilion or bandshell. Both of the latter works, comprised of a single hat, and the more complicated combination of hat forms in the stainless steel, aluminium, painted fibreglass and carbon fibre *Prinz Friedrich von Homburg, Ein Schauspiel, 3X* (1998–2001), all count as part of the 'Heinrich von Kleist' series. The hat meets the smoke form in numerous painted reliefs from that series, and has proceeded to define the hundreds-strong, ongoing 'Scarlatti K' series, begun in 2006. Here, too, we find giants: the unpainted aluminium and stainless steel *K.304 (Full-Size)* (2013), which spans nearly 13 metres, or large painted fibreglass pendant works currently underway in the studio. But most of the 'Scarlatti K' works are smaller – small enough to be 3-D printed by rapid-prototyping means, from the *Protogen RPT of K.37 (Lattice Variation)* (2008), to the *ABS of K.304 (ABS White)* (2012).

Within the 'Scarlatti K' series – in which not only the hat form but occasionally the smoke rings, among others, manifest as well – at times the specificity of any given motif falls away in favour of a new, combinatory specificity.[51] For instance, the particular, computer-modelled tangle of planar loops labelled as, and deployed for, sculptures called *K.37* and *K.43*, respectively, are merged together in *K.81 Combo (K.37 and K.43), Large Size*, a 2009 work in painted Protogen RPT with stainless-steel tubing. In the structurally unorthodox 'Scarlatti K' work *Double K.236*, dominated by an almost creaturely steel stand, the openwork whorl of shapes now known as *K.236* appears twice over, both times in unpainted RPT. Throughout, the 'K' stands for Ralph Kirkpatrick, a musician and musicologist best known for cataloguing, by K-number, eighteenth-century composer Domenico Scarlatti's 555 keyboard sonatas. The externally sourced smoke rings and spiral-cut hat have provided Stella with two distinct lexicons from which to draw, and there is now also a lexicon of internally sourced K-forms – though the Kirkpatrick numbers Stella assigns to his formal combinations are arbitrary, insofar as the forms do not progress or interrelate in either an interpretable or a predictable way from one to the next.

Stella's recent, frequent use of rapid-prototyping processes aptly thematizes both testing and speed; he is not 'developing' a motif, in the musical sense, in order to resolve it, but rather iterating as if ad infinitum.

He has joked about milking single motifs for twenty-five years now, and also about choosing the 'Scarlatti K' sonatas as a titular and structuring device simply because he might never run out. Of course, notions of testing and speed are not exclusive to the works rendered in Protogen RPT or ABS; nor are notions of either the motif or movement exclusive to the work since 1990. Recycling and reuse have been central to both the manic sensibility and the sheer proliferation of printed, painted, relief and sculptural works since the 1970s. Stella revelled in the industrial environments in which he found himself early on for various kinds of metal fabrication, treating them 'like a huge junk yard. There's so much available, it's hard to keep your hands off the things that go flying by you all the time. There's a tremendous physical, material turn-over of things … and [they're] always being thrown out.'[52]

Stella incorporated scraps left over from the machine-cutting of other parts most obviously in the 'Malta' series of the mid-1980s. We know that the components of *Creutzwald* and *Toul* are largely found scraps and fragments as well, even where Toul includes smoke-ring forms, for in the latter case failed casts were not abandoned but instead re-cast. Recent examples abound, too. There is *Kimbul* (2014), a vividly sprayed sculpture made from a husk of sorts, the frame and indentations remaining after spiral-hat and star forms were machine-carved from a block of foam for the creation of another work. There is the carapace-like wall relief *Kraanvogel* (also 2014), an assemblage made from a fragment of broken ceramic retained in the studio since a mid-1980s collaboration with Frank Bosco, along with elements from the 'Alsace-Lorraine' series of 1992.[53]

And then there is a trio of small 2016 works called *Shelf with Marshmallow 05, Segment A & B, Segment C & D,* and *Segment E & F.* On each of three steel shelves sit two unpainted chunks of elasto plastic. The segments labelled E and F have slightly ragged, irregular edges, like archaeological fragments. But otherwise I am hard-pressed to identify by eye alone why these segments never made their way to a larger sculptural work. They are, nevertheless, misprints – retrieved from the fabricator but deemed unusable as initially intended. In more typical works, segments like these would be sutured together and then lusciously shellacked with colours that help to distinguish different motifs from

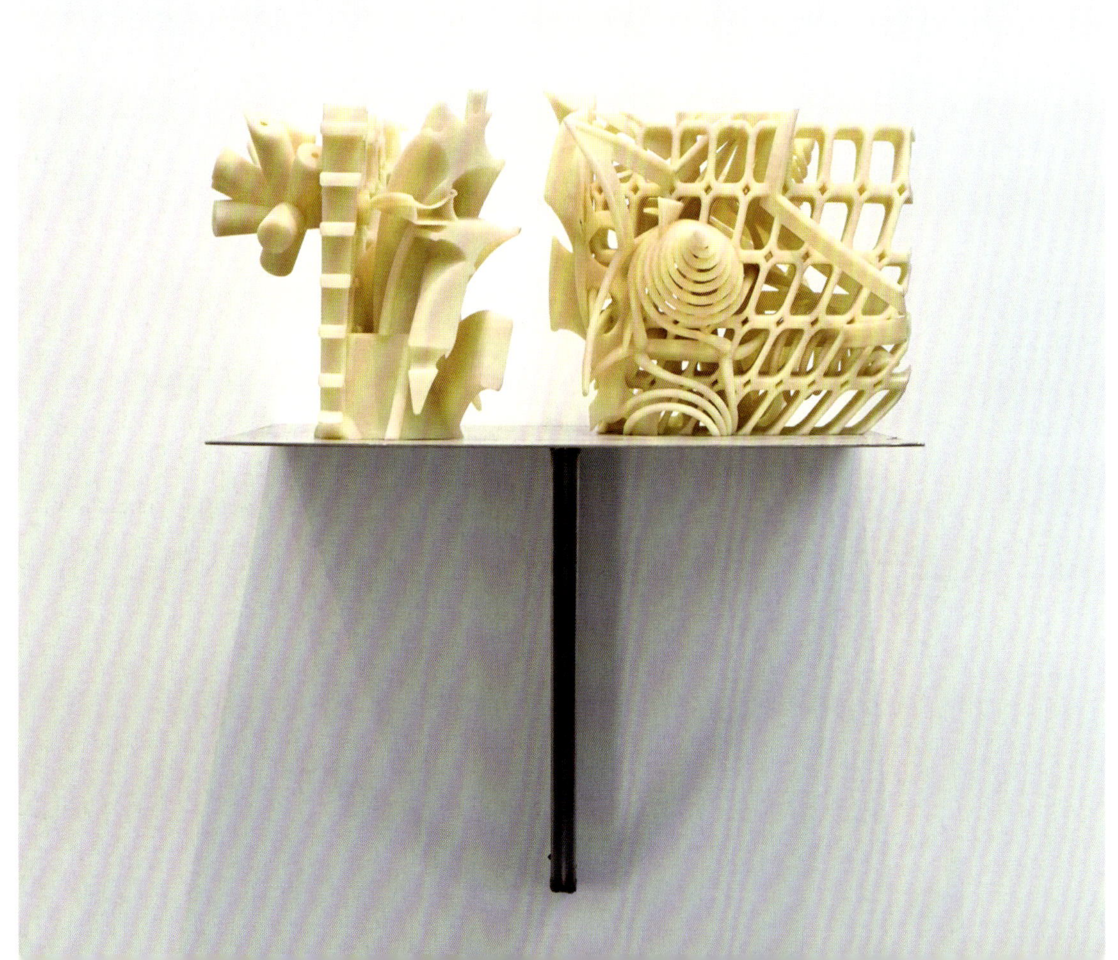

SHELF WITH MARSHMALLOW 05, SEGMENT A & B, 2016
ELASTO PLASTIC RPT
SEGMENT A: 33 X 28 X 30 CM
SEGMENT B: 33 X 33 X 28 CM

KRAANVOGEL, 2014
MIXED MEDIA
160 X 90 X 72 CM

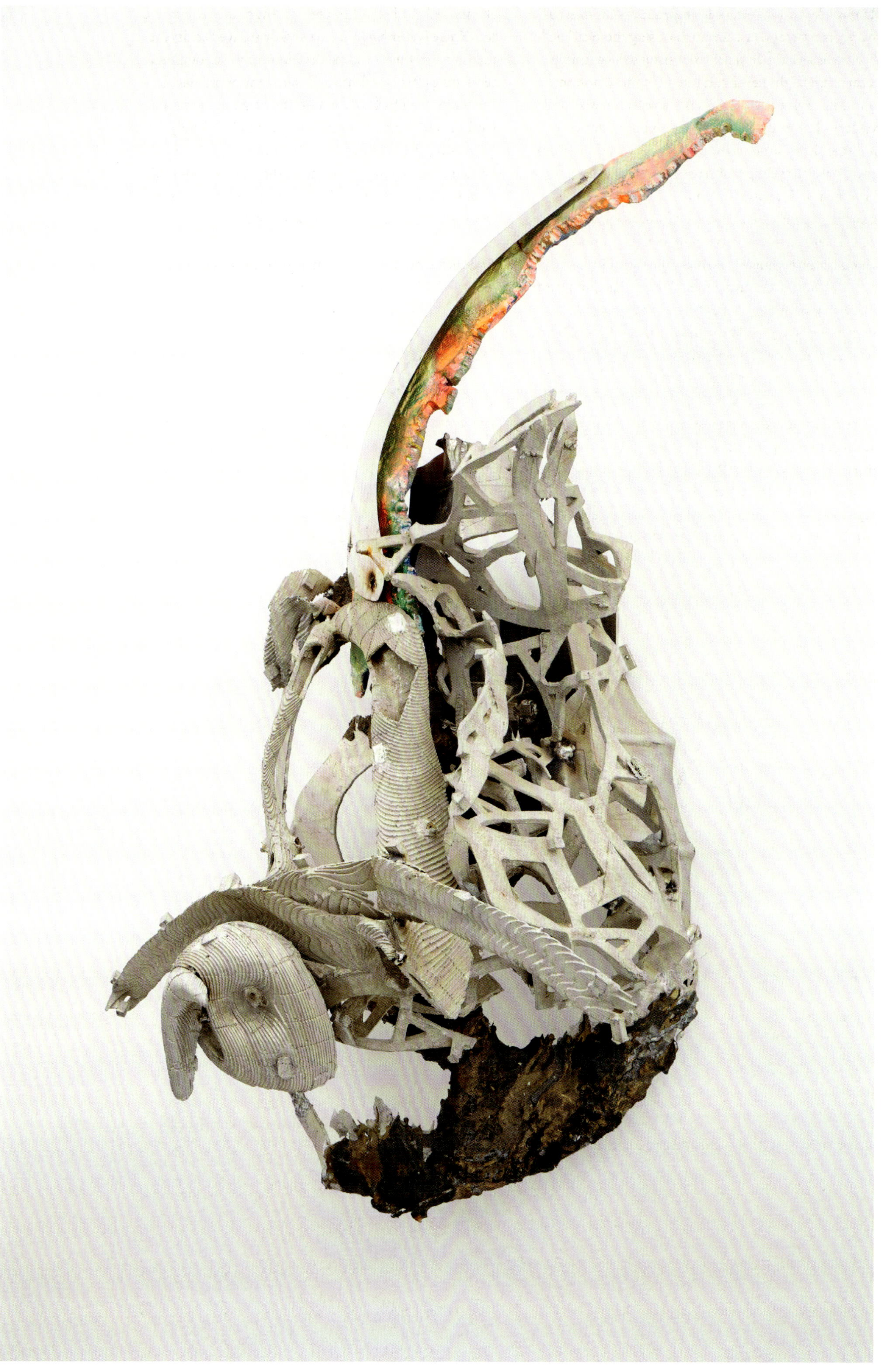

FRENCH TACTICS: AN EXAMPLE FOR ALL [A#2] FRANZOSISCHES EXERZITIUM DAS MAN NACHAHMEN SOLLTE, 1999
PAINTED ALUMINUM SANDCASTING
84 X 128 X 108 CM

one another (star from marshmallow grid, for example) and sometimes different surfaces from one another (the interior of the grid's cells sprayed a different colour from its exterior, for instance) but that otherwise obscure any seams of original segmentation. The edges of the segments are themselves determined by the parameters of fabrication rather than of eventual assembly.

The lofting of these *Marshmallow 05* segments on dark shelves, as specimens for study, reminds us that while Stella's works for some years now consistently begin in the computer, they are finished only in the studio. 'The Bali' series, the last years of which overlapped with the first of the 'Scarlatti K' works, was entirely studio-imagined and studio-made. Even the artist's computer-modelled forms, interrelated within, as we have seen, a 'groundless' space of virtual rendering, must therefore be fitted into real space more or less after the fact. To some degree, and especially where literal mounts are concerned, Stella's choices are simply expedient (also comedic) – most of the smaller 'Scarlatti K' works hang from the wall as if on meathooks. But the plastic forms in these works are themselves intersected, cut through by slender stainless-steel tubing, and this tubing behaves as both armature and arabesque, sometimes spidery, sometimes curling or meandering, spatially extending each sculpture well beyond its efficacy as structural support.

The most elaborate of such steel lineations read first and foremost as decorative flourishes, yet in most cases they also dictate a sculpture's specific disposition against or in relation to the wall. And while the tubes occasionally look as though computer-derived, insofar as they evoke vector lines, for instance, they are formed and determined by Stella in the studio – their calligraphic elegance is of the hand, and if not quite a motif in its own right, increasingly a kind of signature. Even an unorthodox work can be brought to bear in this regard, like the exception that proves the rule. Recall the wire-matrix sculpture earlier described: its armature is clearly constitutive, not decorative. But the wire matrix was modelled within a computer software programme, then built by hand-welding. The sculpture's solid foam and cast-paper fragments are discards or remainders recycled from other projects. Which is to say, the lattice structure was designed in advance, but without the foam and paper contents yet in mind – without a priori knowledge of what, if anything, such a structure might do or hold. It only became an armature for other materials and masses through the process of studio play and assemblage.

The once functional, now extraneous, is often more legible in Stella's work than are the comparatively imagistic motifs. Well before the stainless-steel armature-arabesques of current sculptures, there were the casting gates retained on the surfaces of reliefs and sculptures like *Bear Mountain* (1995) and *French Tactics: An Example for All [A#2]* (1999) or the tangle of rebar that crowns *Mersin XX* (2001). In some cases, of course, the armature is (most of) the sculpture, as in the still nameless wire-matrix work, or as in the prominent 'spine' of *Sanibel to Sobolnoye* (2014). Over the years the artist has established a peculiar economy in which efficiency correlates with exaggeration or elaboration, expediency with excess.

I want to underscore Stella's seemingly tireless activity in any and all 'working spaces', whether computer, factory or studio – the productive coalition of voraciousness and fortuitousness. I also want to underscore, however, what seem to be open questions about agency, which in this context might also be questions about motive and motivation. Who or what is actually tireless, here? Is it the artist's voraciousness or in fact the motif's generosity? Does a form's malleability, its capacity for deformation, ensure its agency, such that Stella remains as if in pursuit, or only its primacy, such that he continues to push it? These are questions more important to ask than to answer, and fittingly, they only beget more: where is the line between a motif and its materiality, or between a motif and its means of manifestation?

Every time I find myself tempted by a stabilizing thesis statement about Stella's relationship to technologies of making, it is contradicted, yet this feels to the point as well. To some extent, since around 1990 (and even before, in terms of machine-cutting of parts, or in terms of printmaking experimentation and innovation), Stella has sought out a new technology, a new expert collaborator or fabricator, with a precise or at least a desired result in mind. In the process, he has inevitably found ways to use what did not work, or what would have been discarded by another artist. In the process, he has been inspired by materials or circumstances beyond either his intention or his expectation (surely he has been disappointed, too). He has, at times, had to wait for

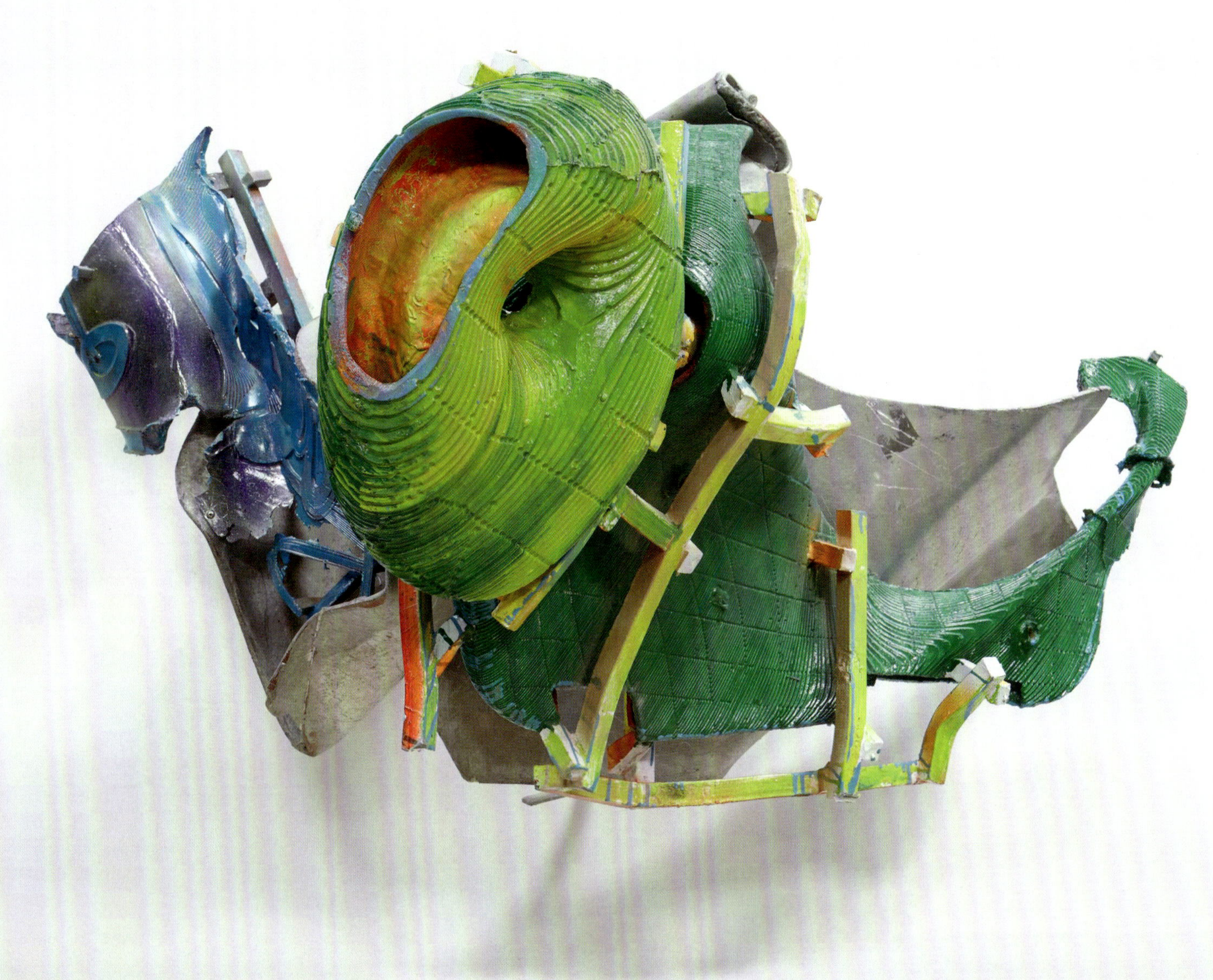

BOEDJOEH, 2004
STAINLESS STEEL TUBING AND
CARBON FIBER
190 X 135 X 104 CM

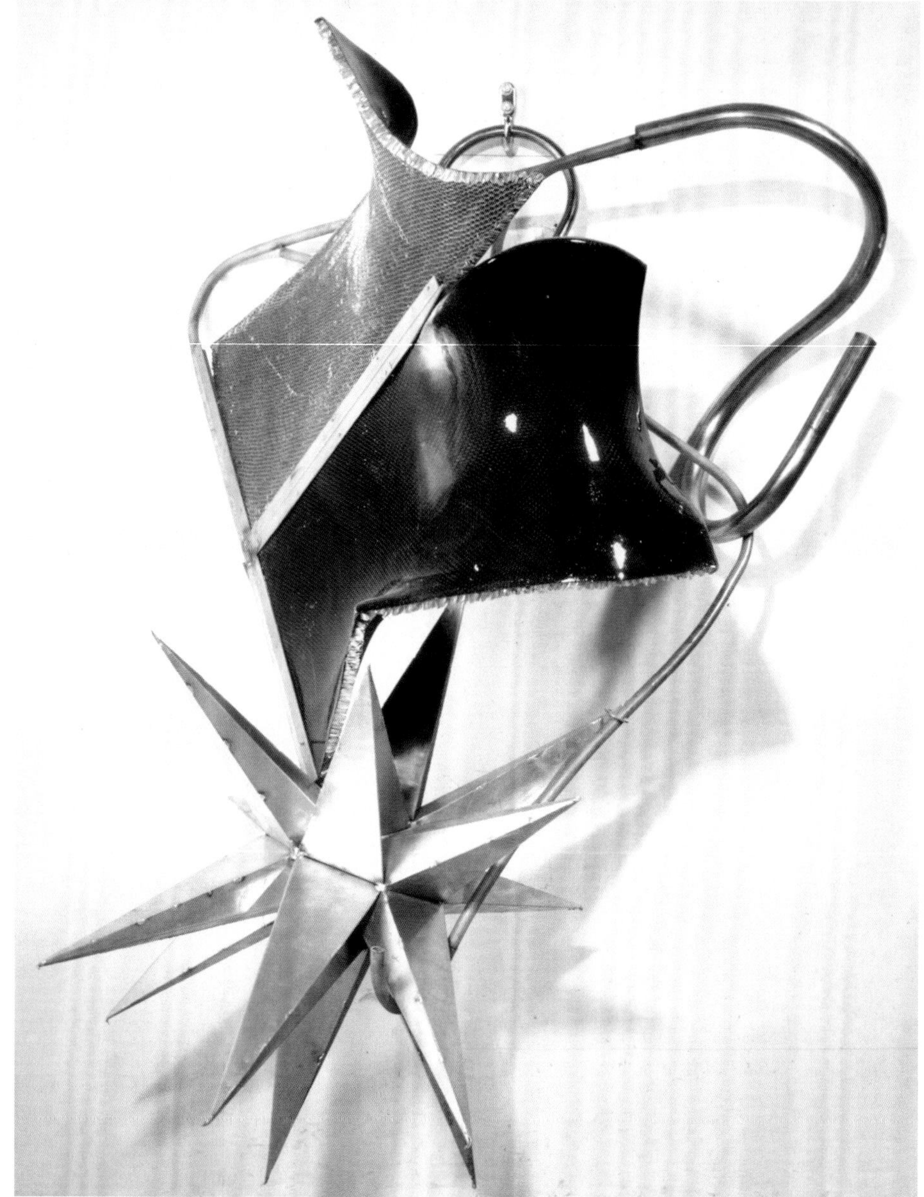

technology to catch up with what he wants it to do for him. He has, at other times, actively pushed technology forward, prompting advances in fabrication.

Stella is swift to try ever-newer modelling programs and 3-D printing technologies, but, despite their advances he isn't after refinement as such. This is true despite, too, the luxuriant, automotive finish of all of the painted sculptures since the early 2000s. He isn't precious. Fabricators have joked that they love to collaborate with him, because nothing is too bad, too crude or failed, for Stella to use. And by all accounts, little in the studio is safe – any supposedly finished work is fair game for repainting, restaging or reworking (as we saw in a materially minor but conceptually useful way with the paired, low-slung display in 2014 of the sculptures *Creutzwald* and *Toul* from 1992). What recurs across Stella's works, or what is reused from one work to another, is also as often what spurs it somewhere, else.

Compared to the drifting and dispersion particular to smoke, and to the spiral-cut hat 'dancing off by itself', the star motif is differently radial, insistently symmetrical. It is also, structurally, far more stable and static than the other two, constructed from triangular panels or, more often, triangular trusses. In fact, the star is Stella's earliest emergent motif – the earliest with a legible shape from which to launch countless deformations and reformations – and given the shape's inherent symmetry, it makes sense that the star first appeared amidst the several years of striped paintings. The canvas for *Port Tampa City* (1963), of the 'Dartmouth' series, takes the form of an octagram, or eight-point star, its stripes nested chevrons painted in the acid ochre of zinc chromate – a toxic, yellow-green compound not unheard of in artist's pigments but most common in industry, used around the mid-twentieth century as an anti-corrosive agent on the aluminium surfaces of commercial and military aircraft.[54]

PORT TAMPA CITY, 1963
RED LEAD ON CANVAS
244 X 244 CM

The star did not figure again until the early 2000s. In 2004, a hand-welded, three-dimensional aluminium star depends from 'The Bali' series work *Boedjoeh*, and since then hundreds of stars have either participated in the central compositions of other series ('Scarlatti K' works in particular), or, quite newly, constituted their own ongoing series. Yet a further question, then: why return to the star after forty years? That Stella's name means 'star' in Italian looms irresistibly, not least thanks to a drawing from 1961 in which the artist sketched shapes for potential 'Purple' series striped paintings, designating each with the name of a friend or peer ('Metallic Aluminum Violet Portraits', the header reads). The sketch for the star-shaped purple painting – unlike most others from the series, this one was never realized – is labelled in unmistakable block letters, 'Frank Stella'.

In assessing his return to the star, on the one hand it seems unreasonable to suspect sentimentality, but on the other hand, it would be unreasonable to ignore playfulness or humour. Here is a humour that is self-

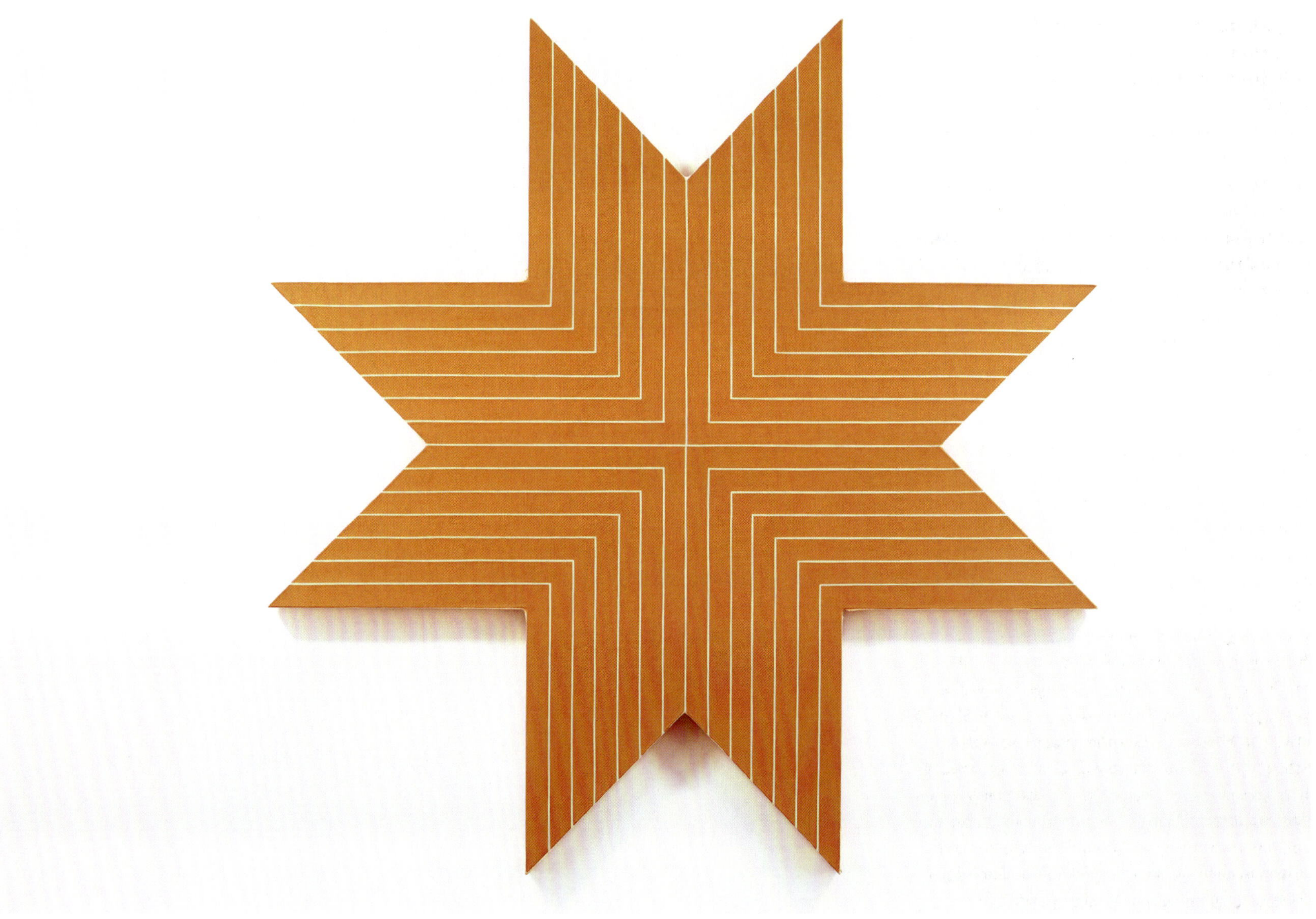

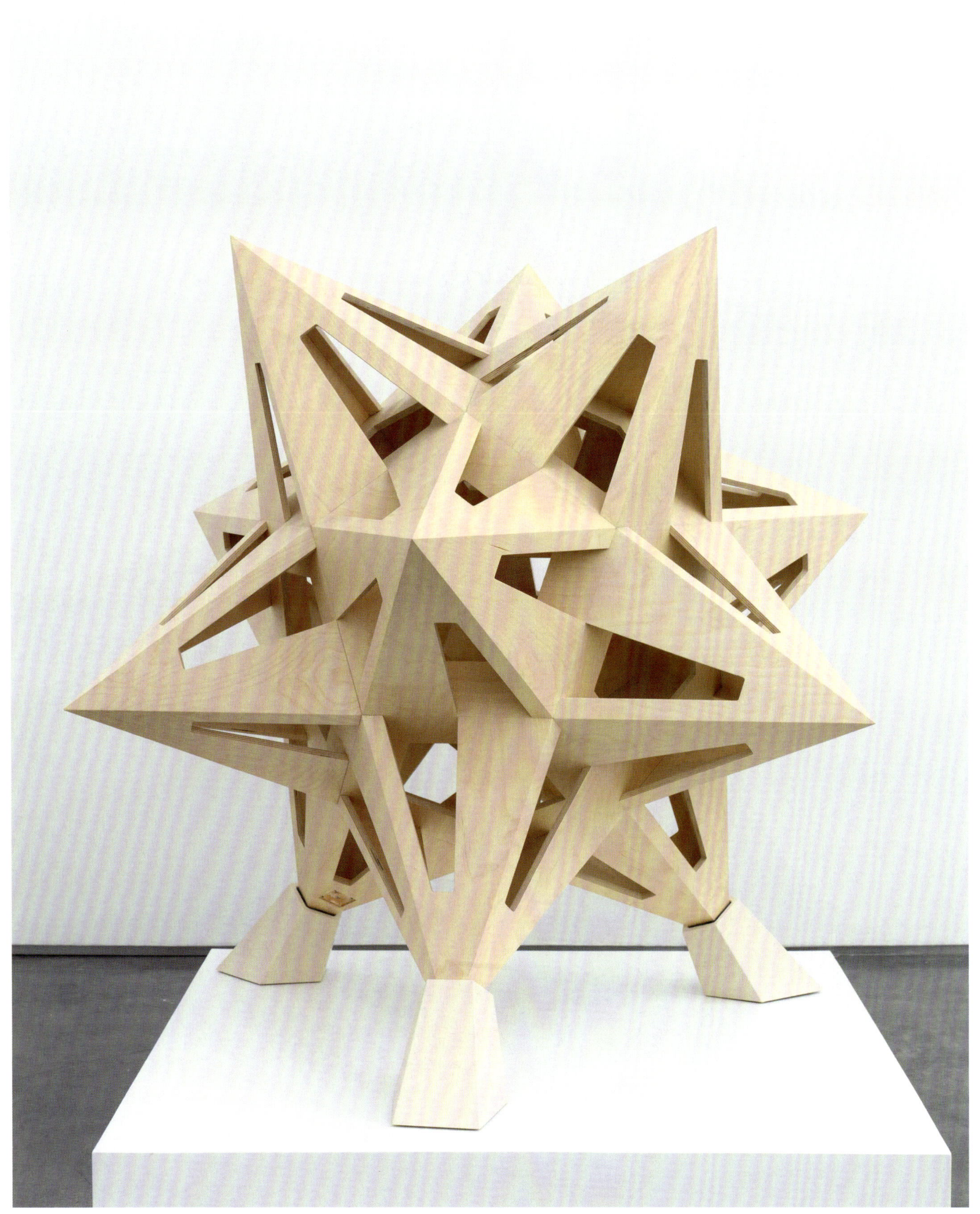

FLAT PACK STAR, 2016
COATED BALTIC BIRCH PLYWOOD
122 X 122 X 122 CM

CORIAN STAR, 2017
CORIAN
119 X 119 X 119 CM

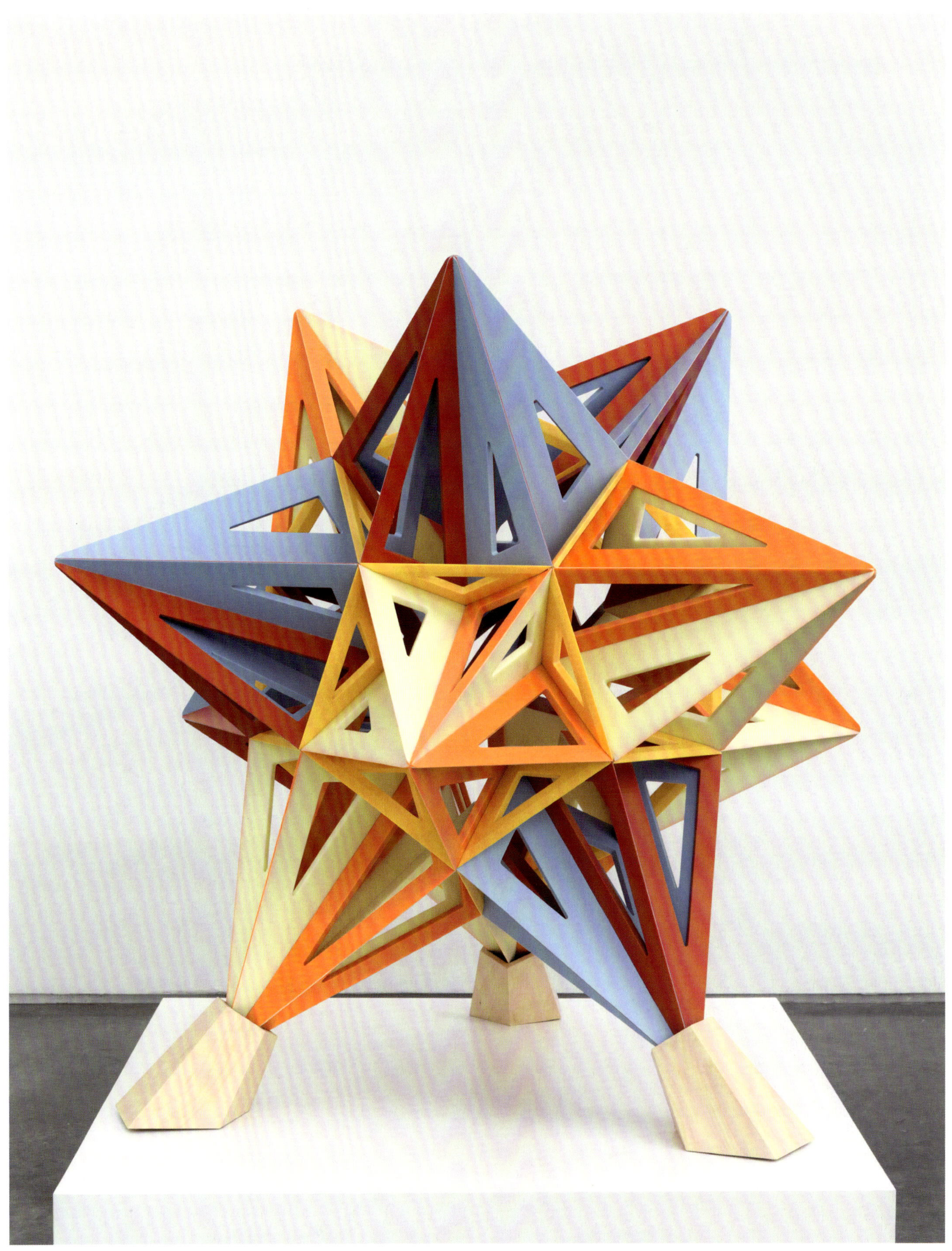

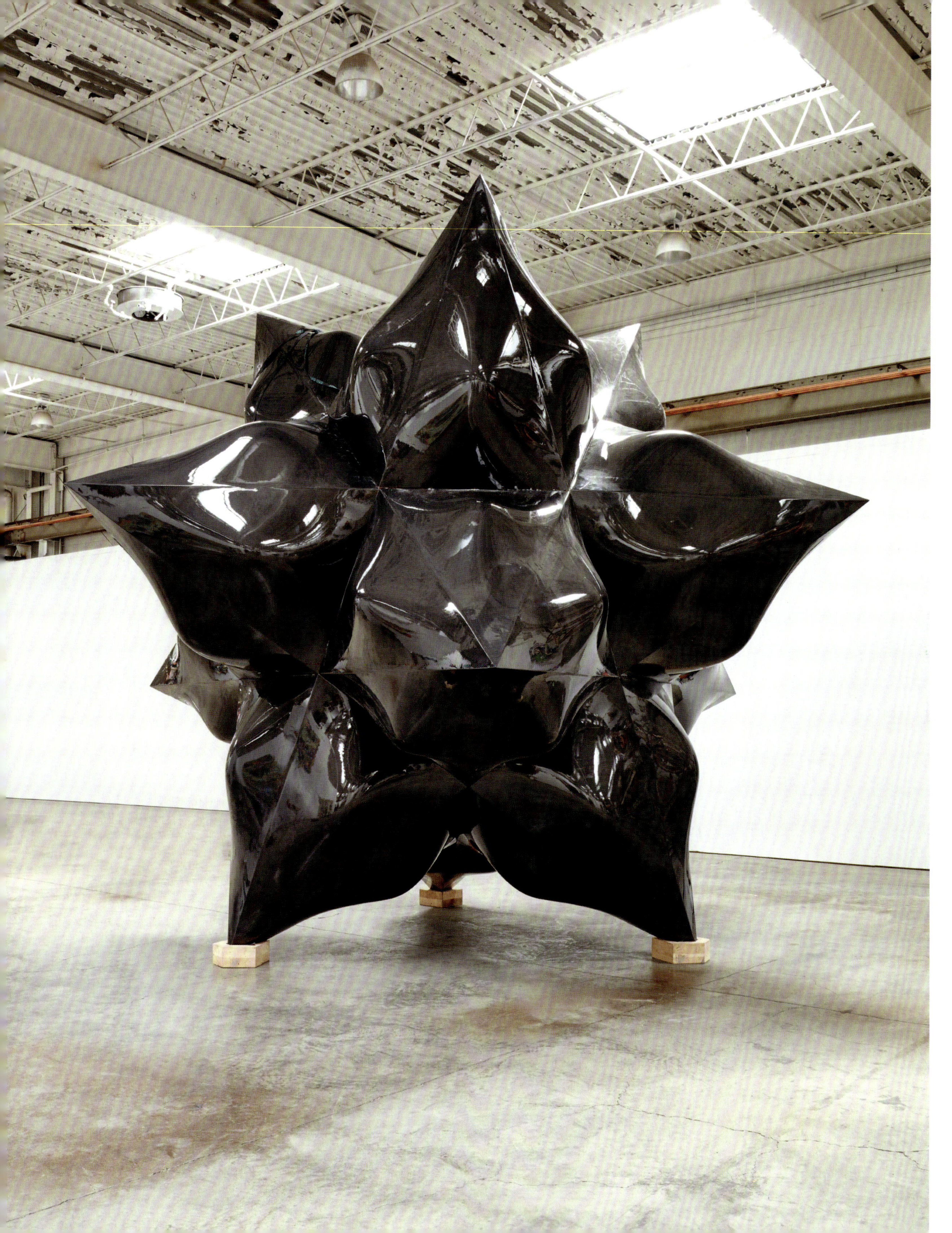

FAT 12 POINT CARBON FIBER STAR, 2016
CARBON FIBRE
580 X 580 X 580 CM

THREE SPLIT STARS, TWO SPLIT STARS AND SMOKE 2, 2016
ELASTO PLASTIC, STAINLESS STEEL, ON STYROFOAM BASE
165 X 234 X 48 CM

deflating just when it seems self-aggrandizing (or a humour that winks in both directions), and Stella plays up this humour in different ways as well. Where and how a star meets the ground is often purposefully awkward – not just because Stella shrugs off elegance in many other contexts, but also because a star isn't *meant* to touch the ground, is otherwise as lofty, even heavenly, a form as one can get. Hence, perhaps, the funny feet on two recent star sculptures, shown together in 2017. *Flat Pack Star* (2016) is made from coated Baltic birch plywood, but perches on three feet made from sandy coloured Corian; *Corian Star* (2017), slightly smaller and slightly different in its contours, is made from primary-coloured Corian, but perches on three unpainted plywood feet. (That these 'feet' touch not quite the ground but rather a low, white-painted platform, as generic as the star's faceted feet are specific, is relevant here, too.)

The titles for all of the star-centred works are atypically literal, descriptive of materials or formal emphases, occasionally both: *Fat 12 Point Carbon Fiber Star* (2012). *Inflated Star and Wooden Star*, in polished and patinated aluminium and teakwood (2015). *Three Split Stars, Two Split Stars and Smoke 2* (2016), in elasto plastic and stainless steel – this sculpture sits on a Styrofoam block, a smudged lightweight base that reads at first glance as marble. *Hercules and Achelous* (2017) is a large aluminium work where the stars' points are unusually curved, more beak-like or wave-like than strictly radiant, tumbling forward from the titular 'jigs' – jigs being devices that secure and align parts for making or assembly during mass production, meant to ensure accuracy and reproducibility. The conceit of the jigs thus registers as a kind of joke: the jigs do, literally, titularly, support this sculpture's stars, yet while accuracy in translation and fabrication are of inceptive importance to Stella, technical errors rule little out of play; and the reproducibility of or fidelity to his core motifs gives way, time and again, to stressing and attenuating them.

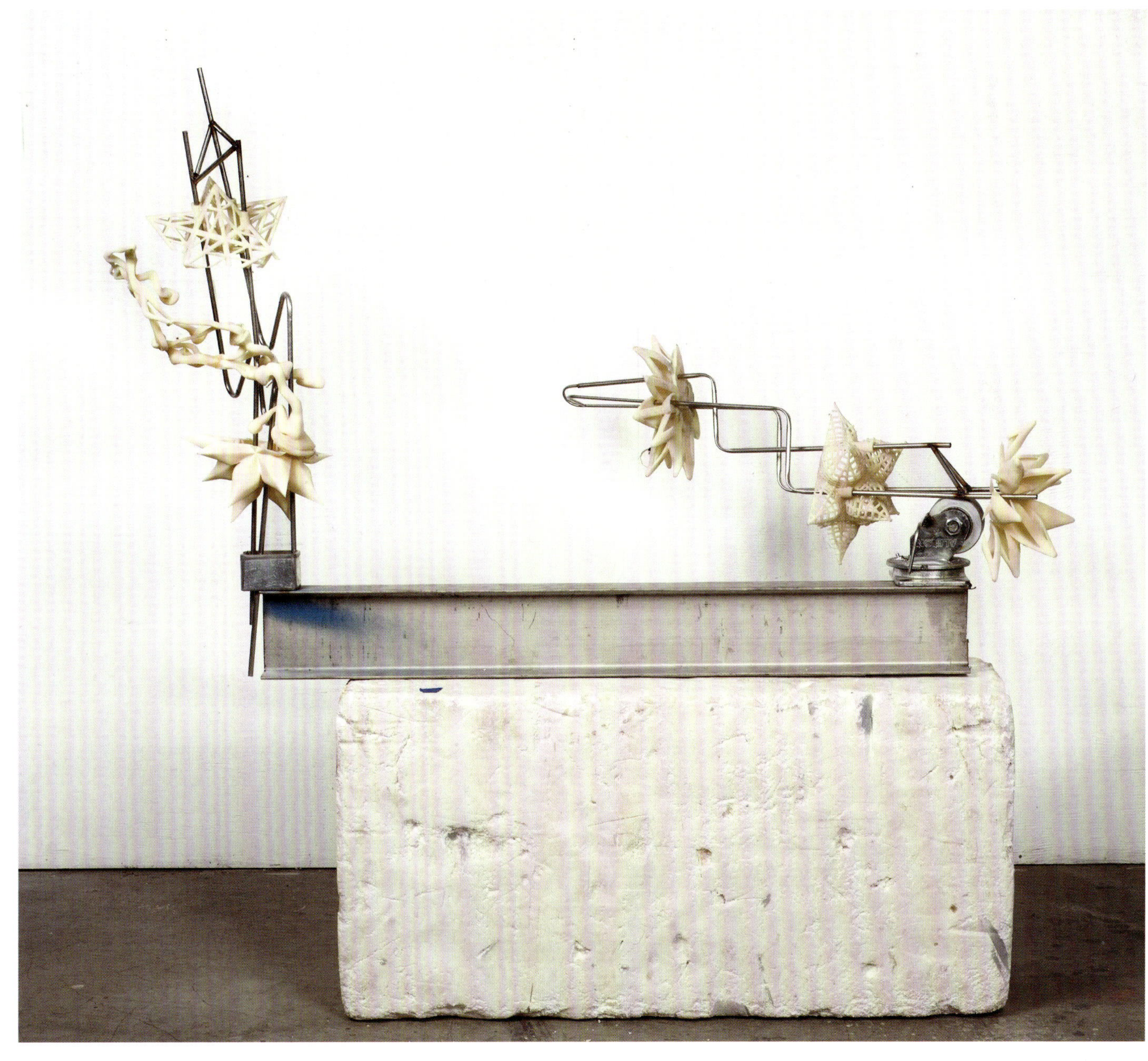

HERCULES AND ACHELOUS,
2017
ALUMINIUM
195 X 309 X 309 CM

That said, the stars are generally less contorted than other motifs in Stella's work, almost always instantly recognizable. This makes sense because the star, unlike the smoke rings or the spiral-cut hat, is a symbol, more or less universal. Stella's literal titles may be a way to exaggerate, underscoring the star's ready legibility while also lampooning it: exaggeration is a kind of distortion. The literal titles may be another way to joke as well, countering the metaphoric intimations of the star as stand-in for Stella, and reminding us that even if the stars can be read in terms of self-insertion or self-reflexivity, a physical signature of sorts, they remain unexpressive. The literal titles and the Stella-stellas remind me, too, of the role of tautology and redundancy in his early work – 'what you see is what you see'. Nor can jokes, flat-footedness, intentional awkwardness or inelegance eradicate our tendency to overinterpret the legible and the symbolic, when encountered in otherwise abstract (hard-to-see) work. The points of Stella's stars demonstrate that they *are,* of course, abstracted: this is how we visually describe light, shimmer, sparkle, pulse. Through such language, we arrive again at a sense of movement – at the 'starburst', which is the name for an image or form and also for an explosion, or for intense galactic activity. (It is difficult not to reference *K.150* once more, the 2014 sculpture in which, among other shapes, a blue star – several of its points cut open and curled back to reveal a black hole inside it – appears to burst through a white plane.) With these star works we also find ourselves as close to figuration or representation as Stella gets, and surely as close to a physical star as we will ever get. Even when considered literally, however, as an actual celestial body rather than as a schematic symbol or shape, the star abstracts, too physically remote and too intangible for most of us to picture otherwise.

This essay cannot pretend to compass Stella's full practice – and that this essay feels, indeed, difficult to end seems, in its own way, appropriate. Stars do have life spans, but ones that are millions and billions of years long, and in this regard also beyond our ken. Compared to Stella's other prominent motifs the star form feels endless. Of course, in the artist's hands (or, via a combination of computer and studio manipulation), all of his motifs are endlessly malleable, at once participating in and seeming to generate the iterative profusion, the again-and-again-and-again and the more-and-more-and-more of his practice; the more you make, the more you learn, Stella has long encouraged. Endlessness is unfathomable, while ongoingness is vital.

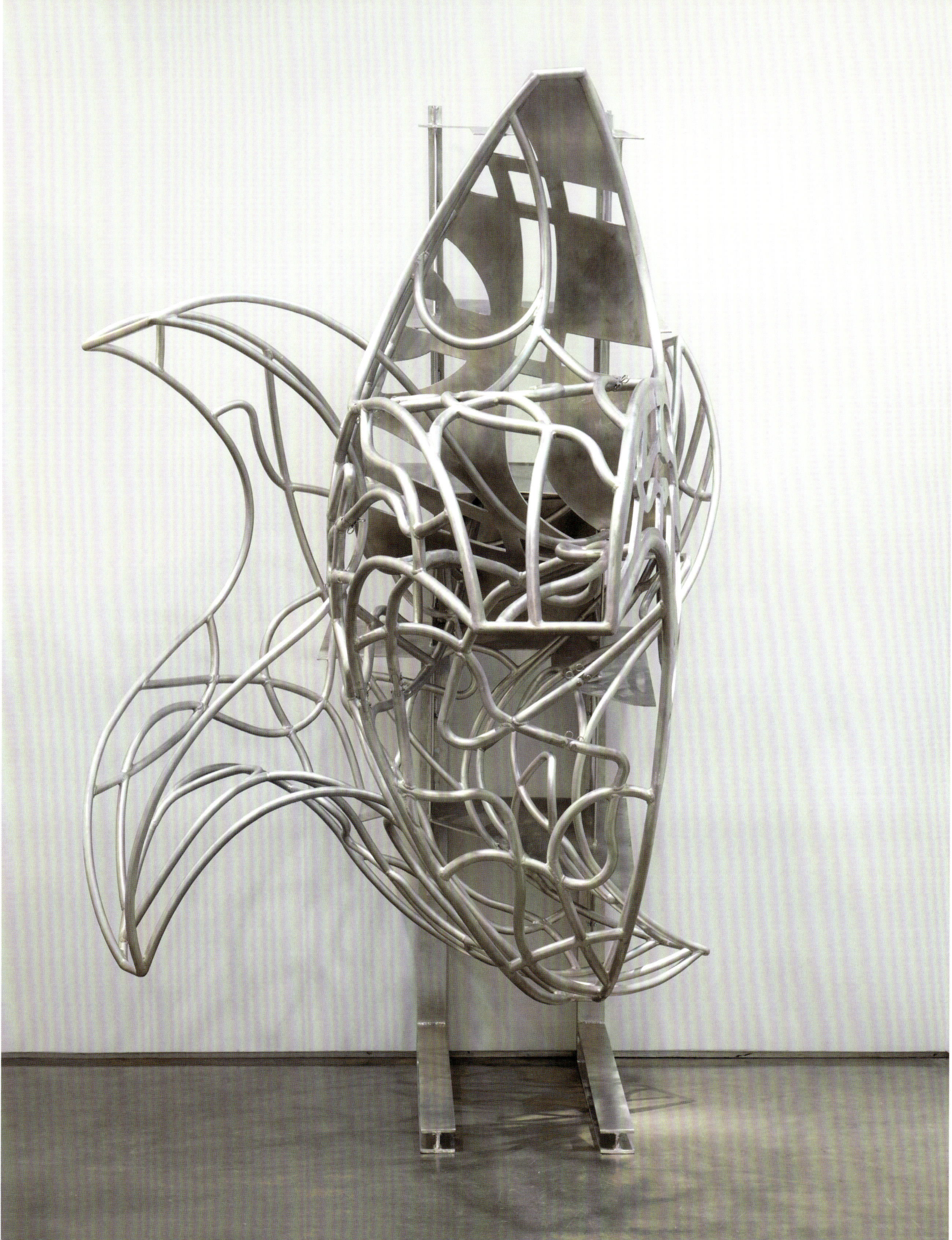

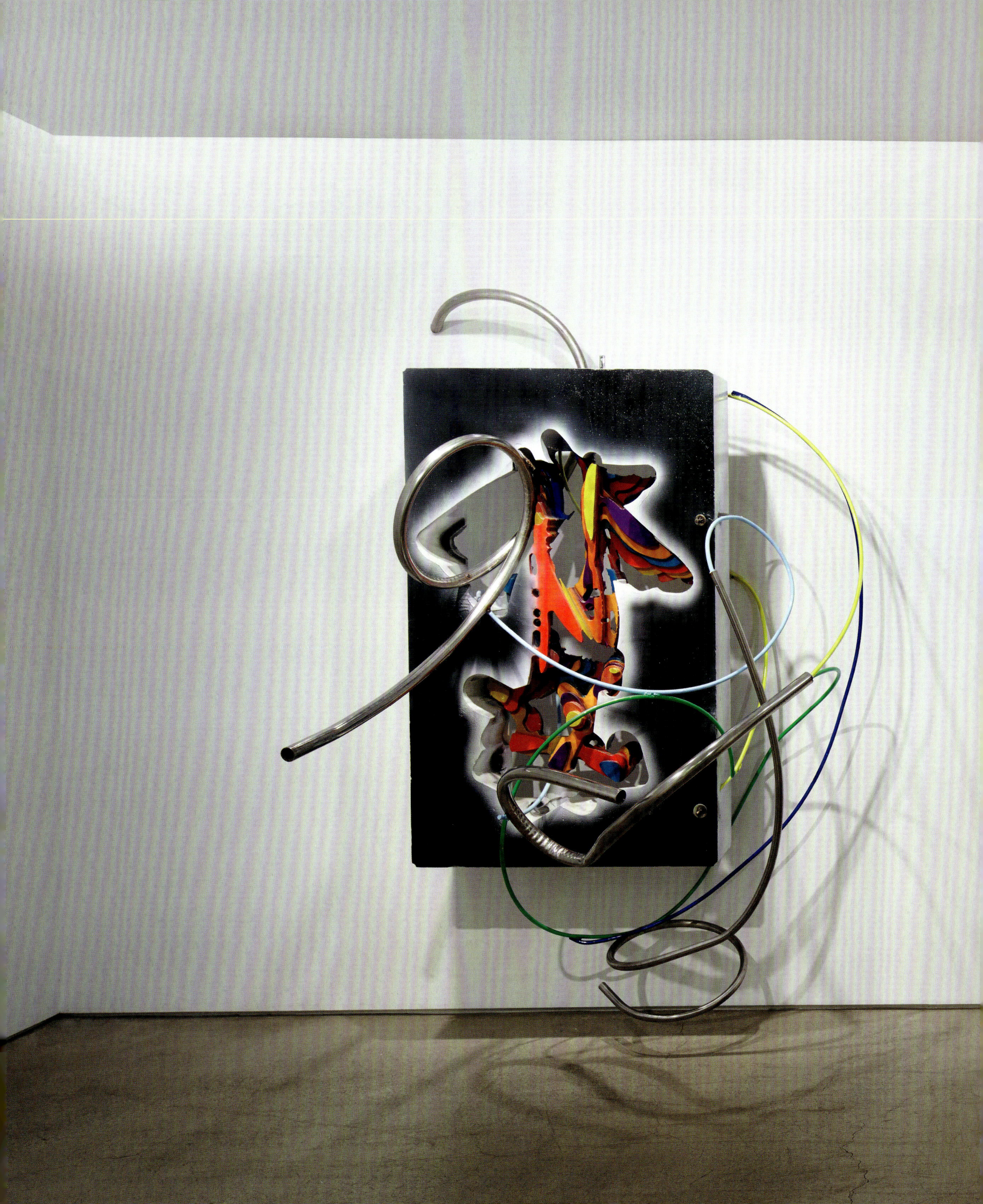

Scarlatti K

Lucas Blalock

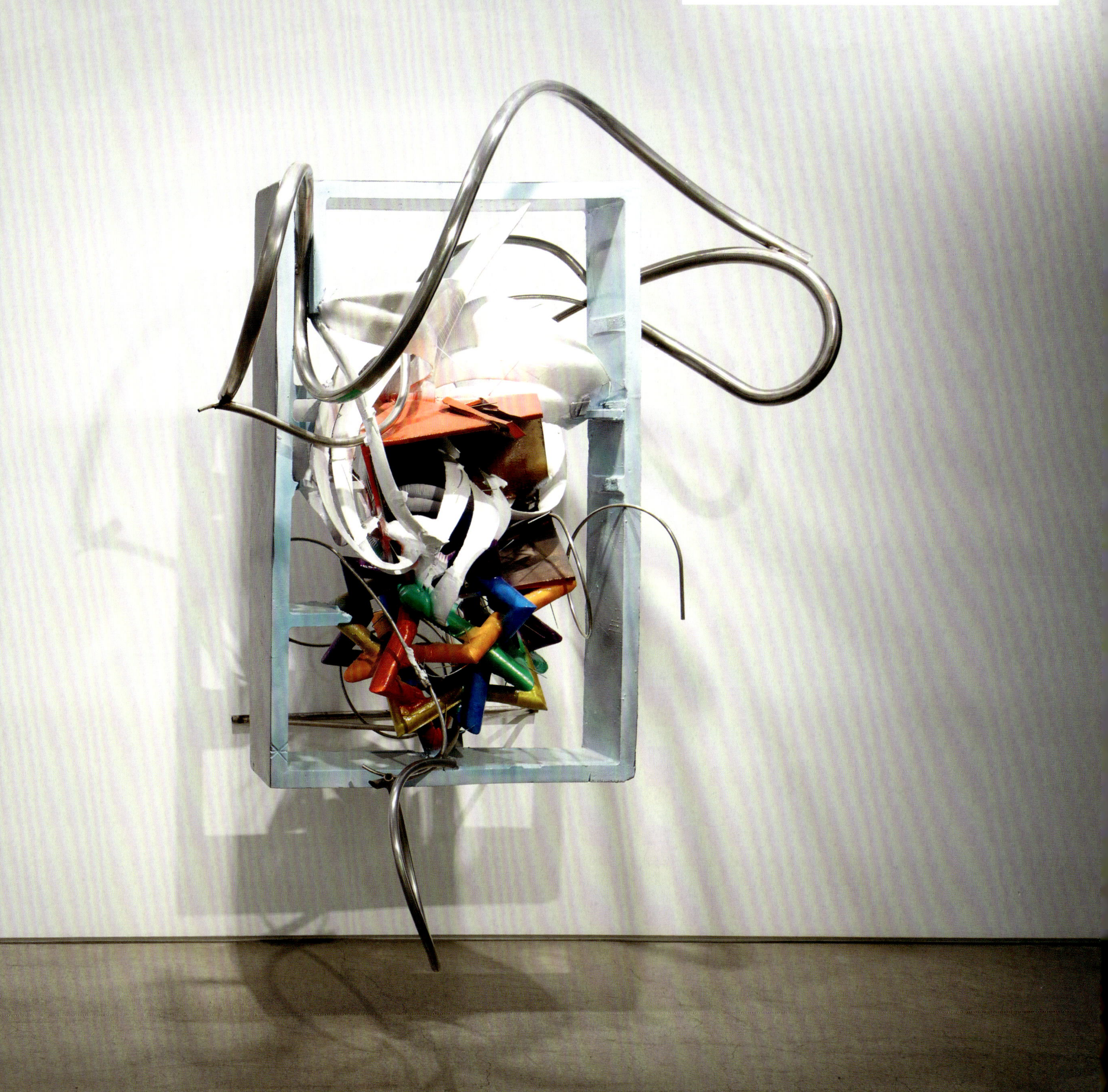

There are two problems in painting. One is to find out what painting is and the other to find out how to make a painting.

– Frank Stella, 1960[1]

Since the work of art, after all, cannot be reality, the elimination of all illusory features accentuates all the more glaringly the illusory characters of its existence. This process is inescapable.

– Theodor Adorno[2]

next page, clockwise from top left,
K 503, 2015
PAINTED ELASTO PLASTIC RPT
WITH METAL
206 X 158 X 121 CM

K 533 (SECOND VERSION), 2016
PAINTED ELASTO PLASTIC RPT
WITH METAL
46 X 74 X 76 CM

K 507, 2016
PAINTED ELASTO PLASTIC RPT
WITH METAL
58 X 46 X 41 CM

K 533 STAR COMBO 02, 2016
PAINTED ELASTO PLASTIC RPT
WITH METAL
56 X 41 X 55 CM

previous pages, from left,
OEKOEN, 2006-14
PAINTED ELASTO PLASTIC RPT
AND CARVED FOAM WITH METAL
229 X 140 X 127 CM

NGEREKA, 2006–14
PAINTED ELASTO PLASTIC RPT
AND CARVED FOAM WITH METAL
216 X 163 X 127 CM

INSTALLATION VIEW AT
LEEAHN GALLERY, DAEGU,
SOUTH KOREA

The works in Frank Stella's recent Scarlatti K series are hard to get to know. They have a basis in the quotidian – in smoke rings, a folding foam sun hat, recycled studio refuse – but these sources have been digested into formal data with the aid of software. By the time we encounter them, they are physical things derived from computer images, and even fully realized, sometimes at massive scale, they feel like visitors in the material universe. This quality of visitation (or perhaps even of misplacement) is amplified by the works' 'transposition': they behave as sculptures presented as paintings or else the other way around. Their exact allure has more to do with this transposition – with the elision of the conventions of painting and of sculpture brightened by the expanding spectre of the virtual – than it does with art's visual seductions. Seductiveness, in fact, is something that Stella actively seems to flout. This purposeful disregard for types and for tastefulness can leave viewers confounded and ready to turn away, but tucked in behind their techno-neon exteriors these works harness a lifetime of deep looking. Stella is laying down a daring wager: intentionally making our grasp on these objects difficult so that we might reconsider painting through the starkness of their unruly presence.

Since emerging as a young artist and proto-Minimalist in a New York still enraptured with Abstract Expressionism – an antagonism soon to be replaced by the incongruity of remaining an heir of modernism in a Pop-inflected postmodern city – Frank Stella has always decisively set the terms for his work. The constant in his now six-decade career is that he has given overwhelming primacy to painting's discursive space in order to synthesize and support his ideas. Painting as a conventional, historical activity has provided Stella with categories to articulate and undermine, and a container to expand and kick against. And though many of his more recent attempts employ the language of sculpture, painting remains by far the most compelling vehicle for considering his works. Stella's friend Michael Fried addressed this back in the 1960s, claiming that painting that

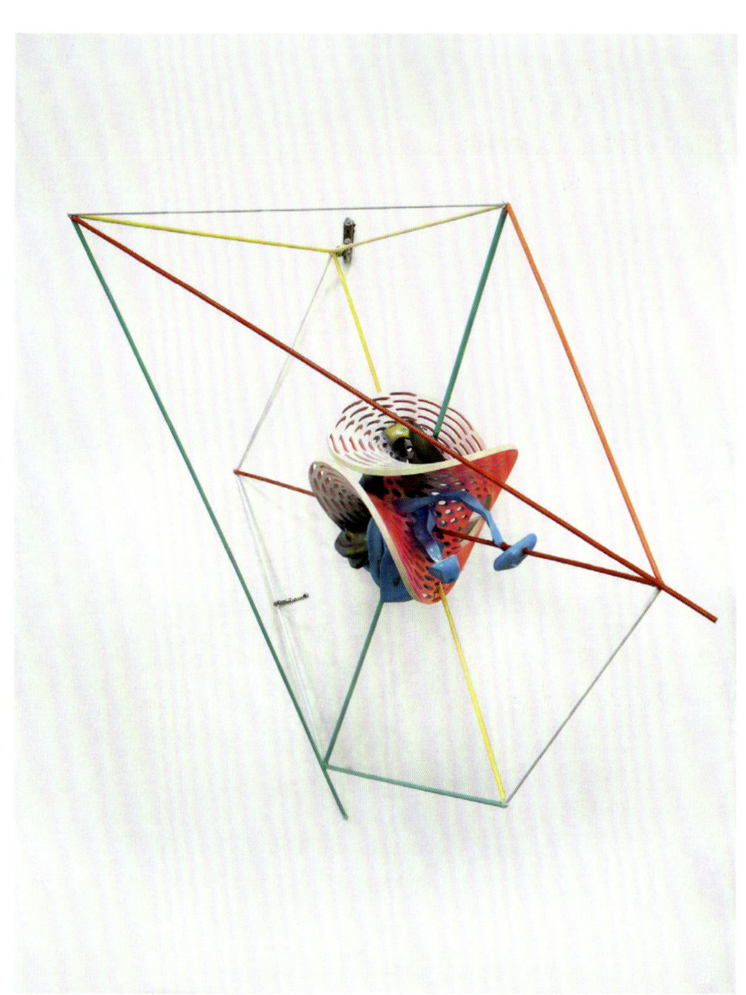

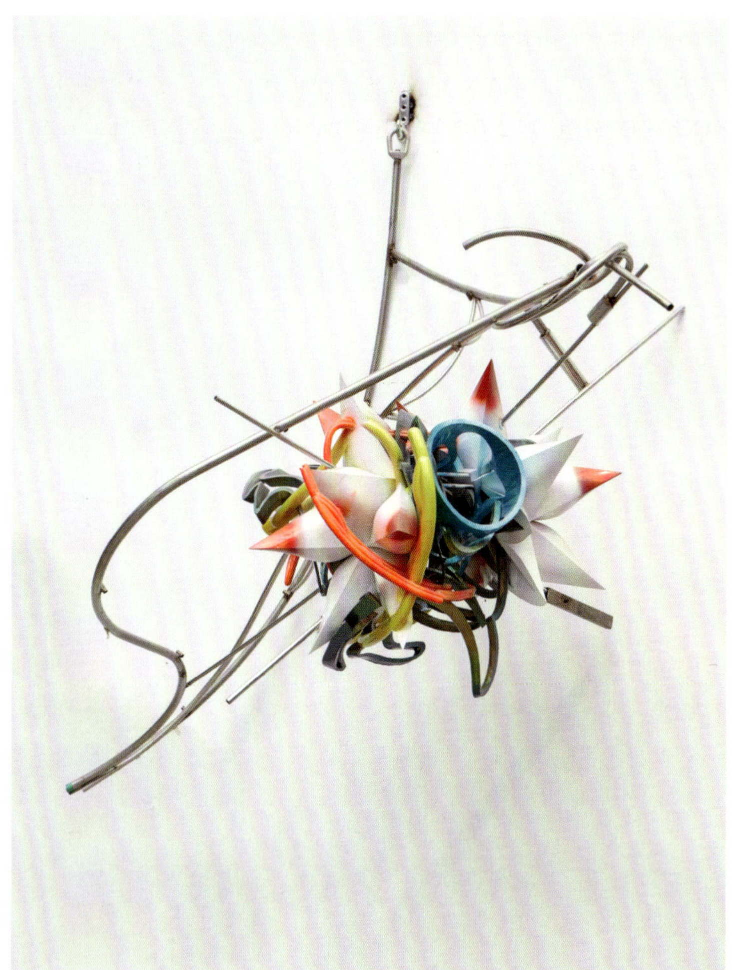

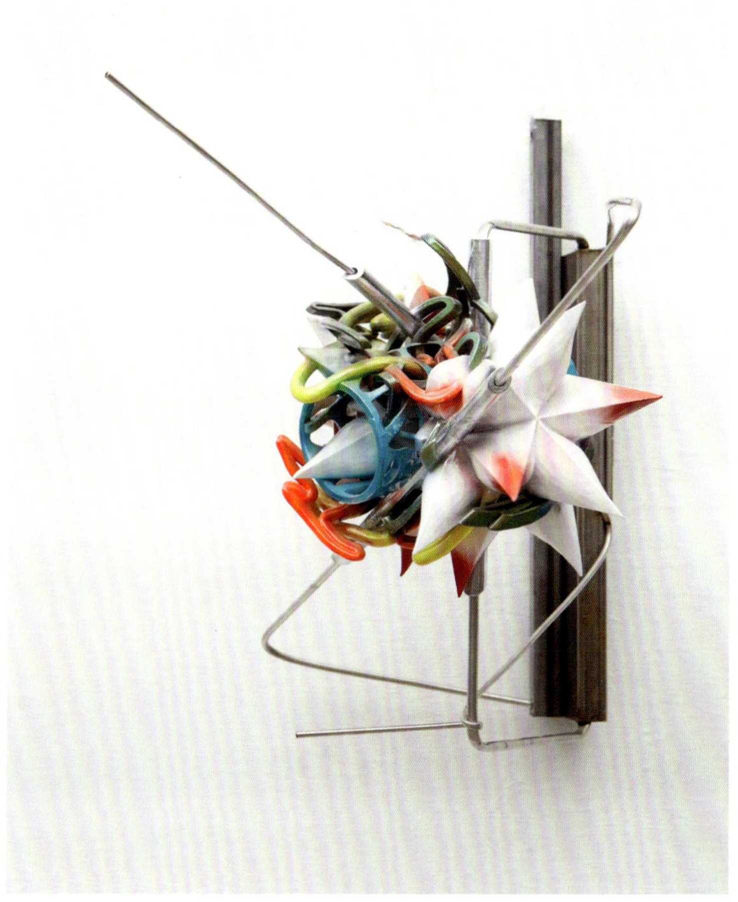

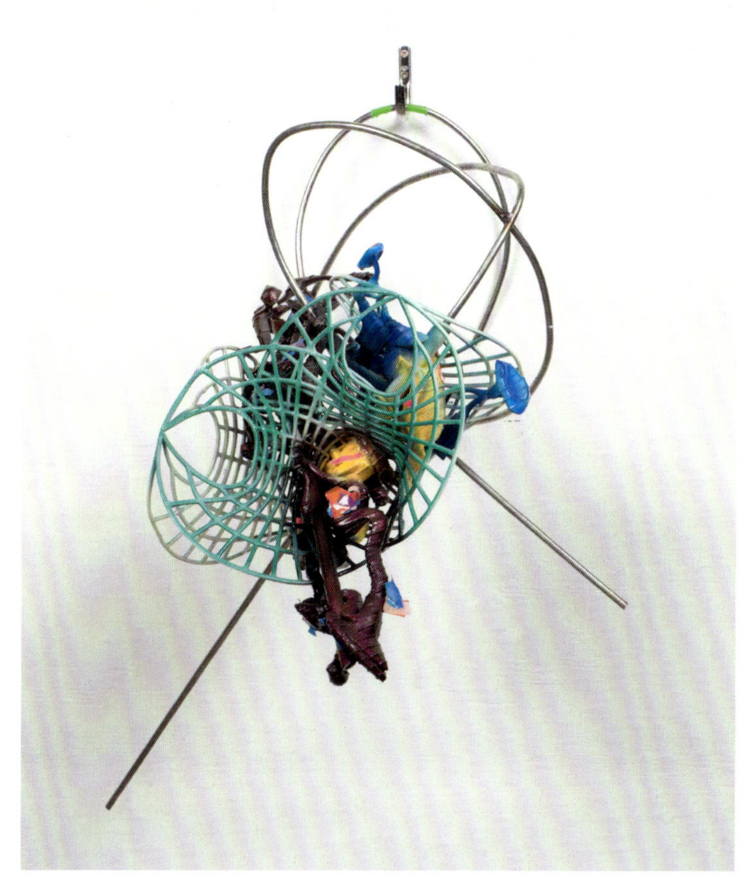

is 'capable of compelling conviction, of succeeding as painting … [must be] largely determined by, and therefore continually change in response to, the vital work of the recent past'. To put it another way: an object is painting if we can be convinced to look at it as such, especially if it is responsive to other painting. But even given this expanded sense of painting's discursive space – and the fact that the works in the Scarlatti K series do indeed build on problems that Stella has addressed previously – it becomes notably less easy to address his work here as painting. This wobbliness, however, can be used to inform our looking.

This is particularly important because the very key to understanding Stella's art has, from the beginning, been in considering the tectonic properties of, capital-P, Painting. He initially attended to the painting as object through its literal support – first in the Black Paintings of the late 1950s, and on through the Protractor and Polish Villages series from the late 1960s and early 1970s – and since then he has, in series after series, reimagined painting's space both through radical autonomy from, and interdependence with, the surrounding architecture.

K.159, 2013
POLYAMIDE (LASER SINTERED PROTOTYPE PART)
99 X 135 X 114 CM

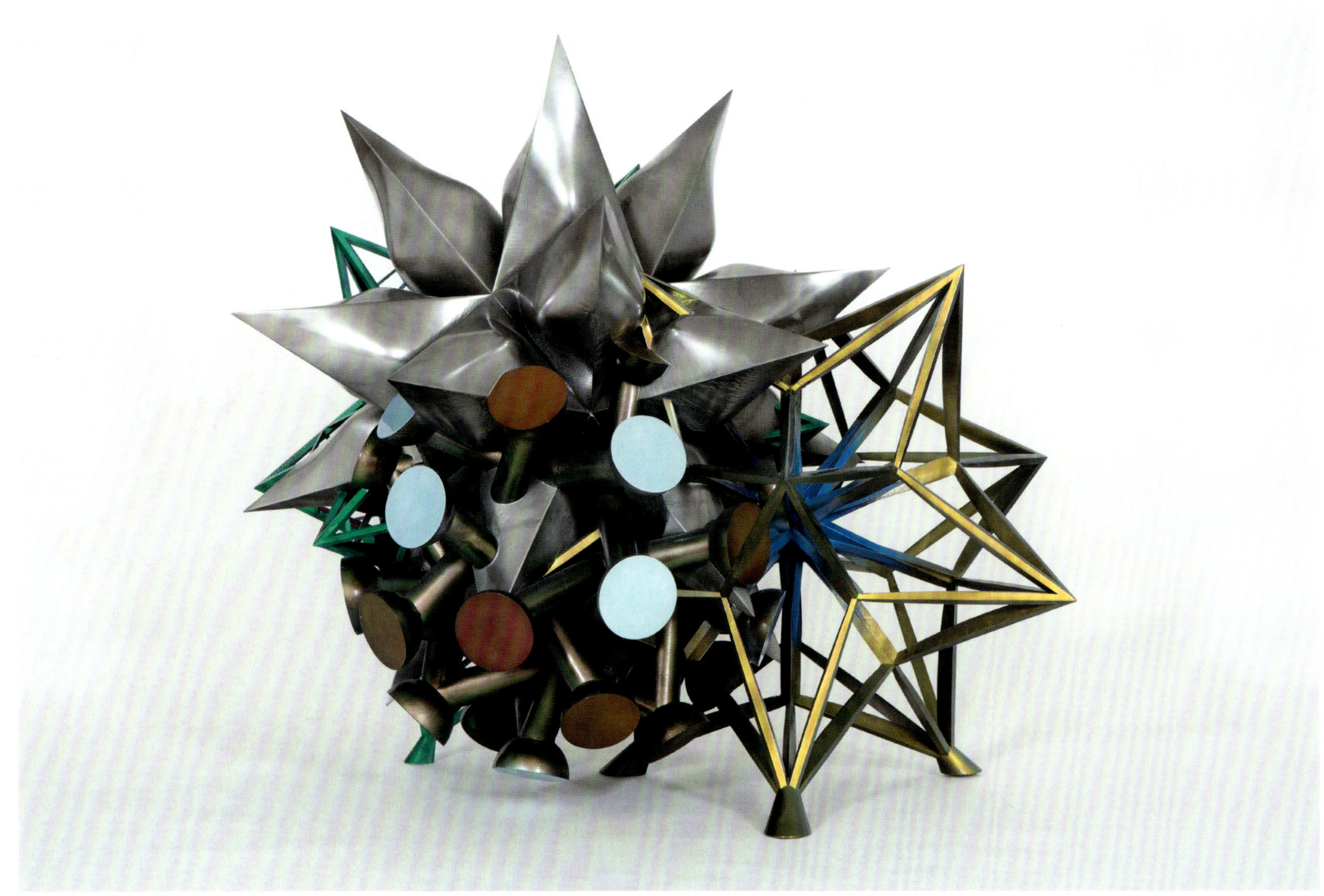

PUFFED NET STAR (SMOKE 1),
2014
PAINTED RPT WITH METAL
53 X 31 X 28 CM

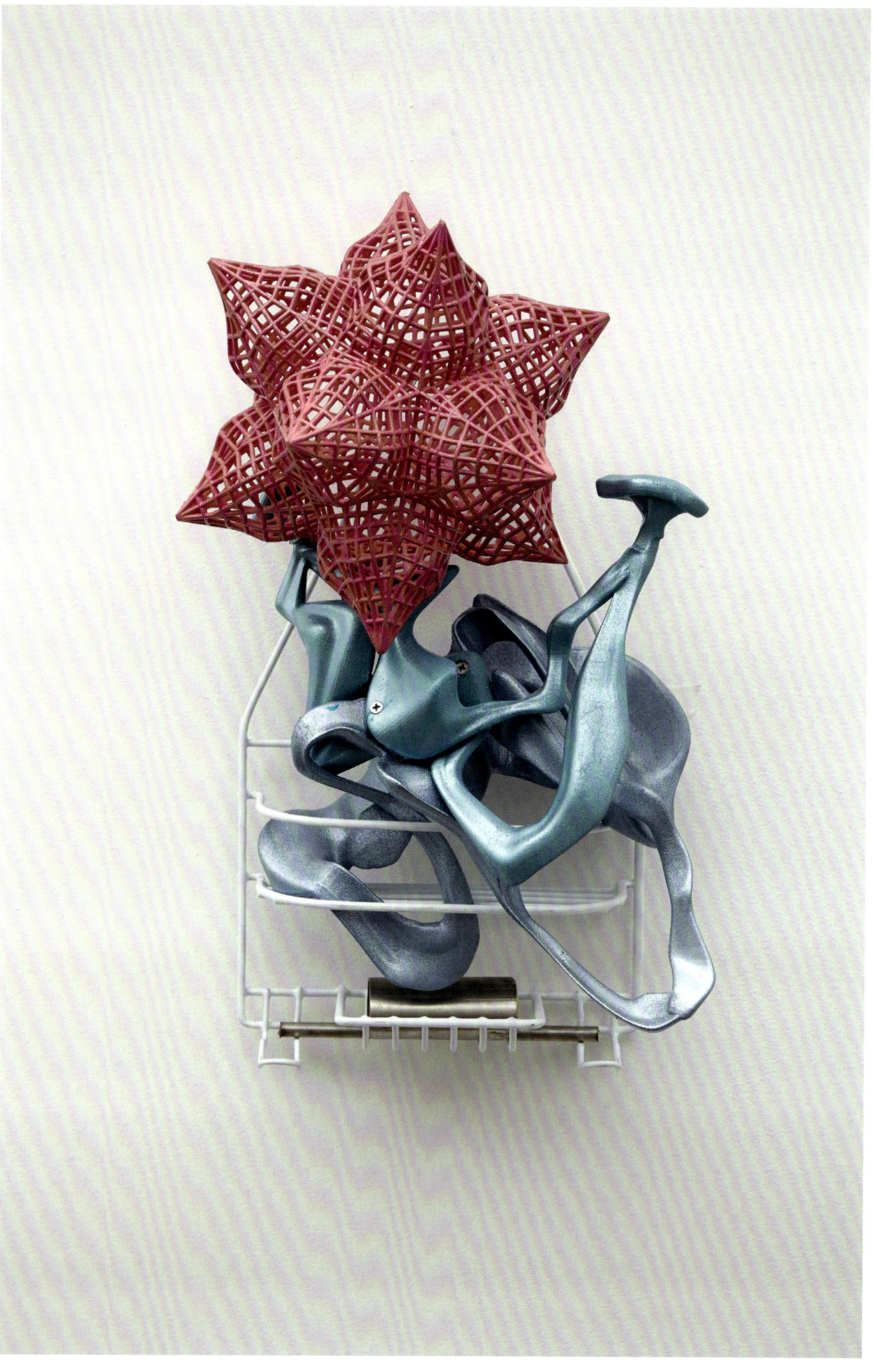

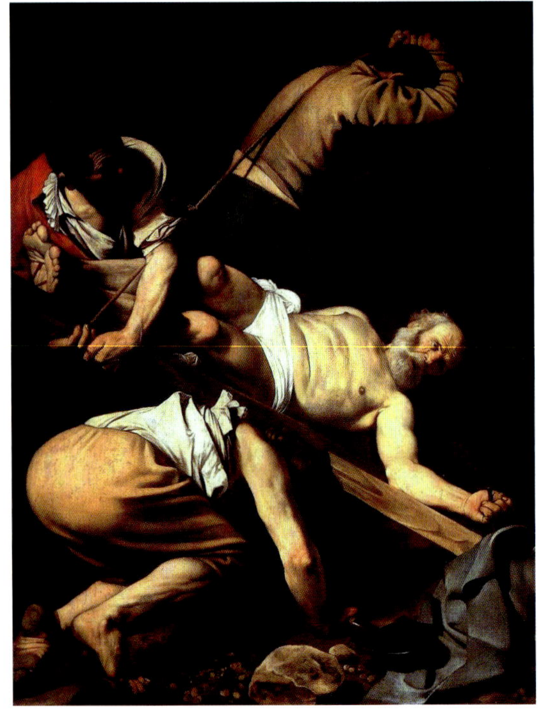

MICHELANGELO MERISI DA CARAVAGGIO
THE CRUCIFIXION OF ST PETER, 1601
OIL ON CANVAS
230 X 175 CM

He grounds his line of inquiry deep in painting's history. In his 1983 Norton Lectures he recounts how the space described in Caravaggio's paintings of the late 1500s and early 1600s challenged and contradicted the space of the cathedrals in which they were hung instead of merely expanding that space as painting had done previously. This he claims, set up the basic terms for modern painting's autonomy. He goes on to argue the case that, despite the immediacy that abstract painting later gained by discarding depiction, the project of abstraction has been structured around an oversimplified spatial condition instead of building on the much more volumetric imaginary introduced by Caravaggio, and later extended by Picasso. Indeed, the untapped confluence that Stella sees between Caravaggio's volume and abstraction's sheer presence draws the plan for his own work. As unconventional an antecedent to Stella as Caravaggio first sounds, if we investigate a painting like The Crucifixion of St Peter (1601), with its discreet intersecting volumes filling out a theatre of action, Stella's claim ceases to seem farfetched. If we take a step further and consider Caravaggio's innovation in relation to architecture, the seed of Stella's post-1983 oeuvre also becomes evident.

Stella has since gobbled up a broad range of approaches and materials as he has extrapolated the potentialities, each more aberrant than the last, of the painting as object. And it is in this trajectory – as he folds computer-based virtuality itself into his programme with the Scarlatti K works – that there is a breach, and the challenge to painting becomes decidedly more complicated. This complication arises because the virtual becomes a 'third space' competing with those of painting space and architectural space, setting up a spatial/conceptual shift with as radical an implication as the one that Stella attributes to Caravaggio. Yet where Caravaggio's was one of pictorial innovation, this new shift relates more to our developing relationship with technology. Previous Stella works had included 3-D prints and other technologically derived elements, but it is only at this juncture that the finished works strike us, with their smooth extraterrestrial volumes, as native to the virtual.

This virtual space was, not long ago, almost entirely relegated to the screen, to CGI effects in cinema and to video games. We might think about something as recent as James Cameron's 2009 3-D blockbuster Avatar,

K 186, 2011
PAINTED PROTOGEN RPT
AND METAL
122 X 97 X 66 CM

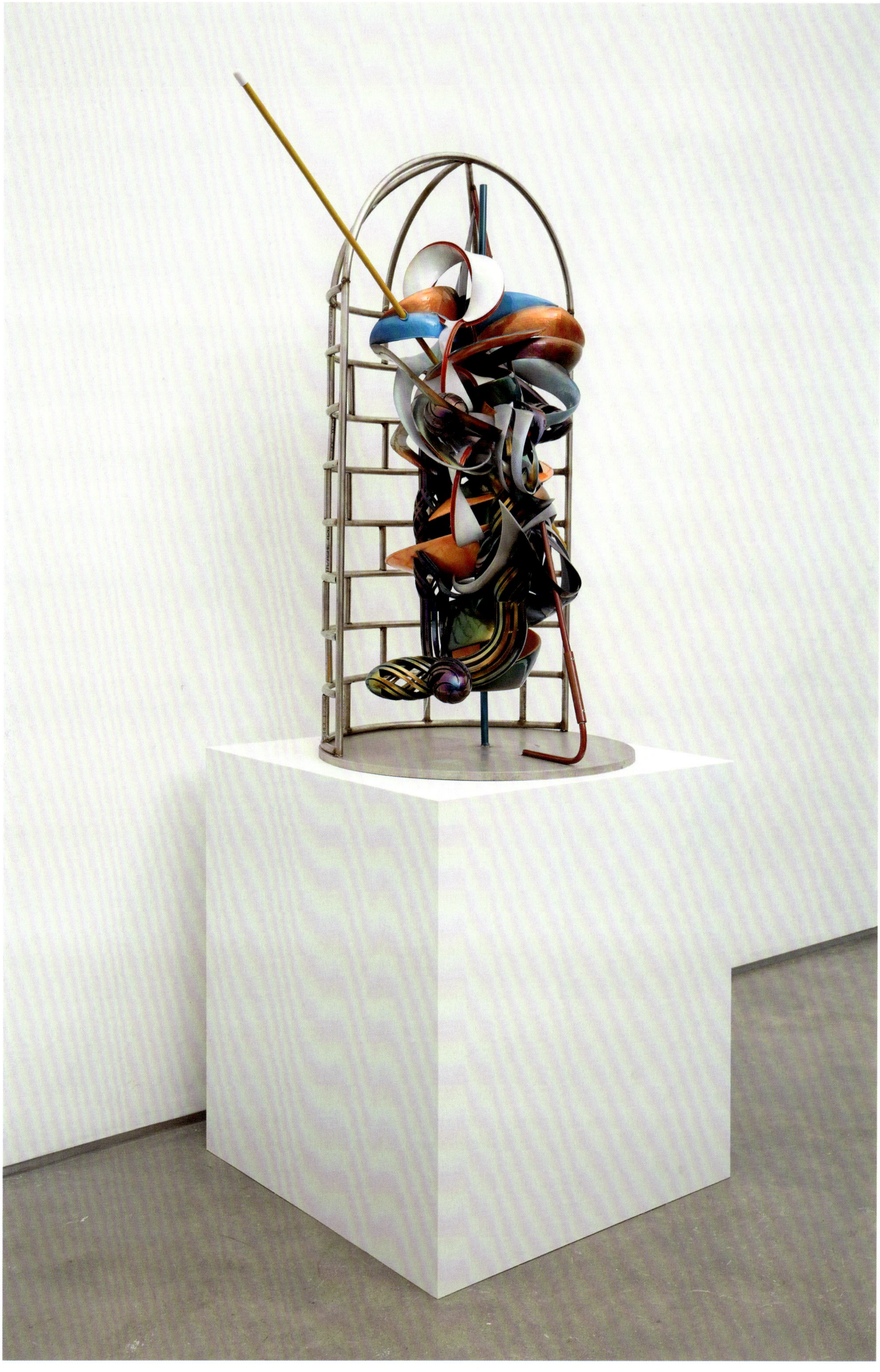

which appeared to bring a fantastical virtual world out of the flat space of the screen, as a shift in the zeitgeist in coming to understand this kind of space as stepping out to join us. But this virtual interpenetration of our environs has in reality come more gradually – through the growing prominence of 3-D printing, celebrity architects like Zaha Hadid and Frank Gehry whose work would be impossible without software, and virtual reality/augmented reality applications, to name a few.

K 150, 2014
PAINTED ABS RPT WITH METAL
244 X 168 X 191 CM

This is important because Stella's construction of painting's autonomy is drawn up as a dialogue – between architecture presented as a concrete, stable space, and painting as a radical one. Painting is radical first in its ability to confront and contradict architecture, and later as a gestural form in its own right. The virtual complicates this by proposing a second 'radical', generative, plastic space that isn't painting, and in so doing brings a second rebellious imaginary into the room. This introduction of the virtual further confounds the situation by seamlessly mapping plasticity onto actual, concrete space, leaving us in a world psychically interpenetrated by the elastic terms of the computer's simulacrum.

The sensible or expected relation of painting to this new virtual space would be to bring it into view as subject matter; that is, to simply draw virtual space into pictorial space, reinforcing the stable, resonant tension between environmental space (now actual and virtual) and picture space – thus keeping painting on track. And a great deal of painting's encounter with computer-based virtuality has been just that. Despite the significant merits of contemporary painters like Avery Singer, Michael Williams, Laura Owens, Jamian Juliano-Villani, or Albert Oehlen, their works play out in a well-rehearsed arrangement, condensing the unruliness of the technological space into the more-or-less traditional picture, directly akin to Duchamp's wry folding of Etienne-Jules Marey's photographic studies into painting with his Nude Descending a Staircase. In these works, painting is 'speaking' technology, and it is a relationship we can enjoy like pop music, without straining to understand how it works. However, it is against just this kind of depiction that Stella has long developed his project. In the Scarlatti K works, he proposes a far more challenging and disruptive encounter by asking painting to leave the canvas and meet technology on its own terms. Stella's wager rests on how he might use the qualities of presence in the virtual to expand the programme of abstraction in painting. In the Scarlatti K works in particular, he does so by asking the formal production newly available through software to 'be' painting or to act 'as' painting, as opposed to being the subject of painting. By asking this, Stella is calling on painting's rich tradition to support these alien objects.

The qualities of painting remain in these works – line, colour, formal relationships and even the sense of a picture plane, though morphed into a sphere or an envelope or a permeable mass. But what is strikingly

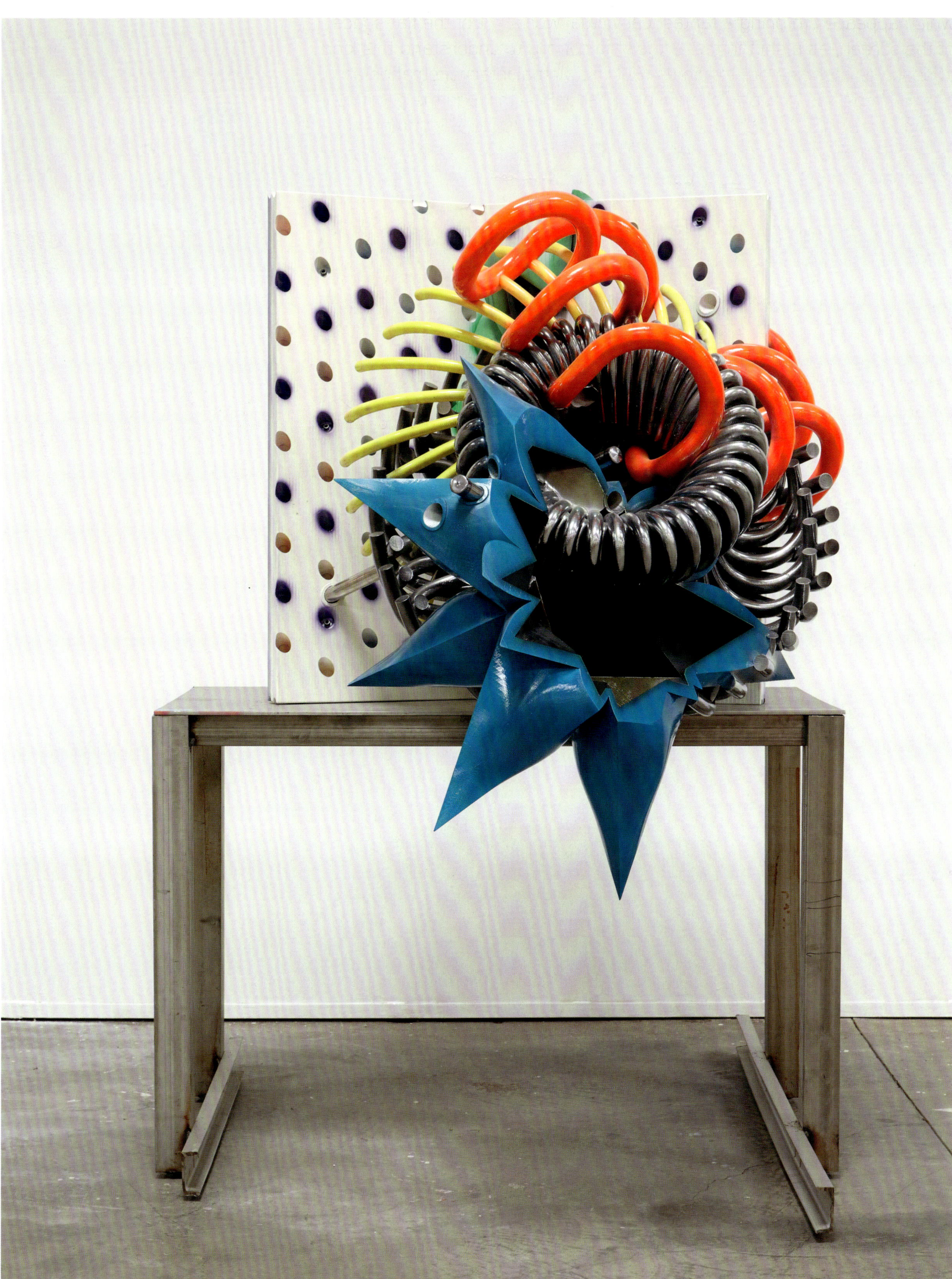

absent in this proposition is painting's dialogical distance and its easy relationship to the human body. Stella is confronting us instead with an algorithmic substitute, a threat displacing one of our most cherished measures, and by doing so he is touching on a deeper unease about our times.

Indeed, there is no way to surrender to these works – no comfortable place to stand in order to consume them or to allow one's self to be seduced by them. The works are simultaneously too much in the room and not of this world, making it hard to understand how to be with them or if such a consideration is even possible.

Given all of this, the artist's gambit here is perverse, brave and funny. Stella, in his eighties, is dismantling the very vehicle that makes his life's work legible and carries it forward. So how do we better understand the proposition in play with these refusing works?

One way out of this conundrum might be through Edward Said's explication of Theodore Adorno's idea of artistic lateness (developed in Adorno's writing about Beethoven),[3] which he describes as an abstruse reformatting in the third act of an artist's career. Said writes of artistic lateness 'as intransigence, difficulty, and unresolved contradiction'; as a catastrophic undoing of the work that comes before; as 'surviving beyond what is acceptable and normal'; and, quoting Adorno, as becoming 'obscure – even to itself'.[4] And there is indeed a sense, looking at these Scarlatti K works, of an idiosyncratic elder decked out in Floridian splendour furiously staring down the void. But lateness is not madness and nor is it senility. It is an outpost in the uncharted territory of a practitioner 'fully conscious, full of memory, and also very (even preternaturally) aware of the present'.[5]

This helps us lay out the field of Stella's inquiry more clearly. To say it again, Stella is intentionally making his work difficult to encounter so that we might again experience the discomforts of sheer presence in painting again. But we can add that he appears willing to be mocked for doing so – the heroic imaginary of modernism furtively giving way to the comic and outlandish. Perhaps, as has been said, only the jester dare speak the truth.

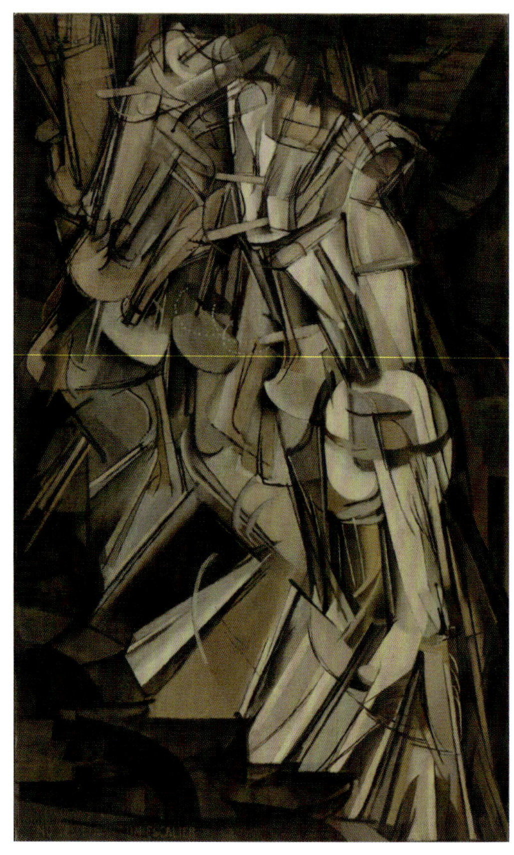

MARCEL DUCHAMP
NUDE DESCENDING A STAIRCASE, NO. 2, 1912
OIL ON CANVAS
147 X 89 CM

K 432, 2013
PAINTED ABS RTP AND METAL
150 X 142 X 132 CM

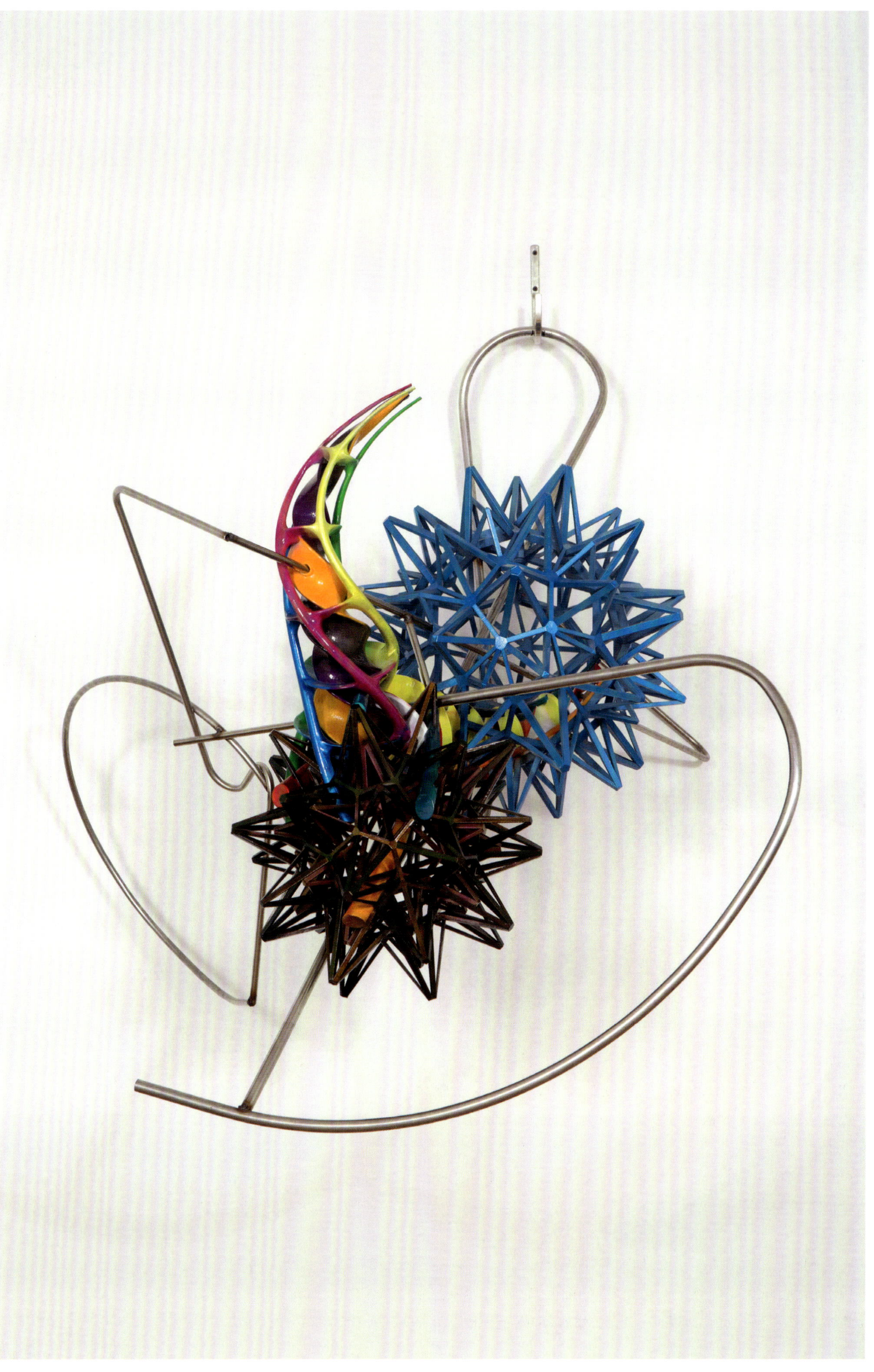

Thus the *Scarlatti K* works become urgent, necessary painting by being really bad at being paintings. But not, say, in the way that painting has been evacuated of the notion of quality at different moments by the likes of René Magritte, Michael Krebber or Josh Smith, through simplification, a suppression of the virtuosic and complex, or else a displacement into language or concept. Stella's volley is quite different in that he is drawing attention to the deeper intelligence that structures painting's spatial terms while simultaneously admitting the object painting's growing anachronism as the dominant, or at least as the only, means of conceptual, phenomenological conveyance. In the process, he is stimulating our discomfort with that passing.

The virtual, as Stella enlists it in the *Scarlatti K* series, stakes out new territory for painting and yet denies painting its clear autonomy. Stella seems to be asking, 'If painting must support the expanse of digital objecthood, will it come apart?' This is indeed a ruse, a negation, but in the tradition of a *Finnegan's Wake*: eviscerating summation at the far end of a profound and expansive practice. And like Joyce, Stella is here using humour and ugliness to do important work as Trojan horses for unpalatable ideas.

Stella claims that his initial attraction to Caravaggio was because the artist's paintings 'looked real' to him. It is this sense of presence that Stella has worked to migrate into abstraction. And if abstraction's ambition was to remove artifice and illusion from painting, then it might be said that the materializing of the drawn object through the computer is the means to take the next step. Perhaps these works are partaking in a relation to the real to which we are still getting used, possessing qualities almost too nervous and uncomfortable for the present. After all, it is with the 'madness' of the late Beethoven that, 200 years on, we find ourselves in love.

K 432 (DETAIL), 2013
PAINTED ABS RTP AND METAL
150 X 142 X 132 CM

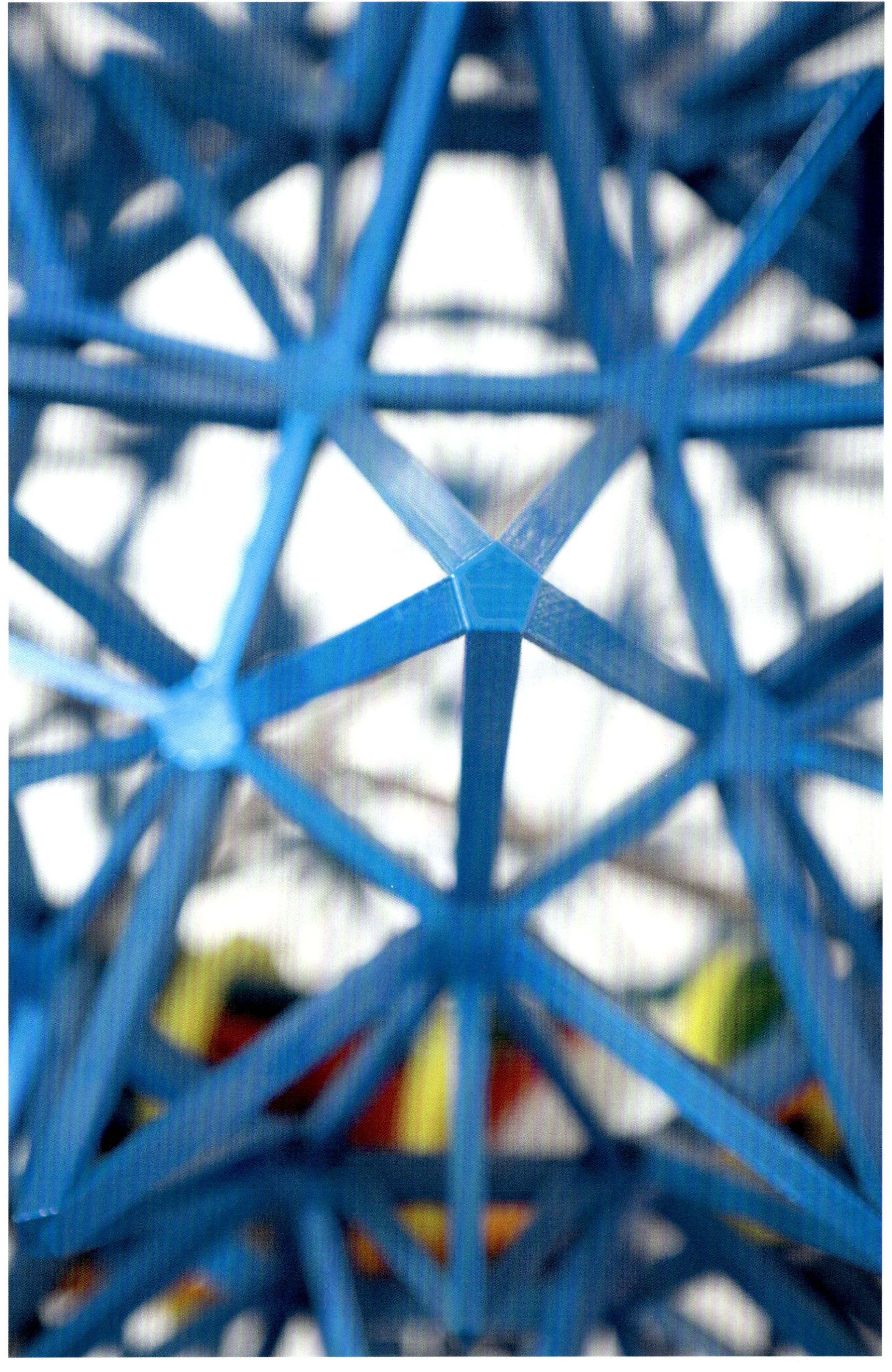

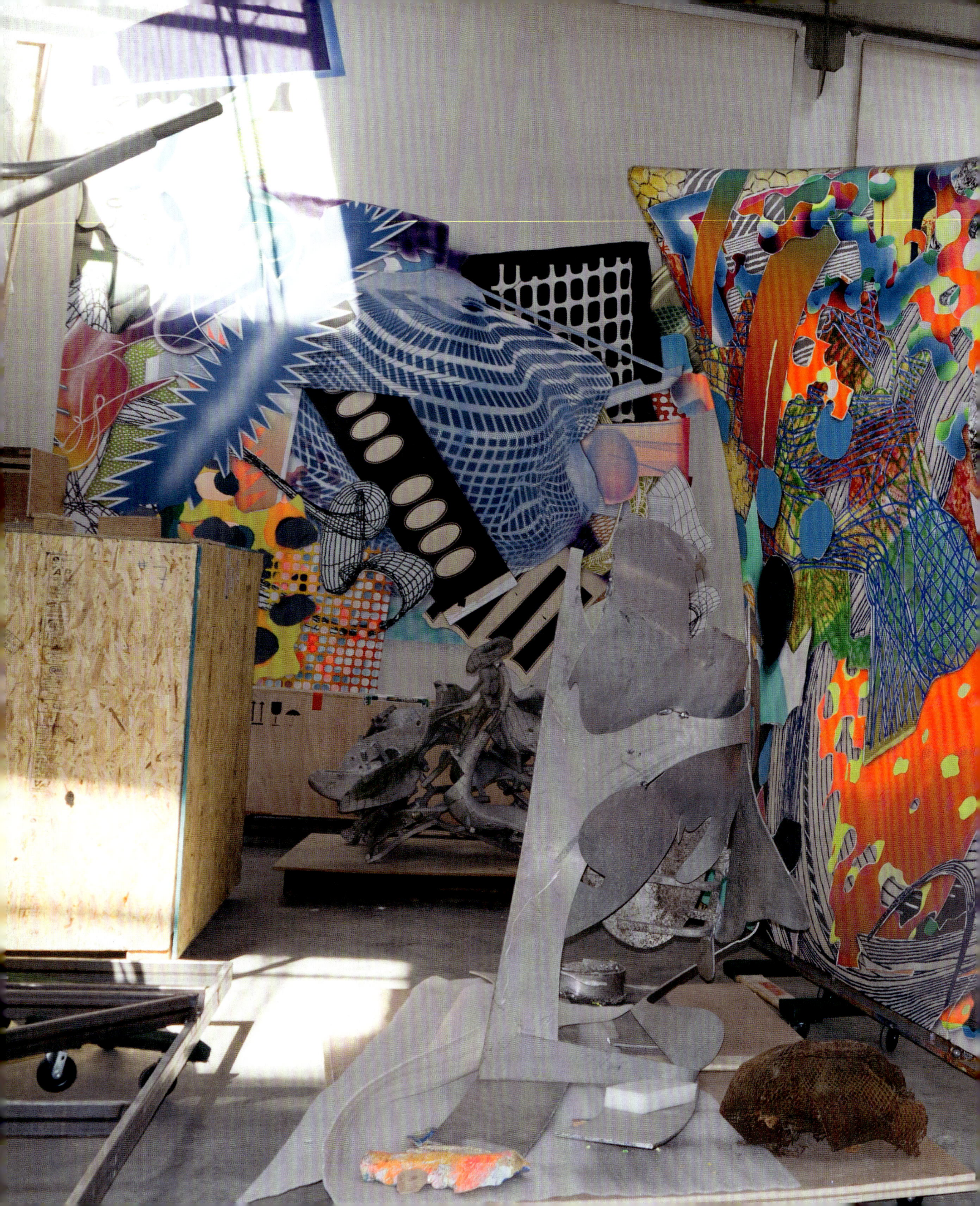

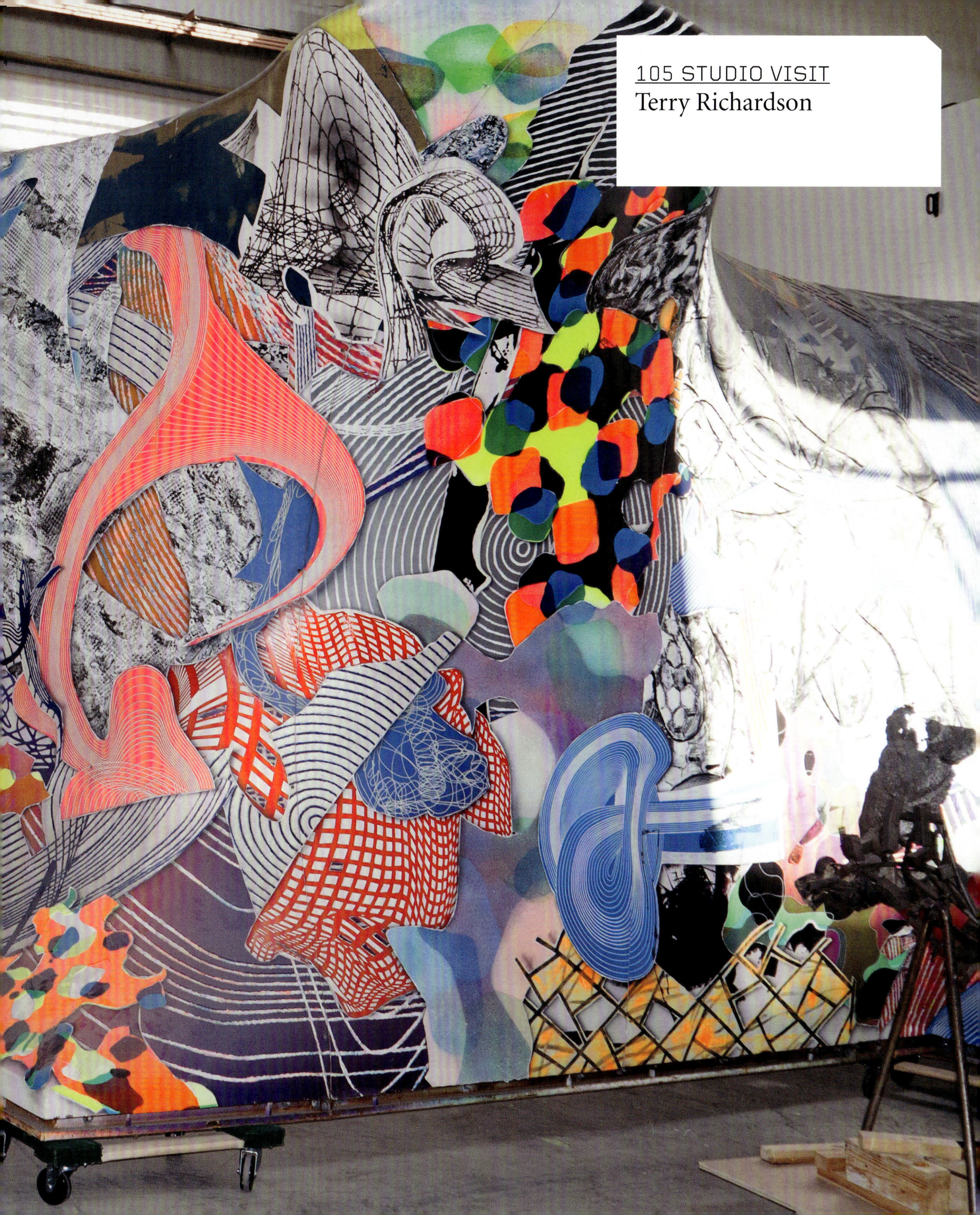

Terry Richardson

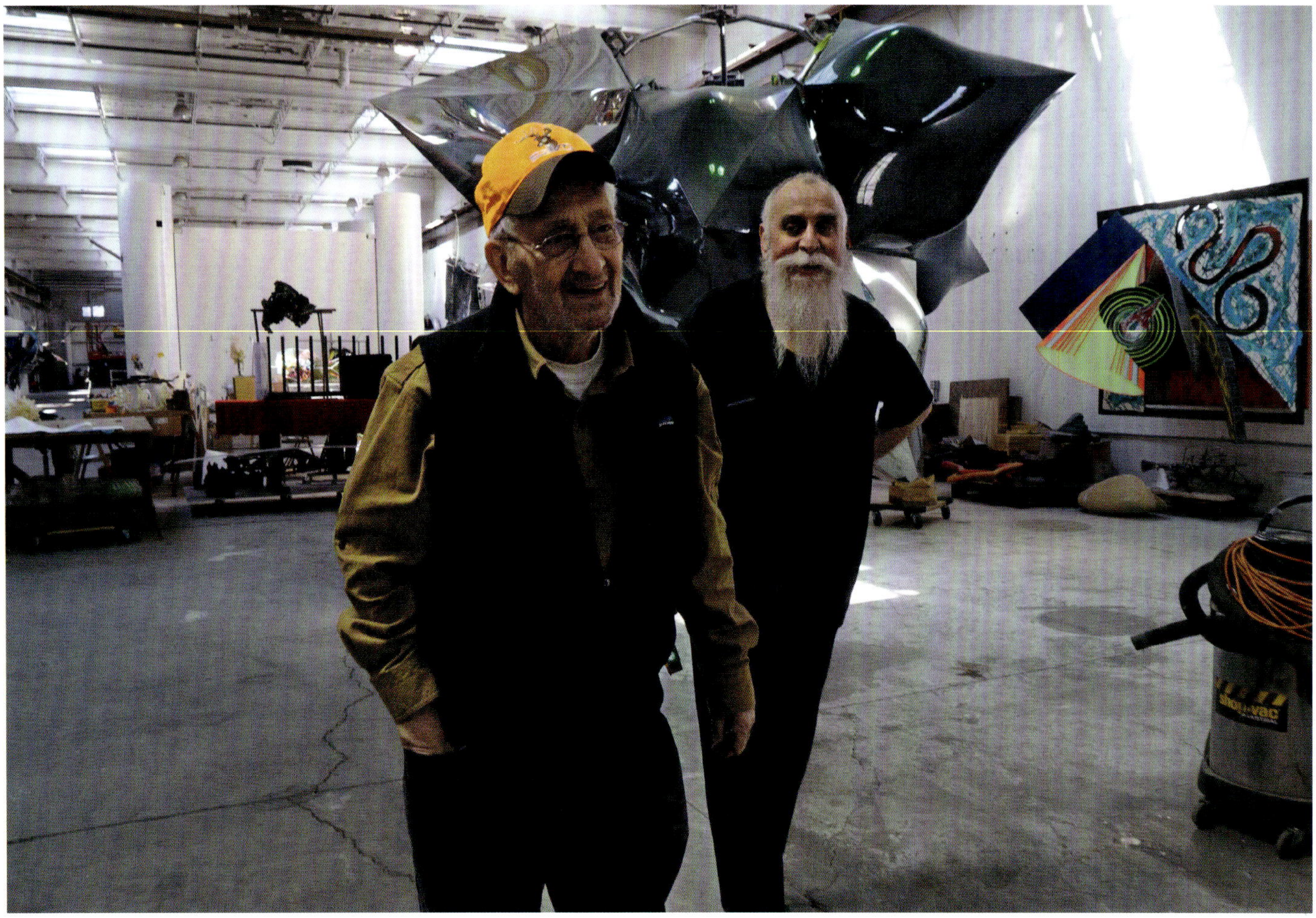

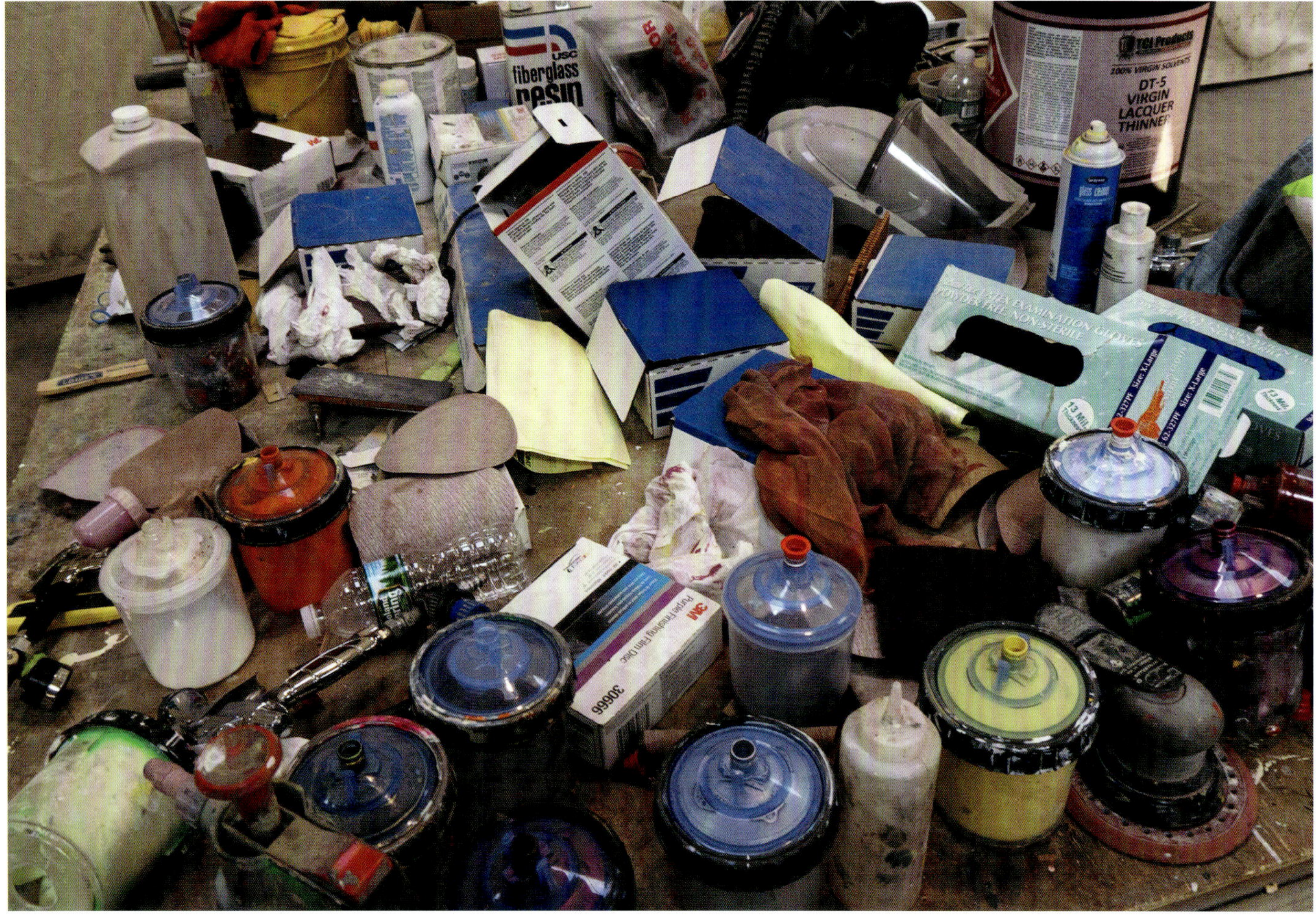
USC
fiberglass
resin
TCI Products
100% VIRGIN SOLVENTS
DT-5
VIRGIN
LACQUER
THINNER
3M
30666

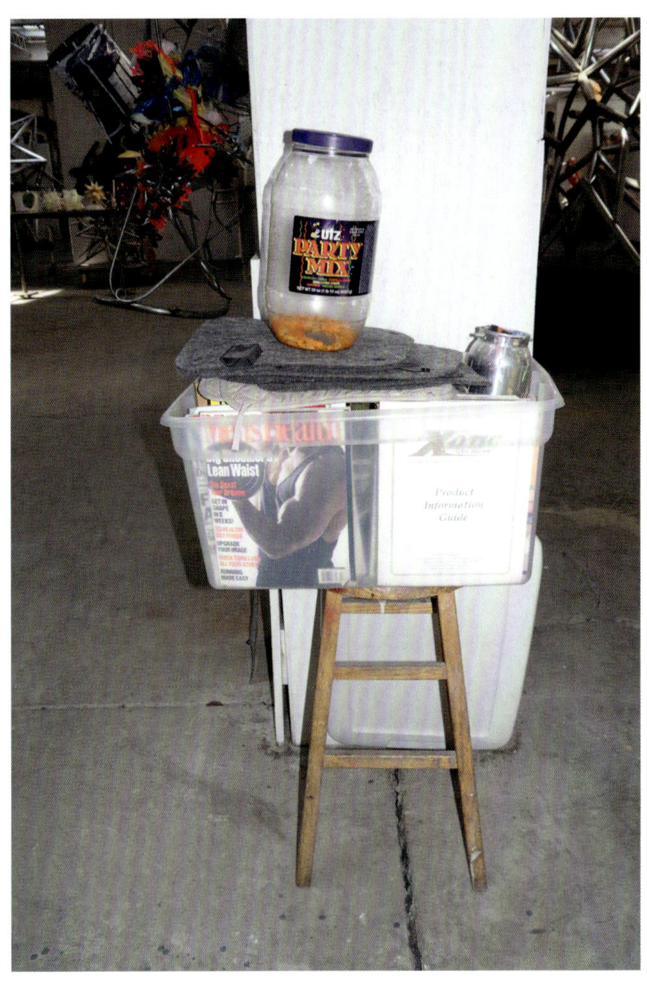
utz
PARTY MIX
Lean Waist
Product
Information
Guide

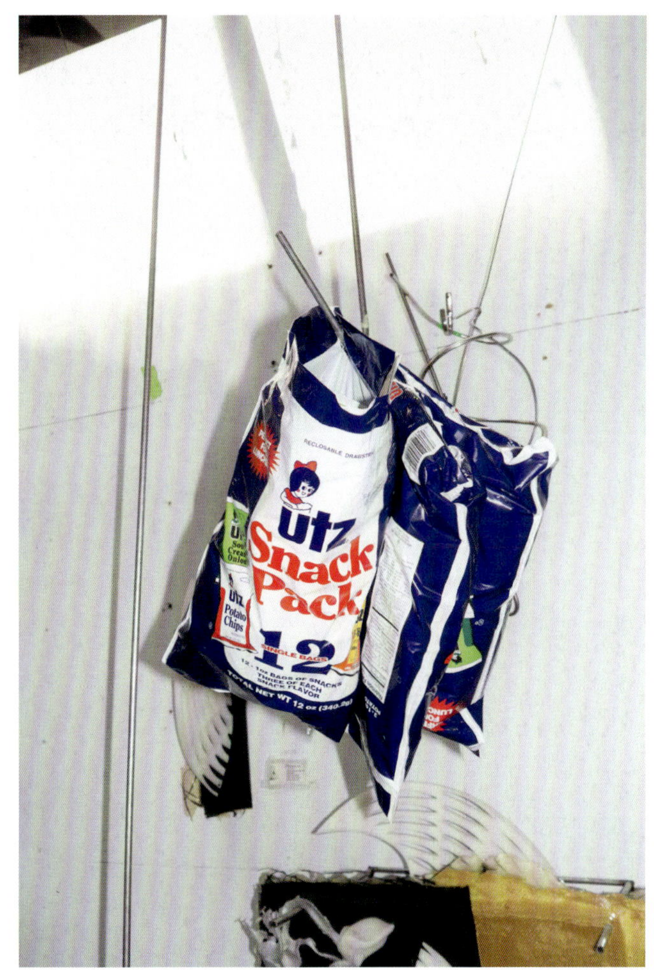
Utz
Snack
Pack
12

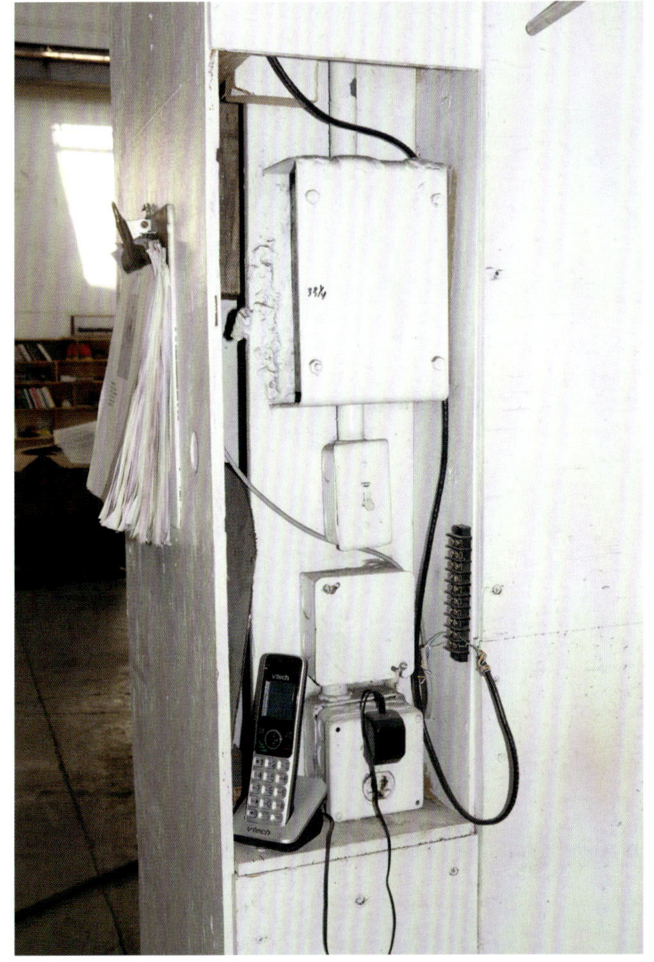

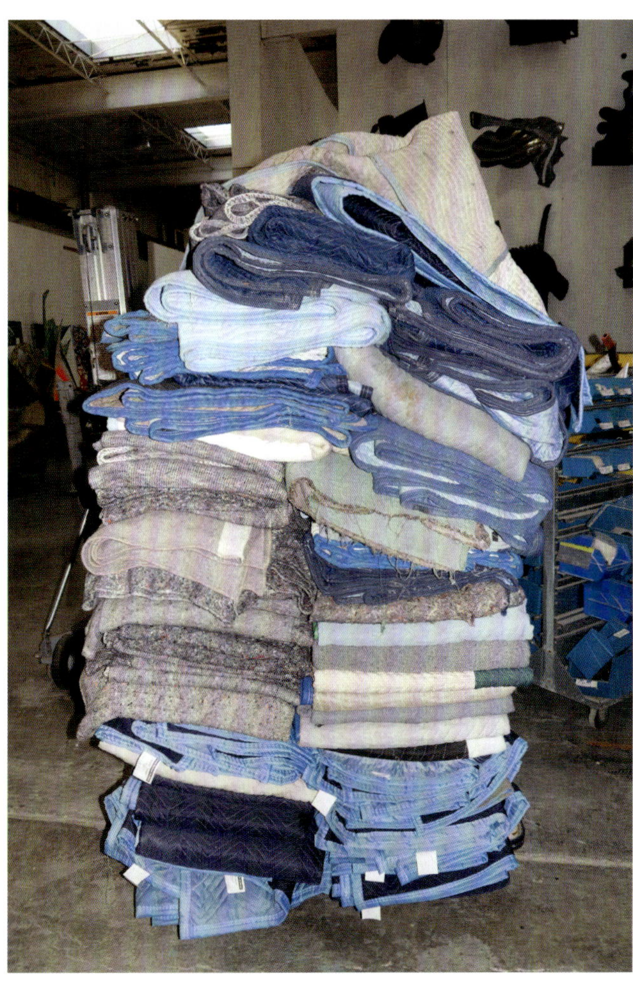

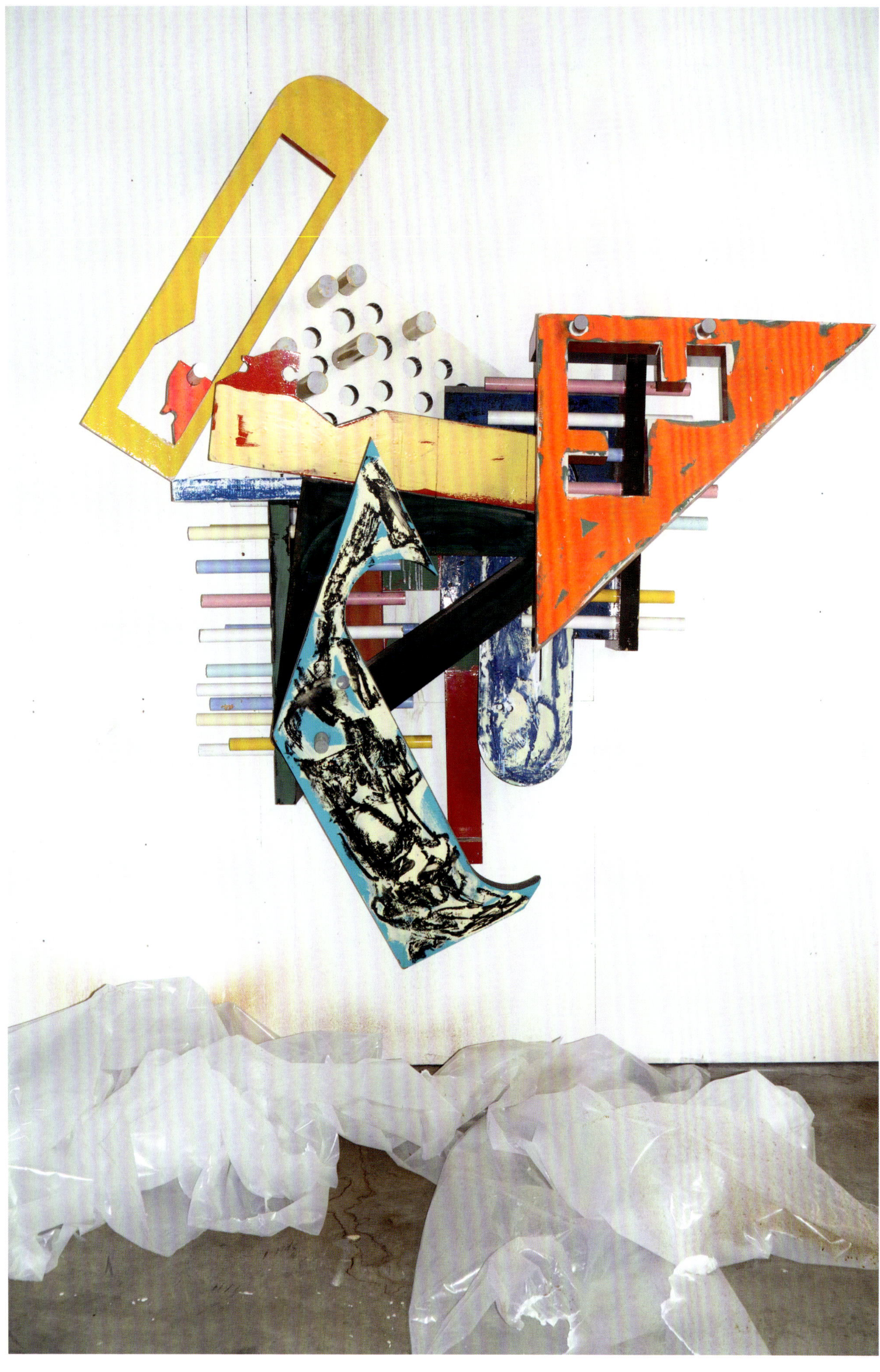

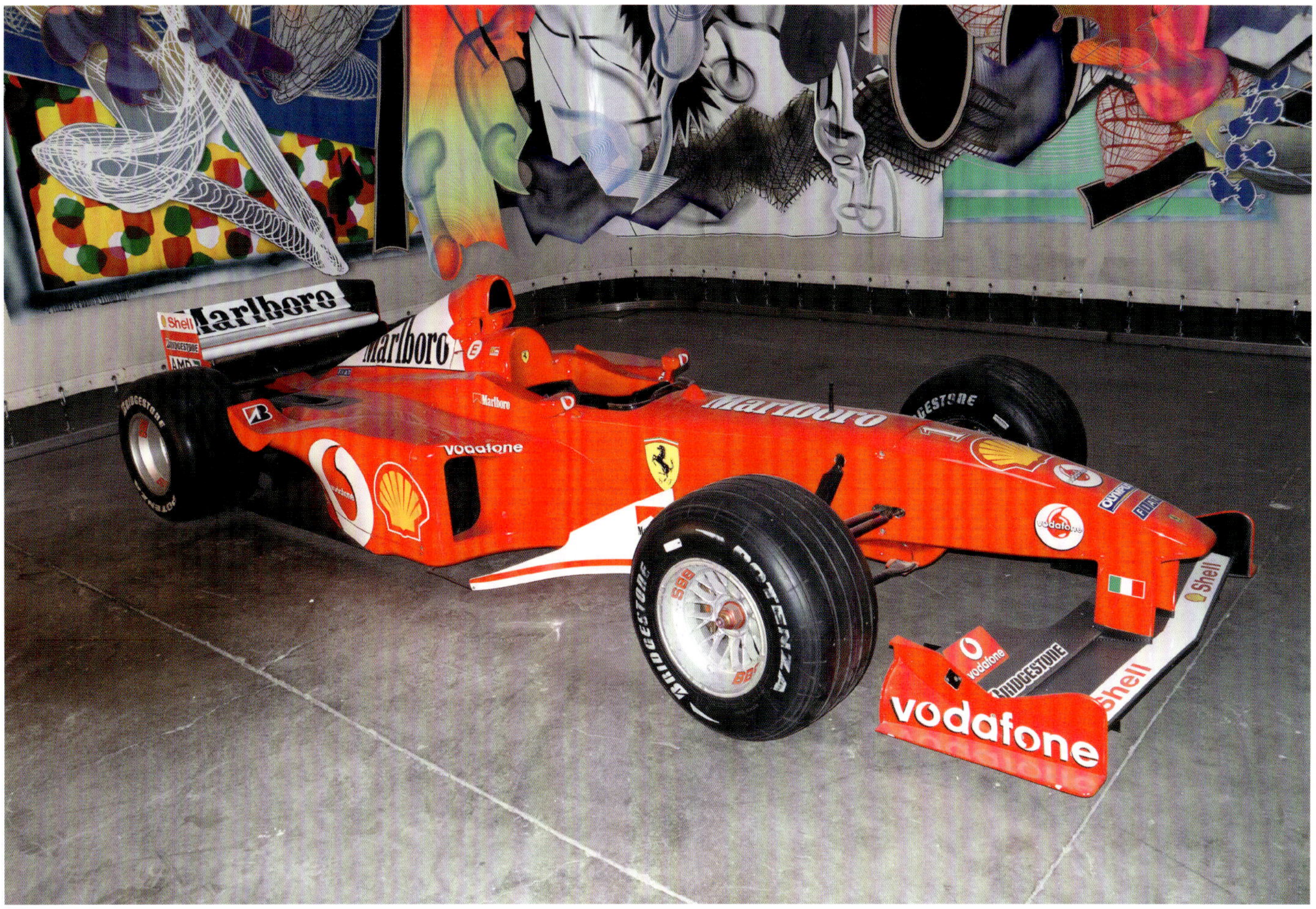

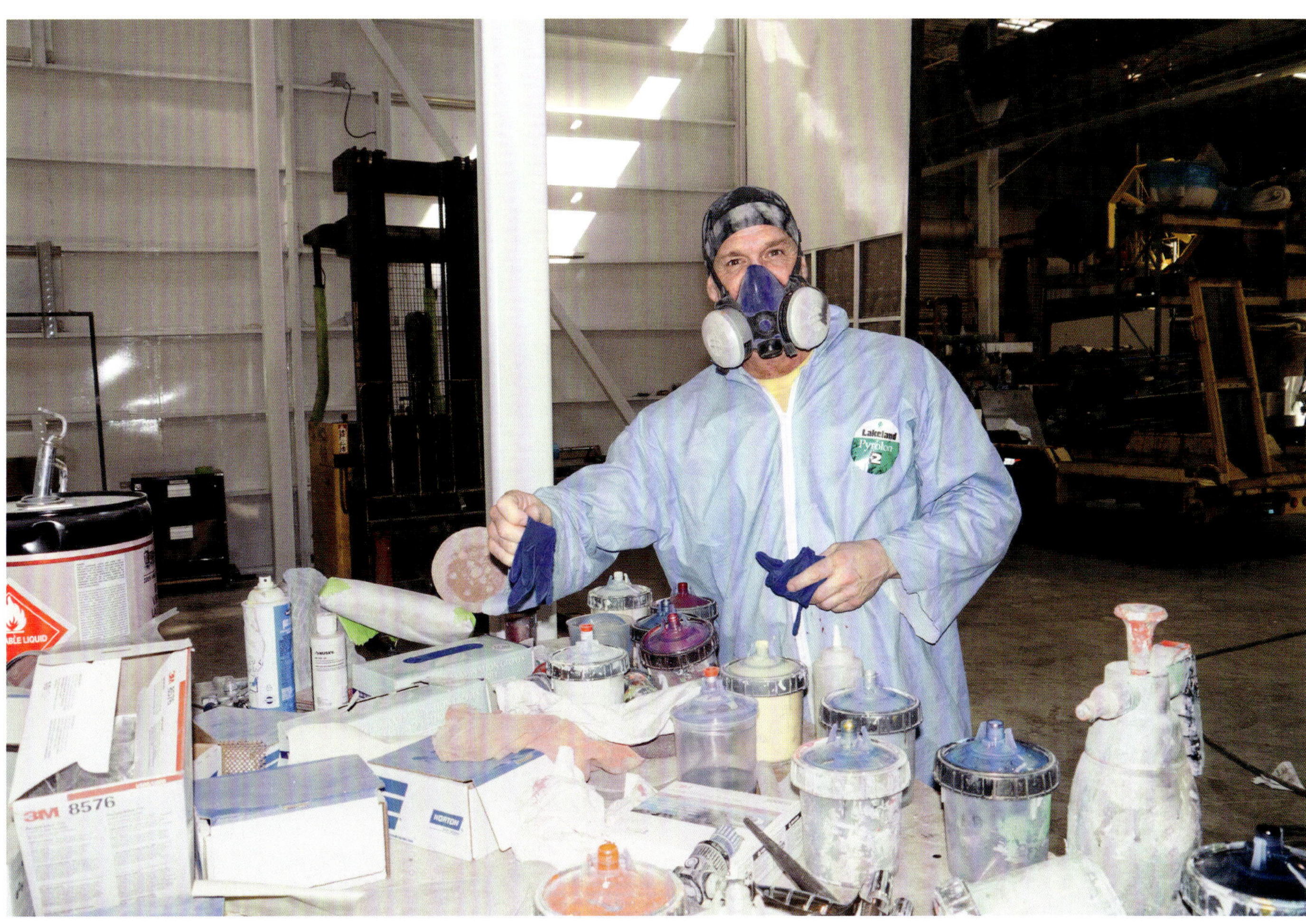
3M 8576

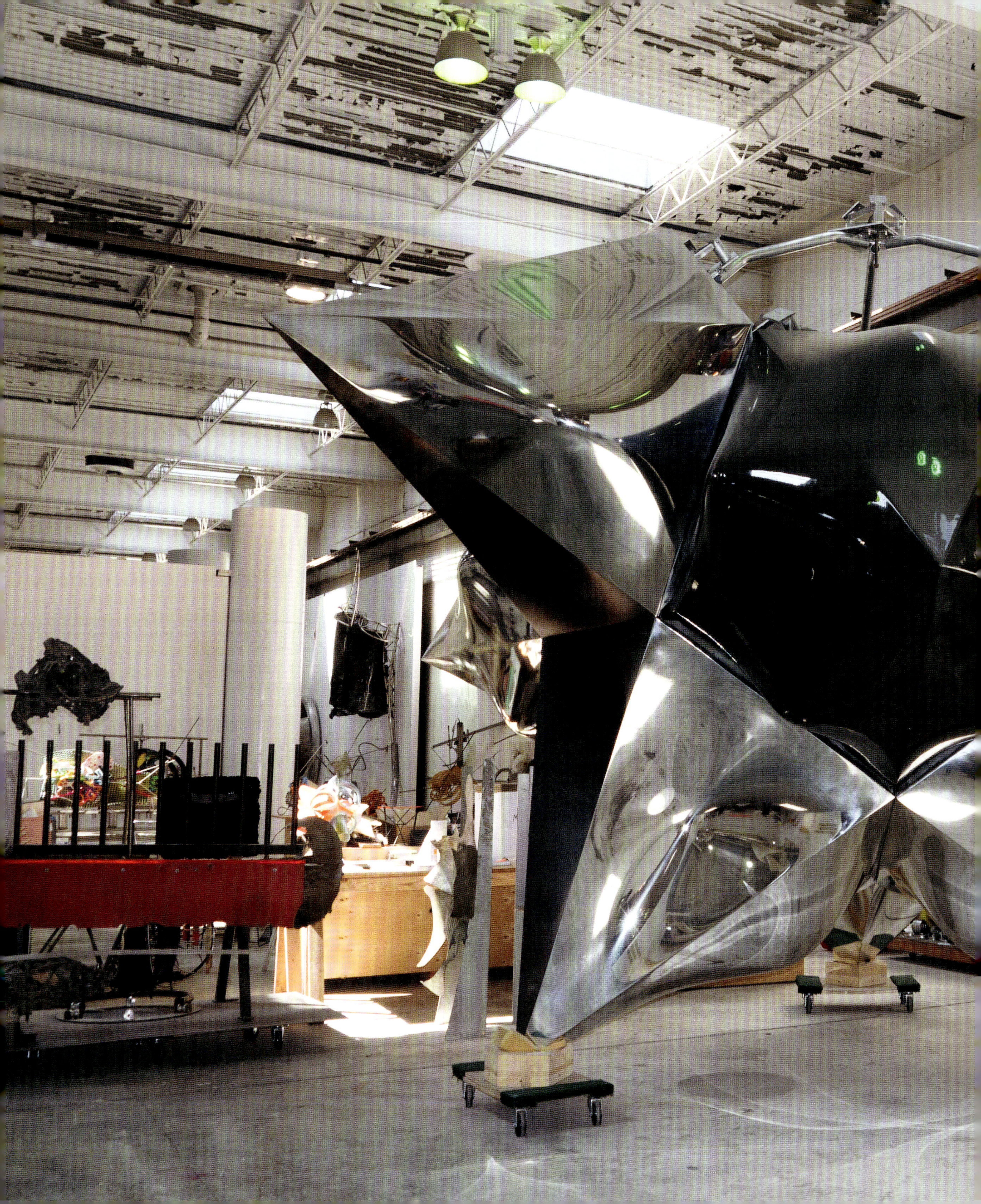

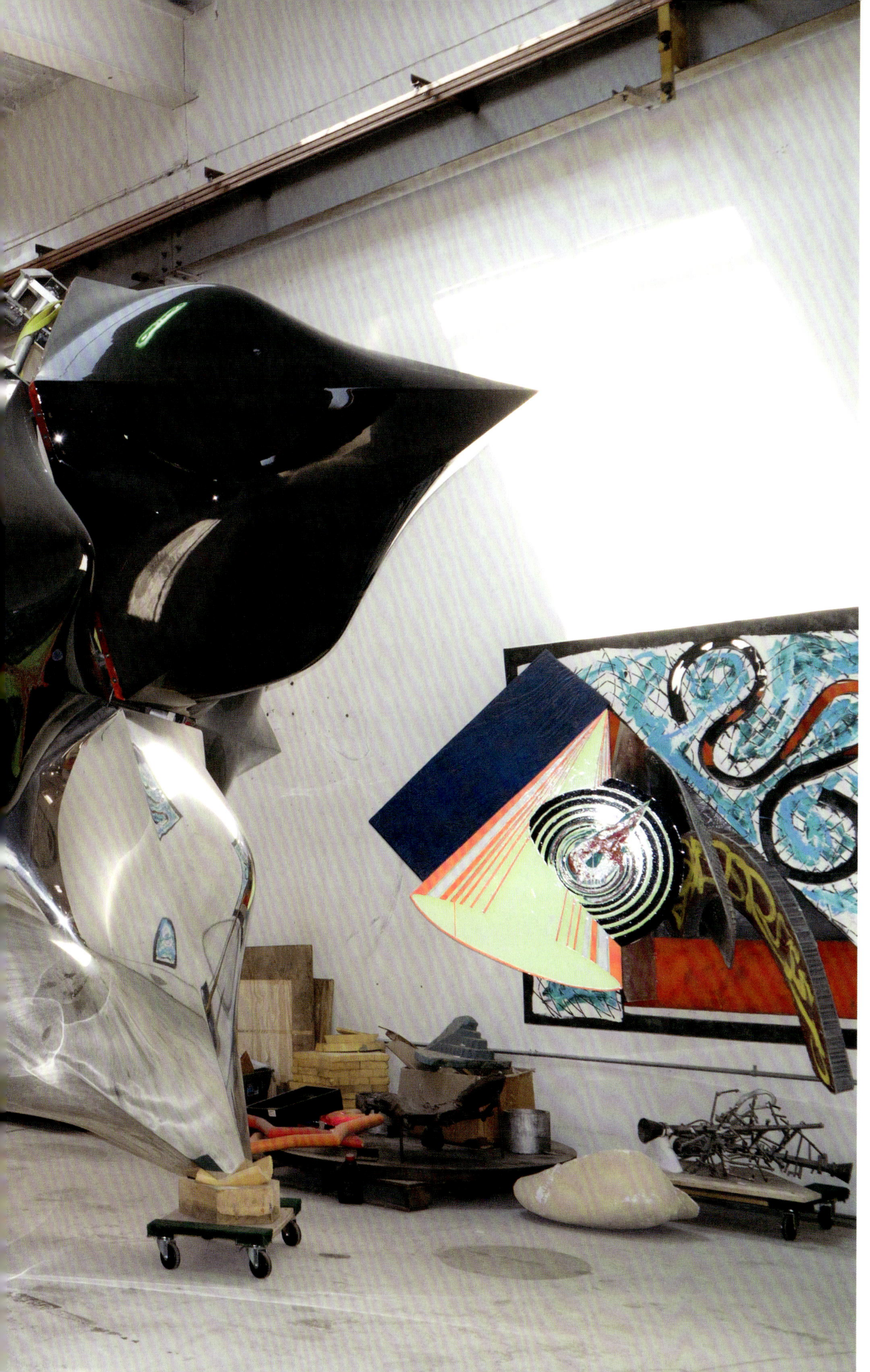

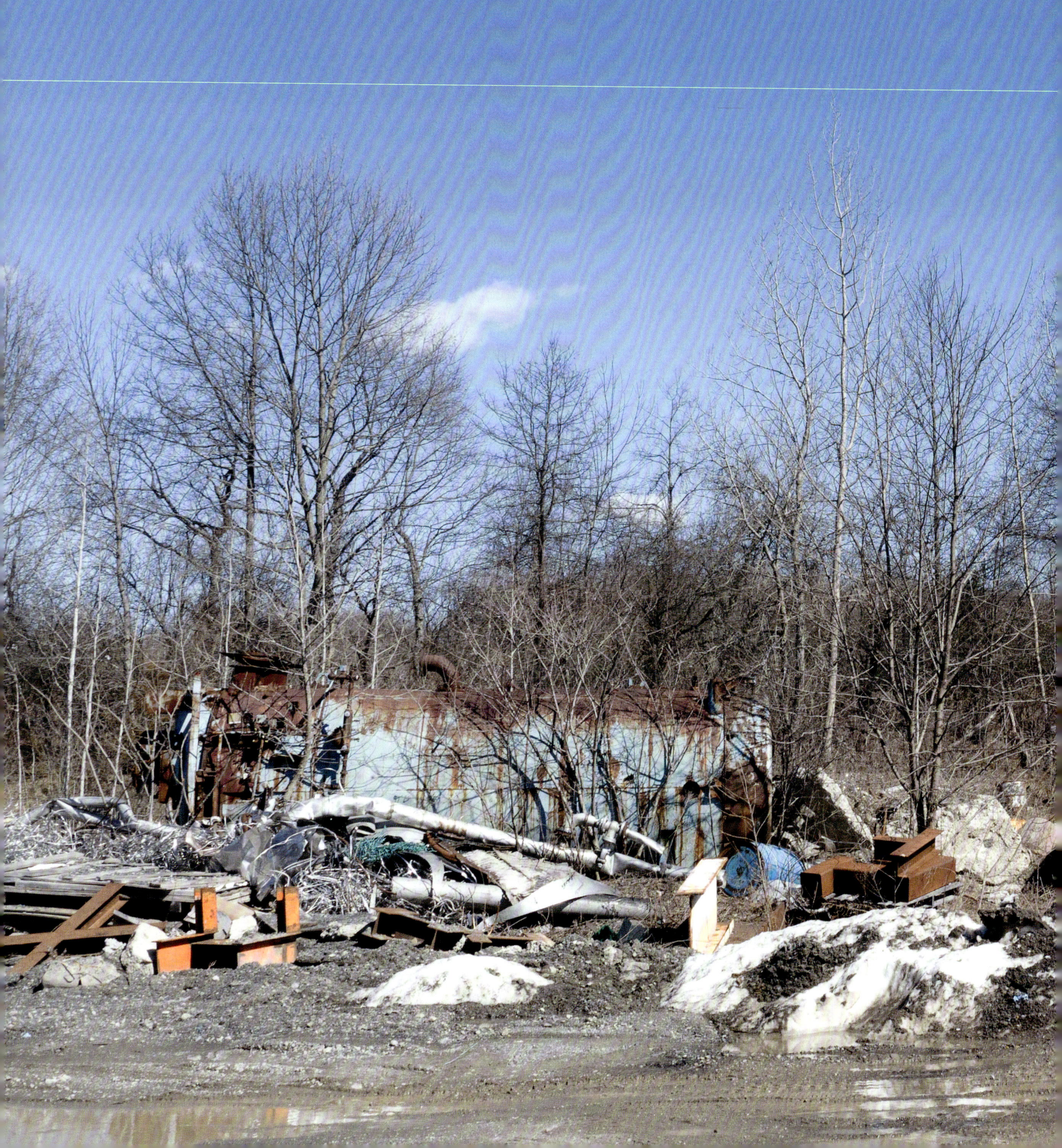

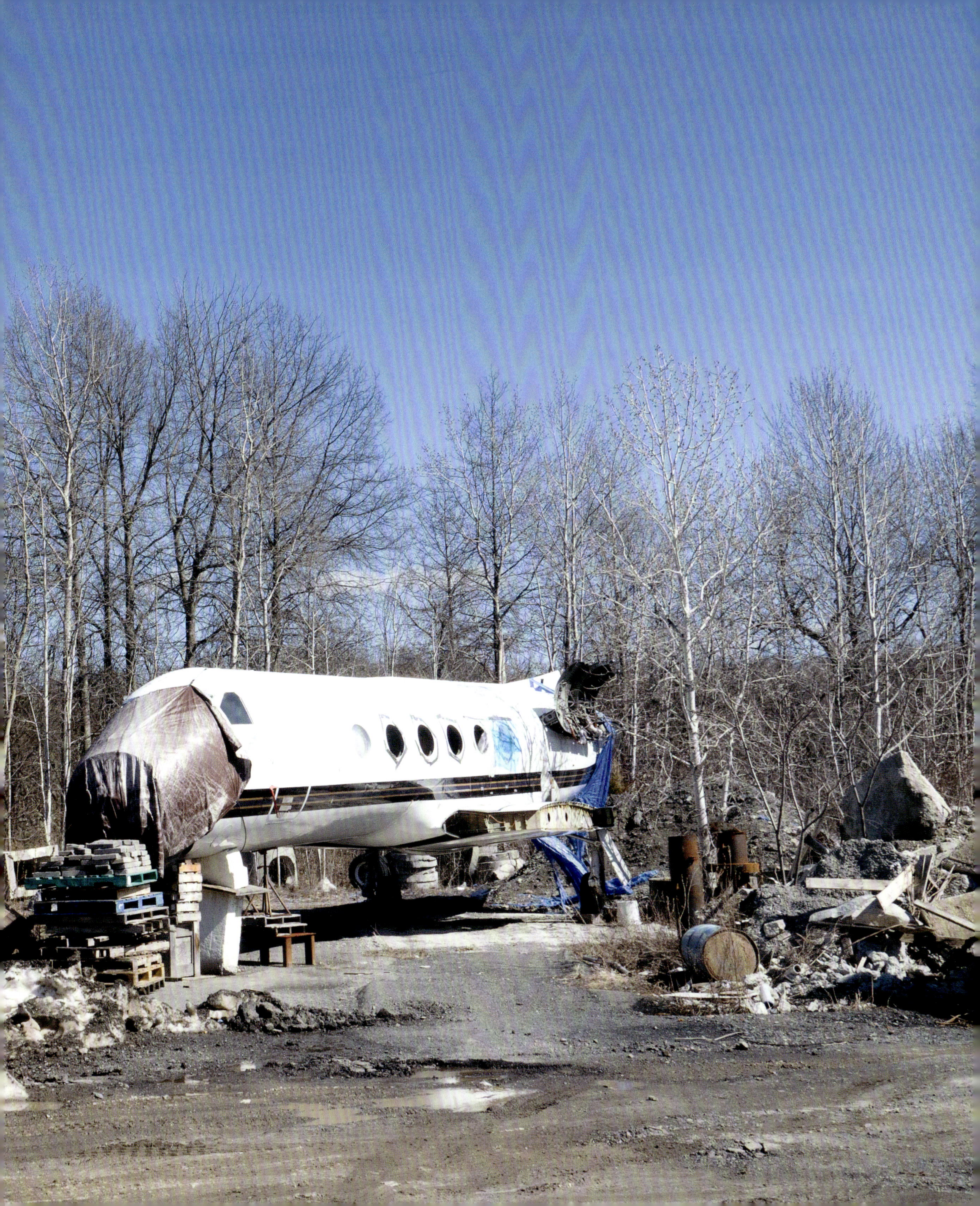

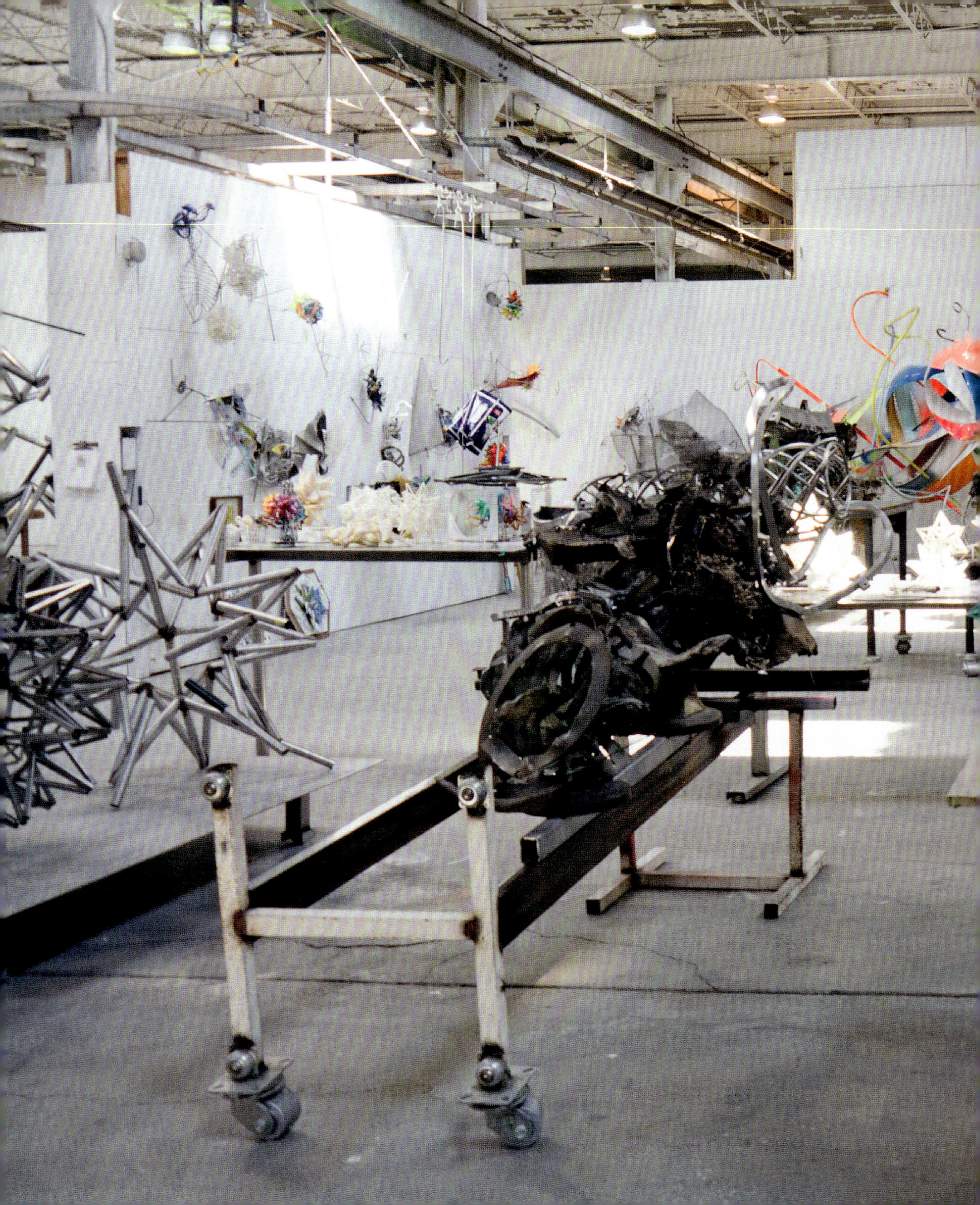

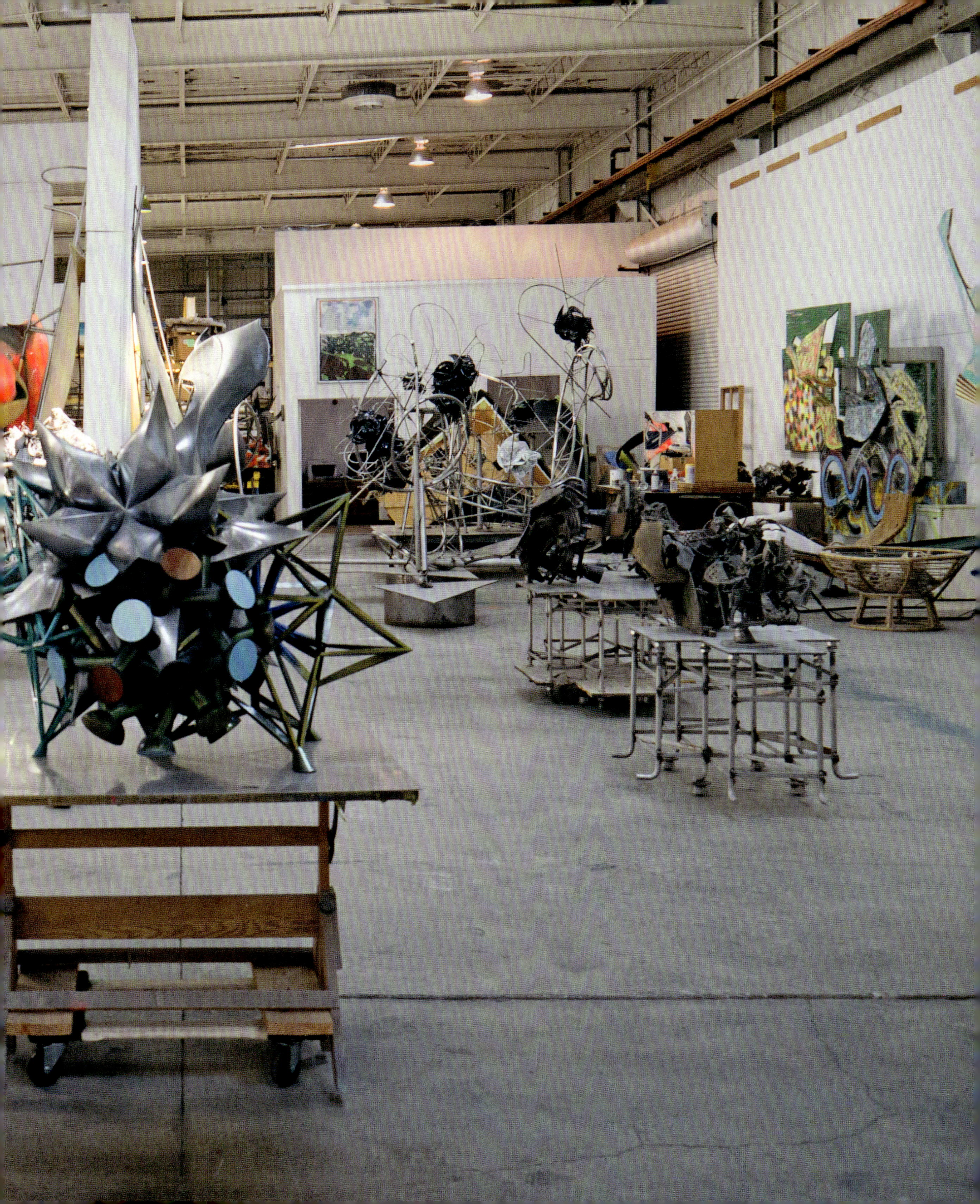

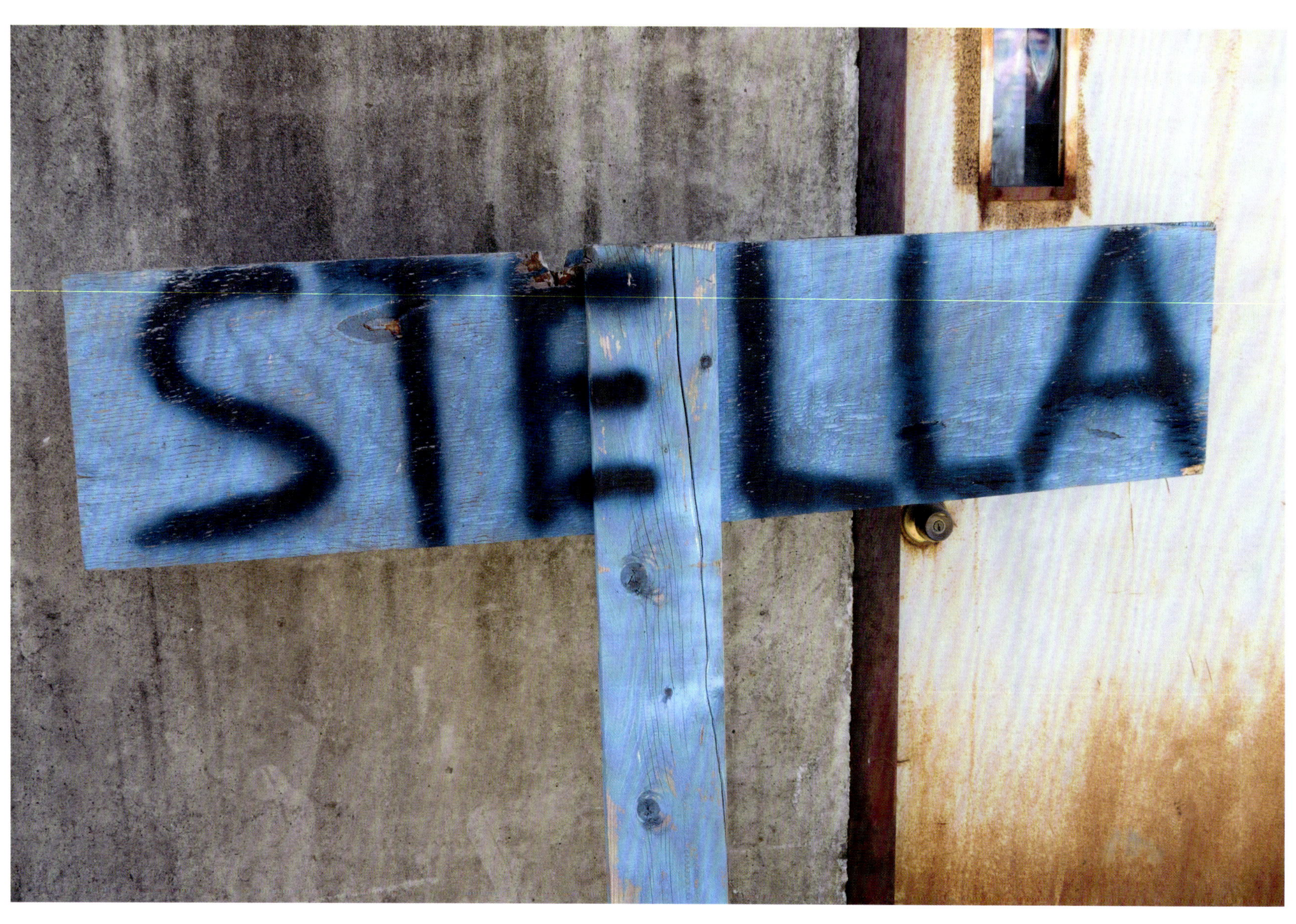
STELLA

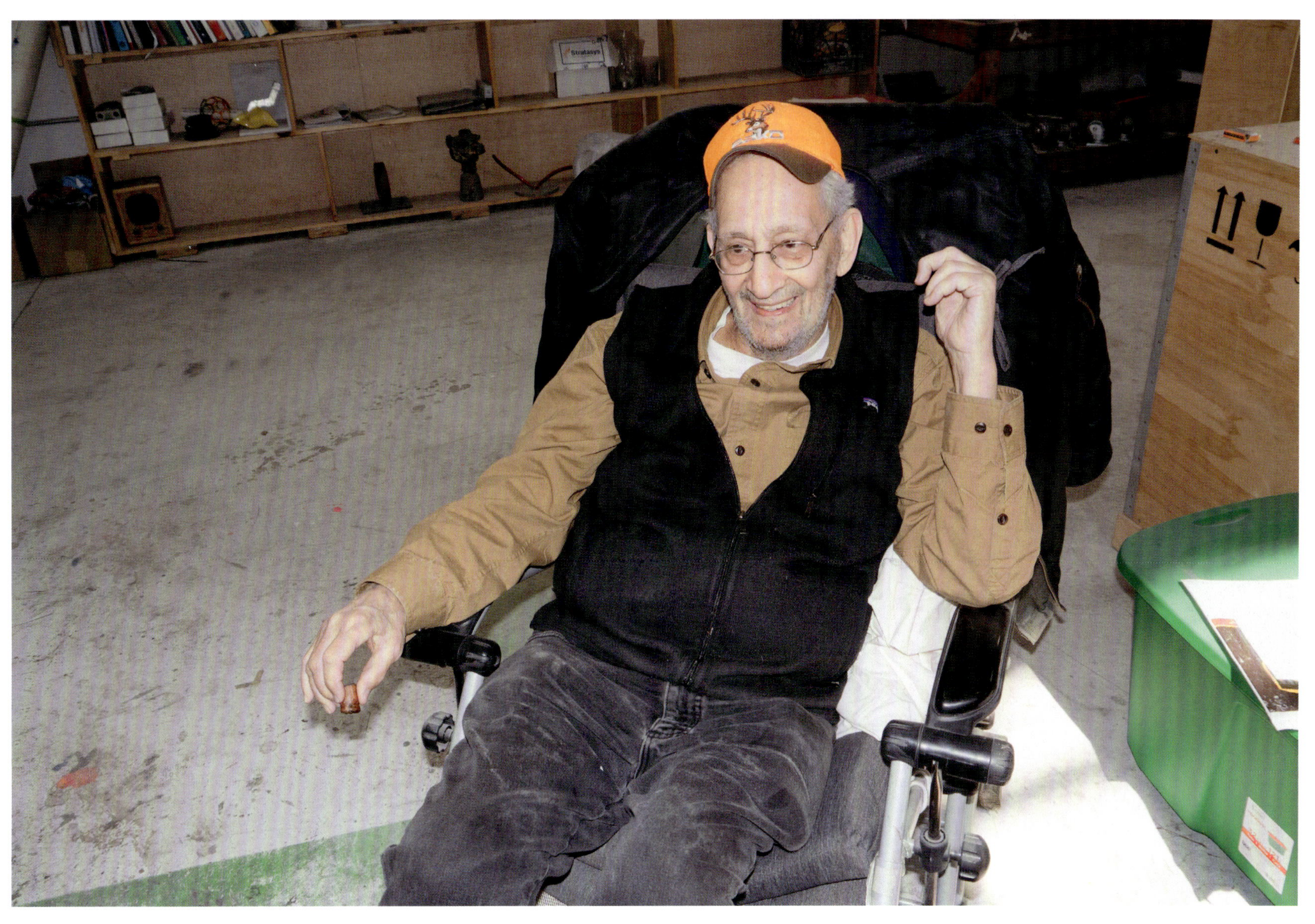

Who are the enemies of
art?
— reproduction
— representation
— recreation

F.S. 10.14.01

Lecture in Havana, 2016

In one sense, you can say that what we have in art now is a more homogenized ethos. From one end of the spectrum to the other, there's a kind of continuity, or almost a kind of amorphism, in which it all seems to be, in a certain sense, not that different.

If we were to look back, say, 100 years, to 1916, what would we see? We'd see a three-part ethos. You'd have Cubism (the Cubism of Picasso and Braque), and you'd have the abstraction from Russia and Germany. You might say that this is the beginning of what will dictate the twentieth century: a push towards abstraction that's not going to be stopped. If you look at 1916, Picasso and Malevich and Kandinsky were dictating the kind of art that was considered the most avant-garde. Yet, in Paris, at the same time, and which you can see now at the Musée de l'Orangerie, are the paintings of Monet. Monet is an old man, but some of the best (or largest) Impressionist masterpieces are being produced at the same time as the most revolutionary and aggressive abstract art.

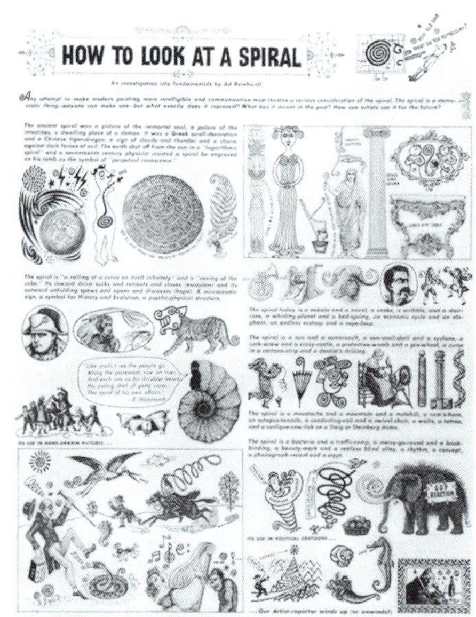

AD REINHARDT
HOW TO LOOK AT A SPIRAL,
1946
COLLAGE, MIXED MEDIA
26 X 33 CM

If you take that for what it's worth, you can stop being too serious about it, and have a look at this cartoon by Ad Reinhardt, *How to Look at a Spiral*. It's from after the war – from 1946. What Ad Reinhardt is doing here is saying something about the art world in which he's functioning, the postwar New York art world, which was a pretty dramatic and powerful art world. It was very serious, especially in that the artists took themselves very seriously. You have to remember that this is a cartoon. It's supposed to be about art; it's supposed to be serious, but it's brutally tongue-in-cheek. It's also worth remembering that his contemporaries didn't like either him or what he had to say, at all. At the top, the cartoon says, 'Any attempt to make modern painting more intelligible and communicative must involve a serious consideration of the spiral. The spiral is a democratic thing – anyone can make one – but what exactly does it represent? What has it meant in the past? How can artists use it for the future?' There you have what, essentially, I'm going to talk about: what art generally is as a problem. It's the past, present and future, and the theme is the spiral.

That's a spiral in a relatively straightforward geometric form.

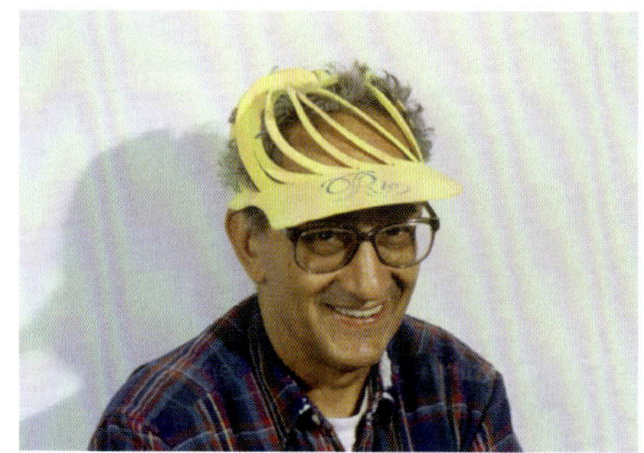

THE ARTIST WEARING A SPIRAL HAT,
NEW YORK, C. 2000

This is also a spiral. You can see where it came from: that's a spiral on your head.

This is what's happening now. This is how, one way or the other, it ends up. This is a way of starting now, and a way to work from now to back to what was, I suppose – the beginning. It's a classic image: if you cut along the line, it can be made into a three-dimensional form.

What you see in these small pieces is the translation of the spiral from a flat plane into three dimensions. I've changed it a bit: I've added a thickness, basically, and it changes it a lot. It becomes a kind of foil, like an air foil, so it's like an airplane wing. Once you change a flat surface into a more complicated curved shape, like the airplane wing, then you have to move that piece through space. Then the geometry becomes too difficult for me. You have a geometry that's asking to do a lot.

If the spiral, a spiral that you've added a thickness to, becomes a quite complicated shape, there are other shapes, or other ways of making things that are, in a certain sense, equally complicated or even more difficult. I'm sure that you can see that

K 304, 2013
ALUMINUM AND STAINLESS STEEL
920 X 1270 X 1170 CM

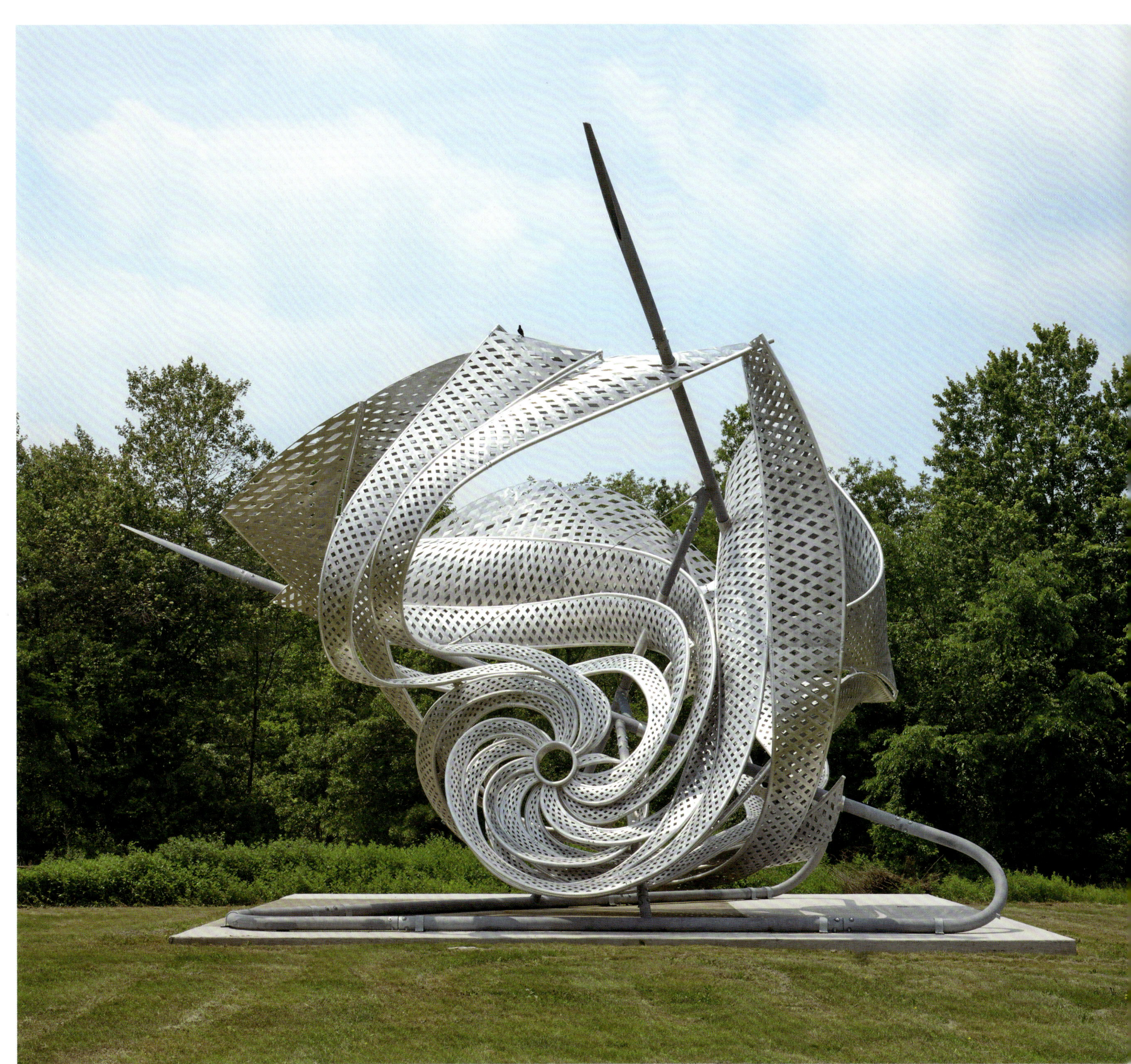

THE ARTIST AND HIS FATHER AT THE ADDISON GALLERY OF AMERICAN ART, ANDOVER, MASSACHUSETTS, C. 1950

BARNETT NEWMAN
TUNDRA, 1950
OIL ON CANVAS
182 X 226 CM

CONSTANCE STELLA
SELF-PORTRAIT, C. 1950
MATERIALS AND DIMENSIONS UNKNOWN

FRANK STELLA
TUNDRA, 1958
OIL ON CANVAS
186 X 252 CM

ROGIER VAN DER WEYDEN
CRUCIFIXION DIPTYCH, C. 1460
OIL ON OAK PANELS
EACH 180 X 94 CM

FRANCISCO DE ZURBARÁN
SAINT BONAVENTURA'S BODY LYING IN STATE, 1629
OIL ON CANVAS
245 X 220 CM

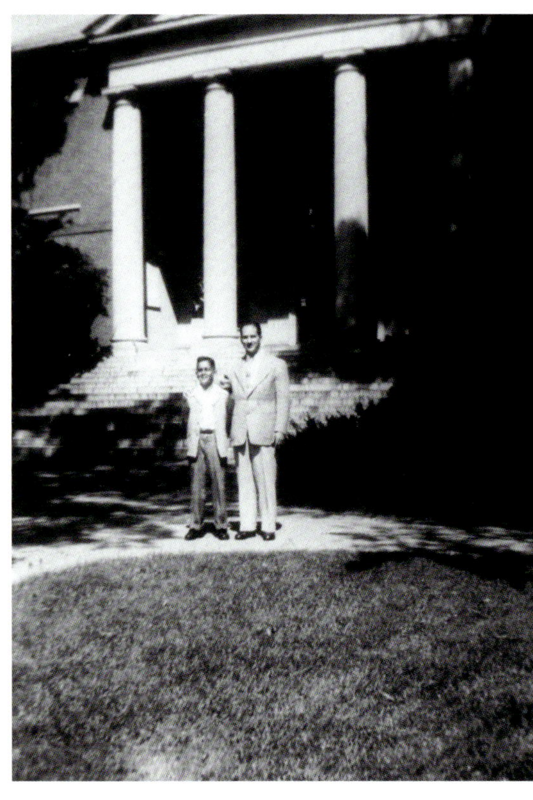

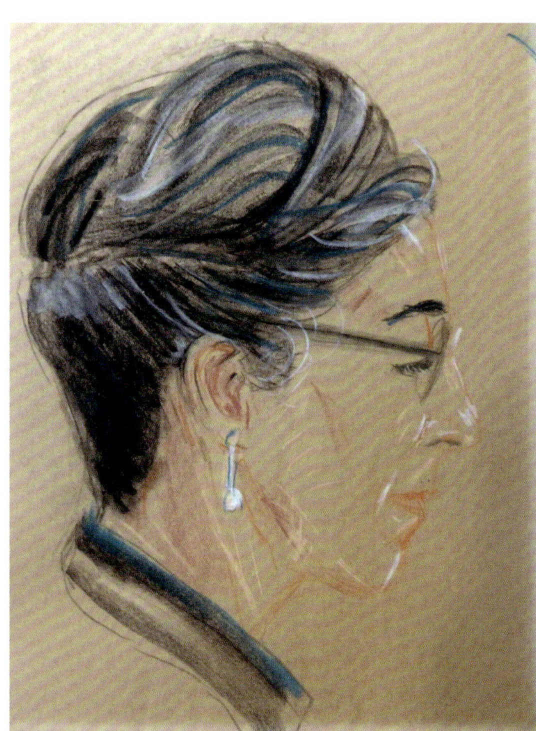

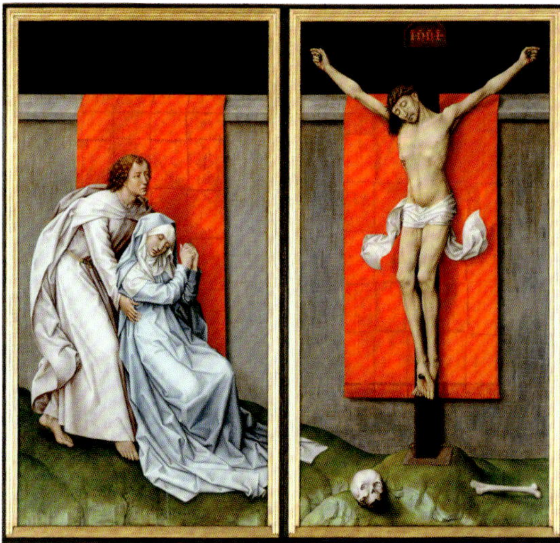

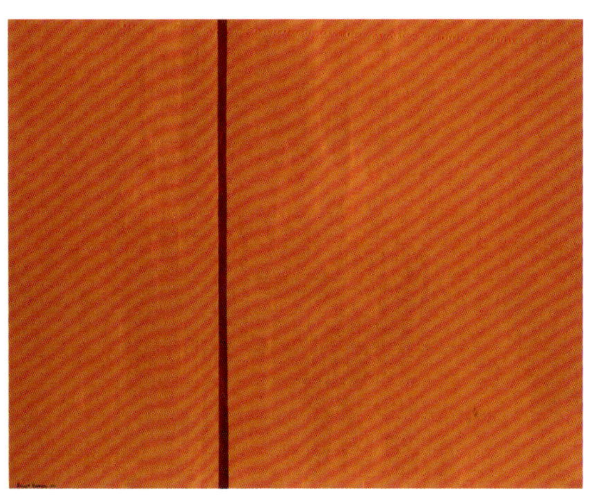

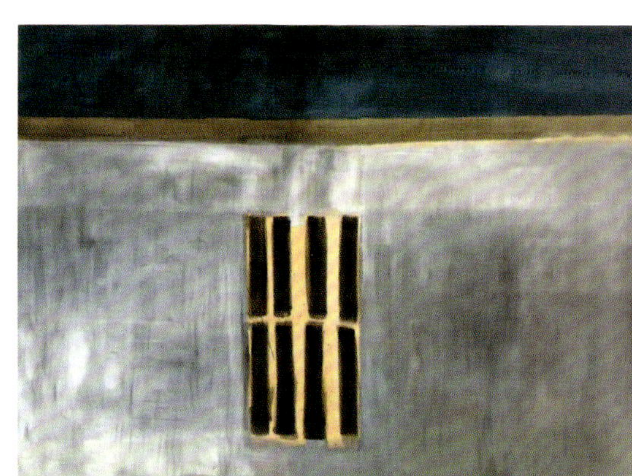

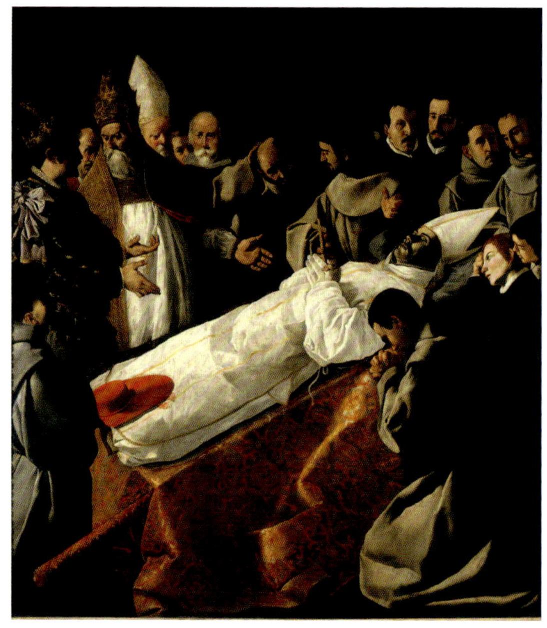

this is smoke; we used Cuban cigars to blow these smoke rings. (That's a joke.) You can make smoke rings yourself, out of your mouth, or you can form a smoke ring by putting smoke in a tube, and hitting the end of it, pushing it out. The fact of the matter is that a smoke ring that comes out of your mouth is far more complicated than the smoke ring that comes out of a tube – that's produced mechanically. What happens with the smoke ring – as it turns, and as it moves through space – it disperses and it bifurcates. There's enough energy in the movement through space to, in effect, produce more smoke rings from one smoke ring.

That's just an example of things that you come across that you have to deal with: the complications of something like smoke, of something like a spiral – these forms. The original spiral, which was a flat painting, was complicated too, in a certain sense. Not so much the geometry, but what was represented. The geometry of the figure is obvious, but what's really there is the path of the gesture. The path of the brush on the canvas follows a spiral gesture.

That's a self-portrait of my mother. Some of the things we talked about, that movement, are available in just about any kind of painting. The hair is flowing down.

I had a father, too. That's both of us in front of the Museum of American Art at the Addison Gallery in Andover, Massachusetts, where I went to school. I'm in front of the building there, but what you can't see is the studio in the basement of the building where I worked. At that school, in that building, the thinking behind the programme was dictated by Josef Albers and Hans Hofmann. In a way, if you're interested in abstraction, you have plenty – you cover all the bases. Between Albers and Hofmann you have geometric art, and then a very painterly art.

This is an example from New York at this time of extreme abstract painting: Barnett Newman's *Tundra*. I made a painting at the same time, while I was in school, which is called *Tundra*. There's a certain kind of similarity, although obviously they're very different. Barnett Newman has a way of making a mark, and the mark is on the surface, but it's from top to bottom. It's a kind of continuity, a kind of gesture. You could call it a strike, but Newman called it a zip. In these pictures, the continuous gesture of going from one side to the other is trying to find a sense of the dimension of the surface that you're working on. A way of thinking about that is to see the difference between my version of *Tundra*, which is a landscape painting, and Barnett Newman's version, which is an image on the *Tundra*. It's one line, and it's one idea, and it's a version of monotheism: the light, what's on the horizon, and what is projected.

At the same time that I was making painting like *Tundra*, I travelled to Philadelphia to see the Arensberg Collection. I was probably wanting to see Marcel Duchamp's *Large Glass*, which I had heard was there, but what I saw was the painting by Rogier van der Weyden. It obviously made a big impression on me, because I'm still talking about it now, and it's quite a few years later. It represented something. If you're making art, or you're interested in making art, this was a goal. In other words, all of a sudden, whether I wanted to be a painter or not, there was something I could reach out to, something that was worth striving for, or a kind of goal.

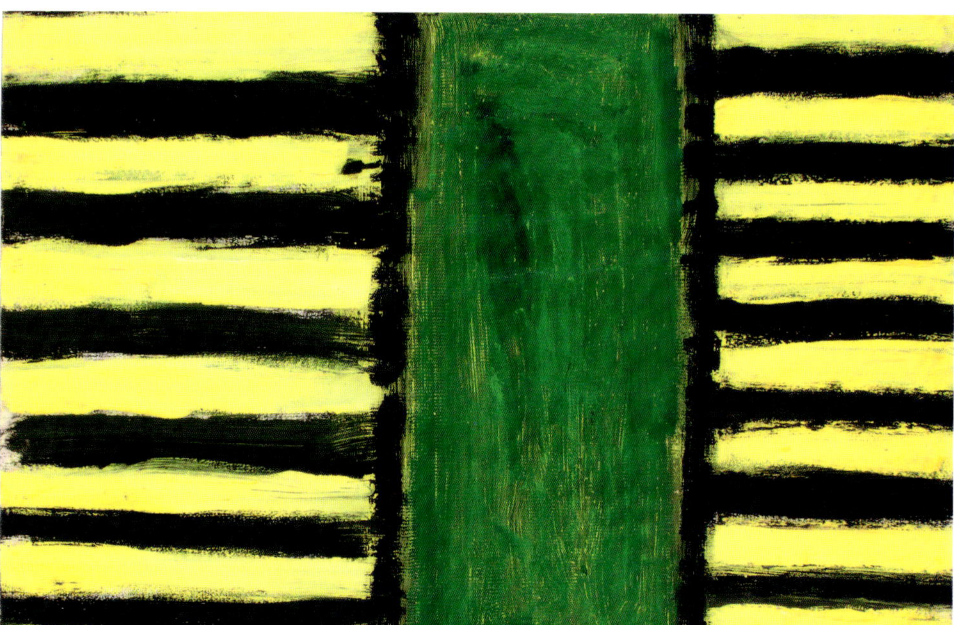

EAST BROADWAY SKETCH, 1958
GOUACHE ON PAPER
34 X 48 CM

In Van der Weyden's *Crucifixion*, I could understand the abstraction that's there, underlying the formalism. It wasn't alien to me. But in *The Deposition*, another painting by Van der Weyden in the Prado, what's happening on the level of composition and complication isn't a sympathetic idea. This is a typical art history problem: it seems that you would go from the *Crucifixion* to the *Deposition*; that would be the normal order. But, of course, the *Crucifixion* came after the *Deposition*. It's not always so easy to find a line of development that's going to make sense, or is even going to be coherent.

This is a relatively recent piece, and in this piece, or in this idea, there's a sense of something that was in the art of the past, particularly medieval art. This would have been a painted relief sculpture. It's like an alter piece.

After I'd seen Van der Weyden's painting in the Prado, I went to Paris and saw *Saint Bonaventura* by Zurbarán. The sum of this painting and Van der Weyden's – it doesn't sound right when I say it, but it's a kind of standard that you're not able to measure yourself against. And since you're not able to measure yourself against it, you can still think about it a lot, and you have a kind of freedom. The easiest way is to hide your excitement and feeling about the piece, and substitute that for a formal understanding of it. You can substitute what you feel about a piece, and what you see in it, with a kind of geometry that, for you, refers back to what you've seen.

In the *Moby Dick* series, specifically in a work called *The Blanket*, what's important is for things to move. They must have a sense of geometry that's arresting, or can be felt.

We started out with the notion of landscape, and the relationship of the landscape to the abstract painting. Willem de Kooning's painting, *Suburb in Havana*, is a very abstract painting, but it's rooted in landscape. My painting, *East Broadway*, which I made in 1958, is a landscape painting, too, but I think it's important to say it's an urban landscape painting. That represents a change, or a way of thinking about both landscape painting and abstraction. A couple of years later, in 1961, I painted *Palmito Ranch*. It's another landscape painting, but it's abstract. This was, for me, the end of the line. It's what was by then known as Minimalism, and for me, it was the end. The painting was quite successful (at least I see it that way), but it was too tight. It's as though the geometry had run dry.

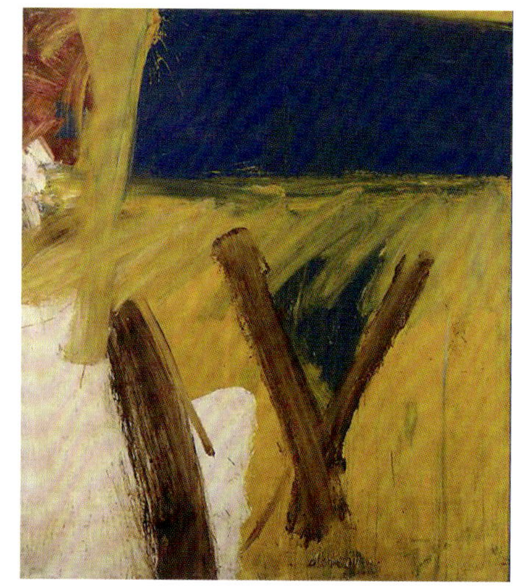

WILLEM DE KOONING
SUBURB IN HAVANA, 1958
OIL ON CANVAS
203 X 178 CM

THE BLANKET (IRS-8,I 875X),
1988
MIXED MEDIA ON CAST
MAGNESIUM AND ALUMINIUM
300 X 580 X 120 CM

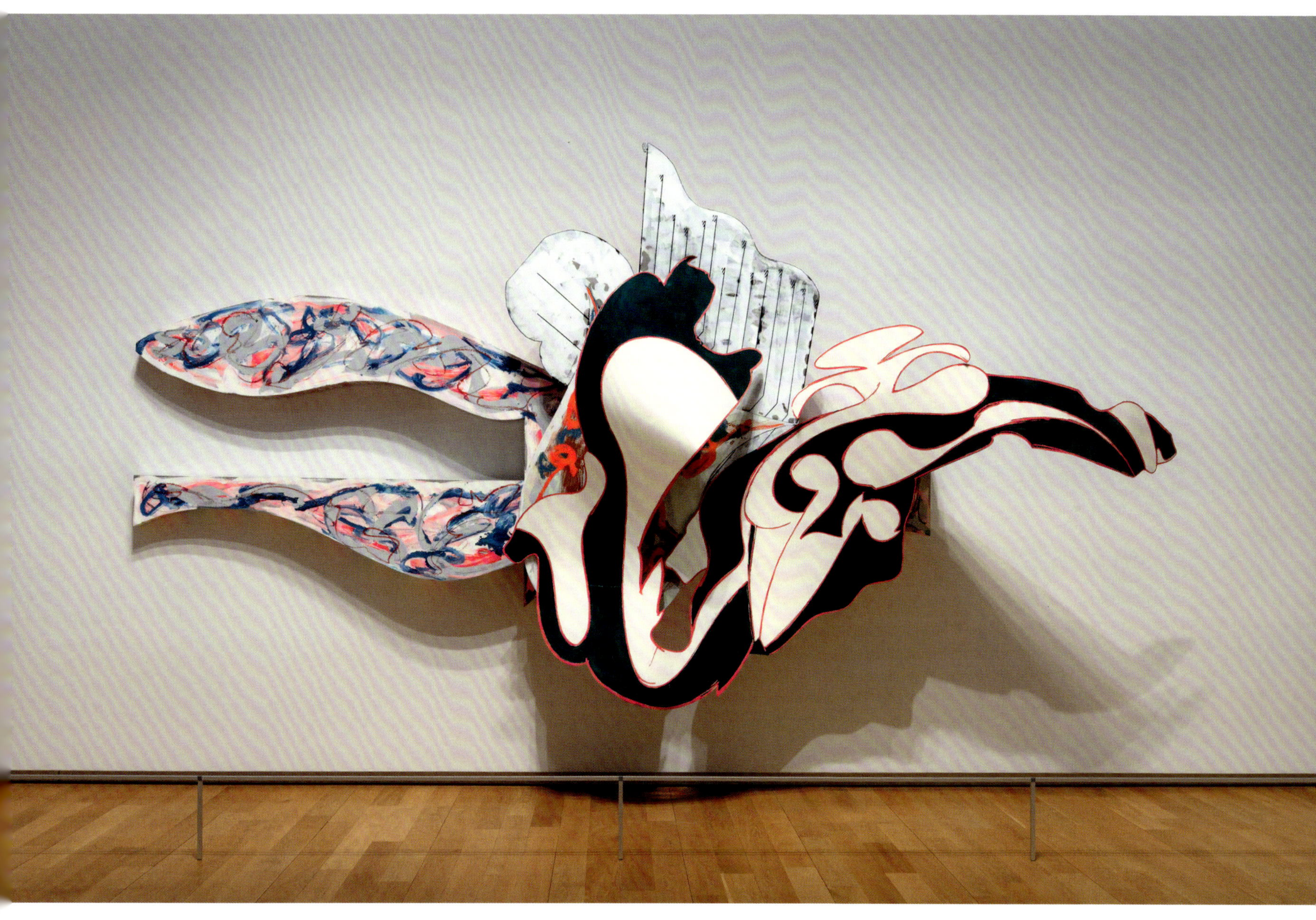

PALMITO RANCH, 1961
ACRYLIC ON CANVAS
196 X 196 CM

LOOMINGS (S-73X–1ST VERSION), 1986
INK AND OIL PAINT ON ETCHED MAGNESIUM AND ALUMINIUM
360 X 410 X 110 CM

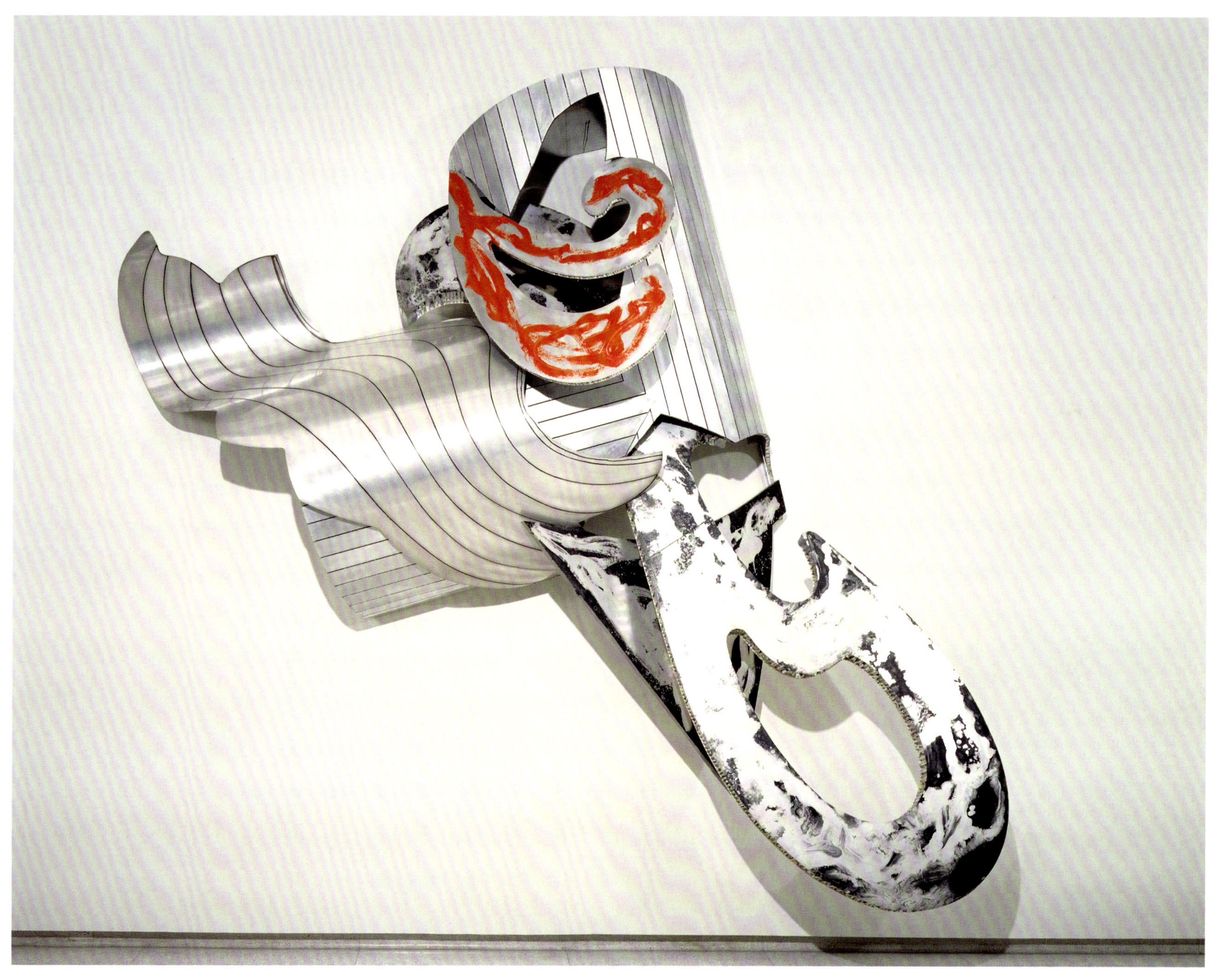

In the *Moby Dick* series, one of the issues is, of course, that it's busier, but it's no longer flat. Surfaces are moving. You can see that it's inevitable that things get more complicated, and somehow seem to tie themselves into knots. Whatever happens, it always goes one way, and then the other. In *Loomings*, you can see the attempt to find a way for the surfaces to flow at the same time, without excessive complication. You might say it's one wave, instead of a lot of waves. The development of movement becomes the central question, but now it's not so much painting, or even my idea of the painting of the spiral's path. Instead, it becomes something about building, about construction.

With the *Moby Dick* pieces you could see the waves; you could see the story actually taking place over the water. In the *Bali Series*, you have an idea of another way of seeing the water, and seeing the things that happen on the water. That's pretty much red sails in the sunset.

Memorias póstumas de Brás Cubas is a novel by a Brazilian writer, Machado de Assis. It's the posthumous story of Brás Cubas, and it's interesting that the two covers are so different. It's relevant here in the sense that a lot depends on how you look at things, or how you look at yourself. This is seeing it from the posthumous point of view. You're looking backwards on what you've done. It's also interesting that Machado introduces a notion of modesty, even if it's a very dramatic story. I think it's relevant because if you look at art making, and you look at yourself, you're a small part of the enterprise of making art in your time. That's still quite large compared to how small a part you are in the evolution of the visual culture.

I introduce Malevich here just to go back to Brazil. This is a painting from a series I did about neighbourhoods in Rio de Janeiro. If you have a little bit of the image of the Malevich still with you, you can see that the connection is kind of obvious.

This is what was very popularly known as Minimalism. These are Minimal paintings with a problem. If you took any more away from either one of these shapes, or their relationship, or what's in these paintings, you'd be left with something that probably wouldn't read as a painting. There's one other thing here: a relationship between the two paintings, although they are, in one sense, the same painting. The way they relate to each other on the wall is important. It represents a possibility for allowing the paintings to make a gesture. The two paintings being near each other make a gesture that you could imagine as being a whole. They could be two parts of a whole painting. It's far fetched, but the way the copper paintings work is something like Guido Reni's *Atalanta e Ippomene*. They each represent the man and the woman, and together they represent their relationship over an imagined pictorial surface. There was also in that painting another kind of relationship, besides the two figures. There was the material of the cloth around them. The action of the drapery is similar to the action in this sculpture. The two main pieces are solid, but derived from imagery of smoke. The notion is that the smoke moves in a kind of diaphanous way. This is a drawing of the imagery that was in the sculpture. That's a version of what the smoke, or the sculpture, the three-dimensional piece, is supposed to be doing.

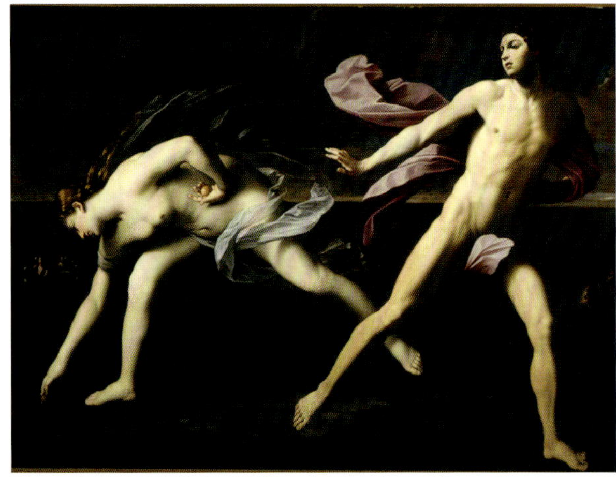

GUIDO RENI
ATLANTA E IPPOMENE, 1620–29
OIL ON CANVAS
191 X 264 CM

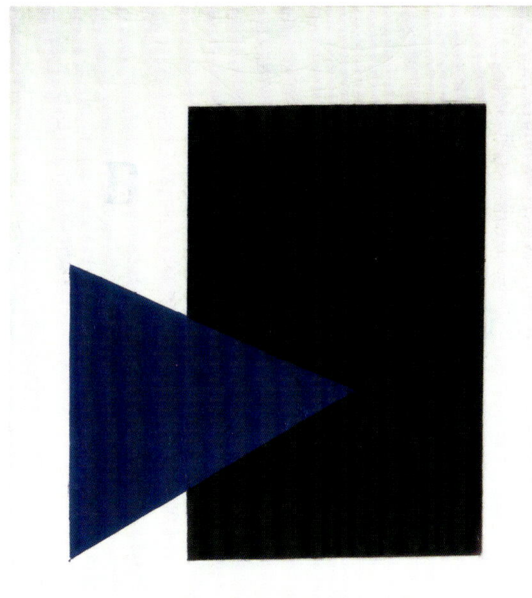

KAZIMIR MALEVICH
SUPREMATISM WITH BLUE TRIANGLE AND BLACK SQUARE,
1915
OIL ON CANVAS
67 X 58 CM

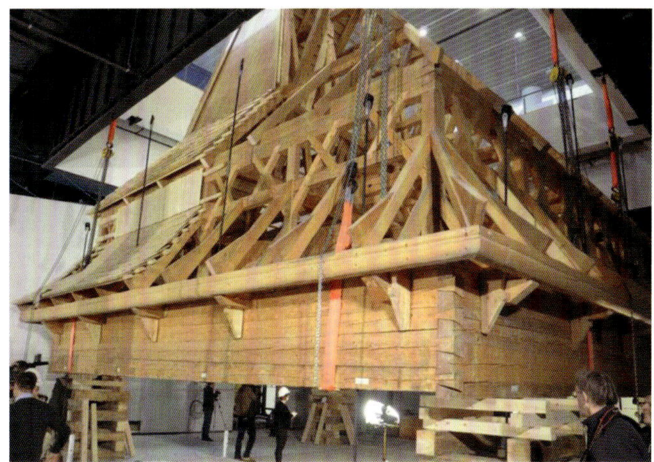

RECONSTRUCTED TIMBER ROOF TRUSS OF A SYNAGOGUE AT THE MUSEUM OF THE HISTORY OF POLISH JEWS, WARSAW, 2016

This is a Malevich painting, and you can see that this is an early painting. It's pretty important in the sense that it's really about what abstract geometry can do. Malevich said – I'd almost say he claimed – that the advantage of abstraction was that it was the expression of pure feeling. That would mean that the blue triangle is more powerful than a blue triangle. A blue triangle, how anyone would express it, has a feeling. The feelings are enlarged, or made more present by its relationship to the black rectangle. It seems now to be a very conventional kind of geometry.

This geometry has lasted a long time, but it represents a kind of problem, which is that the blue triangle, and it's relationship to the black rectangle, is one of simply being present, overlaid, so they're one on top of each other. Another way of looking at the same problem, which is straightforward geometry, a triangle and a rectangle, is to see if they can do something more than relate to each other as one on top of each other. In this case, the triangle is penetrating the green rectangle. The result is, it's not really overlaid – they exist in the same plane – yet it becomes a situation that we would call spring-loaded. There's the possibility that the rectangle could expel the triangle. There's a kind of tension between the two elements that's a different way of putting the geometry together, rather than laying it one on top of each other, so that they're simply measurable. It's implying that there's a force there.

This is another version of dealing with geometry in that way, in which there's a rectangle sitting on another rectangle, and they have a relationship, a kind of tension, and a sense of force. This is another example of the same kind of thinking, and it produces again, the kind of geometry that's not so obvious in what it allows you to do. It's not so obvious in terms of what we call compositional balance, because it is, in a certain sense, almost a kind of pirouette. It does get close to sculpture.

This is in Warsaw, and it's a reconstruction of a Polish synagogue, probably from the seventeenth century. These synagogues were destroyed during the war, and there were two things interesting about them. One was that there was a kind of geometry in the construction, the wooden construction, which I would call interlocking-ness:

CHODROW II, 1971
FELT, PAPER, AND CANVAS
275 X 270 CM

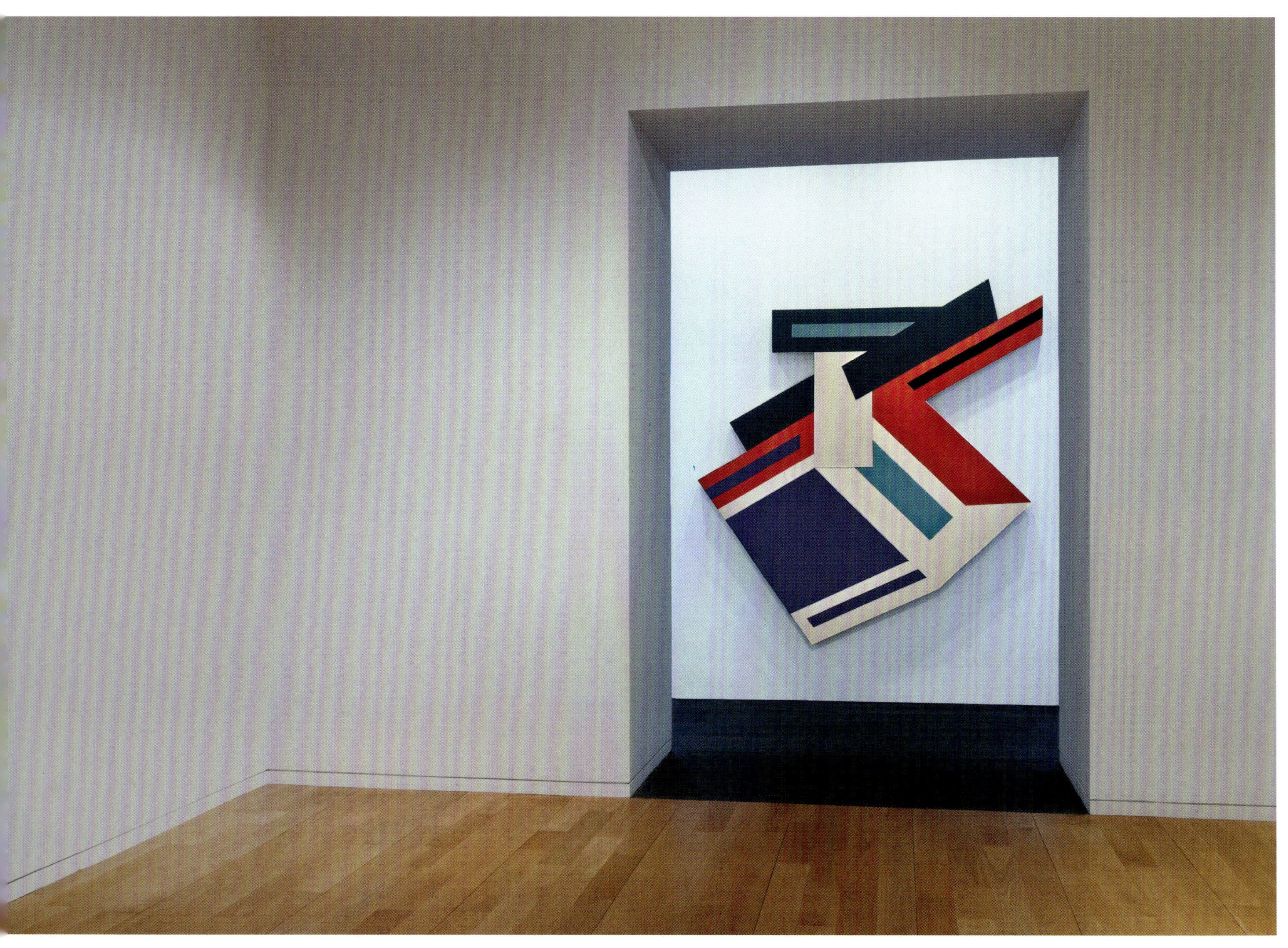

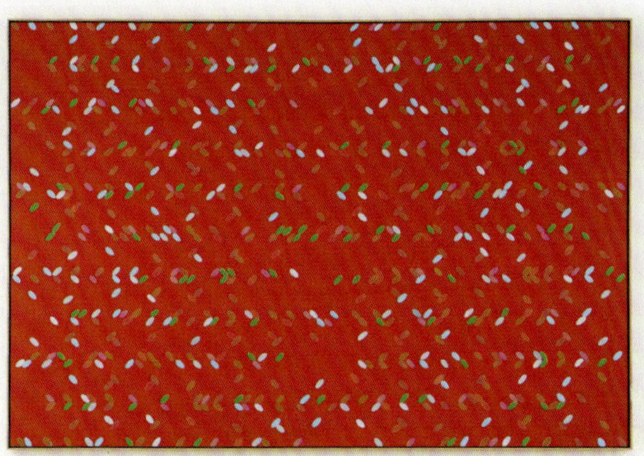

LARRY POONS
LITTLE SANGRE DE CHRISTO,
1964
ACRYLIC ON CANVAS
242 X 343 CM

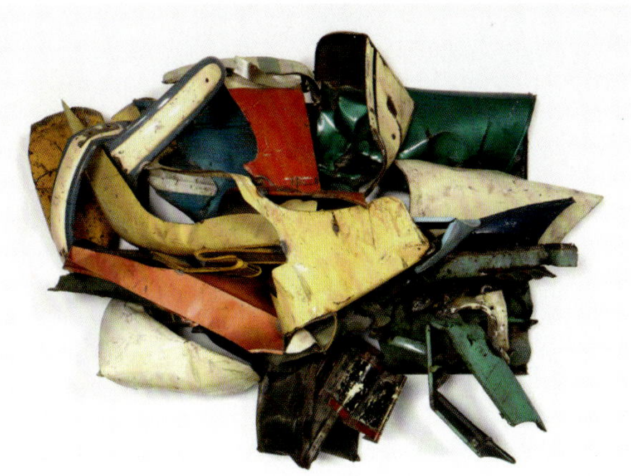

JOHN CHAMBERLAIN
DOLORES JAMES, 1962
WELDED AND PAINTED STEEL
184 X 258 X 118 CM

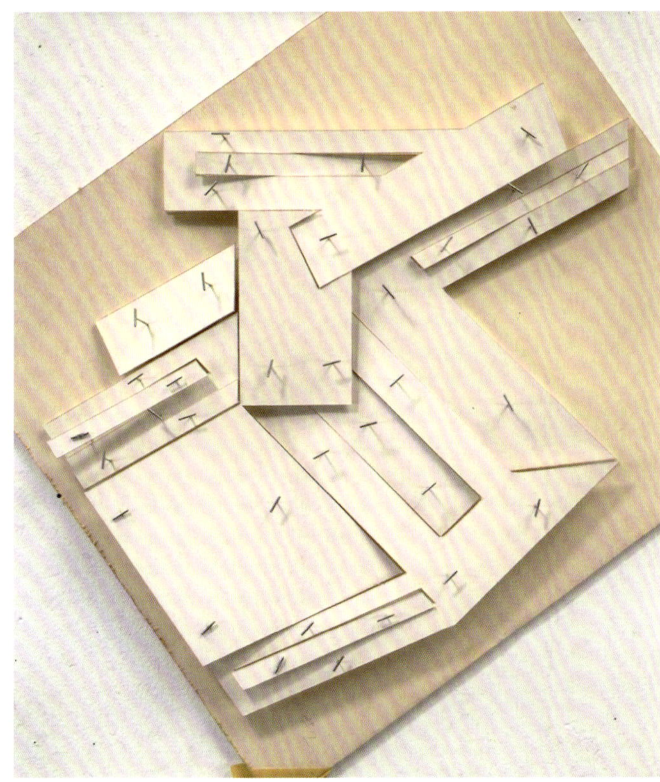

MAQUETTE FOR CHODOROW,
1971–74
BRISTOL BOARD
47 X 45 CM

interlocking parts that are interesting as a kind of geometry. The other thing that was compelling was that the trace of the destruction of these synagogues was from Berlin to Warsaw to Moscow. The development of abstraction in the twentieth century traces that same path, from Moscow to Warsaw to Berlin and back.

This is a paper model. You can see that there's a geometry there that's a little different from the geometry preceding it. It's a more complicated geometry, but in a certain sense, it's a more traditional geometry. This geometry is clearly owing to Russian Constructivism. That's the painted version of *Chodorow. Kamionka Strumilowa* is another Polish synagogue piece, and this is clearly about the geometry of the parts, and their relationship in regard to surface, as they come out and change, as they project themselves, or recess.

This is a drawing by the artist Larry Poons. This is in some ways typical of what was going on in New York in 1960. That's the geometry that you saw: you saw the pattern, you saw the way it went, and this is how it expressed itself as a painting.

This is John Chamberlain, and this is probably from the early 1960s too. I bring this up because I like John a lot, but mostly because that's the kind of thing that eventually happens to my way of working.

That's a recent sculpture from this year. That's at the Whitney Museum, and that's the Hudson River in the background. That would be a work from 2015.

Those are two works in the Whitney Museum. They're from 1960. That's the *Marriage of Reason and Squalor*, and that's the end, or the beginning, depending on how you want to see it. Thank you for your patience.

WOODEN STAR I, 2004
WOOD
399 X 399 X 399 CM

INSTALLATION VIEW AT
THE WHITNEY MUSEUM
OF AMERICAN ART,
NEW YORK, 2015

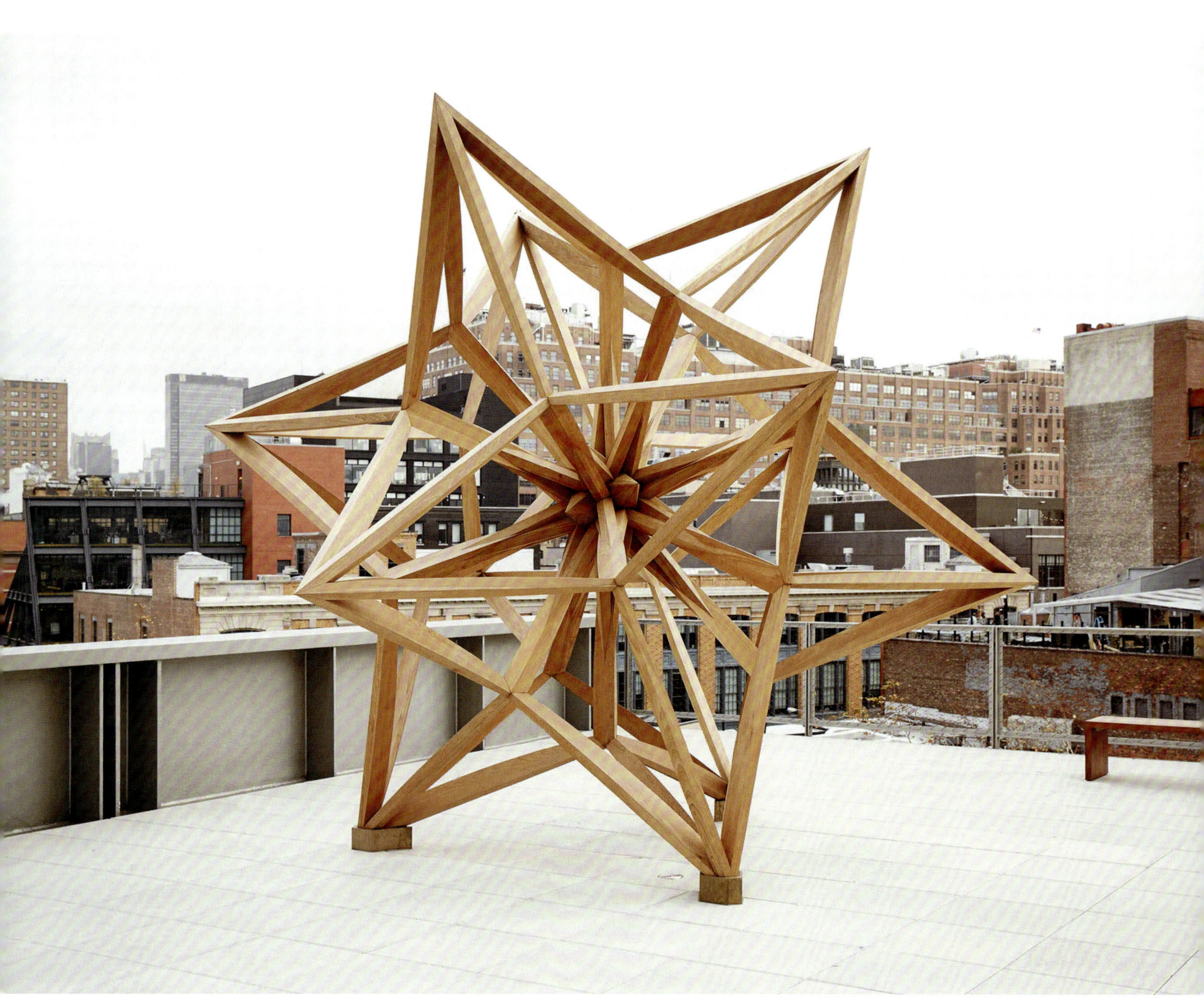

THE MARRIAGE OF REASON AND SQUALOR II, 1959
ENAMEL ON CANVAS
231 X 337 CM

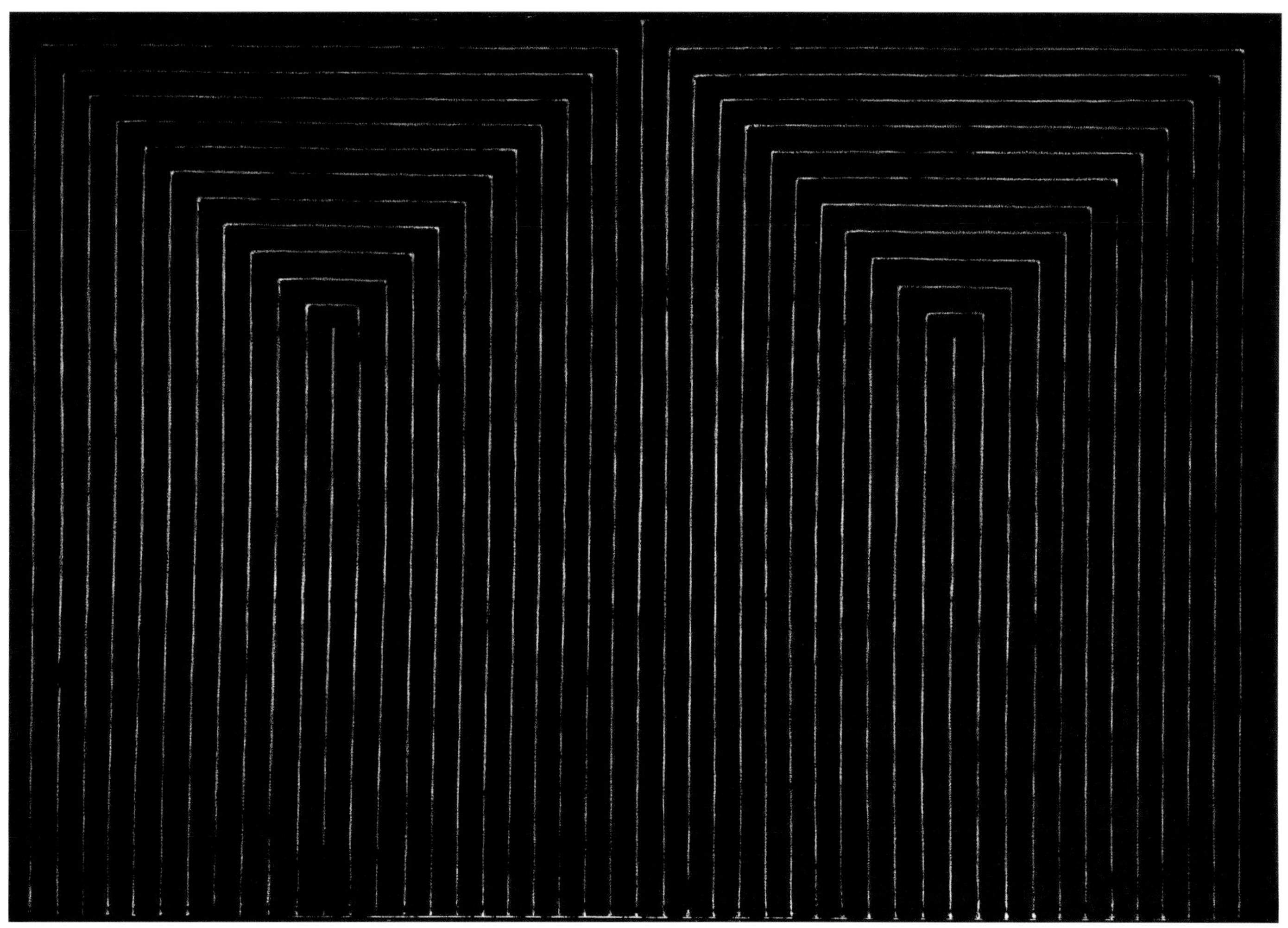

NOTES

SURVEY PAGES 035–089

1 In his review of the artist's 2015 retrospective at the Whitney Museum of American Art Thomas Crow offered up, as both diagnosis and thought experiment, the identification of one 'un-Stella' after another; if only we could free Stella from the presumptions of singularity or cohesion, we might find ourselves able to locate relevant contexts for his diverse bodies of work. See Crow, 'Frank Stella', *Artforum*, February 2016, pp. 224–25.

2 This phrase, 'the sculpture threshold', appears both in the headline and the body of Michael Kimmelman's review of a 1992 exhibition at M. Knoedler & Company, New York; see Kimmelman, 'Frank Stella Crosses the Sculpture Threshold', *The New York Times*, 16 October 1992. The exhibition itself was called 'Frank Stella: New Work. Projects and Sculpture'. For what it's worth, all three of Stella's exhibitions since 2014, upon joining Marianne Boesky Gallery, have shown new work billed more or less explicitly as sculpture as well.

3 This show was 'Frank Stella: New Work: Projects and Sculpture', at M. Knoedler & Company, New York, 10 October–11 November 1992.

4 See, for instance, the extended catalogue essay for the first exhibition to formalize 'assemblage' as an art-historical category, William C. Seitz's *The Art of Assemblage*, Museum of Modern Art, New York, 1961.

5 My language here echoes that of art historian and critic Rosalind Krauss, whose writing in the 1970s remains essential to histories of modern and contemporary sculpture today. For her assessment of the 'logic of the monument' and sculpture's subsequent nomadic state, see Krauss, 'Sculpture in the Expanded Field', *October*, no. 8, Spring 1979, especially pp. 33–34. In light of my own emphasis in these opening pages on words like threshold and transit, I must mention Krauss's landmark book *Passages in Modern Sculpture* as well (MIT Press, Cambridge, Massachusetts, 1977–1981).

6 These debates are typically referred to as the paragone, which means 'comparison' in Italian, and included architecture and sometimes drawing as competitors as well. In 1547 Benedetto Varchi surveyed seven artists on their respective positions, among them Benvenuto Cellini, Michelangelo, and Giorgio Vasari. Cellini (as well as Michelangelo) sided with sculpture, calling painting 'nothing more than the reflection in a fountain of a tree, a man or some other thing. The difference between painting and sculpture is immense; it is like the difference between a shadow and the thing that cast it'. More often than not, however, painting dominated – proponents like Leonardo da Vinci appraising sculpture as primarily mechanical, the product of workmanship, rather than as primarily intellectual. For Cellini's quotation, and for a comprehensive account of the paragone, see Jacqueline Lichtenstein, *The Blind Spot: An Essay on the Relations between Painting and Sculpture in the Modern Age*, Getty Research Institute, Los Angeles, 2008, p. 4. As it happens, across the seventeenth century the paragone gradually gave way to the querelle ('quarrel' in French), which pitched line against color, though the former persisted as sculptural and the latter as painterly.

7 William S. Rubin, *Frank Stella 1970–1987*, Museum of Modern Art, New York, 1987, p. 8.

8 The film is thirteen minutes long, made with cinematographer Sacha Vierny and its voiceover narration voiced by actor Pierre Dux and written (entirely in the rhyming, metrical form of the alexandrine) by novelist Raymond Queneau. For an analysis of the documentary that considers the very materiality of the celluloid of film itself, see Edward Dimendberg, 'These Are Not Exercises in Style": Le Chant du Styrène', *October*, no. 112, Spring 2005, pp. 63–88.

9 'I guess it's not very surprising, but it took me quite a while to notice it (as it did to notice the rooted-out plywood boards of the "Circuits" Series) – that working with sculpture in a painterly way would yield a powerful printing tool. Surely, though, it is surprising that the tool, poured molten aluminum, made such a perfect frozen gesture. Used as a printed device, poured metal had a nice relationship to the painting of the past I so admired. It was easy to see the hardened metal and its printed traces as an appropriate way of working parallel to that of the abstract expressionist masters.... With its link to the immediate past, and its own inherent power, poured metal used as a printed device has helped confound my impression of the difference between real motion and depicted motion, to the point that I no longer worry about the distinction.... The poured metal is an advance because it does more than the touché splash, applied to stone, aluminum, or silkscreen, can do. The poured metal gets closer to the heart of printing by pressing the relief version of its image, just as the ink outlines the surface impression of its image into the paper. The image made by the poured metal simply yields a stronger and deeper impression, showing that poured metal plates are better than conventional plates at doing what printing does best, creating a stamped-out image'. See Frank Stella, 'Melrose Avenue' (1999), reprinted in Franz-Joachim Verspohl (ed.), with Ulrich Müller and Reinhard Wegner, *The Writings of Frank Stella*, Walther König, Cologne, 2001), p. 215. In 'Melrose Avenue', first delivered as a lecture at Keio University in Fukushima, Japan, Stella wrote at length about experimental techniques and unexpected recognitions as key to his work in printmaking in particular – as well as about the bearing such discoveries have had on his work in other mediums, and vice versa. Indeed, while my emphasis in this essay will remain on painting and sculpture, questions of medium boundaries, and of the porousness of such boundaries, apply to Stella's work in printmaking and architecture as well.

10 I am grateful to Lisa Lee for her own deep work on plastics and plasticity, as well as for her specific conversations with me on the topic in recent weeks. See, for example, her chapter 'Plastic Allegories' in Lisa Lee, *Isa Genzken: Sculpture as World Receiver*, University of Chicago Press, Chicago, 2017.

11 See Roland Barthes, 'Plastic', reprinted in Penny Sparke (ed.), *The Plastics Age: From Modernity to Post-Modernity*, Victoria and Albert Museum, London, 1990, p. 110. See also Lee, *Isa Genzken*, p. 101.

12 Caveats abound, to be sure: Casting, while an ancient process, is a technology, too.

13 In closing his 1999 talk on printmaking, Stella indicates that *The Fountain* isn't only culminatory, however, but must itself be pushed farther still: 'we have to imagine adding to *The Fountain*' ('Melrose Avenue', p. 223).

14 Stella, in 'Questions to Stella and Judd: Interview by Bruce Glaser, Edited by Lucy Lippard', in Gregory Battcock (ed.), *Minimal Art: A Critical Anthology*, University of California Press, Berkeley, 1968–1995, p. 158; the interview was broadcast on WBAI-FM, New York, in February 1964 under the title 'New Nihilism or New Art?' and was conducted by Glaser with Stella, Judd, and Dan Flavin. The edited transcript, published by Lippard in *ARTNews* in September 1966, removed Flavin's contributions, apparently at the artist's request.

15 The term 'presentness' here is lifted from Michael Fried's polemical 1967 essay 'Art and Objecthood'('I want to claim', for instance, 'that it is by virtue of their presentness and instantaneousness that modernist painting and sculpture defeat' the 'theatre' and 'presence' of literalist art and the encounters it generated.); the term 'literalism', itself, was Fried's name for (and charge against) minimal art. See Fried, 'Art and Objecthood', *Artforum*, Summer 1967, which in fact appeared in an issue devoted to 'American Sculpture'.

16 Fried, 'An Introduction to My Criticism', in *Art and Objecthood: Essays and Reviews*, University of Chicago Press, Chicago, 1998, note 67, p. 71. He waged such a battle with, for example, minimalist sculptor Carl Andre, who wrote the first published text on Stella's 'Black Paintings' (see 'Preface to Stripe Painting', *Sixteen Americans*, Museum of Modern Art, New York, 1959) and has frequently cited the significance of the series for his own work. Stella was close to both Fried and Andre during these years. James Meyer provides a nuanced assessment of any such battle through the lens of an exhibition Stella co-curated at the time called 'Shape and Structure' (1965); see Meyer, 'Shape and Structure: 1965: The battle for Stella's "soul"', in *Minimalism: Art and Polemics in the Sixties*, Yale University Press, New Haven, 2004.

17 In his 1964 radio interview Stella refers to the extreme Greenberg, too, reached: 'Clement Greenberg talked about the ideas or possibilities of painting in, I think, the After Abstract Expressionism article [1962], and he allows a blank canvas to be an idea for a painting. It might not be a good idea, but it's certainly valid'; see Stella, 'Questions to Stella and Judd', p. 161. For Fried's point see Fried, *Art and Objecthood*, p. 36.

18 This trajectory, starting from the 'Black Paintings', leaves out Stella's earlier work, of course, for which see the excellent catalogue Frank Stella 1958 by Harry Cooper and Megan R. Luke. Luke's essay, in fact, proceeds backwards, chronologically speaking, in order to avoid the otherwise unavoidable sense of teleology. See Luke, 'Objecting to Things', *Frank Stella 1958*, Fogg Art Museum, Cambridge, Massachusetts, 2006.

19 Elizabeth C. Baker, 'Frank Stella Perspectives', *ARTnews*, May 1970, republished online at http://www.artnews.com/2015/10/30/his-ability-to-change-has-been-amazing-a-review-of-momas-frank-stella-survey-from-1970/ (accessed 23 May 2017).

20 Stella, 'Text of a Lecture at the Pratt Institute' (Winter 1959–60), in *The Writings of Frank Stella*, op. cit., p. 9.

21 For his indication of 'less illusionism', see Stella, 'Questions to Stella and Judd', p. 149; and for his explanation of the 'element of fantasy' see the transcript of a 1966 radio interview for KPFA, Berkeley, California, between Henry Geldzahler, Larry Poons, Roy Lichtenstein and Stella, quoted in Harry Cooper, 'What You See and What He Said', *Frank Stella 1958*, p. 74. Indeed, Cooper's essay provides a careful reading of optical effects in Stella's earliest work, as well as of such shifts in his articulation of or around them (especially pp. 73–79).

22 Meyer, *Minimalism: Art and Polemics*, p. 121. Also in that year, Stella was included in the Museum of Modern Art's first show of Op, or optical, art, *The Responsive Eye*, curated by William C. Seitz.
23 See Lucy R. Lippard, 'Perverse Perspectives', *Art International*, no. 11, March 1967, reprinted in Lucy R. Lippard, *Changing: Essays on Art*, E.P. Dutton, New York, 1971, pp. 168–69.
24 As Judd explained – what Stella offered has one 'near' exception: 'Almost all paintings are spatial in one way or another. Yves Klein's blue paintings are the only ones that are unspatial, and there is little that is nearly unspatial, mainly Stella's work. It's possible that not much can be done with both an upright rectangular plane and an absence of space. Anything on a surface has space behind it. Two colors on the same surface almost always lie on different depths'. See Donald Judd, 'Specific Objects', *Arts Yearbook*, no. 8, 1965, reprinted in Judd, *Complete Writings 1959–1975*, Press of the Nova Scotia College of Art and Design, Halifax, and New York University Press, New York, 1975, p. 182.
25 Almost right away, some critics began to insist on the buried or inescapable illusionism in Judd's emphatically three-dimensional work, too – earliest and most notably artist Robert Smithson and art historian Rosalind Krauss, for instance. Judd's materials – polished metals, colored Plexiglas, and often the negative space of wall or room between his serially arrayed box forms – convened disorienting perceptual effects that threw sculptural solidity and material facticity into question. As James Meyer summarizes, 'Both Smithson and Krauss suggest that they were drawn to Judd's work because it was not easily seen, was not so 'specific' as Judd claimed. A good Judd gave a lot to look at. It was not at all minimal, as Judd's detractors asserted but, on the contrary, visually complex…. Although Smithson and Krauss were the first to note these contradictions, the illusionistic quality of Judd's work, and the tension between his theory and his practice this implied, became a topos of the Judd literature' (Meyer, *Minimalism: Art and Polemics*, p. 138). For an interesting analysis of both Judd's and Krauss's various claims and positions in this regard, see David Raskin, 'The Shiny Illusionism of Krauss and Judd', *Art Journal*, no. 1, 2006, pp. 6–21.
26 See Krauss, 'Sculpture in the Expanded Field', published in 1979 (full citation in endnote 5). In his review of Stella's 2015 retrospective at the Whitney Museum, Jerry Saltz proffers the phrase 'expanded field of painting' (Saltz, 'Toward a Unified Theory of Frank Stella', *New York Magazine*, Vulture.com (15 October 2015), http://www.vulture.com/2015/10/toward-a-unified-theory-of-frank-stella.html.
27 Stella, quoted in Rubin, *Frank Stella*, 1970, p. 68.
28 Stella in interview with Juliet Steyn, 'Frank Stella Talks about His Recent Work', *Art Monthly*, May 1977, p. 13.
29 Stella, quoted in Rubin, *Frank Stella 1970–1987*, p. 77.
30 Alina Payne, 'On sculptural relief: Malerisch, the autonomy of artistic media and the beginnings of Baroque studies', in Helen Hills (ed.), *Rethinking the Baroque*, Ashgate, Farnham, England, 2011, p. 57.
31 Ibid, p. 59. (This phrase is Heinrich Wölfflin's, from a review of Hildebrand's book in year of its publication.)
32 As Payne continues, 'For him sculpture had evolved from drawing (the relief being its three-dimensional impression into stone); even free-standing sculpture was tributary to the picture plane, according to him, since in its origin it derived from the sculptural ensembles set up against the pediment wall of the Greek temple' (Ibid.). For a good historical summary of Hildebrand's writing and of shifting responses to it – he was, for instance, later taken 'sternly to task for his painterly notion that a free-standing sculpture should be structured formally like a bas-relief', such a conception of sculpture deemed 'excessively pictorial' – see Alex Potts, *The Sculptural Imagination: Figurative, Modernist, Minimalist*, Yale University Press, New Haven and London, 2000, pp. 124–131.
33 These texts were specifically prepared as the Charles Eliot Norton Lectures at Harvard (1983–84). For quotations see, Stella, Working Space (Harvard University Press, Cambridge, 1986)), pp. 12, 17, 22.
34 Stella, *Working Space*, p. 19.
35 Ibid, p. 35.
36 Michael Auping has estimated the works from this series as closer to 2.8 or 2.9 on Stella's relief scale. Auping, 'The Phenomenology of Frank: "Materiality and Gesture Make Space"', in Auping (ed.), *Frank Stella: A Retrospective*, Yale University Press, New Haven, Connecticut; Whitney Museum of American Art, New York; and Modern Art Museum of Fort Worth, 2015, p. 32.
37 Stella, 'Grimm's Ecstasy', in *The Writings of Frank Stella*, p. 157.
38 For 'pigmented objects', see Ibid., pp. 159 and 167; for 'habitable illusion', see 165; for the long quotation about 'normal vision', see p. 167. Stella proceeds to clarify: 'Normal vision actually has a greater knack than we give it credit for in terms of handling sensations of what might be called multidimensional space… We see a lot at a time without worrying about it. Only when we get wound up trying to translate normal vision into artistic vision do we seem to get into trouble. We get tangled up trying to frame what we see and confused trying to fit it into the boxes marked X, Y, and Z'.
39 Ibid., p. 169.
40 Ibid., p. 171.
41 Ibid., p. 183
42 Ibid.
43 Stella, quoted in Auping, 'The Phenomenology of Frank', p. 36.
44 Ibid.
45 It is worth quoting Stella at length on these discoveries, not least for his emphasis on 'endless variation', which will return to us later in this essay: In California in 1975 Stella came across a set of ship curves, used for nautical design, and bought them on a whim. Numbering nearly a hundred, 'There were many more templates than I could ever possibly use, because the size gradations were so tiny – you could get what seemed like thirty different versions of one shape. But I liked the repetitious quality, the endless variations. Later I purchased sets of railroad curves'. He described his process of deploying these templates as well: One 'important aspect of using the templates was that they permitted me to effect my own version of coming free on the surface. I was now free to do easily what most people did the hard way. I could make so-called relational paintings or, rather, the structural schemas for such paintings, just by sliding the templates around the surface. No need to erase, paint out, or redo. Only when I had the composition the way I wanted was it transferred to the graph paper – directly into a mechanically drawing – and then into a three-dimensional Foamcore maquette, where I turned the template forms at angles to the picture surface'. All quotations Stella, in Rubin, *Frank Stella: 1970–1987*, p. 64.
46 Stella, quoted in Auping, 'The Phenomenology of Frank', p. 36.
47 For a thorough account of these processes, see Michael O'Rourke, 'The Digital Modeling of Frank Stella's Smoke Sculpture', http://www.michaelorourke.com/pubs/Maquette93/Maquette93.pdf (accessed May 23, 2017).
48 Ibid.
49 It is likely, in fact, that Stella received the hat in the 1980s, but could not figure out how to access or apply its inherent manipulability within his work until he began using CAD software in the early 1990s.
50 Stella, 'Grimm's Ecstasy', p. 159; the above passage begins, 'It happened by accident, more or less, that I found something that linked me to the dome in Parma and to the notion of extending pictorial illusionism. It was a hat…'
51 Nor is it the case that all the 'Scarlatti K' works revolve around a hat form. The 2016 painted Elasto plastic and stainless steel sculpture *K.507* clearly prioritizes the smoke rings, for instance.
52 Stella, quoted in Caroline A. Jones, *Machine in the Studio: Constructing the Postwar American Artist*, University of Chicago Press, Chicago, 1996, pp. 181–82.
53 For Frank Bosco's memories of their collaboration, see Bosco, 'History File | 1984: Frank Bosco and Frank Stella Collaboration', cfile.daily, 3 February 2014, https://cfileonline.org/history-file-1984-frank-bosco-frank-stella-collaboration/ (accessed 23 May 2017).
54 Stella traveled to Iran and Central Asia in 1963, and the slightly different eight-point star of Persian ceramic tiles is worth noting here, given that he painted Plant City in the same year. In 1967 as well Stella made a series of prints called Star of Persia.

FOCUS PAGES 091–103

1 *The Writings of Frank Stella*, op. cit., p. 9.
2 Theodor W. Adorno, *Philosophy of New Music*, translation by Anne G. Mitchell and Wesley V. Blomster, Continuum, New York and London, 2004, p. 70.
3 Theodor W. Adorno, 'Late Style in Beethoven', in Richard Leppert (ed.), *Theodor W. Adorno: Essays On Music*, with new translations by Susan H. Gillespie, University of California Press, Berkeley, 2002.
4 Adorno, *Philosophy of New Music*, p. 19.
5 Edward W. Said, *On Late Style: Music and Literature Against the Grain*, Vintage Books, New York, 2007, p. 14.

Frank Stella

22 juin – 12 août 1995 **L'Usine**
37 rue de Longvic 21000 Dijon

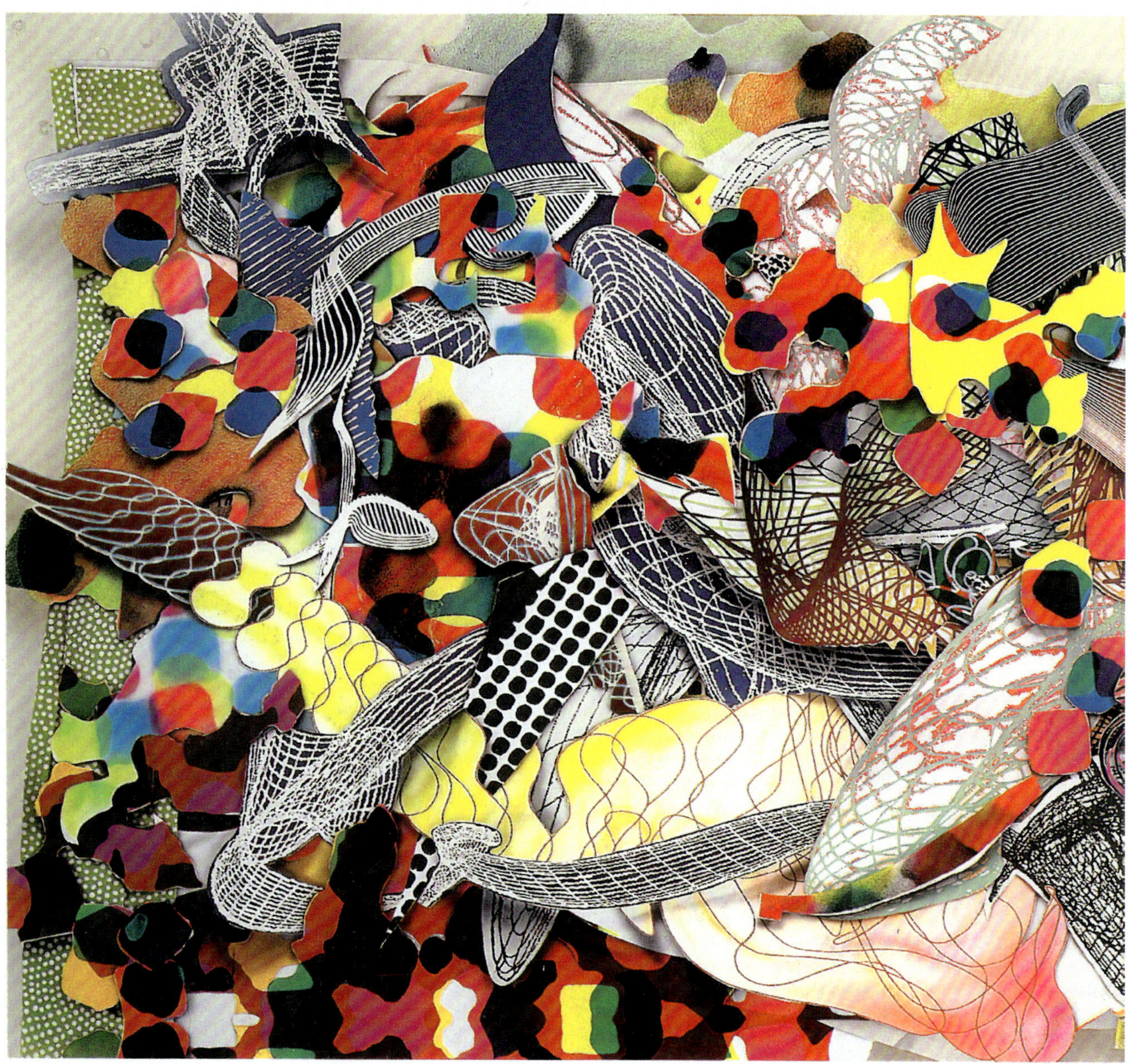

vernissage le jeudi 22 juin 1995
à partir de 18h

ouvert du mardi au samedi de 14h30 à 18h30
tél. : 80 31 67 44
fax : 80 30 59 74

SIXTEEN AMERICANS

J. De Feo, Wally Hedrick, James Jarvaise, Jasper Johns
Ellsworth Kelly, Alfred Leslie, Landes Lewitin, Richard Lytle
Robert Mallary, Louise Nevelson, Robert Rauschenberg, Julius Schmidt
Richard Stankiewicz, Frank Stella, Albert Urban, Jack Youngerman

The President and Trustees of The Museum of Modern Art request the pleasure of your company at the Members' preview of the exhibition *Sixteen Americans* on Tuesday evening, December the fifteenth, from five to eleven o'clock. 11 West 53 Street, New York 19. This invitation admits two.

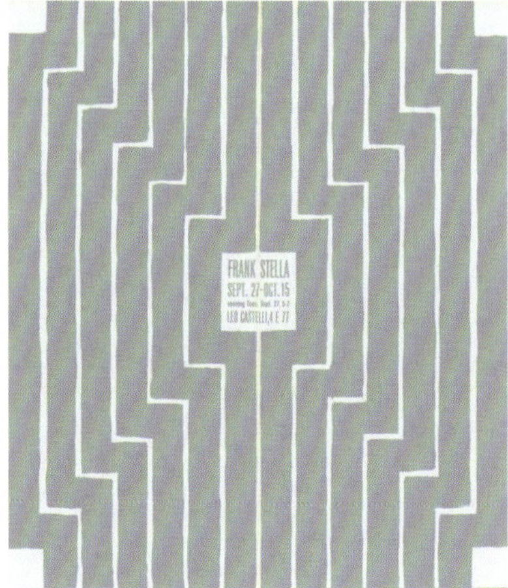

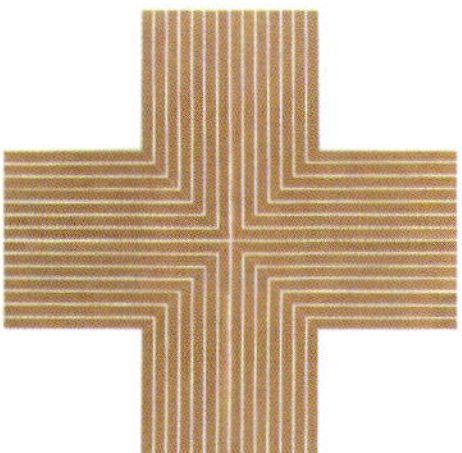

EAST 77TH ST NY NY APRIL 28–MAY
STELLA PAINTINGS LEO CASTELLI 4
MAY 19 OPENING SATURDAY ALL
LEO CASTELLI 4 EAST 77TH ST
OPENING SATURDAY ALL DAY
LEO CASTELLI 4 EAST 77TH
12 OPENING SATURDAY

CHRONOLOGY: Frank Stella, born 1936 in Malden, Massachusetts. Lives and works in New York.

SELECTED SOLO EXHIBITIONS AND PROJECTS
1950–1965

SELECTED ARTICLES AND INTERVIEWS
1950–1965

1950
Attends the Phillips Academy in Andover, Massachusetts

1954
Attends Princeton University, New Jersey

1959
MALDEN PUBLIC LIBRARY, Massachusetts

1959
Genauer, Emily, '16-Artist Show Is On Today at Museum of Modern Art', New York Herald Tribune, 16 December

Stella, Frank, 'An Artist Writes to Correct and Explain', New York Herald Tribune, 27 December

---

1960
LEO CASTELLI GALLERY, New York

1960
'The Higher Criticism', Time, 11 January

Preston, Stuart, 'Housing in Art's Many Mansions', The New York Times, 2 October

Fried, Michael, 'New York Letter: John Chamberlain and Frank Stella at Leo Castelli Gallery', Art International, 25 November

Preston, Valerie, 'Reviews and Previews', ARTnews, November

1961
GALERIE LAWRENCE, Paris

1961
Ashbery, John, 'Can Art be Excellent if Anybody Could Do It?', New York Herald Tribune, 8 November

---

1962
'Frank Stella: Copper Series',
LEO CASTELLI GALLERY, New York

1962
Campbell, Lawrence, 'Reviews and Previews', ARTnews, Summer

Judd, Donald, 'Exhibition at the Castelli Gallery', Arts Magazine, September

---

1963
FERUS GALLERY, Los Angeles

1963
Langsner, Jules, 'Los Angeles Letter', Art International, 25 March

Factor, Donald, 'Los Angeles', Artforum, May

1964
LEO CASTELLI GALLERY, New York

GALERIE LAWRENCE, Paris

'Frank Stella: Recent Paintings',
KASMIN LIMITED, London

1964
O'Doherty, Brian, 'Frank Stella and a Crisis of Nothingness', The New York Times, 19 January

Tillim, Sidney, 'The New Avant-Garde', Arts Magazine, February

Lippard, Lucy, 'New York', Artforum, March

Lynton, Norbert, 'London Letter', Art International, December

---

1965
'Frank Stella in an Exhibition of New Work',
FERUS GALLERY, Los Angeles

1965
Baro, Gene, 'London Exhibition', Arts Magazine, January

Sandler, Irving, ' The Cool New Art', Art in America, January

Leider, Philip, 'Small but Select', Frontier (Los Angeles), March

Marmer, Nancy, 'Los Angeles Letter', Art International, May

Lippard, Lucy R., 'The Third Stream: Constructed Paintings and Painted Structures', Art Voices, Spring

Rosenblum, Robert, 'Frank Stella: Five Years of Variations on an "Irreducible" Theme', Artforum, June

Judd, Donald, 'Specific Objects', Arts Yearbook, no. 8

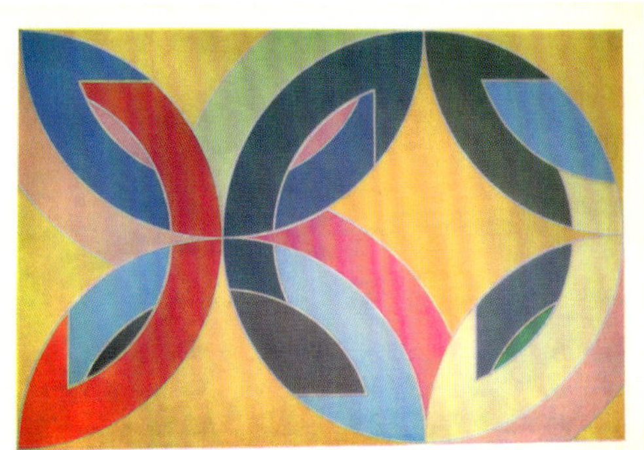

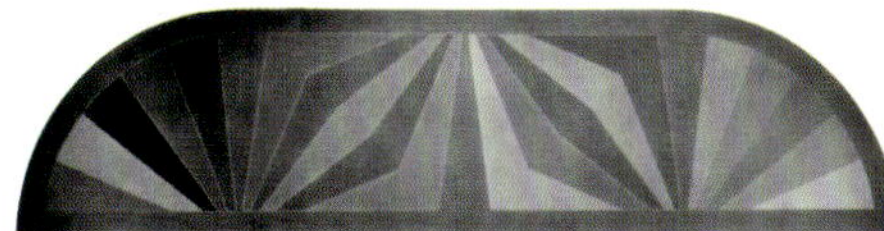

Frank Stella New paintings

Private view 3-6 Thursday 5 December
Exhibition from 6 December 1968
Mondays-Fridays 10-5-30
Saturdays 10-1

Kasmin Limited
118 New Bond Street
London W1
Telephone: 01-629 2821/2

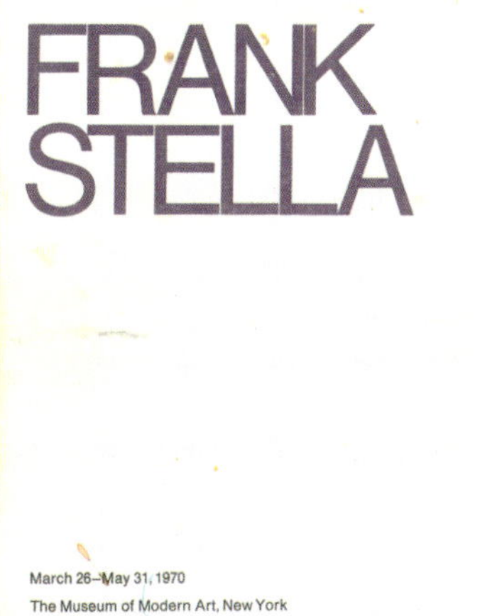

SELECTED SOLO EXHIBITIONS AND PROJECTS
1966–70

1966
'Frank Stella: Irregular Polygon Series',
LEO CASTELLI GALLERY, New York

'Frank Stella: Irregular Polygons',
DAVID MIRVISH GALLERY, Toronto

'Frank Stella: An Exhibition of Recent Paintings',
PASADENA ART MUSEUM, California, toured to SEATTLE ART MUSEUM PAVILION

'Frank Stella: A Selection of Paintings and Recent Drawings',
KASMIN LIMITED, London

1967
GALERIE BISCHOFBERGER, Zurich

DOUGLAS GALLERY, Vancouver

LEO CASTELLI GALLERY, New York

Recieves the First Prize at the International Biennial Exhibition of Paintings, Tokyo

1968
'Frank Stella: An Exhibition of Recent Paintings and Drawings',
WASHINGTON GALLERY OF MODERN ART, D.C.

IRVING BLUM GALLERY, Los Angeles

'Frank Stella: Recent Paintings',
DAVID MIRVISH GALLERY, Toronto

BENNINGTON COLLEGE, Vermont

'Frank Stella: Recent Paintings',
KASMIN LIMITED, London

1969
MAYAGUEZ CAMPUS OF THE UNIVERSITY OF PUERTO RICO

'The First Lithographic Projects of Frank Stella',
HARCUS/KRAKOW GALLERY, Boston

'Recent Paintings by Frank Stella',
ROSE ART MUSEUM AT BRANDEIS UNIVERSITY

IRVING BLUM GALLERY, Los Angeles

LEO CASTELLI GALLERY, New York

1970
LAWRENCE RUBIN GALLERY, New York

GALERIE RENÉE ZIEGLER, Zurich

SELECTED ARTICLES AND INTERVIEWS
1966–70

1966
Kramer, Hilton, 'Representative of the 1960s', The New York Times, March

Ashton, Dore, 'Conditioned Historic Reactions', Studio International, no. 171, May

Bochner, Mel, 'In the Galleries', Arts Magazine, May

Krauss, Rosalind, 'New York', Artforum, May

Glaser, Bruce, 'New Nihilism or New Art?', ARTnews, September

Fried, Michael, 'Shape as Form: Frank Stella's New Paintings', Artforum, November

1967
Crujel, Hans, 'Ausstellungen: Zurich', Werk, April

Fried, Michael, 'Art and Objecthood', Artforum, June

Livingston, Jane, 'Los Angeles: Frank Stella, Lithograohs, Gemini', Artforum, November

Harrison Cone, Jane, 'Frank Stella's New Paintings', Artforum, December

Kramer, Hilton, 'Frank Stella: What You See Is What You See', The New York Times, 10 December

1968
Castle, Friederick, 'What's That, the '68 Stella? Wow!', ARTnews, January

Ashton, Dore, 'Stella at Castelli'; Joeph Masheck, 'Frank Stella at Kasmin', Studio International, February

Gold, Barbara, 'Stella exhibits in Washington', Baltimore Sun, 3 March

Russell, Paul, 'Exhibition at David Mirvish Gallery', Arts Canada, June

Kane, George, 'Stripes and Shapes by Stella', Boston Sunday Globe Magazine, 14 July

Goldman, Judith, 'Frank Stella: Black Series and Star of Persia Prints', Artist's Proof, no. 8

1969
Ruiz de la Mata, Ernesto, 'Frank Stella', San Juan Star Sunday Magazine, 23 March

Driscoll, Edgar Jr, 'Stella Shines at Brandeis', Boston Morning Globe, 15 April

Giuliano, Charles, 'Mr. Stella d'Oro of the Art World', Boston After Dark, 16 April

Rosenblum, Robert, 'Frank Stella: An Exhilarating Adventure', Vogue, 15 November

1970
Pincus-Witten, Robert, 'New York', Artforum, January

Kramer, Hilton, 'Art: A Retrospective of Frank Stella', The New York Times, 25 March

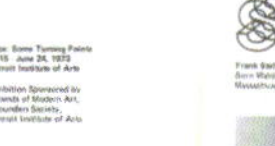

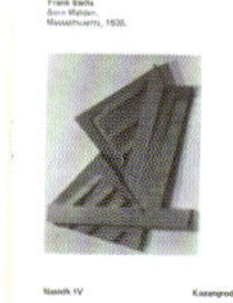

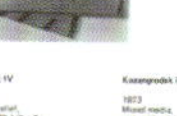

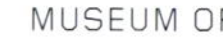

SELECTED SOLO EXHIBITIONS AND PROJECTS
1970–75

1970 (cont.)
MUSEUM OF MODERN ART, New York, toured to HAYWARD GALLERY, London; STEDELIJK MUSEUM, Amsterdam; PASADENA ART MUSEUM, California; ART GALLERY OF ONTARIO, Toronto

JOSEPH HELMAN GALLERY, St. Louis, Missouri

1971
HANSEN FULLER GALLERY, San Francisco

IRVING BLUM GALLERY, Los Angeles

DAVID MIRVISH GALLERY, Toronto

ART GALLERY OF ONTARIO, Toronto

'Frank Stella: Prinzip Seriell, Grafik 1967-1970', KUNSTMUSEUM DÜSSELDORF, toured to KUNSTHALLE BIELEFELD; AARHUS KUNSTMUSEUM, Denmark

KASMIN LIMITED, London

LAWRENCE RUBIN GALLERY, New York

1972
IRVING BLUM GALLERY, Los Angeles

1973
'Frank Stella: Polish Village Series', LEO CASTELLI GALLERY, New York

THE PHILLIPS COLLECTION, Washington, D.C.

KNOEDLER GALLERY, New York

JANIE C. LEE GALLERY, Dallas

1974
'Frank Stella: Recent Constructions and Earlier Paintings', PORTLAND CENTER FOR THE VISUAL ARTS, Oregon, toured to HENRY GALLERY AT THE UNIVERSITY OF WASHINGTON, Seattle, Washington; ACE GALLERY, Vancouver

1975
'Frank Stella: Metal Reliefs', LEO CASTELLI GALLERY, New York

'Frank Stella: Variations on the Square 1960-1974', JANIE C. LEE GALLERY, Houston

'Frank Stella: Recent Paintings', GALERIE TEMPLON, Paris

GALLERIA DELL'ARIETE, Milan

'Frank Stella: High-Relief Aluminum Paintings', ACE VENICE GALLERY, Venice, California

SELECTED ARTICLES AND INTERVIEWS
1970–75

1970 (cont.)
Leider, Philip, 'Literalism and Abstraction: Frank Stella's Retrospective at the Modern', Artforum, April

Baker, Elizabeth C., 'Frank Stella: Perspectives', ARTnews, May

Rosenberg, Harold, 'The Art World: Young Masters, New Critics', The New Yorker, 9 May

1971
'Frank Stella by Stedelijk Museum', The Print Collector's Newsletter, January–February

Richardson, Brenda, 'Bay Area', Arts Magazine, April

Terbell, Melinda, 'Review', Arts Magazine, May

Kramer, Hilton, 'Two Uses of the Shaped Canvas', The New York Times, 16 October

Baker, Elizabeth, 'Frank Stella: Revival and Relief', ARTnews, November

Krauss, Rosalind E., 'Stella's New York and the Problem of Series', Artforum, December

1972
Sandler, Irving, 'Stella at Rubin', Art in America, January–February

Gibbs, Mary Laura, 'Albers and Stella', Record of the Art Museum Princeton University, no. 1

1973
Schjeldhal, Peter, 'Frank Stella: The Best – and Last of His Breed?', The New York Times, 21 January

Domingo, Willis, 'Intuition of Form: Michael Fried's Reading of Stella's Moultonboro Series', Arts Magazine, February–March

White, Edmund, 'Frank Stella Explores a New Dimension', Saturday Review of the Arts, 3 March

Fikelstein, Louis, 'Seeing Stella', Artforum, June

Richard, Paul, 'Stella: Not So Simple Anymore', Washington Post, 10 November

1974
Gilbert-Rolfe, Jeremy, 'Review', Artforum, February

Smith, Roberta, 'Frank Stella's New Paintings: The Thrill Is Back', Art in America, November–December

1975
Russell, John, 'Review', The New York Times, 18 May

Bourdon, David, 'Frank Stella', Village Voice, 19 May

Battcock, Gregory, 'Assailing Technology', Domus, September

Herrera, Hayden, 'Review', Artforum, September

Welling, James, 'New Work by Frank Stella', Artweek, 29 November

Millet, Catherine, 'Un Peintre: Frank Stella–Histoire (ou contre-histoire) de l'éspace littéral', Art Press, November–December

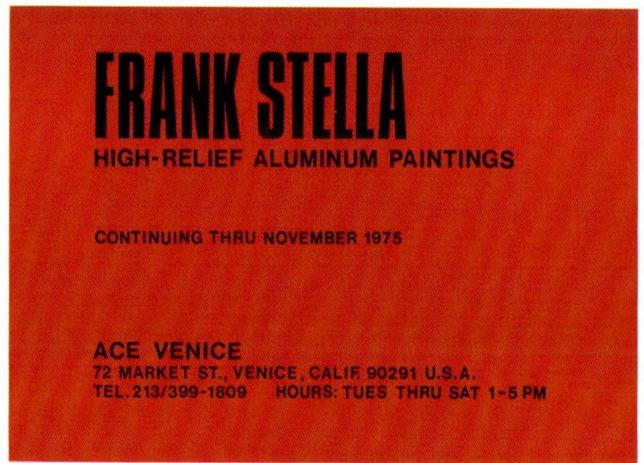

Frank Stella (American, b. 1936)
Jill, 1959
enamel on canvas, 90¾" × 70¾"
Gift of Seymour H. Knox, 1962

Hans Strelow und Rudolf Zwirner zeigen

Frank Stella

Metallreliefs aus dem Jahre 1976

Eröffnung am Freitag, 4. Februar 1977, 20.00 Uhr
Dauer der Ausstellung bis 12. März 1977

Frank Stella wird anwesend sein

Galerie Rudolf Zwirner 5 Köln 1 Albertusstraße 18 Tel. 235837+235838

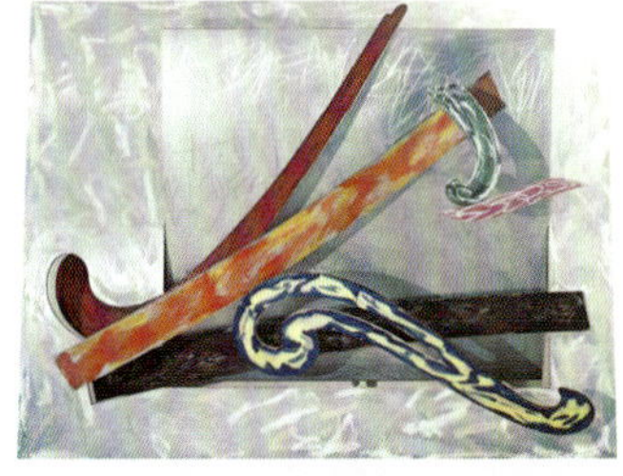

FRANK STELLA

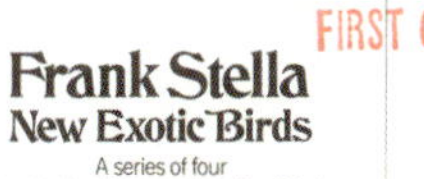

FIRST CLASS

Frank Stella
New Exotic Birds
A series of four
hand-colored screenprints, 5 × 7 feet.
September 15-October 6, 1979

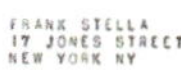

Castelli Graphics
4 East 77th Street New York, N.Y. 10021

SELECTED SOLO EXHIBITIONS AND PROJECTS
1976–79

1976
'Frank Stella: Neue Reliefs',
ANDRÉ EMMERICH GALLERY, Zurich

'Frank Stella: Paintings and Graphics',
SEARS BANK AND TRUST COMPANY, Chicago

'Frank Stella: Neue Reliefbilder, Bilder und Graphik',
KUNSTHALLE BASEL

M. KNOEDLER & CO., New York

'Frank Stella: The Black Paintings',
THE BALTIMORE MUSEUM OF ART

'Frank Stella: A Historical Selection',
DAVID MIRVISH GALLERY, Toronto

1977
'Frank Stella: Metal Reliefs from the Year 1976',
HANS STRELOW AND RUDOLF ZWIRNER GALLERY, Cologne

'Shaped Canvases',
GALERIE M, Bochum, Germany

'Frank Stella: Werke 1958-1976',
KUNSTHALLE BIELEFELD, toured to KUNSTHALLE TÜBINGEN,

'Frank Stella: Aluminum Reliefs 1976-77',
MUSEUM OF MODERN ART, Oxford, toured to the FRUIT MARKET, Edinburgh

'Frank Stella: Paintings and Recent Prints',
JOHN BERGGRUEN GALLERY, San Francisco

'Frank Stella: Paintings, Drawings, and Prints 1959-1977',
M. KNOEDLER & CO., London

'Frank Stella: Sinjerli Variations',
LINDA FARRIS GALLERY, Seattle

1978
'Frank Stella Prints',
GETLER/PALL GALLERY, New York

SABLE-CASTELLI GALLERY, Toronto

'Stella Since 1970',
FORT WORTH ART MUSEUM, Texas, toured to NEWPORT HARBOR ART MUSEUM, Newport Beach, California; MONTREAL MUSEUM OF FINE ARTS; THE VANCOUVER ART GALLERY; THE CORCORAN GALLERY OF ART, Washington, D.C.; MISSISSIPPI MUSEUM OF ART, Jackson; DENVER ART MUSEUM; THE MINNEAPOLIS INSTITUTE OF ARTS; DES MOINES ART CENTER, Iowa

'Frank Stella: Prints',
GALERIE VALEUR, Nagoya

The Series within a Series',
SCHOOL OF VISUAL ARTS MUSEUM, New York

1979
'Frank Stella: Indian Birds, Painted Metal Reliefs',
LEO CASTELLI GALLERY, New York

SELECTED ARTICLES AND INTERVIEWS
1976–79

1976
Henry, Gerrit, 'Is New York Still the Artistic Place to Be?', ARTnews, November

Lebensztejn, Jean-Claude, and John Johnston, 'Star', October, Spring

Hess, Thomas, 'Stella Means Star', New York Magazine, 1 November

Frackman, Noel, 'Frank Stella's Abstract Aerie: A Reading of Stella's New Paintings', Arts Magazine, no. 51, December

Hopkins, Budd, 'Frank Stella's New Work: A Personal Note', Artforum, December

Perone, Jeff, 'Review', Artforum, December

Ward, Mary Martha, 'Frank Stella', Arts Magazine, December

1977
Richard, Paul, 'Frank Stella at 40: A Fierce and Entertaining Logic', Washington Post, 9 January

Richard, Paul, 'Stella: High Energy', Buffalo Evening News, 12 February

Goldin, Amy, 'Frank Stella at Knoedler Gallery', Art in America, January–February

Steyn, Juliet, 'Frank Stella Talks about his Recent Work', Art Monthly, May

Feaver, William, 'The Stella Collection', Observer, 8 May

Overy, Paul, 'Frank Stella's Exhilarating Vitality', Times, 17 May

Rippon, Peter, Terence Maloon and Ben Jones, 'Frank Stella', Artscribe, July

Smith, Roberta, 'Review', Art in America, July–August

Rosenbaum, Allen, John Rewald and Frank Stella, 'The William C. Seitz Collection', Art Journal, no. 1, Autumn

1978
Rubinfien, Leo, 'Frank Stella', Artforum, February

Leider, Philip, 'Stella since 1970', Art in America, March

Hunter, J., 'Stella's Captivating Color', Dallas Morning News, 11 March

Hughes, Robert, 'Stella And The Painted Bird In Fort Worth, a major show', Time, 3 April

Richard, Paul, 'Stella the Daring', Washington Post, 21 April

Marvel, Bill, 'Stella at Fort Worth', Horizon, May

Leder, Dennis, 'Endings and Beginnings', America, 15 July

Toupin, Gilles, 'Frank Stella: Evolution ou révolution?', La Presse, 11 November

1979
Russell, John, 'Stella Shows His Metal in SoHo', The New York Times, 19 January

Perlberg, Deborah, 'Frank Stella', Artforum, March

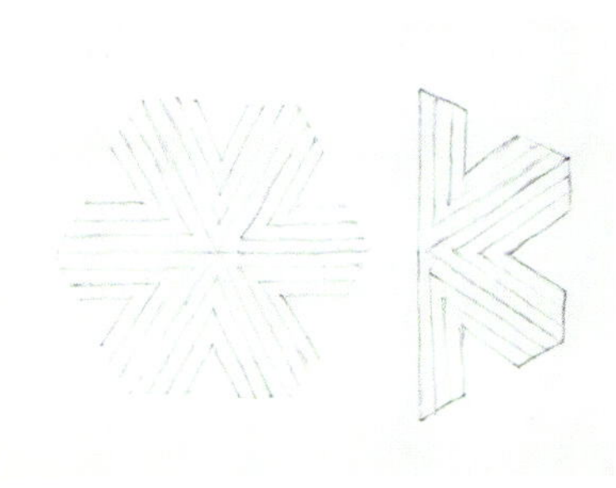

Kunstmuseum Basel

Frank Stella
Working Drawings – Zeichnungen
1956–1970

Einladung
zur Eröffnung der Ausstellung
am Mittwoch
21 Mai 1980, 20.15 Uhr

Es sprachen Prof. Dr. Frank Vischer
und Dr. Christian Geelhaar

Die Ausstellung dauert bis zum 27. Juli 1980

Los Angeles County
Museum of Art

Members' Calendar
December 1980

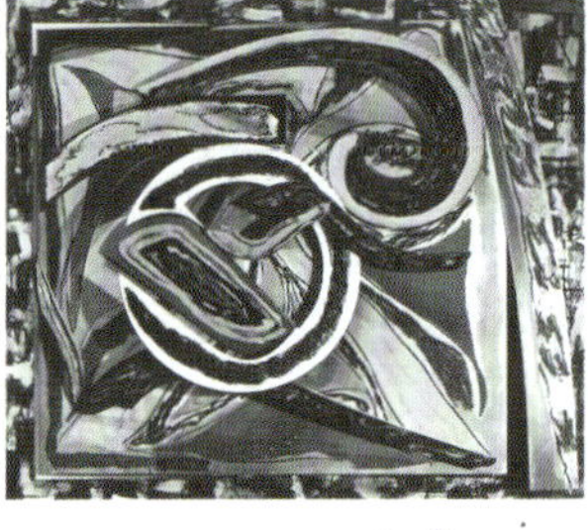

for Frank, cordially, Maurice

Volume 18/Number 12

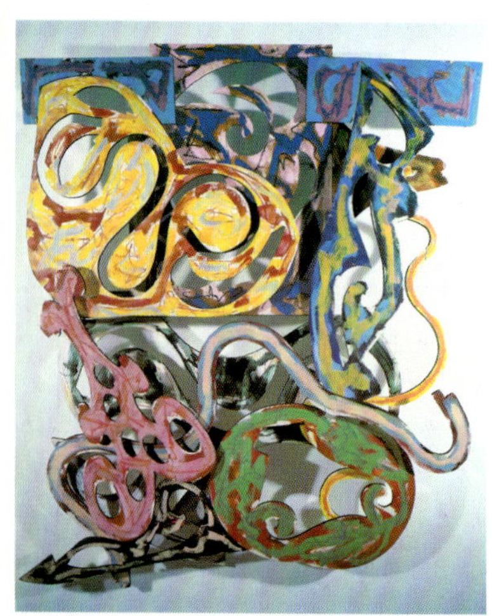

FRANK STELLA IMOLA 1981 206 x 183 cm

SELECTED SOLO EXHIBITIONS AND PROJECTS
1979–81

1979 (cont.)

'Frank Stella: The Indian Bird Maquettes',
MUSEUM OF MODERN ART, New York

'Frank Stella: Metallic Reliefs',
ROSE ART MUSEUM AT BRANDEIS UNIVERSITY

'Frank Stella: 8 Drawings; 1976 Sketch Sinjerli Variation; 1977 Exotic Bird Series',
AKIRA IKEDA GALLERY, Nagoya

Receives the Claude M. Fuess Distinguished Service Award, Phillips Academy, Andover, Massachusetts

1980

'Frank Stella: Paintings and Prints',
GALERIE NINETY-NINE, Bay Harbor Islands, Florida

KOH GALLERY, Tokyo

'Frank Stella: Works on Paper',
M. KNOEDLER & CO., London

'Frank Stella: Peintures 1970-1979',
CENTRE D'ARTS PLASTIQUES CONTEMPORAINS DE BORDEAUX

'Frank Stella: Recent Works',
GALERIE VALEUR, Nagoya

'Frank Stella: Polar Coordinates, for Ronnie Peterson',
L.A. LOUVER, Los Angeles

'Frank Stella: Working Drawings/Zeichnungen 1956-1970',
KUNSTMUSEUM BASEL, toured to STAATLICHE GRAPHISCHE SAMMLUNG, Munich

GALERIE VALEUR, Nagoya

'Frank Stella: Polar Co-ordinates',
AKIRA IKEDA GALLERY, Nagoya

GETLER/PALL GALLERY, New York

1981

'Frank Stella: Recent Graphics',
ALBERT WHITE GALLERY, Toronto

'Frank Stella: The Prints',
BELL GALLERY LIST ART CENTER at BROWN UNIVERSITY

'Frank Stella: Works from 1970 to 1980',
GALERIE TEMPLON, Paris

'Frank Stella: Metal Reliefs',
M. KNOEDLER & CO., New York

'Frank Stella: New Work',
GALERIE HANS STRELOW, Düsseldorf

Receives the New York City Mayor's Award for Arts and Culture, New York

Receives the Medal for Painting, Skowhegan School of Painting and Sculpture, Skowhegan, Maine

Awarded the Honorary Fellowship, Bezalel Academy of Arts and Design, Jerusalem

SELECTED ARTICLES AND INTERVIEWS
1979–81

1979 (cont.)

Lawson, Thomas, 'Frank Stella at Leo Castelli', Flash Art, March–April

Kramer, Hilton, 'Frank Stella's Brash and Lyric Flight', Portfolio, April–May

Taylor, R., 'Frank Stella Hits his Stride', Boston Sunday Globe, May

Hughes, Robert, 'Ten Years that Buried the Avant-Garde', Sunday Times Magazine, 30 December

1980

Bonito Oliva, Achille, 'The Bewildered Image', Flash Art, no. 96–97, January–February

Axsom, Richard, 'Frank Stella's Graphics', Print Collector's Newsletter, no. 1, March–April

Gintz, Claude, 'Entretien avec Frank Stella', Artistes, April–May

Tomkins, Calvin, 'A Good Eye and a Good Ear', The New Yorker, 26 May

1981

Crimp, Douglas, 'The End of Painting', October 16, Spring

Meir, Ronnen, 'Frank Stella on Making Art', Jerusalem Post Magazine, 22 May

'Frank Stella: Working Drawings/Zeichnungen 1956-70 by Kunstmuseum Basel', The Print Collector's Newsletter, July–August

Kipnis, Jeff, 'Stella Forgery in Atlanta', Art Papers, August

Kramer, Hilton, 'Review', The New York Times, 6 November

Larson, Kay, 'Art: The Odd Couple', New York Magazine, 23 November

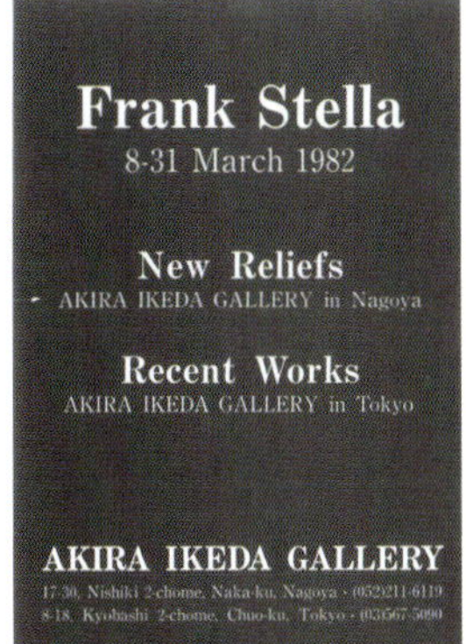

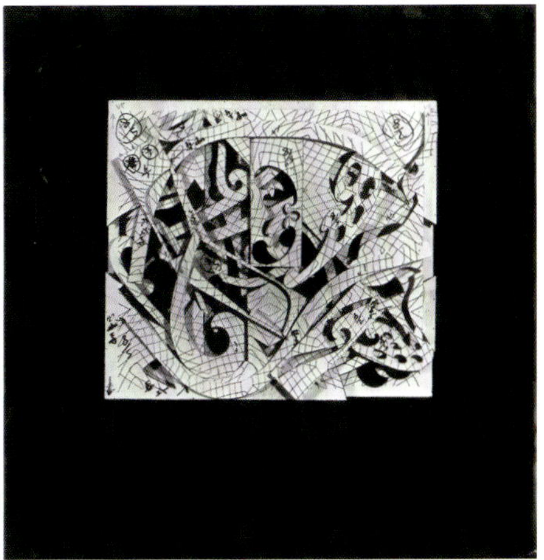

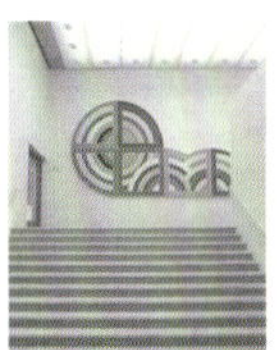

LOUISIANA 3050 Humlebæk. Danmark

SELECTED SOLO EXHIBITIONS AND PROJECTS
1982–83

1982
'Frank Stella: Polar Co-ordinates',
FAY GOLD GALLERY, Atlanta

New Reliefs and Recent Works',
AKIRA IKEDA GALLERY, Nagoya and Tokyo

'Frank Stella: New Prints',
AKIRA IKEDA GALLERY, Nagoya

'Frank Stella: Circuits',
L.A. LOUVER, Los Angeles

M. KNOEDLER & CO., London

'Stella by Starlight',
MUSEUM OF FINE ARTS, Houston

'Frank Stella: Polar Coordinates for Ronnie Peterson',
MUSEUM OF MODERN ART, New York, toured to the UNIVERSITY OF ARIZONA MUSEUM OF ART, Tucson; THE WILLIAM BENTON MUSEUM OF ART at UNIVERSITY OF CONNECTICUT, Storrs; GLENBOW MUSEUM, Calgary; ART GALLERY OF HAMILTON, Ontario; MADISON ART CENTER, Wisconsin.

'Frank Stella: Prints 1967-1982',
THE UNIVERSITY OF MICHIGAN MUSEUM OF ART, Ann Arbor, toured to WHITNEY MUSEUM OF AMERICAN ART, New York; HUNTSVILLE MUSEUM OF ART, Alabama; SARAH CAMPBELL BLAFFER GALLERY, University of Houston; BRUNNIER GALLERY AND MUSEUM, Ames, Iowa; CLEVELAND MUSEUM OF ART; MARY AND LEIGH BLOCK GALLERY at NORTHWESTERN UNIVERSITY, Evanston, Illinois; PENNSYLVANIA ACADEMY OF FINE ARTS, Philadelphia; MEMORIAL ART GALLERY at UNIVERSITY OF ROCHESTER; LAGUNA GLORIA ART MUSEUM, Austin; BROOKS MEMORIAL ART GALLERY, Memphis; BEAUMONT ART MUSEUM, Texas; THE NELSON-ATKINS MUSEUM OF ART, Kansas City, Missouri; COLUMBUS GALLERY OF FINE ARTS, Ohio; LOS ANGELES COUNTY MUSEUM OF ART

'Frank Stella: Swan Engravings',
CASTELLI GRAPHICS, New York

'Frank Stella: From Start to Finish',
ADDISON GALLERY OF AMERICAN ART at the PHILLIPS ACADEMY, ANDOVER, Massachusetts

'Frank Stella: Exhibition of South African Mines',
LEO CASTELLI GALLERY, New York

'Frank Stella: Working Drawings from the Artist's Collection',
KITAKYUSHU MUNICIPAL MUSEUM OF ART

'Frank Stella: Works on Paper',
GETLER/PALL GALLERY, New York

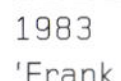

1983
'Frank Stella: Recent Works',
JACKSONVILLE ART MUSEUM

'Frank Stella: Polish Wooden Synagogues. Constructions of the 1970s',
THE JEWISH MUSEUM, New York

'Frank Stella: The Circuit Series and the Swan Engravings',
MARIANNE FRIEDLAND GALLERY, Toronto

'Resource/Response/Reservoir: Stella Survey 1959-1982',
SAN FRANCISCO MUSEUM OF MODERN ART

SELECTED ARTICLES AND INTERVIEWS
1982–83

1982
Foster, Hal, 'Frank Stella at Knoedler Gallery', Art in America, February

1982 (cont.)
Guberman, Sidney T., 'Frank Stella', Art Papers, March

De Antonio, Emile, 'Frank Stella: A Passion for Painting', GEO, March

Frackman, Noel, 'Tracking Frank Stella's Circuit Series', Arts Magazine, no. 56, April

Cohen, Arthur, 'Frank Stella', Art Magazine, May

Hogrefe, Jeffrey, 'Stella Ties Record', Washington Post, 6 May

Raynor, Vivien, 'Gallery View; Frank Stella Exhibits at His Alma Mater', The New York Times, 7 November

Ruhe, Barnaby, 'Frank Stella', Art World, November

Smith, Roberta, 'Abstraction: Simple and Complex', Village Voice, 23 November

1983
Feinstein, Roni, 'Stella's Diamonds: Frank Stella's New Work', Arts Magazine, no. 5, January

Glueck, Grace, 'Art: Frank Stella's Prints at the Whitney', The New York Times, 14 January

Wolff, Theodore, 'Frank Stella: As Important a Printmaker as He Is a Painter', Christian Science Monitor, 25 January

Ackley, Clifford, 'Frank Stella's Big Football Weekend', Print Collector's Newsletter, no. 6, January–February

Corbett, Patricia, 'Frank Stella', Art & Auction, February

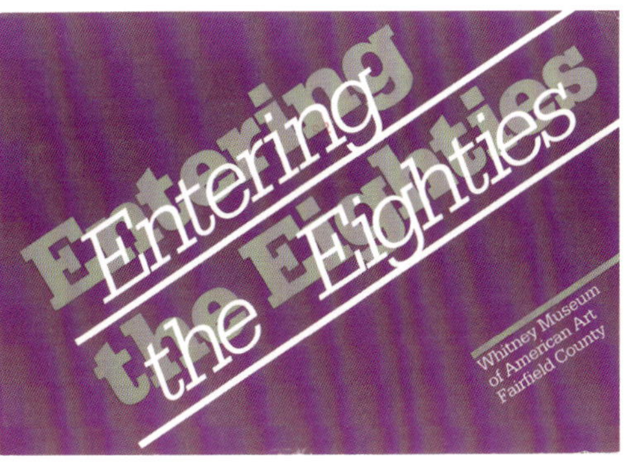

WHY NEW YORK

Milton Resnick · Idelle Weber · Michelle Stuart · Mattie Berhang
John Kacere · James Rosenquist · John Baeder · Robert Stackhouse
Tom Wesselmann · Frank Stella · Mary Beth Edelson · Pat Lasch
Richard Smith · Mel Edwards · Chuck Close · Keith Haring

FRANK STELLA
Early Paintings
March 15—April 20, 1985
Akira Ikeda Gallery/Tokyo
8-18, Kyobashi 2-chome, Chuo-ku, Tokyo

フランク ステラ
ペインティング 1960年代
3月15日(金)—4月20日(土) 1985
アキラ イケダ ギャラリー/東京

アキラ イケダ ギャラリー
東京都中央区京橋2-8-18 昭和ビルB1 (03)567-5090

Panel Discussion chaired by Clifton C. Olds,
Barry Professor of Art History and Criticism,
Bowdoin College, Brunswick, Maine

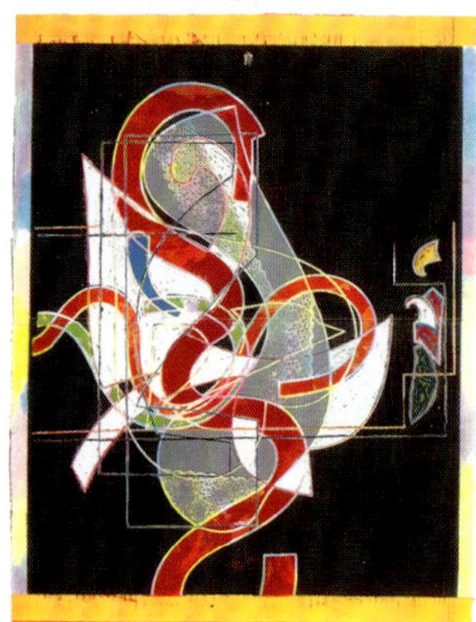

SELECTED SOLO EXHIBITIONS AND PROJECTS
1983–85

1983 (cont.)
'Frank Stella: Prints',
L.A. LOUVER, Los Angeles

GOLDMAN-KRAFT GALLERY, Chicago

'Frank Stella: Works from the Permanent Collection',
ALBRIGHT-KNOX GALLERY, Buffalo, New York

'Focus on Frank Stella: Nasielk II, a Polish Wooden Synagogue Construction',
SKIRBALL MUSEUM at HEBREW UNION COLLEGE, Los Angeles

'Frank Stella: Graphics and Mixed Media',
HARCUS GALLERY, Boston

'Frank Stella: Fourteen Prints with Drawings, Collages, and Working Proofs',
THE ART MUSEUM at PRINCETON UNIVERSITY, New Jersey

'Frank Stella: Selected Works',
FOGG ART MUSEUM at HARVARD UNIVERSITY, Cambridge, Massachusetts

'Recent Work',
M. KNOEDLER, Zurich, toured to GALERIE WÜRTHLE, Vienna

'Frank Stella: The Swan Engravings',
THE FORT WORTH ART MUSEUM

Appointed Charles Eliot Norton Professor of Poetry, Harvard University, Cambridge, Massachusetts

1984
Honorary Doctor of Arts, Princeton University, Princeton, NJ

1985
'Frank Stella: Relief Paintings',
M. KNOEDLER & CO., New York

'Frank Stella: New Prints',
PORT WASHINGTON PUBLIC LIBRARY, New York

'Frank Stella: Illustrations after El Lissitzky's 'Had Gadya,'
L.A. LOUVER, Los Angeles

'Illustrations after El Lissitzky's Had Gadya 1982–84',
WADDINGTON GRAPHICS, London

BARBARA KRAKOW GALLERY, Boston

AKIRA IKEDA GALLERY, Tokyo

'Frank Stella: Early Paintings',
AKIRA IKEDA GALLERY, Nagoya

'Frank Stella: Ceramic Reliefs and Steel Reliefs',
M. KNOEDLER & CO., London

'Frank Stella: Works and New Graphics',
INSTITUTE OF CONTEMPORARY ARTS, London, toured to DOUGLAS HYDE GALLERY, Trinity College, Dublin; THIRD EYE CENTRE, Glasgow

'Frank Stella: New Prints',
AKIRA IKEDA GALLERY, Nagoya

SELECTED ARTICLES AND INTERVIEWS
1983–85

1983 (cont.)
Hughes, Robert, 'Expanding What Prints Can Do', Time, 28 February

Ratcliff, Carter, 'Stella: Flirting with Geometry', Vogue, February

Silverthorne, Jeanne, 'Review', Artforum, February

Feinstein, Roni, 'Frank Stella's Prints 1967–1982', Arts Magazine, March

Taylor, Sarah, 'Frank Stella at Leo Castelli', Flash Art, no. 111, March

'Frank Stella', American Art, Summer

Curtis, Charlotte, 'Frank Stella and Art', The New York Times, 28 June

Berman, Avis, 'Artist's Dialogue: A conversation with Frank Stella', Architectural Digest, September

Morrow, Elizabeth Chase, 'Frank Stella', Art Papers, September–October

Rosenblum, Robert, 'Stella's Third Dimension', Vanity Fair, November

Shirley, David, 'Princeton Belatedly Honours a Graduate', The New York Times, 27 November

Taylor, Robert, 'Frank Stella: Fresh, Brilliant and Abstract', Boston Globe, 11 December

1984
Russell, John, 'Art View: Frank Stella at Harvard – The Artist as Lecturer', The New York Times, 18 March

Tomkins, Calvin, 'Profiles: The Space Around Real Things', The New Yorker, 10 September

1985
Braff, Phyllis, 'Prints Confirm Stella's Mastery', The New York Times, 24 February

Flam, Jack, 'The Gallery: Surprises from Frank Stella', Wall Street Journal, 12 February

Ratcliff, Carter, 'Frank Stella: Portrait of the Artist as Image Administrator'; Robert Storr, 'Frank Stella's Norton Lectures: A Response', Art in America, February

Russell, John, 'The Power of Frank Stella', The New York Times, 1 February

Stella, Frank, 'On Caravaggio', The New York Times Magazine, 3 February

Feaver, William, 'New Editions: Frank Stella', ARTnews, March

Cohen, Ronny, 'New York Previews: Frank Stella', ARTnews, May

O'Brien, Glenn, 'Frank Stella at Knoedler Gallery', Artforum, May

Turner, Norman, 'Stella on Caravaggio', Arts Magazine, Summer

Fallon, Brian, 'Frank Stella Exhibition at Douglas Hyde', Irish Times, 15 August

Fowler, Joan, 'Frankie Says', Circa, no. 24, September–October

Media Preview

Frank Stella
1970–1987

The
Museum
of
Modern
Art

Wednesday, October 7, 1987
11:00 a.m. to 2:00 p.m.

The artist and William Rubin, Director of the Department of Painting and Sculpture, will be present. Refreshments will be served.

11 West 53 Street
New York

On view from October 12, 1987, to January 5, 1988, the exhibition is made possible by a generous grant from PaineWebber Group Inc.

RSVP 212/708-9750
Department of Public Information

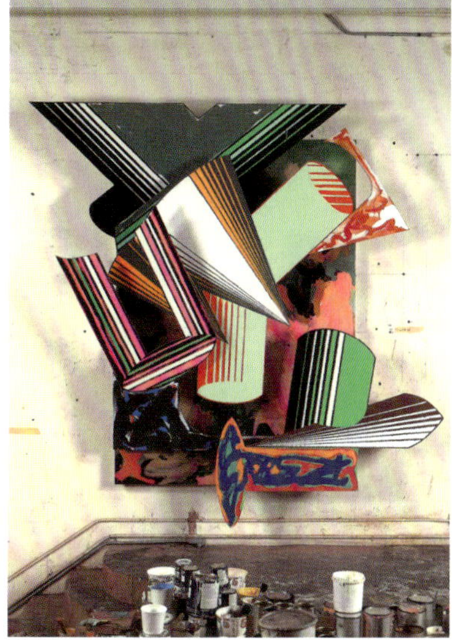

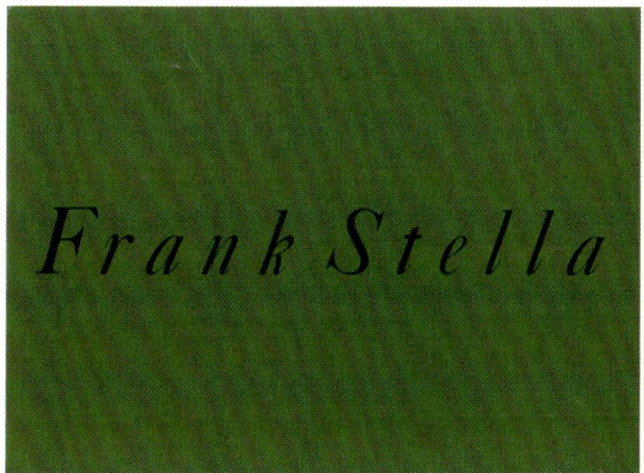

SELECTED SOLO EXHIBITIONS AND PROJECTS
1985–87

1985 (cont.)
'Frank Stella: Classic Prints',
GETLER/SAPER GALLERY, New York

'Frank Stella: Pillars and Cones Series',
THE GREENBERG GALLERY, St. Louis, Missouri

Receives the Award of American Art, Pennsylvania Academy of Fine Arts, Philadelphia, Pennsylvania

Honorary Degree, Dartmouth College, Hanover, New Hampshire

1986
'Frank Stella: Illustrations after El Lissitzky's Had Gadya',
RICHARD GREEN GALLERY, New York

'Frank Stella: Had Gadya, after El Lissitzky—A Series of Prints, 1982-1984',
TEL AVIV MUSEUM

'Stella at Laumeier: Frank Stella from St. Louis Collections',
LAUMEIER SCULPTURE PARK, St. Louis

'Frank Stella: Color and Form on Paper',
CARNEGIE MELLON UNIVERSITY ART GALLERY, Pittsburgh

'Frank Stella: New Reliefs',
AKIRA IKEDA GALLERY, Tokyo

Receives a Honorary Degree from the Brandeis University, Waltham, Massachusetts

1987
'Frank Stella: The Pre-Black Paintings 1958',
GAGOSIAN GALLERY, New York

'Frank Stella: Reliefs',
AKIRA IKEDA GALLERY, Nagoya

'Frank Stella: New Work',
GALERIE HANS STRELOW, Düsseldorf

'Frank Stella: New Works',
M. KNOEDLER & CO., London

'Frank Stella: 1970-1987',
MUSEUM OF MODERN ART, New York, toured to STEDELIJK MUSEUM, Amsterdam; CENTRE POMPIDOU, Paris; WALKER ART CENTER, Minneapolis; CONTEMPORARY ART MUSEUM, Houston; LOS ANGELES COUNTY MUSEUM OF ART

SELECTED ARTICLES AND INTERVIEWS
1985–87

1986
Halley, Peter, 'Frank Stella... and the Simulacrum', Flash Art, no. 126, January–February

Golding, John, 'The Expansive Imagination', Times Literary Supplement, 27 March

McGill, Douglas C, 'Art People: A New Stella in Office Lobby', The New York Times, 25 April

Ceysson, Bernard, 'Ut picture pictura: Frank Stella ou l'abstraction accomplie', Artstudio, Summer

McGee, Celia, 'Art takes its Chances and it Knocks: Interview with Frank Stella', Newsday, 9 July

Smith, Roberta, 'Oh, the Pity', Connoisseur, August

Kramer, Hilton, 'The Crisis in Abstract Art', Atlantic Monthly, October

McGill, Douglas C., 'Stella's elucidates Abstract Art's links to Realism', The New York Times, 7 December

1987
Carrier, David, 'The Era of Post-Historical Art', Leonardo, no. 3

Bankowsky, Jack, 'Frank Stella at Gagosian Gallery', Flash Art, no. 135, Summer

Beaumont, Mary Rose, 'Frank Stella', Arts Review 39, July

Lyon, Christopher, 'Frank Stella's Working Space', MoMA Magazine, no. 45, Autumn

Solomon, Deborah, 'Keep Your Eye on a Stellar Performer', Harper's Bazaar, September

Weschler, Lawrence, 'Stella's Flying Ships', ARTnews, September

Dorsey, John, 'Exploring Abstraction', Baltimore Sun, 11 October

Grundberg, Andy, 'Frank Stella Finds Space for Cosmic Reliefs', The New York Times, 11 October

Richard, Paul, 'Stella's Frontiers of Astonishment', Washington Post, 14 October

McGill, Douglas, 'Art People: Stella's Art', The New York Times, 16 October

Russell, John, 'Risky Works from Stella at the Museum of Modern Art', The New York Times, 16 October

Flam, Jack, 'Stargazing: MoMA puts Stella in Perspective', Wall Street Journal, 22 October

Sozanski, Edward, 'Exhibit Traces the Artistry of Frank Stella Since 1970', Philadelphia Inquirer, 25 October

G A G O S I A N

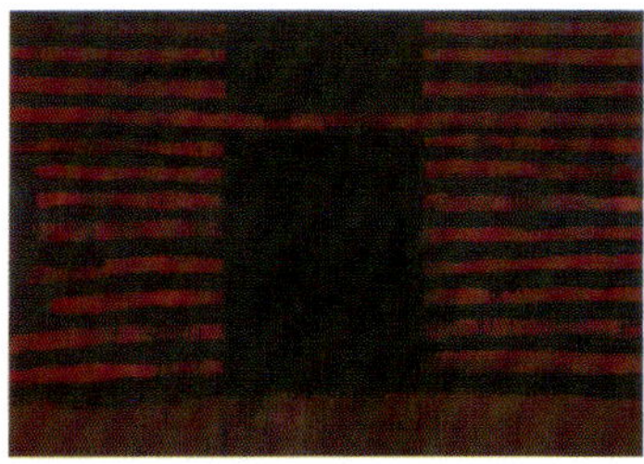

FRANK STELLA Great Jones Street, 1958, Enamel on Canvas, 8' x 9'6," two panels. Collection: Mr. and Mrs. Norman Braman

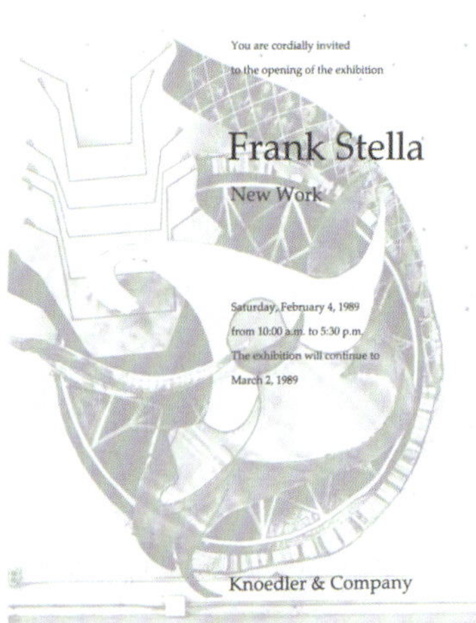

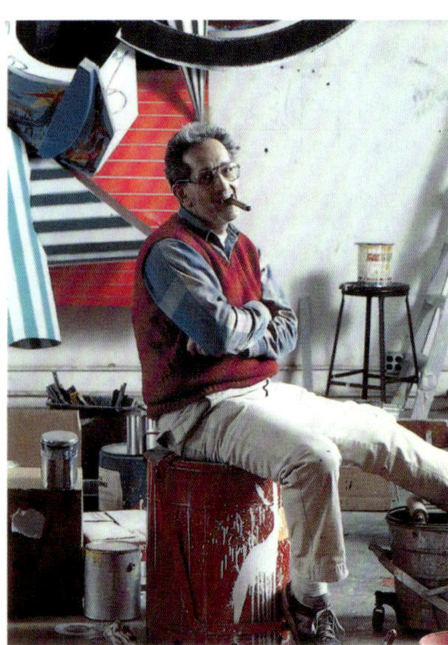

SELECTED SOLO EXHIBITIONS AND PROJECTS
1987–89

1988
'Frank Stella: Reliefs',
JAMES CORCORAN GALLERY, Santa Monica

'Frank Stella: Reliefs',
NATIONAL MUSEUM OF ART, Osaka

'Frank Stella: Recent Prints',
JOHN BERGGRUEN GALLERY, San Francisco

'Frank Stella: The Waves',
L.A. LOUVER, Venice, California

'Frank Stella: The Circuits Prints',
WALKER ART CENTER, Minneapolis, toured to the GRUNWALD CENTER FOR THE GRAPHIC ARTS WIGHT ART GALLERY at UNIVERSITY OF CALIFORNIA, Los Angeles; THE UNIVERSITY OF OKLAHOMA MUSEUM OF ART, Norman; ALLENTOWN ART MUSEUM, Pennsylvania; MILWAUKEE ART MUSEUM; MUNSON-WILLIAMS-PROCTOR INSTITUTE MUSEUM OF ART, Utica, New York; HOOD MUSEUM OF ART at DARTMOUTH COLLEGE, Hanover, New Hampshire

'Frank Stella: Waves',
NAN MILLER GALLERY, Rochester, New York

'Frank Stella: Swan Engraving V',
SMITHSONIAN AMERICAN ART MUSEUM, Washington, D.C.

'Frank Stella: Reliefs',
AKIRA IKEDA GALLERY, Taura

'Frank Stella: Black Paintings 1958-1960, Cones and Pillars 1984-1987',
STAATSGALERIE STUTTGART

1989
'Frank Stella: The Waves 1985-88',
AKIRA IKEDA GALLERY, Nagoya

'Frank Stella: Prints, 1967-88',
AC&T GALLERY, Tokyo

'Frank Stella: New Work',
M. KNOEDLER & CO., New York

'Frank Stella: A Selection of Works from 1968 to the Present',
EVELYN AIMIS GALLERY, Aventura, Florida

'Frank Stella: Waves II',
RICHARD GREEN GALLERY, Los Angeles

'The Waves',
GALERIE ALICE PAULI, Lausanne, Switzerland

'Frank Stella: The Waves',
WADDINGTON GRAPHICS, London

SELECTED ARTICLES AND INTERVIEWS
1987–89

1987 (cont.)
Schwabsky, Barry, 'Frank Stella', Arts Magazine 62, October

Hughes, Robert, 'The Grand Maximalist', Time, 2 November

Baker, Kenneth, 'Frank Stella, 1970–1987', San Francisco Chronicle, 22 November

Kenner, H., 'Frank Stella: America's Genuis of Insignificant Form', Art & Antiques, November

Kuspit, Donald, 'Review', Artforum, December

1988
'Frank Stella, 1970–1987', Museumjounaal 33

Salvioni, Daniela, 'Frank Stella at Museum of Modern Art', Flash Art, no. 138, January–February

Gopnik, Adam, 'Stella in Relief', The New Yorker, 4 January

Gardner, J., 'Stelliferous Stella, a Real "Momma's Boy"', Commonweal, 29 January

Kleyn, Robert, 'Abstraction Defeated in Victory: Frank Stella', Tema Celeste, no. 14, February

Perl, Jed, 'Stellar Turns', New Republic, February

Welchman, John, 'Geometer, Photographer, Bloodhound', Art International, Spring

Kingsley, April, 'Frank Stella: Works 1970-1987. Amsterdam, Stedelijk Museum', The Burlington Magazine, no. 1021, April

De Bure, Gilles, 'Frank Stella: Étoile de l'Amérique', Vogue, May

Grundberg, Andy, 'Frank Stella: Abstraction and Mannerism', Art Press, no. 125, May

Criqui, Jean-Pierre, 'Exposition Stella', Beaux Arts, no. 58, June

Coupland, Ken, 'Stella at Berggruen: Bad Boy Frank', San Francisco Sentinel, 2 September

Tilghman, B. R., 'Picture Space and Moral Space', British Journal of Aesthetics, Autumn

1989
Smith, Roberta, 'Frank Stella's 1988', The New York Times, 10 February

Camargo, José Carlos, 'Frank Stella', Folha de São Paulo, 14 May

Plagens, Peter, 'Is bigger necessarily better?', Newsweek, 17 April

Kaufman, Jason Edward, 'Frank Stella', Art Papers, May–June

Harrison, Katharine, 'Spotlight: Frank Stella', Flash Art, no. 147, Summer

Blaisdell, Gus, 'Frank Stella: The Whiteness of the Whale', Artspace, no. 13, July–August

Stella, Frank, 'Willem de Kooning', Art Journal, Autumn

Stella, Frank, 'How Velazquez Seizes the Truth of What is Art', The New York Times, 1 October

SELECTED SOLO EXHIBITIONS AND PROJECTS
1989–91

SELECTED ARTICLES AND INTERVIEWS
1989–91

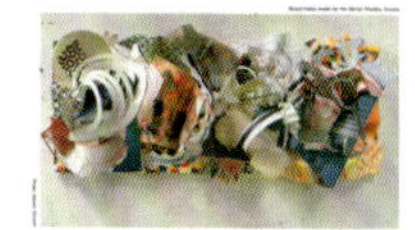

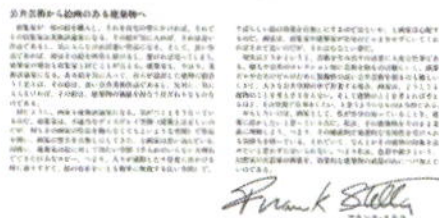

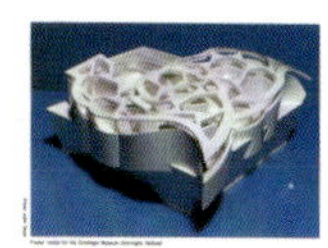

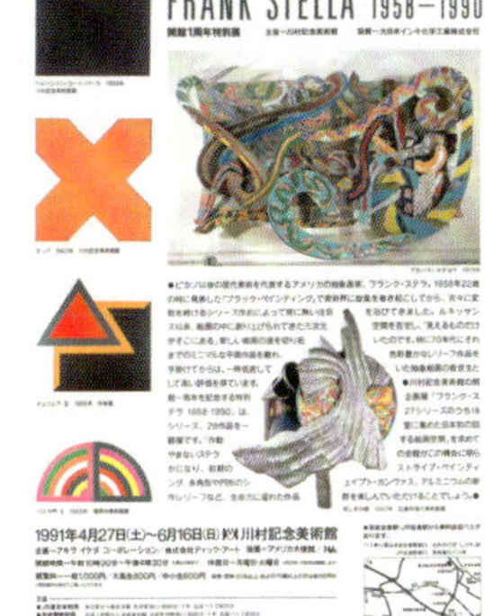

1989 (cont.)
'Frank Stella: New Work, Mixed Media Prints 1988-89',
ERIKA MEYEROVICH GALLERY, San Francisco

'Frank Stella: Waves II',
CARL SOLWAY GALLERY, Cincinnati

'Frank Stella: The Waves',
DOLAN/MAXWELL, Philadelphia

Receives the Ordre des Arts et des Lettres from the French Government

1989 (cont.)
Burn, Guy, 'Prints: Frank Stella', Arts Review, 17 November

Mauron, Véronique, 'La jubilation formelle de Frank Stella', Paribas, 15 November

Sozanski, Edward J., 'Set of 13 Frank Stella Prints Together for 1st Time in East', Philadelphia Inquirer, 28 December

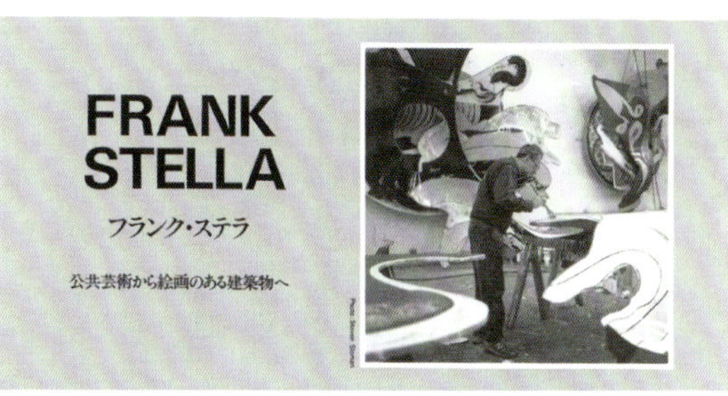

1990
'Waves, Part 2 and Wall Reliefs 1985–87',
GREENBERG GALLERY ANNEX, St. Louis

'Frank Stella: Prints and Wall Constructions',
GERALD PETERS GALLERY, Dallas

GALERIE JAMILEH WEBER, Zurich

'Frank Stella: Les Années 1980',
GALERIE BEAUBOURG, Paris

'Frank Stella: New Prints',
AKIRA IKEDA GALLERY, Nagoya

KNOEDLER KASMIN, London

'Frank Stella: Black and Metallic Paintings 1959–1964',
GAGOSIAN GALLERY, New York

'Frank Stella: Recent Paintings',
GALERIE KAJ FORSBLOM, Helsinki

'Frank Stella: Waves',
HOKIN GALLERY, Bay Harbor Islands, Florida

'Frank Stella: New Works',
HELAND WETTERLING GALLERY, Stockholm

'Frank Stella: New Work',
65 THOMPSON STREET (CASTELLI/GAGOSIAN)

1990
Brun, Ursula, 'Stellas monumentale Werke', Tagblatt der Stadt Zürich, 12 February

Peter, Charlotte, 'Frank Stella: Der Maximalist aus USA', Züri Woche, 15 February

Wallace, Robert K., 'Frank Stella', New Art Examiner, February

Bourriad, Nicholas, 'Théorie de la baleine', Globe, March

Legros, Hervé, 'Frank Stella: L'intelligence de la série', Beaux Arts, no. 134, March

Lévy, Bernard-Henri, 'Frank Stella: Les Années 80', Art Press, no. 145, March

Hilton, Tim, 'Critics' Choice: Stella Gets Off the Wall', Guardian, 20 June

Wheeler, Colin, 'Frank Stella: Reassuringly Expensive?', The Independent, 10 July

Leider, Philip, 'Shakespearean fish: Frank Stella Meets Moby Dick', Art in America, October

Avgikos, Jan, 'Frank Stella', Artforum, December

Smith, Roberta, 'Review', The New York Times, 14 December

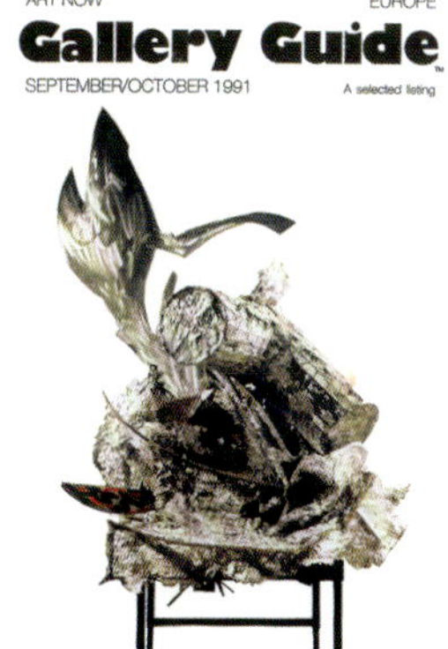

1991
GALERIE HANS STRELOW, Düsseldorf

AKIRA IKEDA GALLERY, Tokyo

'Frank Stella 1958-1990',
KAWAMURA MEMORIAL DIC MUSEUM OF ART, Sakura

'Frank Stella: Recent works',
AKIRA IKEDA GALLERY, Taura, Japan

CASINO KNOKKE, Knokke

'Frank Stella: Paintings, Reliefs, Hand-Coloring, Lithographs with Collage',
GALERIE ERIC VAN DE WEGHE, Brussels

'Frank Stella: Paintings and Reliefs',
NATIONAL MUSEUM OF ART, Osaka

LEO CASTELLI GALLERY, New York

'Frank Stella: Prints 1967-1988',
AC&T CORPORATION, Tokyo

1991
Anfam, David, 'Clyfford Still and Frank Stella', The Burlington Magazine, no. 1054, January

Larson, Kay, '65 Thomson Street', New York Magazine, 7 January

Wallace, Robert K., 'Sightings of the White Whale', Contemporanea, no. 24, January

Cotter, Holland, 'Deconstructed Painting: Some Younger Artists in the 1980s'; Frances Colpitt, 'The Shape of Painting in the 1960s', Art Journal, March

Rimanelli, David, 'Frank Stella', Artforum, April

Millet, Catherine, 'Frank Stella: Moby-Dick Series', Art Press, no. 159, June

Sugawara, Norio, 'An Interview with Frank Stella in Japan', Kenhi Otsubo, 'A Transformation of Frank Stella', Mizue, no. 959, Summer

Hiromoto, Nobuyuki, 'Review of Frank Stella: 1958–1990'; Sumi Hayashi, 'Interview with Frank Stella', Aura, August

Muchnic, Suzanne, 'Whaling Wall', Los Angeles Times, 7 August

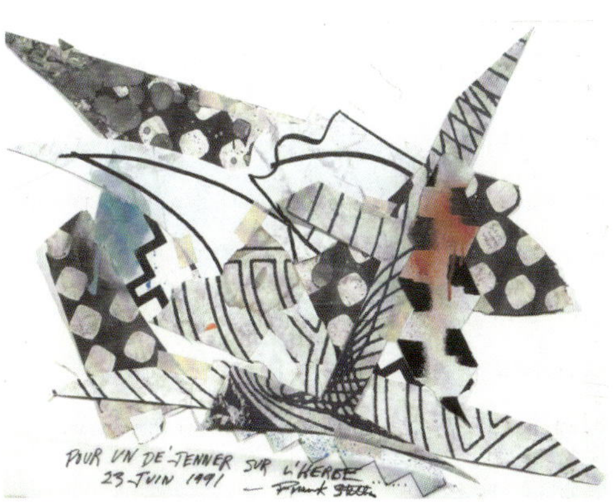

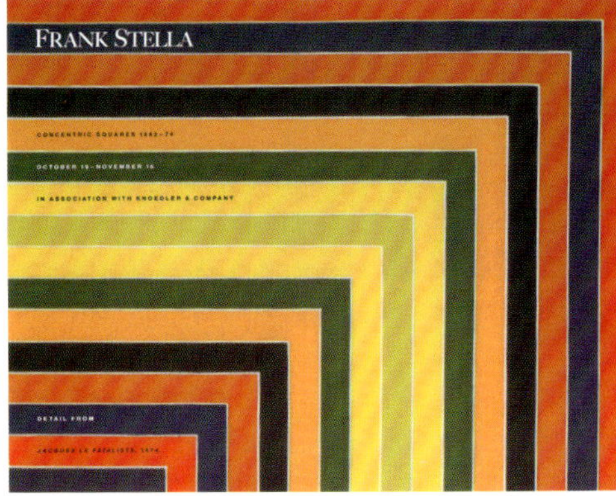

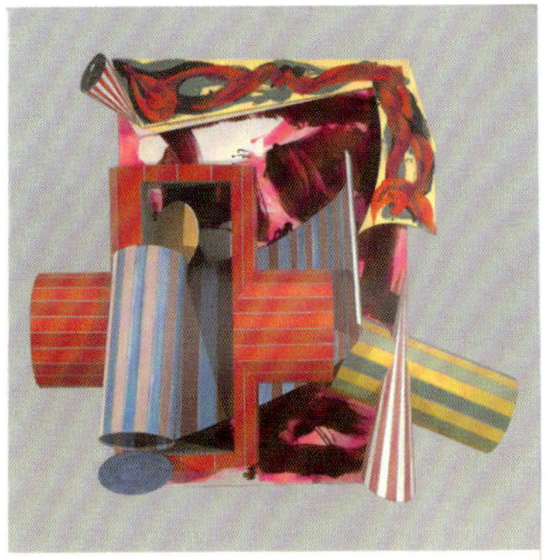

The Honor and the Glory of Whaling
1992; painted aluminum maquette 93" x 101" x 40"

SELECTED SOLO EXHIBITIONS AND PROJECTS
1991–93

1991 (cont.)
'Frank Stella: Construction, Prints',
FAY GOLD GALLERY, Atlanta

'Frank Stella: Recent Sculpture',
GALERIE DANIEL TEMPLON, Paris

'Frank Stella: Moby-Dick Engravings',
STELLAR GRAPHICS, Paris

'Concentric Squares, 1962-1974',
RUBIN-SPANGLE, New York

1992
'Frank Stella: The Fountain',
TYLER GRAPHICS LTD., Mount Kisco, New York

'Frank Stella: Works from 1972-1991',
EVELYN AMIS GALLERY, Boca Raton, Florida

'Frank Stella: Dome Prints',
BOBBIE GREENFIELD FINE ART, Venice, California

'Frank Stella: Prints from the Collection',
HIRSHHORN MUSEUM AND SCULPTURE GARDEN, Washington, D.C.

'Frank Stella: The Moby-Dick Series',
ERIKA MEYEROVICH GALLERY, San Francisco

'Frank Stella: Architectural Projects',
TOKYO AMERICAN CENTER, toured to FUKUOKA AMERICAN CENTER; SAPPORO AMERICAN CENTER; JETTY EAST, Nagoya; KYOTO INTERNATIONAL COMMUNITY HOUSE

'Moby-Dick Reliefs',
JAMILEH WEBER GALLERY, Zurich

'Frank Stella: New Sculpture',
AKIRA IKEDA GALLERY, Nagoya

'Frank Stella: A Selection of Prints 1967-1989',
RICHARD GREEN GALLERY, Santa Monica

'Frank Stella: New Work. Projects & Sculpture',
M. KNOEDLER & CO., New York

Awarded the Barnard Medal of Distinction, Columbia University, New York

1993
'Frank Stella: New Work; Sculpture and Woodcuts',
GALERIE KAJ FORSBLOM, Zurich

'Reliefs from the Moby-Dick Series',
MEREDITH LONG & COMPANY, Houston

KUKJE GALLERY, Seoul

'Stella! Archives of American Art',
SMITHSONIAN INSTITUTION, New York

'Frank Stella: Moby-Dick Deckle Edges',
NATIONAL GALLERY OF ART, Washington, D.C.

'Moby Dick Deckle Edges',
TYLER GRAPHICS LTD., Mount Kisco, New York

'Frank Stella: Moby Dick Series/Engravings, Domes, and Deckle Edges',
ULMER MUSEUM, Ulm, Germany

SELECTED ARTICLES AND INTERVIEWS
1991–93

1991 (cont.)
Dagen, Philippe, 'Flots argentés' and 'Stella: Étoile américaine', Le Monde, 2 October

Sorman, Guy, 'Stella: LÁbstraction en couleurs', Le Figaro Magazine, 30 November

'Stella Over L.A.', Flash Art, no. 161, November–December

1992
Macleish, Archibald, 'Frank Stella: Ars poética', Litoral, no.193/194

Peatross, Paula, 'Frank Stella', Art Papers, March–April

'Frank Stella: Su "Moby Dick"', Vanidades, no. 10, May

Matake, Makiko, 'Frank Stella: Expanding Possibilites through Complex Process and Experiments'; Yuke Takagi, 'An Introduction to Tyler Graphics', Mizue, no. 963, Summer

Wallace, Robert K., 'Frank Stella's Embassy Print, "The Symphony"', Print Collector's Newsletter, no. 3, July–August

Jodidio, Philip, 'La forme d'abord, la function ensuite', Connaissance des arts, no. 487, September

'Art World hits the Hustings for 1992', Art in America, October

Kimmelman, Michael, 'Frank Stella Crosses the Sculpture Threshold', The New York Times, 16 October

Levin, Kim, 'Frank Stella', Village Voice, 10 November

1993
Bass, Ruth, 'Stella's New Elegance', ARTnews, January

Galloway, David, 'Stella's Deep-Dish Pie', ARTnews, February

Merz, Michael, 'Pop-Art-Künstler Stella stellt Skulpturen aus', Blick, 20 March

Schwabsky, Barry, 'Frank Stella: Knoedler & Company', Sculpture, no. 2, March–April

Hume, Christopher, 'Artist Makes Big Splash on Theatre's Wall', Toronto Star, 10 September

Stella, Frank, 'Complex Surfaces', Connaissance des arts, September

O'Rourke, Michael, 'The Digital Modeling of Frank Stella's Smoke Sculpture', Maquette, November

Stella, Frank, 'Painting is Dead', Washington Post, 21 November

Frank Stella
April 3—May 1
1993

Kukje Gallery
59-1 SOKYUK-DONG
CHONGRO-KU SEOUL
KOREA

frank stella

IBERIA

Free Standing Murals

November 11 through December 16, 1995

Leo Castelli
420 West Broadway, New York

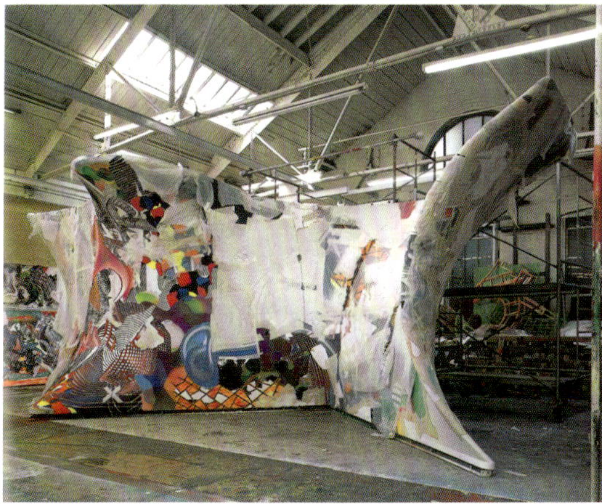

SELECTED SOLO EXHIBITIONS AND PROJECTS
1993–95

1993 (cont.)
'Frank Stella: New Prints from Tyler Graphics',
LEO CASTELLI GALLERY, New York

'Frank Stella: Moby Dick Deckle Edges',
BOBBIE GREENFIELD GALLERY, Venice, California

1994
'Frank Stella: New Editions',
GALERIE KAJ FORSBLOM, Zurich

'Frank Stella: Moby-Dick Deckle Edges Series',
MEREDITH LONG & COMPANY, Houston

'Frank Stella: Moby-Dick Deckle Edges',
AUBURN UNIVERSITY ART DEPARTMENT, Georgia

'Frank Stella: 1960s-1990s',
AKIRA IKEDA GALLERY, Taura, Japan

'Frank Stella: Space in Progress',
KAWAMURA MEMORIAL MUSEUM OF ART, Sakura

'Imaginary Places. New York: Painting, Relief, and Sculpture',
WADDINGTON GALLERIES, London

'Frank Stella: Large-Scale Constructions',
GREENBERG VAN DOREN, St. Louis

'Frank Stella: Recent Paintings',
M. KNOEDLER & CO., New York

1995
'Frank Stella: Prints from the 1960s and 1970s',
JONI MOISANT WEYL, New York

'Frank Stella: Prints, Black Series, 1967',
AKIRA IKEDA GALLERY, Nagoya

'Imaginary Places',
TYLER GRAPHICS, Mount Kisco, New York

'Frank Stella: Imaginary Places',
LEO CASTELLI GALLERY, New York

L'USINE, Dijon

VREJ BAGHOOMIAN GALLERY, New York

MUSEO NACIONAL CENTRO DE ARTE REINA SOFIA, Madrid,
toured to HAUS DER KUNST, Munich

'Frank Stella: Imaginary Places,
MORRIS MUSEUM OF ART, Augusta, Georgia

'Frank Stella: New Sculpture',
GAGOSIAN GALLERY, Los Angeles

'Imaginary Places: New Prints',
NANCY SOLOMON GALLERY, Atlanta

'Frank Stella: Imaginary Places; New Paintings and Prints',
KNOEDLER & COMPANY, New York

'Frank Stella: Freestanding Murals',
LEO CASTELLI GALLERY, New York

'New Works',
WETTERLING TEO GALLERY, Singapore

SELECTED ARTICLES AND INTERVIEWS
1993–95

1993 (cont.)
Elkins, James, 'Abstraction's Sense of History: Frank Stella's "Working Space" Revisited', American Art, Winter

Snodgrass, Susan, 'Stella Sculpture prompts Protest', Art in America, December

1994
Pacheco, Patrick, 'Letter from Toronto: Now Staring–Stella!', Art & Antiques, no. 16, January

Howlett, Margaret, ed., 'Frank Stella: Abstraction', Scholastic Art, 24 February

Stephens, Suzanne, 'Frank Stella: Blurring the Line between Art and Architecture', Architectural Digest, July

Finstein, Roni, 'Stella and the Princess of Wales', Art in America, July

Jocks, Heinz-Norbert, 'Frank Stella: Ich benutze den Stil, der mir gerade in den Kram passt', Kunstforum International, no. 127, July

'Frank Stella', Art in America, August

Smith, Roberta, 'Frank Stella's New Direction', The New York Times, 21 October

Criqui, Jean-Pierre, 'Country Sculpture', Artforum, November

Geldzahler, Henry, 'Oversize Prints', Graphis, November–December

1995
Landi, Ann, 'Frank Stella in "The 50 Most Powerful People in the Art World"', ARTnews, January

Edelman, Robert G., 'Frank Stella at Knoedler and American Fine Arts', Art in America, January

Drolet, Owen, 'Frank Stella at Knoedler & Company', Flash Art, no. 180, January–February

Daspin, Ellen, 'Stella Performance', W, February

Wallace, Robert K., 'Frank Stella: Sous le signe de Melville, encore', Art Press, March

Bergoffen, Celia, 'Architecture Dominates New Stella Works', Villager, 22 March

Hertzberg, Hendrik and John Lahr, 'Stella's Ring Cycle', The New Yorker, 15 May

Nuridsany, Michel, 'Stella: Encore une métamorphose', Le Figaro, 29 August

Schwabsky, Barry, 'Frank Stella', Artforum, September

Wolfon, Nancy, 'The Stella Story: Rings of Art', Cigar Aficionado, September

Muschamp, Herbert, 'A 'Monster' of a Masterpiece in Connecticut', The New York Times, September

Serraller, Francisco, 'Frank Stella reinventa el arte moderno', El Pais, 26 September

Fernández-Cid, Miguel, 'La actitud de Frank Stella', ABC, 29 September

SELECTED SOLO EXHIBITIONS AND PROJECTS
1995–97

1995 (cont.)
'Frank Stella: Editions',
LEO CASTELLI GALLERY, New York

1996
'Frank Stella: Master Prints',
WASSERMANN GALERIE, Munich

'Frank Stella: Smoke Sculptures',
AKIRA IKEDA GALLERY, Nagoya

'Frank Stella: New Works',
AKIRA IKEDA GALLERY, Nagoya

'Pictor Laureatus: In Honor of Frank Stella. With Drawings and a Collage',
GALERIE DER JENOPTIK AG, Jena

'Frank Stella: Exposition personnelle',
GALERIE PILTZER, Paris

PYO GALLERY, Seoul

'Frank Stella: A Collection of Prints 1967-1995',
MONTGOMERY MUSEUM OF FINE ARTS, Alabama, toured to HUNTSVILLE MUSEUM OF ART, Alabama; WIREGRASS MUSEUM, Dothan, Alabama

'Frank Stella 1970-1990: Twenty Years of Prints',
SUSAN SHEEHAN GALLERY, New York

'Imaginary Places II: Project Notes',
TYLER GRAPHICS, Mount Kisco, New York

'Frank Stella: Imaginary Places II',
WETTERLING TEO GALLERY, Singapore

1997
'Stella in Studio: The Public Art of Frank Stella 1982-1997',
UNIVERSITY OF HOUSTON BLAFFER GALLERY

'Frank Stella's obra gráphica (1982-1996)',
COLECCIÓN TYLER GRAPHICS, MUSEO DE ARTE ABSTRACTO ESPAÑOL FUNDACIÓN JUAN MARCH, Cuenca, Ecuador, toured to MUSEU D'ART ESPANYOL CONTEMPORANI FUNDACIÓN JUAN MARCH, Palma de Mallorca, Spain

'Frank Stella: New Sculpture',
GAGOSIAN GALLERY, New York

CITY MUSEUM OF ART, Kagoshima

'Frank Stella: Three-Dimensional Paintings 1977–91',
MEYERSON & NOWINSKI GALLERY, Seattle

'Frank Stella at Tyler Graphics',
WALKER ART CENTER, Minneapolis, Minnesota, toured to AUSTIN MUSEUM OF ART; ADDISON GALLERY OF AMERICAN ART at the PHILLIPS ACADEMY, Andover, Massachusetts; JACKSONVILLE MUSEUM OF CONTEMPORARY ART, Florida; ART MUSEUM OF SOUTH TEXAS, Corpus Christi

'Frank Stella: Transformation',
KAWAMURA MEMORIAL DIC MUSEUM OF ART, Sakura City

SELECTED ARTICLES AND INTERVIEWS
1995–97

1995 (cont.)
Pagel, David, 'Some Metal Monsters from Frank Stella', Los Angeles Times, 26 October

Karmel, Pepe, 'Frank Stella: "Free Standing Murals" and "Imaginary places"', The New York Times, 8 December

1996
Hantover, Jeffrey, 'Frank Stella at Wetterling Teo Gallery', Asian Art News, January–February

Baumer, Dorothea, 'Actuell in Münchner Galerien', Süddeutsche Zeitung, 22 February

'Fusion of Energies', Mainichi-Shimbun, 22 February

Vogel, Carol, 'A Museum Tackles a Monster: Abstraction', The New York Times, 22 February

Burchard, Hank, 'New Prints: Medium Message', Washington Post, 24 May

Stella, Frank, 'American Archives: Frank Stella', American Art, Summer

1997
Ellis, Jessica, 'Work of Artist Frank Stella Has Always Been Part of Local Color', Daily Couger, 23 January

Johnson, Patricia, 'Stella Show is Dizzying Affair', Houston Chronicle, 11 February

Abbe, Mary, 'Art: Frank Stella at Tyler Graphics', Minneapolis Star Tribune, 18 May

McTaggert, Tom, 'New Geometry: Frank Stella's 3D Paintings', Stranger, 29 May

Diehl, Carol, 'Frank Stella: Gagosian' and Carter Wiseman, 'Flights of Fancy', ARTnews, June

Villani, John, 'Visual Riddle: Pixels and Patterns Build Multiple Dimensions in a Frank Stella Mural', Continental, June

Vincens, Miguel, 'La última abstracción de Frank Stella llega a Palma', Diario de Mallorca, 1 July

Rubinstein, Raphael, 'Abstraction out of bounds', Art in America, November

Gilmour, Pat, 'Frank Stella at Tyler Graphics', Print Quaterly, December

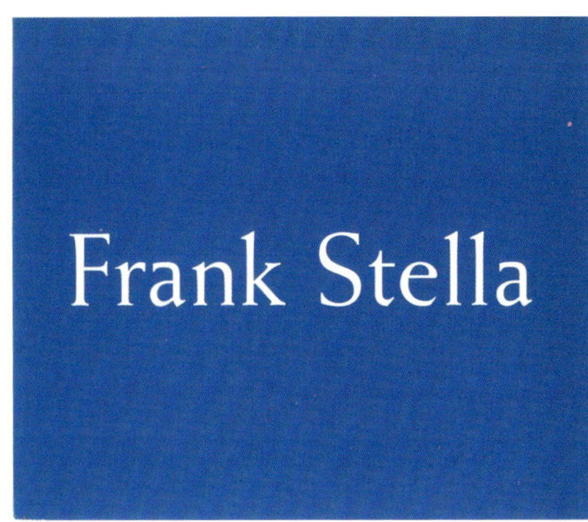

FRANK STELLA. NEW SCULPTURE. HUDSON RIVER VALLEY SERIES Einladung.

Bernard Jacobson
invites you to celebrate his
30th year in business
and
Frank Stella 'Easel Paintings'
on the
29th June 1999

Reception 6-8pm
Bernard Jacobson Gallery
14a Clifford Street
London
W1

and afterwards at
Legends
12 Old Burlington Street
London
W1

RSVP
Janey McAllester
tel 0171 495 8575 fax 0171 495 6210
Bernard Jacobson Gallery 14a Clifford Street London W1X 1RF

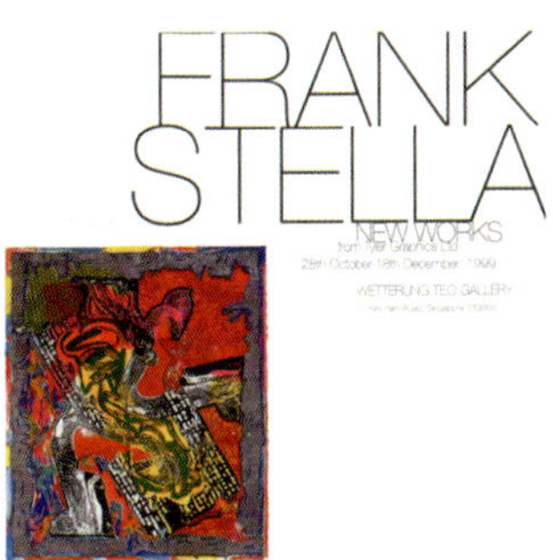

BARBARA MATHES GALLERY

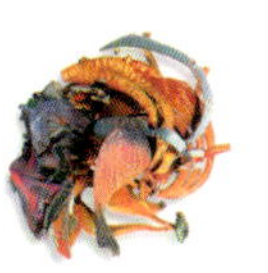

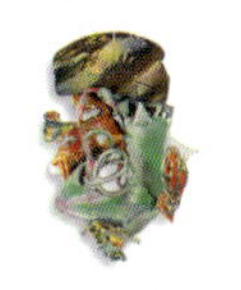

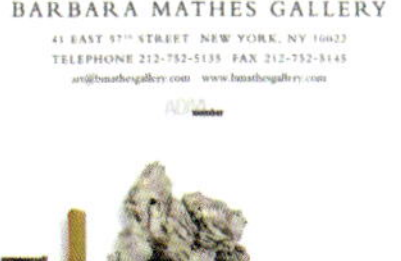

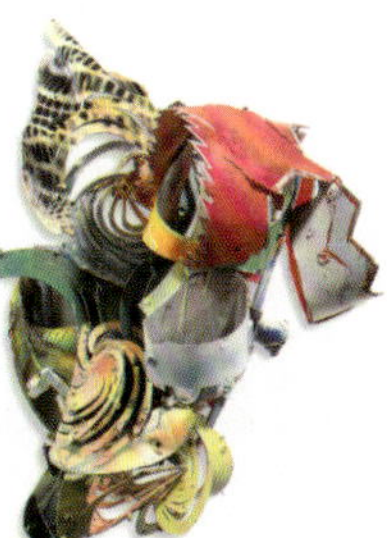

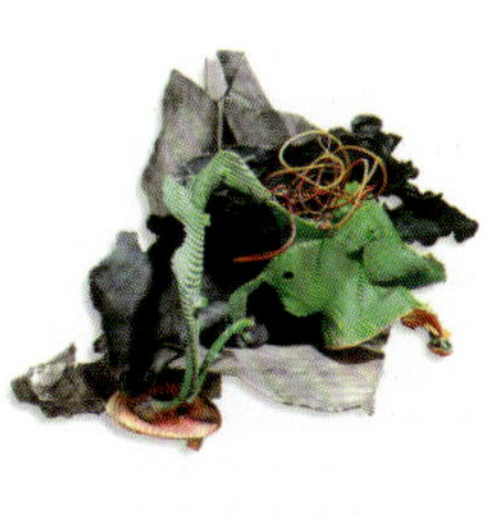

SELECTED SOLO EXHIBITIONS AND PROJECTS
1998–2001

1998
'Frank Stella and Kenneth Tyler: A Unique 30-Year Collaboration, CENTER FOR CONTEMPORARY GRAPHIC ART AND TYLER GRAPHICS ARCHIVE COLLECTION, Sukagawa, toured to TAKAMATSU CITY MUSEUM OF ART; MACHIDA CITY MUSEUM OF GRAPHIC ARTS; KAWAMURA MEMORIAL MUSEUM OF ART, Sakura

'Frank Stella: Multiple Dimensions in the 1990s',
KNOEDLER & COMPANY, New York

'Frank Stella: New Paintings',
BERNARD JACOBSON GALLERY, London

Receives the Gold Medal for Graphic Art Award, American Academy of Arts and Letters, New York

1999
'Stella: Work from the Leo Castelli Collection and Other Private Collections',
BRENAU UNIVERSITY GALLERIES, Gainesville, Georgia

'Frank Stella: Easel Paintings',
BERNARD JACOBSON GALLERY, London

KUKJE GALLERY, Seoul

'Stella and Tyler: Masterworks in Print',
NATIONAL GALLERY OF AUSTRALIA, Canberra

'Frank Stella: New Work',
SPERONE WESTWATER, New York

'Frank Stella: Hand-Colored Variations and New Editions',
BOBBIE GREENFIELD GALLERY, Santa Monica

'Frank Stella: Die Marquise von O',
BONINGTON GALLERY at NOTTINGHAM TRENT UNIVERSITY, England

'Frank Stella: New Works from Tyler Graphics Ltd.',
WETTERLING TEO GALLERY, Singapore

'Frank Stella at 2000: Changing the Rules',
MUSEUM OF CONTEMPORARY ART, Miami

2000
WADDINGTON GALLERIES, London

'Frank Stella: Recent Paintings and Sculpture',
RICHARD GRAY GALLERY, Chicago

'Frank Stella: Recent Work',
LOCKS GALLERY, Philadelphia, Pennsylvania

'Frank Stella Love Letters and Correspondence',
BARBARA MATHES GALLERY, New York

2001
'Frank Stella: vortex Engravings #1-12',
DAVID MIRVISH DESIGNS, Toronto

'Heinrich von Kleist by Frank Stella',
GALERIE DER JENOPTIK AG, toured to ROEMER- UND PELIZAEUS-MUSEUM, Hildesheim; WÜRTTEMBERGISCHER KUNSTVEREIN, Stuttgart; GALERIE AKIRA IKEDA, Berlin; SINGAPORE TYLER PRINT INSTITUTE LIMITED, Singapore

WADDINGTON GALLERIES, London

SELECTED ARTICLES AND INTERVIEWS
1998–2001

1998
Kramer, Hilton, 'Frank Stella, Rank Amateur, in an Overhyped New Show', New York Observer, 25 May

Grayford, Martin, 'The Journey into Stella Space', Sunday Telegraph, 14 June

Barber, Lynn, 'Spent: Interview', Observer (London), 14 June

Tully, Jud, 'Frank Stella', Art and Auction 20, June

Reed, Robert, 'Printmaking Dynamic Duo', Daily Yomiuri (Tokyo), 7 July

Unger, Miles, 'Spotlight: Frank Stella at Tyler Graphics', Art New England, December

1999
Silberman, Steve, 'Stella', Wired, March

Kinsman, Jane, 'The Fountain: A Print Epic – Frank Stella and Ken Tyler', Art on View, no.19 Spring

Rickerd, Julie Rekai, 'Stella by Stagelight', Entertainment Design, August–September

'Frank Stella at 2000: Changing the Rules' review, Art in America, August

Adelman, Jacob, 'American Abstract painter Stella Displays Works in Seoul Gallery', Korea Herald, 9 September

Jackson, Sally, 'Master of a Minimalist Stripe', Australian, 8 October

McCulloch-Euhlin, Susan, 'Inspiring Perspective', Weekend Australian, 23 October

Smith, Sue, 'Masterful Showing', Courier Mail (Queensland), 30 October

Johnson, Ken, 'Art in Review', The New York Times, 26 November

Jay, Sian, 'Don't Fear Riot of Colours and Shapes', Strait Times (Singapore), 26 November

2000
Ostrow, Saul, 'Frank Stella', Bomb, no. 71, Spring

Turner, Elisa, 'Frank Stella at 2000', ARTnews, March

Siegel, Katy, 'Frank Stella', Artforum, April

Schulze, Franz, 'Frank Stella as Architect', Art in America, June

Takashima, Miki, 'Bare Necessities Suit Stella', Daily Yomiuri (Tokyo), 20 July

2001
Landi, Ann, 'Frank Stella' and Elisa Turner, 'Off the Waterfront', ARTnews, February

Jones, Jonathan, 'The Prince of Whales', Guardian, 5 April

Gayford, Martin, 'Artists on Art: Frank Stella on Caravaggio's St John the Baptist (c. 1602)', Daily Telegraph, 28 April

Jay, Sian, 'Hail the Artist in the Printer', Straits Times (Singapore), 9 April

SELECTED SOLO EXHIBITIONS AND PROJECTS
2001–04

2001 (cont.)
'Frank Stella: Imaginary Landscapes',
GIBBES MUSEUM, Charleston, South Carolina

'Frank Stella: Recent Paintings and Sculpture',
RICHARD GRAY GALLERY, Chicago

'Stella at Arrowhead: An Exhibition in Honor of the 150th Anniversary of Moby Dick',
BERKSHIRE COUNTY HISTORICAL SOCIETY AT ARROWHEAD, Pittsfield, Massachusetts

'Frank Stella: The Waves',
SOUTH STREET SEAPORT, New York

GALERIE HANS STRELOW, Dusseldorf

'Frank Stella: Recent Work',
PAUL KASMIN GALLERY, New York

'Off the Wall: Prints by Frank Stella',
IRIS AND B. GERALD CANTOR CENTER FOR VISUAL ARTS at STANFORD UNIVERSITY, Palo Alto, California

'Frank Stella: Heinrich von Kleist',
AKIRA IKEDA GALLERY, Berlin

Receives the Gold Medal of the National Arts Club, New York

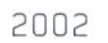

2002
'Frank Stella: Hacilar 1999-2001',
ARTEMIS GREENBERG VAN DOREN GALLERY, New York

2003
'Frank Stella: An Empty Space',
AKIRA IKEDA GALLERY, New York

NAGOYA CITY ART MUSEUM, toured to IWATE MUSEUM OF ART, Morioka

BERNARD JACOBSON GALLERY, London

'Frank Stella: Recent Work',
PAUL KASMIN GALLERY, New York

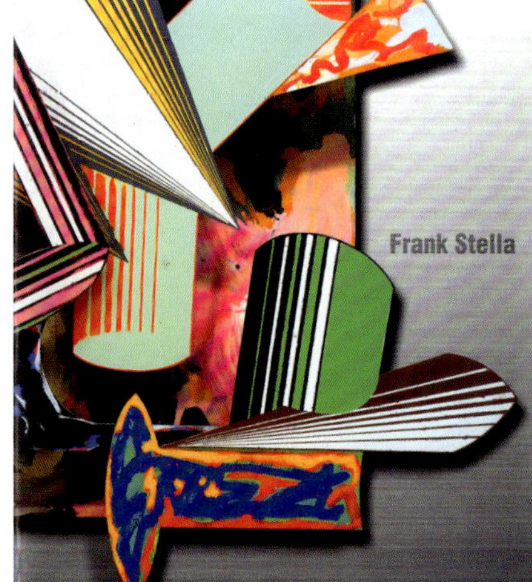

2004
JACOBSON HOWARD GALLERY, New York

'Frank Stella: A Breakthrough in Abstraction: Exotic Birds',
GAGOSIAN GALLERY, New York

'What You See Is What You See: Frank Stella and the Anderson Collection at SFMOMA',
SAN FRANCISCO MUSEUM OF MODERN ART

'Frank Stella: Moby Dick and Imaginary Places',
GALERIE JAMILEH WEBER, Zurich

GALERIE TERMINUS, Munich

'Frank Stella: New Works',
MCCLAIN GALLERY, Houston, Texas

'Frank Stella: The Marquise of O Paintings',
JACOBSON HOWARD GALLERY, New York

SELECTED ARTICLES AND INTERVIEWS
2001–04

2001 (cont.)
Russell, John, 'Critic's Notebook: Frank Stella Builds a Landmark Out of Romanticism and Steel; A Monumental Sculpture is Headed for Washington', The New York Times, 17 May

Lewis, Jo Ann, 'Stella Sculpture to Land at National Gallery', Washington Post, 18 May

Leider, Philip, 'Stella's Quest', Art in America, October

Shawn-Eagle, Joanna, 'Spectacular "Prince" Rises', Washington Times, 27 October

Gilmour, Pat, 'Frank Stella's "Moby Dick"', Print Quarterly, December

Gopnik, Blake, 'Frank Stella's Twisted Prince of a Sculpture', Washington Post, 11 December

Myers, Chuck, 'A Massine Monument to the Abstract', Philadelphia Inquirer, 22 December

Puente, Maria, 'Sculpture Swoops into D.C.', USA Today, 12 December

2002
Rimanelli, David, 'Frank Stella', Artforum, March

2003
Smee, Sebastian, 'Frank Stella: I Never Felt That Minimal', Daily Telegraph, 30 April

Solomon, Deborah, 'Frank Stella's Expressionist Phase', The New York Times Magazine, 4 May

James, Victoria, 'Frank Stella Fills the Space between Sculpture and Painting', Japan Times, 2 July

Stella, Frank, 'Special Section on James Rosenquist', Artforum, October

2004
'Frank Stella, 'Kastura, 1979', Arts & Activities, February

Hubbard, Guy, 'Clip and Save Art Notes', Arts & Activities, February

Johnson, Ken, 'Review', The New York Times, 7 May

Fischer, Jack, 'Frank Stella: Shaping a Life in Art', San Jose Mercury News, 13 June

Ayers, Robert, 'Frank Stella', ARTnews, October

Hainley, Bruce, 'Best of 2004', Artforum, December

SELECTED SOLO EXHIBITIONS AND PROJECTS 2005–08

2005

'Frank Stella: Painting in Three Dimensions', NASHER SCULPTURE CENTER, Dallas

ROSENBAUM CONTEMPORARY, Bal Harbour, Florida

JOHN BERGGRUEN GALLERY, San Francisco

PAUL KASMIN GALLERY, New York

'Frank Stella's Moby Dick Series Prints', NATIONAL MUSEUM OF FINE ARTS, Santiago, toured to THE MUSEUM OF LATIN AMERICAN ART IN BUENOS AIRES (MALBA) COLLECTION CONSTANTINI

WADDINGTON GALLERIES, London

2006

'Frank Stella 1958', HARVARD UNIVERSITY ART MUSEUMS, Cambridge, Massachusetts, toured to THE MENIL COLLECTION, Houston; WEXNER CENTER FOR THE ARTS UNIVERSITY, Columbus

'Illustrations after El Lissitzky's "Had Gadya" 1982-84', CONNELLY CENTER, Villanova University, Pennsylvania

GALERIE THOMAS, Munich

'Collages and Related Sculpture from the von Kleist Series', JACOBSON HOWARD GALLERY, New York

SAMUELIS BAUMGARTE GALERIE, Bielefeld

'Frank Stella: Major Works from the von Kleist Series', DANESE GALLERY, New York

2007

'Frank Stella: Painting into Architecture', METROPOLITAN MUSEUM, New York

'Frank Stella on the Roof', METROPOLITAN MUSEUM, New York

'Frank Stella: New Work', PAUL KASMIN GALLERY, New York

'Frank Stella: Bali Series', GALERIE FICHER ROHR, Basel

'Frank Stella: Paintings 1958-1965', PETER FREEMAN INC., Paris

GALERIE HAAS & FUCHS, Berlin

'Frank Stella: Space', GALERIE TERMINUS, Munich

'Frank Stella: Five Decades of Painting & Sculpture, GARY NADER FINE ART, Miami

2008

WETTERLING GALLERY, Stockholm

'Frank Stella: K Series', JACOBSON HOWARD GALLERY, New York

'Frank Stella Prints 1980-2008', JACOBSON HOWARD GALLERY, New York

SELECTED ARTICLES AND INTERVIEWS 2005–08

2005

Kuspit, Donald, 'Frank Stella', Artforum, February

Kunitz, Daniel, 'Review', New York Sun, 14 April

Naves, Mario, 'Review', New York Observer, 9 May

Scheb, Ronnie, 'Who gets to call it art?', Variety, no. 13, November

Westfall, Stephen, 'Frank Stella at Paul Kasmin', Art in America, November

Rosenblum, Robert, 'Best of 2005: 11 Top Tens', Artforum, December

2006

Smith, Roberta, 'A Vivid Back Story for a Stella Legend', The New York Times, 10 February

Stella, Frank, 'One Life Twice Lived', Artforum, May

Lawrence, James, 'Frank Stella: Cambridge MA, Houston and Columbus', The Burlington Magazine, no. 1238, May

Silver, Joanne, 'Frank Stella, 1958', ARTnews, April

Shiff, Richard, 'Frank Stella 1958', Artforum, Summer

Michael, Amy, 'Cambridge: Frank Stella at the Sackler Museum, Harvard University', Art in America, June

Carrier, David, 'Frank Stella', ArtUS, no. 14, July–August

2007

Gough, Maria, 'Frank Stella is a Constructivist', October, no. 119, Winter

Tupitsyn, Margarita, 'Black Paintings: Haus der Kunst', Artforum, January

Foxley, David, 'Big Sky, Big Art', New York Observer, 24 April

White, Renée Minus, 'Artist Frank Stella's Solo Exhibitions at the Met', New York Amsterdam News, 3 May

Niel, Jonathan T. D., 'First to arrive', Art Review, May

Wilkin, Karen, 'Frank Stella Three Ways', New Criterion, June

Lawrence, James, 'Frank Stella. New York', The Burlington Magazine, no. 1254, September

Turvey, Lisa, 'Painting into Architecture', Artforum, October

Castro, Jan Garden, 'The Age of Abstraction: A Conversation with Frank Stella', Sculpture, December

2008

Carmean Jr, E. A., 'Stella's Places', Art & Antiques, February

'Frank Stella', Arte y Parte, February

Feder, Theodore, and Frank Stella, 'The Proposed New Law is a Nightmare for Artists', Arts Newspaper 17, 28 June

Knelman, Martin, 'AGO's Franks Admiration', Toronto Star, 29 October

FRANK STELLA
Irregular Polygons

A Guide to the Exhibition

Hood Museum of Art, Dartmouth College
October 9, 2010–March 13, 2011

FRANK STELLA

BLACK

ALUMINUM

COPPER

PAINTINGS

FRANK STELLA

NEW WORK

OPENING MAY 17, 2012

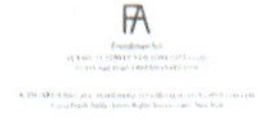

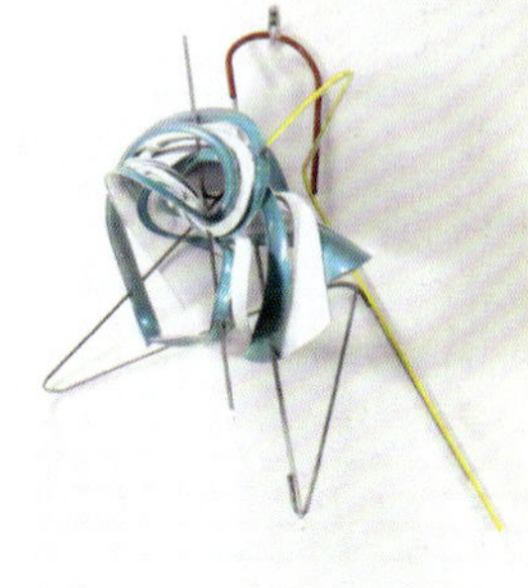

SELECTED SOLO EXHIBITIONS AND PROJECTS
2008–12

2008 (cont.)
'Frank Stella: Scarlatti and Bali Series',
PARACELSUS BUILDING, St. Moritz, Switzerland

'Polygons to Printmaking: The Work of Frank Stella 1958–1997',
PRINCETON UNIVERSITY ART MUSEUM, New Jersey

'Frank Stella: Work on Canvas from the 1960s',
VAN DE WEGHE FINE ART, New York

2009
'Moby Dick: Frank Stella and Herman Melville',
GRAND RAPIDS ART MUSEUM, Michigan

'Frank Stella: Prints 1977–1982',
AKIRA IKEDA GALLERY, Taura, Japan

'Frank Stella: Polychrome Relief',
PAUL KASMIN GALLERY, New York

2010
'Frank Stella: New Works',
WETTERLING GALLERY, Stockholm

'Frank Stella: Verdichtung und Ausdehnung; Arbeiten von 1974 bis 2000',
GALERIE FICHER ROHR, Basel, Switzerland

'Frank Stella: Irregular Polygons 1965–66',
HOOD MUSEUM OF ART at DARTMOUTH COLLEGE, Hanover, New Hampshire, toured to TOLEDO MUSEUM OF ART, Ohio

Receives the 2009 National Medal of Arts, the White House, Washington, D.C.

2011
Stella Sounds: The Scarlatti K Series',
THE PHILLIPS COLLECTION, Washington, D.C.

'Frank Stella: Study for Watson and the Shark 1991',
MORE GALLERY, Giswell, Switzerland

'Frank Stella: American Master',
THE BASCOM: A CENTER FOR THE VISUAL ARTS, Highlands, North Carolina

'Frank Stella: Recent Work',
GALERIE DER STADT, Tuttlingen, Germany, toured to FRIEDRICH-SCHILLER-UNIVERSITAT, Jena, Germany

'Frank Stella: Geometric Variations',
PAUL KASMIN GALLERY, New York

'Frank Stella: Connections',
HAUNCH OF VENISON, London

2012
'Frank Stella: Black, Aluminum, Copper Paintings',
L&M ARTS, New York

'Frank Stella: New Work',
FREEDMANART, New York

'Frank Stella: From Strictness to Baroque',
INSTITUT VALENCIÀ D'ART MODERN, Spain

'Frank Stella: The Retrospective. Works 1958–2012',
KUNSTMUSEUM WOLFSBURG, Germany

SELECTED ARTICLES AND INTERVIEWS
2008–12

2008 (cont.)
Sheila Heti, 'Interview with Frank Stella', Believer 6, no. 9, November–December

Smith, Roberta, 'Works on Canvas from the '60s', The New York Times, November 14

2009
Tomkins, Calvin, 'Is it Art?', The New Yorker, 16 March

Carlin, T.J., 'Frank Stella: The Heavyweight Champion of Abstraction Talks about Risk Taking and Flourescence', Time Out New York, 1 October

Smith, Roberta, 'Frank Stella: Polychrome Relief at Paul Kasmin Gallery', The New York Times, 30 October

2010
Salus, Carol, 'Frank Stella's Polish Village Series and Related Works: Heritage and Alliance', Shofar: An Interdisciplinary Journal of Jewish Studies, January

Fiz, Testo Alberto, 'Frank Stella: Predecessor delle archistar' Domus 941, November

Smee, Sebastian, 'Frank Stella: Tilting at Minimalism', Boston Globe, 12 December

2011
Trescott, Jacqueline, 'The Phillips Collection plans Wassily Kandinsky and Frank Stella', Washington Post, 9 March

Ottoman, Klaus, 'Action and Spatial Engagement', Sculpture, April

Kennicott, Philip, 'Two new Phillips Collection exhibitions involve Tie between Abstraction and Music', Washington Post, 10 June

Wilkin, Karen, 'Complementary Abstractionists', Wall Street Journal, 23 June

Ziegler, Yvonne, 'Frank Stella: You See What You See', Kunst Bulletin, July–August

Stella, Frank, 'American Artists Must Fight for Resale Rights', The Art Newspaper, 4 August

Luke, Ben, 'Throwing Shapes', Evening Standard, 30 September

2012
De Albornoz, Cristina Carrillo, 'Being Frank in Zaragoza', The Art Newspaper, January

Saltz, Jerry, 'Where Minimalism Began', New York Magazine, May

Levin, Kim, 'Frank Stella', ARTnews, Summer

Smith, Roberta, 'Frank Stella: New Work', The New York Times, 6 July

Allen, Jennifer and Prince, Mark, 'Hands-On', Frieze d/e, no. 6, September

FRANK STELLA
Recent Work
9 January - 22 February 2014

PETER FREEMAN, INC.

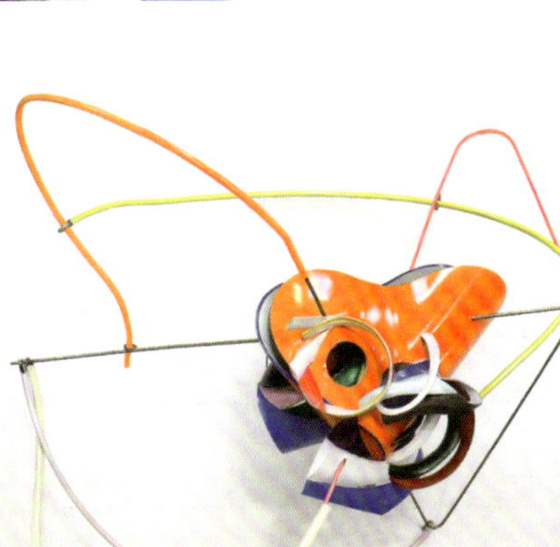

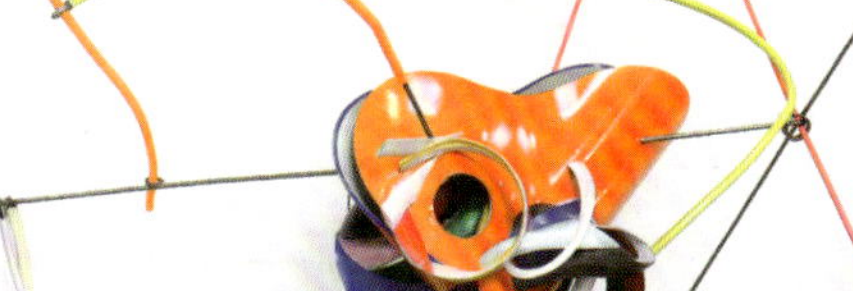

SELECTED SOLO EXHIBITIONS AND PROJECTS 2012–15

2012 (cont.)

'How a Stripe Works: Frank Stella's Early Gemini Prints 1967–1970',
IRIS AND B. GERALD CANTOR CENTER FOR VISUAL ARTS at STANFORD UNIVERSITY, California

'Frank Stella: Scarlatti Kirkpatrick',
GLASS HOUSE, New Canaan, Connecticut

2013

'Frank Stella: Drawings 1960–1975',
LEO CASTELLI GALLERY, New York

'Frank Stella: Recent Work',
WETTERLING GALLERY, Stockholm

'Frank Stella Room',
KAWAMURA MEMORIAL DIC MUSEUM OF ART, Sakura

'Frank Stella: Prints from the Permanent Collection',
WIREGRASS MUSEUM OF ART, Dothan, Alabama

2014

'Frank Stella: Recent Work',
PETER FREEMAN INC., New York

'Frank Stella: Polish Village',
VAN DOREN WAXTER GALLERY, New York

'Frank Stella: Works from 1971–1987',
LESLIE FEELY GALLERY, New York

'Frank Stella: Big Works in Progress',
MORE GALLERY, Giswil, Switzerland

'Frank Stella: Sculpture',
MARIANNE BOESKY GALLERY, New York

'Frank Stella, Illustrations after El Lissitzky's 'Had Gadya': The Unique Colour Variants',
WADDINGTON CUSTOT GALLERIES, London, UK

2015

'Frank Stella: Paintings and Drawings',
MUSEUM FÜR GEGENWARTSKUNST, Basel

Inflated Star and Wood Star',
ROYAL ACADEMY, London, toured to ARTZUID, Amsterdam

'Frank Stella: Shape as Form',
PAUL KASMIN GALLERY, New York

BERNARD JACOBSON GALLERY, London

'Frank Stella at Gemini G.E.L',
JONI MOISANT WEYL, New York

'Frank Stella: Retrospective',
THE WHITNEY MUSEUM OF AMERICAN ART, New York, toured to MODERN ART MUSEUM OF FORT WORTH, Texas; DE YOUNG MUSEUM, San Francisco

SELECTED ARTICLES AND INTERVIEWS 2012–15

2012 (cont.)

Allen, Emma, 'Frank Stella Visits Da Monsta', The New Yorker, 25 October

Cooper, Harry, 'Frank Stella: The Retrospective. Works 1958–2012', Artforum, October

Whitfield, Sarah, 'Frank Stella: Black Aluminium Copper Paintings', The Burlington Magazine, no. 1315, October

Bohel, Sabine, 'Frank Stella: The 2.7th and Further Dimensions', RES, no. 9, November

Prince, Mark, 'Anarchy and Objecthood', Art in America, December

2013

Buchloh, Benjamin H. D., 'Painting as Diagram: Five Notes on Frank Stella's Early Paintings, 1958–1959', October, Winter

Ruas, Charles, 'Frank Stella Drawings, 1960–1975', ARTnews, May

'Art enters the Third Dimension', The Art Newspaper, July–August

Dorfman, J., 'Working in Space: Frank Stella's Expansion Plan Continues with a Foray into Computer-Assisted 3D Fabrication', Art and Antiques, no. 9, October

2014

Rosenberg, Karen, 'Review', The New York Times, 19 June

Vankin, Deborah, 'Abstract Frank Stella Sculpture 'Adjoeman' Joins Cedars-Sinai Artworks', Los Angeles Times, 7 July

'Stella Joke That Made Minimalist Car Andre's Career', Evening Standard, 31 July

Dimock, Wai Chee, 'Epic Relays: C. L. R. James, Herman Melville, Frank Stella', Comparatist, October

McCartney, Stella, 'Frank Stella', Interview, November

2015

Niel, Jonathan T. D., 'Frank Stella', Art Review, January–February

Asfour, Nana, 'A New Art Exhibit Breaks Out the Traditional Square', Vogue, May

Schnitzer, Jordan, 'Frank Stella', Art in America, August

Heartney, Eleanor, 'Frank Stella: l'espace paradoxal', Art Press, September

Sayer, Nadja, 'Frank stella: If you get into art to make money, you are deluded', The Guardian, 1 September

Solomon, Deborah, 'No Slowing Down', The New York Times, 13 September

Braithwaite, Hunter, 'Q&A: Frank Stella Gets Candid About His Long Career', Modern Painters, October

Kunitz, Daniel, 'State of the Game', Modern Painters, October

SELECTED SOLO EXHIBITIONS AND PROJECTS
2015–17

2015 (cont.)
'Frank Stella Sculpture: One Man Show',
GARY NADER ART CENTER, New York

'Frank Stella: Recent Works',
LEEAHN GALLERY, Seoul

Receives the National Artist Award, The Anderson Ranch Arts Center, Aspen

2016
'Frank Stella Prints',
MADISON MUSEUM OF CONTEMPORARY ART, Wisconsin, toured to ADDISON GALLERY OF AMERICAN ART at the PHILLIPS ACADEMY, Andover, Massachusetts

'Frank Stella: Circuit Prints',
ANDERS WAHLSTEDT FINE ART, New York

'Frank Stella and the Synagogues of Old Poland',
POLIN MUSEUM OF THE HISTORY OF POLISH JEWS, Warsaw

'Frank 'Stella',
SPRÜTH MAGERS, Berlin

'Frank Stella: From the Line to the Line',
KEITELMAN GALLERY, Brussels

LEILA HELLER GALLERY, Dubai

2017
'Frank Stella: Works from Three Decades',
GALERIE HANS STRELOW, Dusseldorf

CHARLES RIVA COLLECTION, Brussels

MARIANNE BOESKY GALLERY, New York

'Frank Stella: Recent Work',
WETTERLING GALLERY, Stockholm

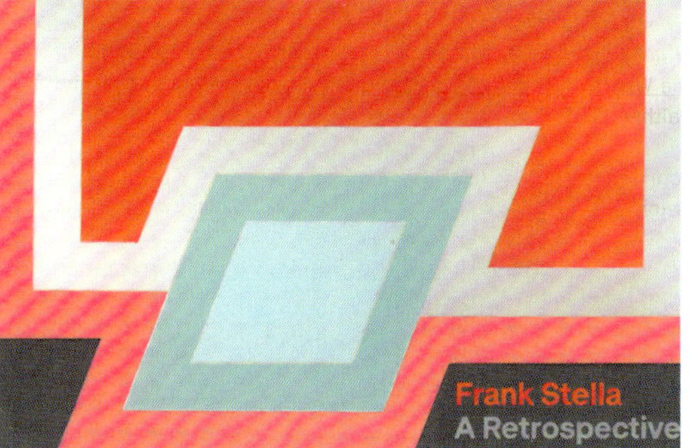

SELECTED ARTICLES AND INTERVIEWS
2015–17

2015 (cont.)
Pobric, Pac, 'Frank Stella Retrospective charts the Development of Minimalism into Maximalism', The Art Newspaper, October

'Portfolio by Frank Stella', Art in America, October

''His Ability to Change Has Been Amazing': A Review of MoMA's Frank Stella Survey from 1970', ARTnews, October

Green, Dominic, 'Ingenious Individual', Art & Antiques, November

Tuchman, Phyllis, 'Everything You Ever Wanted to Know About Abstraction: Frank Stella stuns at the Whitney', ARTnews, November

Campbell, Andrianna, 'Frank Stella', Artforum, November

Schjeldahl, Peter, 'Big Ideas', The New Yorker, 9 November

Obrist, Hans Ulrich, and Susanne Cotter, 'There is no Art without Geometry', Mousse, no. 50, December

Wilkin, Karen, 'Stella at the Whitney', New Criterion, December

McGlynn, Tom, 'The Clamor of Reason: Frank Stella. A Retrospective', The Brooklyn Rail, December

Smith, Roberta, 'Best Art of 2015: Frank Stella. A Retrospective', The New York Times, 9 December

2016
Ghorashi, Hannah, 'This person is multiple, this practice is multiple, and this might be confusing: a roundtable discussion on Frank Stella at the Whitney', ARTnews, January

Greenberger, Alex, 'Coast to Coast: Frank Stella and Larry Bell on the 1960s Los Angeles Art Scene', ARTnews, February

Scheffler, Dan, 'Colliding Worlds: Frank Stella and the Synagogues of Historic Poland', Wallpaper, February

Crow, Thomas, 'Frank Stella', Artforum, February

Geers, David, 'Frank Stella', Frieze, no. 177, March

Forrest, Nicholas, 'Frank Stella's Spatial Symphonics at Sprüth Magers Berlin', Art + Auction, 21 July

Prince, Mark, 'Abstraction', Art Monthly, no. 402, December–January

2017
Luke, Megan R., 'Frank Stella: New York, Fort Worth and San Francisco', The Burlington Magazine, no. 1368, March

McQuaid, Cate, 'A very full survey of prints by Frank Stella', The Boston Globe, 4 May

BIBLIOGRAPHY

SELECTED MONOGRAPHS AND ARTIST'S BOOKS

Fried, Michael, Frank Stella: An Exhibition of Recent Paintings, Pasadena Art Museum, California, 1966

Frank Stella, Galerie Bruno Bischofberger, Zurich, 1967

Frank Stella: Recent Prints, Douglas Gallery, Vancouver, 1967

Frank Stella: Recent Paintings, Kasmin Limited, London, 1968

Frank Stella: Recent Paintings and Drawings, Washington Gallery of Modern Art, Washington D.C., 1968

Seitz, William C., Recent Paintings by Frank Stella, Brandeis University Press, Waltham, Massachusetts, 1969

Campbell, Robin, and John McLean, Frank Stella, Hayward Gallery, London, 1970

Imdahl, Max, Frank Stella: Sanbornville II, Werkmonographien zur bildenden Kunst, Reclams Universal-Bibliothek, Stuttgart, Germany, 1970

Keers, Frits, Frank Stella, Stedelijk Museum, Amsterdam, 1970

Rubin, William S., Frank Stella, Museum of Modern Art, New York, 1970

Heckmanns, Friedrich, Frank Stella: Prinzip Seriell, Graphik 1967–1970, Kunstmuseum Düsseldorf, Kunsthalle Bielefeld, Germany, and Aarhus Kunstmuseum, Denmark, 1971

Rosenblum, Robert, Frank Stella, Penguin, Harmondsworth, England, 1971

Friedman, Richard, Frank Stella at the Phillips Collection, Phillips Collection, Washington D.C., 1973

Meyer, Franz, Frank Stella: Neue Reliefbilder. Bilder und Graphik, Kunsthalle Basel, Switzerland, 1976

Richardson, Brenda, Frank Stella: The Black Paintings, Baltimore Museum of Art, 1976

Pauseback, Michael, Frank Stella: Werke 1958–1976, Kunsthalle Bielefeld and Kunsthalle Tübingen, Germany, 1977

Leider, Philip, Stella since 1970, Modern Art Museum of Fort Worth, Texas, 1978

Frank Stella: Metalic Reliefs, Brandeis University Press, Waltham, Massachusetts, 1979

Frank Stella: 8 Drawings: 1976 Sketch Sinjerli Variation/1977 Exotic Bird Series, Galerie Valeur, Nagoya, Japan, 1979

Froment, Jean-Louis, Philip Leider and Marcelin Pleynet, Frank Stella: Peintures 1970–1979, Centre d'Arts Plastiques Contemporains de Bordeaux, 1980

Geelhaar, Christian, Frank Stella: Working Drawings/ Zeichrmngen 1956-1970, Kunstmuseum Basel, 1980

Stella, Frank, Frank Stella: Working Drawings from the Artist's Collection, Kitakyushu Municipal Museum of Art, Japan, 1982

Meier, Richard, and Frank Stella, Shards, Petersburg, New York, 1983

Frank Stella: Polish Wooden Synagogues; Constructions of the 1970s, Jewish Museum, New York, 1983

Resource/Response/ Reservoir: Stella Survey 1959–1982, San Francisco Museum of Modern Art, 1983

Axsom, Richard H., The Prints of Frank Stella: A Catalogue Raisonné 1967–1982, Hudson Hills Press, Manchester, Vermont, 1983

Goldman, Judith, Frank Stella: Fourteen Prints with Drawings, Collages, and Working Proofs, Princeton University Art Museum, New Jersey, 1983

Hughes, Robert, Frank Stella: The Swan Engravings, Modern Art Museum of Fort Worth, Texas, 1984

Rubin, Lawrence, and Robert Rosenblum, Frank Stella: Paintings 1958 to 1965. A Catalogue Raisonné, Stewart, Tabori & Chang, New York, 1986

Stella, Frank, Working Space: The Charles Eliot Norton Lectures, Harvard University Press, Cambridge, Massachusetts, 1986

Rubin, William S., Frank Stella 1970-1987, Museum of Modern Art, New York, 1987

Armstrong, Elizabeth, and Richard H. Axsom, Frank Stella: The Circuits Prints, Walker Art Center, Minneapolis, 1988

Amagasaki, Kikuko, Frank Stella: Reliefs, Akira Ikeda Gallery, Taura, Japan, 1988

Inboden, Gudrun, Frank Stella: Black Paintings 1958–1960; Cones and Pillars, 1984–1987, Staatsgalerie Stuttgart, 1988

Pacquement, Alfred, Frank Stella, Flammarion, Paris, 1988

Lévy, Bernard-Henri, Frank Stella: Les Années 80, Galerie Beaubourg, Paris, 1990

Kuroiwa, Kyosuke, and Juniki Nakashima, Frank Stella: 1958–1990, Kawamura Memorial Museum of Art, Sakura, 1991

Millet, Catherine, Frank Stella: Recent Sculpture, Galerie Daniel Templon, Paris, 1991

Stella, Frank, and Eddy Devolder, Frank Stella: Conversations with/avec Eddy Devolder, Éditions Tandem, Gerpinnes, Belgium, 1991

Costanzo, Michele, Vincenzo Giorgi and Maria Grazia Tolomeo, Richard Meier & Frank Stella: Arte e Architettura, Palazzo delle Esposizioni, Rome, and Electa Mondadori, Milan, 1993

Baas, Jacquelynn, Frank Stella: Moby Dick Deckle Edges, Tyler Graphics, Mount Kisco, New York, 1993

Reinhardt, Brigitte and Robert K. Wallace, Frank Stella: Moby-Dick Series; Engravings, Domes and Deckle Edges, Ulm Museum, Germany, 1993

Pearson, James, Frank Stella, Joe's Press, Kidderminster, England, 1994

Stella, Frank, A Vision for Public Art, Tankosha Publishing, Kyoto, 1994

Frank Stella: New Works, 1995, Wetterling Teo Gallery, Singapore, 1995

Goldman, Judith, Hubert Gassner, et al, Frank Stella: The Retrospective, Museo Nacional Centro de Arte Reina Sofía, Madrid, and Haus der Kunst, Munich 1995

Guberman, Sidney, Frank Stella: An Illustrated Biography, Rizzoli, New York, 1995

Frank Stella, Pyo Gallery, Seoul, South Korea, 1996

Ausfeld, Margaret Lynne, Frank Stella: A Collection of Prints, 1967–1995, Montgomery Museum of Fine Arts, Alabama, 1996

Childress, Earl, David Galloway and Masahiko Haito, Richard Meier & Frank Stella: Architecture and Art, Prefectural Museum of Art, Nagoya, Japan, 1996

Hoffmann, Rolf, and Erika Hoffmann, Kunsthalle Desden: Ein Prjekt Architectur. Frank Stella, Kunsthalle Dresden, Germany, 1996

Frank Stella's obra gráphica (1982–1996): Colección Tyler Graphics, Museu Fundación Juan March, Palma de Mallorca, Spain, 1997

Stella, Frank, Lilar, Axel Springer, Hamburg, 1997

Engberg, Siri, Frank Stella at Tyler Graphics, Walker Art Center, Minneapolis, 1997

Stella, Frank, Broadsides: Architecture and Art, Cooper Union, New York, 1997

Yaguchi, Yuzo, Frank Stella, Kagoshima City Museum of Art, Japan, 1997

Wallace, Robert K., and Frank Stella, Frank Stella: Juam, Juam, Juam, State 1; From Imaginary Places, Tyler Graphics, Mount Kisco, New York, 1997

Tyler, Kenneth H., and Frank Stella, Frank Stella and Kenneth Tyler: A Unique 30 Year Collaboration, Center for Contemporary Graphic Art, Sukagawa, Japan, 1998

Clearwater, Bonnie, and Frank Stella, Frank Stella at Two Thousand: Changing the Rules, Museum of Contemporary Art, Miami, 1999

Wallace, Robert K., Frank Stella's Moby-Dick: Worm and Shapes, University of Michigan Press, Ann Arbor, 2000

Guberman, Sidney, Frank Stella: Imaginary Landscapes, Gibbes Museum, Charleston, South Carolina, 2001

Verspohl, Franz-Joachim (ed.), Ulrich Müller, Reinhard Wegner and Frank Stella, The Writings of Frank Stella, Walther König, Cologne, 2001

Hogrebe, Wolfram, Franz-Joachim Verspohl, Robert K. Wallace and Martin Warnke, Henrich von Kleist by Frank Stella, Walther König, Cologne, 2002

Clearwater, Bonnie, Frank Stella, Nagoya City Art Museum and Iwate Museum of Art, Japan, 2003

Cooper, Harry, and Megan R. Luke, Frank Stella 1958, Yale University Press, New Haven, 2006

Frank Stella: For his 70th Birthday, Galerie Thomas, Munich, Germany, 2006

Goldberger, Paul, Frank Stella: Painting into Architecture, Metropolitan Museum of Art, New York, 2007

Rubin, William H., Moby Dick: Frank Stella and Herman Melville, Grand Rapids Art Museum, Minnesota, 2009

Stella, Frank, and Giovanni Pietro Bellori, Su Caravaggio, Abscondita, Milan, 2010

Kennedy, Brian P., Frank Stella: Irregular Polygons 1965–66, Hood Museum of Art, Hanover, New Hampshire, 2010

Stella Sounds: The Scarlatti K Series, Phillips Collection, Washington D.C., 2011

Hobbs, Robert, Tom Hunt, Karen Wilken and Ben Tufnell (ed.), Frank Stella: Connections, Hatje Cantz, Ostfildern, Germany, 2011

Klébaner, Daniel, Frank Stella: La Jubilation traversière, Ides et Calendes, Neuchâtel, Switzerland, 2011

Frank Stella: American Master, The Bascom, Highlands, North Carolina, 2011

Pincus-Witten, Robert, and Katy Siegel, Frank Stella Paintings: Black Aluminum Copper, L & M Arts, New York, 2012

Brüderlin, Markus (ed.), Holger Bröker and Gregor Stemmrich, Frank Stella: The Retrospective Works. 1959–2012, Hatje Cantz, Ostfildern, and Kunstmuseum Wolfsburg, Germany, 2012

Pearson, James, Frank Stella: American Abstract Artist, Crescent Moon, Maidstone, England, 2013

Pfab, Tina, Frank Stella Shaped Canvases, Grin, Munich, 2013

Axsom, Richard H., and Leah Kolb, Frank Stella Prints: A Catalogue Raisonné, Jordan Schnitzer Family Foundation and Madison Museum of Contemporary Art, Winsconsin, 2013

Auping, Michael, Adam D. Weinberg, Jordan Kamor and Laura Owens, Frank Stella: A Retrospective, Yale University Press, New Haven, Modern Art Museum of Fort Worth, Texas and Whitney Museum of American Art, New York, 2015

Stella, Frank, Andrianna Campbell, Kate Nesin, Lucas Blalock, Terry Richardson and Michele Robecchi (ed.), Frank Stella, Phaidon, London, 2017

ILLUSTRATED WORKS

COMPARATIVE IMAGES

PUBLIC COLLECTIONS

ADDISON GALLERY OF AMERICAN ART AT THE PHILLIPS ACADEMY, Andover

ALBRIGHT-KNOX ART GALLERY, Buffalo

ART GALLERY OF NEW SOUTH WALES, Sydney

ART GALLERY OF ONTARIO, Toronto

ART INSTITUTE OF CHICAGO

BALTIMORE MUSEUM

BROOKLYN MUSEUM, New York

CENTRE POMPIDOU, Paris

CLEVELAND ART MUSEUM

CONTEMPORARY ARTS MUSEUM, Houston

CORCORAN GALLERY OF ART, Washington

DALLAS MUSEUM OF ART

DENVER ART MUSEUM

DETROIT INSTITUTE OF ARTS

FINE ARTS MUSEUMS OF SAN FRANCISCO

FOLKWANG MUSEUM, Essen, Germany

HARVARD UNIVERSITY ART MUSEUMS, Cambridge

HARA MUSEUM OF CONTEMPORARY ART, Tokyo

HIGH MUSEUM OF ART, Atlanta

HIRSHHORN MUSEUM AND SCULPTURE GARDEN, Washington

INDIANAPOLIS MUSEUM OF ART

INSTITUTE OF CONTEMPORARY ART, Philadelphia

KAWAMURA MEMORIAL MUSEUM OF ART, Sakura

KEMPER MUSEUM OF CONTEMPORARY ART, Kansas City

KITAKYUSHU MUNICIPAL MUSEUM, Japan

KUNSTMUSEUM BASEL

LIST ART CENTER AT BROWN UNIVERSITY, Providence, Rhode Island

LOS ANGELES COUNTY MUSEUM OF ART

LOUISIANA MUSEUM, Humlebæk, Denmark

METROPOLITAN MUSEUM OF ART, New York

MINNEAPOLIS INSTITUTE OF ARTS

MODERN ART MUSEUM OF FORT WORTH, Indiana

MODERNA MUSEET, Stockholm

MUSEUM BOCHUM, Germany

MUSEUM BOYMANS VON BEUNINGEN, Rotterdam

MUSEUM OF CONTEMPORARY ART, Chicago

MUSEUM OF CONTEMPORARY ART, Los Angeles

MUSEUM OF FINE ARTS, Boston

MUSEUM OF FINE ARTS, Houston

MUSEUM OF MODERN ART, New York

NASHER SCULPTURE CENTER, Dallas

NATIONAL GALLERY OF ART, Washington

NATIONALGALERIE, Berlin

NATIONAL GALLERY OF AUSTRALIA, Canberra

NELSON-ATKINS MUSEUM OF ART, Kansas City

PHILADELPHIA ART MUSEUM

THE PHILLIPS COLLECTION, Washington

PRINCETON UNIVERSITY ART MUSEUM, New Jersey

SAINT LOUIS ART MUSEUM

SAN FRANCISCO MUSEUM OF MODERN ART

SEATTLE ART MUSEUM

SMITHSONIAN AMERICAN ART MUSEUM, Washington

SOLOMON R. GUGGENHEIM MUSEUM, New York

STEDELIJK MUSEUM, Amsterdam

STEDELIJK VAN ABBEMUSEUM, Eindhoven

TATE, London

UNIVERSITY OF MICHIGAN ART MUSEUM, East Lansing

VANCOUVER ART MUSEUM

VIRGINIA MUSEUM OF FINE ARTS, Richmond

WADSWORTH ATHENEUM MUSEUM OF ART, Hartford, Connecticut

WALKER ART CENTER, Minneapolis

WALLRAF-RICHARTZ MUSEUM, Cologne

WHITNEY MUSEUM OF AMERICAN ART, New York

YALE UNIVERSITY ART GALLERY, New Haven

PHAIDON PRESS LTD.
REGENT'S WHARF
ALL SAINTS STREET
LONDON N1 9PA

PHAIDON PRESS INC.
65 BLEECKER STREET
NEW YORK, NY 10012

PHAIDON.COM

First published 2017

ISBN:
978-0-7148-7459-3

A CIP catalogue record of this book is available from the British Library and the Library of Congress.

Commissioning Editor:
Michele Robecchi

Production Controller:
Sarah Kramer

Design:
Melanie Mues, Mues Design, London

Printed in Hong Kong

PUBLISHER'S ACKNOWLEDGEMENTS

Special thanks to Rebecca Ann Siegel at Frank Stella Studio, New York; Marianne Boesky, Ricky Manne and Savannah Downs at Marianne Boesky Gallery, New York; Dominique Lévy and Brett Gorvy at Lévy Gorvy, London; Guggenheim Museum, New York; Whitney Museum of American Art, New York; Philadelphia Museum of Art; Stedelijk Museum, Amsterdam; the Barnett Newman Foundation, New York; the Willem de Kooning Estate, New York; Mnuchin Gallery, New York; DACS, London; Scala, Florence, Melissa Larner, João Mota.

Very special thanks to Catalina Imizcoz and Sarah Scott for their editorial assistance.

Photographers: Ron Amstutz, Christopher Burke, David Cohen, Terry Richardson, Steven Sloman, Jason Wyche.

ARTIST'SACKNOWLEDGEMENTS

Special thanks to Rebecca Ann Siegel and Ricky Manne; Marianne Boesky; Dominique Lévy and Brett Gorvy; Paula Pelosi and Allison Martone; David Lukowski and Dominic Nurre; Michele Otero; Arturo Martinez; Julia Mazur, Bauby Tan, Victoria Faller and Savannah Downs.

Thank you to Lucas Blalock, Andrianna Campbell, Kate Nesin and Terry Richardson for their contributions, and to Michele Robecchi and the team at Phaidon for their vision and dedication.

The most thanks to Harriet McGurk.

CONTEMPORARY ARTISTS:

Contemporary Artists is a series of authoritative and extensively illustrated studies of today's most important artists. Each title offers a comprehensive survey of an individual artist's work and a range of art writing contributed by an international spectrum of authors, all leading figures in their fields, from art history and criticism to philosophy, cultural theory and fiction. Each study provides incisive analysis and multiple perspectives on contemporary art and its inspiration. These are essential source books for everyone concerned with art today.

MARINA ABRAMOVIĆ KLAUS BIESENBACH, KRISTINE STILES, CHRISSIE ILES / VITO ACCONCI FRAZER WARD, MARK C. TAYLOR, JENNIFER BLOOMER / AI WEIWEI HANS ULRICH OBRIST, KAREN SMITH, BERNARD FIBICHER / DOUG AITKEN DANIEL BIRNBAUM, AMANDA SHARP, JÖRG HEISER / PAWEŁ ALTHAMER ADAM SZYMCZYK, ROMAN KURZMEYER, SUZANNE COTTER / FRANCIS ALŸS CUAUHTÉMOC MEDINA, RUSSELL FERGUSON, JEAN FISHER / UTA BARTH PAMELA M. LEE, MATTHEW HIGGS, JEREMY GILBERT-ROLFE / CHRISTIAN BOLTANSKI DIDIER SEMIN, TAMAR GARB, DONALD KUSPIT / MONICA BONVICINI ALEXANDER ALBERRO, JANET KRAYNAK, JULIANE REBENTISCH / LOUISE BOURGEOIS PAULO HERKENHOFF (WITH THYRZA GOODEVE), ROBERT STORR, ALLAN SCHWARTZMAN / MARK BRADFORD ANITA HILL, SEBASTIAN SMEE, CONNIE BUTLER / CAI GUO-QIANG DANA FRIIS-HANSEN, OCTAVIO ZAYA, TAKASHI SERIZAWA / MAURIZIO CATTELAN NANCY SPECTOR, FRANCESCO BONAMI, BARBARA VANDERLINDEN, MASSIMILIANO GIONI / VIJA CELMINS ROBERT GOBER, LANE RELYEA, BRIONY FER / NIGEL COOKE DARIAN LEADER, TONY GODFREY, MARIE DARRIEUSSECQ / RICHARD DEACON PIER LUIGI TAZZI, JON THOMPSON, PETER SCHJELDAHL, PENELOPE CURTIS / TACITA DEAN JEAN-CHRISTOPHE ROYOUX, MARINA WARNER, GERMAINE GREER / MARK DION LISA GRAZIOSE CORRIN, MIWON KWON, NORMAN BRYSON / PETER DOIG ADRIAN SEARLE, KITTY SCOTT, CATHERINE GRENIER / STAN DOUGLAS SCOTT WATSON, DIANA THATER, CAROL J. CLOVER / MARLENE DUMAS DOMINIC VAN DEN BOOGERD, BARBARA BLOOM, MARIUCCIA CASADIO, ILARIA BONACOSSA / JIMMIE DURHAM LAURA MULVEY, DIRK SNAUWAERT, MARK ALICE DURANT, KATE NESIN / OLAFUR ELIASSON MADELEINE GRYNSZTEJN, DANIEL BIRNBAUM, MICHAEL SPEAKS / PETER FISCHLI AND DAVID WEISS ROBERT FLECK, BEATE SÖNTGEN, ARTHUR C. DANTO / TOM FRIEDMAN DENNIS COOPER, BRUCE HAINLEY, ADRIAN SEARLE / THEASTER GATES CAROL BECKER, LISA YUN LEE, ACHIM BORCHARDT-HUME / ISA GENZKEN ALEX FARQUHARSON, DIEDRICH DIEDERICHSEN, SABINE BREITWIESER / ANTONY GORMLEY ERNST GOMBRICH, JOHN HUTCHINSON, LELA B. NJATIN, W. J. T. MITCHELL / DAN GRAHAM BIRGIT PELZER, MARK FRANCIS, BEATRIZ COLOMINA / PAUL GRAHAM ANDREW WILSON, GILLIAN WEARING, CAROL SQUIERS / HANS HAACKE WALTER GRASSKAMP, MOLLY NESBIT, JON BIRD / MONA HATOUM GUY BRETT, MICHAEL ARCHER, CATHERINE DE ZEGHER, NANCY SPECTOR / THOMAS HIRSCHHORN BENJAMIN H. D. BUCHLOH, ALISON M. GINGERAS, CARLOS BASUALDO / JENNY HOLZER DAVID JOSELIT, JOAN SIMON, RENATA SALECL / RONI HORN LOUISE NERI, LYNNE COOKE, THIERRY DE DUVE / CHRIS JOHANSON CORRINA PEIPON, BOB NICKAS, JULIE DEAMER / ILYA KABAKOV BORIS GROYS, DAVID A. ROSS, IWONA BLAZWICK / ALEX KATZ ROBERT STORR, CARTER RATCLIFF, IWONA BLAZWICK, BARRY SCHWABSKY / ON KAWARA 'TRIBUTE', JONATHAN WATKINS, RENÉ DENIZOT / MIKE KELLEY ISABELLE GRAW, JOHN C. WELCHMAN, ANTHONY VIDLER / MARY KELLY MARGARET IVERSEN, DOUGLAS CRIMP, HOMI K. BHABHA / WILLIAM KENTRIDGE CAROLYN CHRISTOV-BAKARGIEV, DAN CAMERON, J. M. COETZEE / YAYOI KUSAMA AKIRA TATEHATA, LAURA HOPTMAN, UDO KULTERMANN, CATHERINE TAFT CHRISTIAN MARCLAY JENNIFER GONZALEZ, KIM GORDON, MATTHEW HIGGS / KERRY JAMES MARSHALL CHARLES GAINES, GREGORY TATE, LAURENCE RASSEL / PAUL McCARTHY KRISTINE STILES, RALPH RUGOFF, MASSIMILIANO GIONI, ROBERT STORR / CILDO MEIRELES PAULO HERKENHOFF, GERARDO MOSQUERA, DAN CAMERON LUCY ORTA ROBERTO PINTO, NICOLAS BOURRIAUD, MAIA DAMIANOVIC / JORGE PARDO CHRISTINE VÉGH, LANE RELYEA, CHRIS KRAUS / RAYMOND PETTIBON DENNIS COOPER, ROBERT STORR, ULRICH LOOCK / RICHARD PRINCE ROSETTA BROOKS, JEFF RIAN, LUC SANTE / PIPILOTTI RIST HANS ULRICH OBRIST, PEGGY PHELAN, ELIZABETH BRONFEN / STERLING RUBY KATE FOWLE, FRANKLIN SIRMANS, JESSICA MORGAN / ANRI SALA HANS ULRICH OBRIST, MARK GODFREY, LIAM GILLICK / DORIS SALCEDO NANCY PRINCENTHAL, CARLOS BASUALDO, ANDREAS HUYSSEN / WILHELM SASNAL ANDRZEJ PRZYWARA, DOMINIC EICHLER, JÖRG HEISER / THOMAS SCHÜTTE JULIAN HEYNEN, JAMES LINGWOOD, ANGELA VETTESE / STEPHEN SHORE MICHAEL FRIED, CHRISTY LANGE, JOEL STERNFELD / ROMAN SIGNER PAULA VAN DEN BOSCH, GERHARD MACK, JEREMY MILLAR / LORNA SIMPSON KELLIE JONES, THELMA GOLDEN, CHRISSIE ILES / NANCY SPERO JON BIRD, JO ANNA ISAAK, SYLVÈRE LOTRINGER / SIMON STARLING FRANCESCO MANACORDA, DIETER ROELSTRAETE, JANET HARBORD / FRANK STELLA ANDRIANNA CAMPBELL, KATE NESIN, LUCAS BLALOCK, TERRY RICHARDSON / JESSICA STOCKHOLDER BARRY SCHWABSKY, LYNNE TILLMAN, LYNNE COOKE, GERMANO CELANT / SARAH SZE OKWUI ENWEZOR, BENJAMIN H. D. BUCHLOH, LAURA HOPTMAN / WOLFGANG TILLMANS PETER HALLEY, JAN VERWOERT, MIDORI MATSUI, JOHANNA BURTON / LUC TUYMANS ULRICH LOOCK, JUAN VICENTE ALIAGA, NANCY SPECTOR, HANS RUDOLF REUST / JEFF WALL THIERRY DE DUVE, ARIELLE PÉLENC, BORIS GROYS, JEAN-FRANÇOIS CHEVRIER, MARK LEWIS / GILLIAN WEARING RUSSELL FERGUSON, DONNA DE SALVO, JOHN SLYCE / LAWRENCE WEINER BENJAMIN H. D. BUCHLOH, ALEXANDER ALBERRO AND ALICE ZIMMERMAN, DAVID BATCHELOR / FRANZ WEST ROBERT FLECK, BICE CURIGER, NEAL BENEZRA / YIN XIUZHEN HOU HANRU, WU HUNG, STEPHANIE ROSENTHAL / ZHANG HUAN ROSELEE GOLDBERG, YILMAZ DZIEWOR, ROBERT STORR